CAMBRIDGE TEXTBOOKS IN LINGUISTICS

General Editors: B. COMRIE, R. HUDDLESTON, R. LASS, D. LIGHTFOOT,
J. LYONS, P. H. MATTHEWS, R. POSNER, S. ROMAINE, N. V. SMITH, N. VINCE

PRAGMATICS

In this series:

P. H. MATTHEWS *Morphology* Second edition
B. COMRIE *Aspect*
R. M. KEMPSON *Semantic Theory*
T. BYNON *Historical Linguistics*
J. ALLWOOD, L.-G. ANDERSON and O. DAHL *Logic in Linguistics*
D. B. FRY *The Physics of Speech*
R. A. HUDSON *Sociolinguistics*
J. K. CHAMBERS and P. TRUDGILL *Dialectology*
A. J. ELLIOT *Child Language*
P. H. MATTHEWS *Syntax*
A. RADFORD *Transformational Syntax*
L. BAUER *English Word-formation*
S. C. LEVINSON *Pragmatics*
G. BROWN and G. YULE *Discourse Analysis*
R. HUDDLESTON *Introduction to the Grammar of English*
R. LASS *Phonology*
B. COMRIE *Tense*
W. KLEIN *Second Language Acquisition*
A. CRUTTENDON *Intonation*
A. J. WOODS, P. FLETCHER and
A. HUGHES *Statistics in Language Studies*
D. A. CRUSE *Lexical Semantics*
F. R. PALMER *Mood and Modality*
A. RADFORD *Transformational Grammar*
M. GARMAN *Psycholinguistics*
W. CROFT *Typology and Universals*
G. CORBETT *Gender*

PRAGMATICS

STEPHEN C. LEVINSON

FORSCHUNGSGRUPPE KOGNITIVE ANTHROPOLOGIE
MAX–PLANCK–INSTITUT FÜR PSYCHOLINGUISTIK,
NIJMEGEN

CAMBRIDGE
UNIVERSITY PRESS

PUBLISHED BY THE PRESS SYNDICATE OF THE UNIVERSITY OF CAMBRIDGE
The Pitt Building, Trumpington Street, Cambridge, United Kingdom

CAMBRIDGE UNIVERSITY PRESS
The Edinburgh Building, Cambridge CB2 2RU, UK   http://www.cup.cam.ac.uk
40 West 20th Street, New York, NY 10011–4211, USA   http://www.cup.org
10 Stamford Road, Oakleigh, Melbourne 3166, Australia
Ruiz de Alarcón 13, 28014 Madrid, Spain

First published 1983
Reprinted 1984, 1985 (twice), 1987 (twice), 1989, 1991, 1992, 1994,
1995, 1997, 2000

Printed in the United Kingdom at the University Press, Cambridge

Library of Congress Catalogue card number: 82–14701

British Library Cataloguing in Publication Data
Levinson, Stephen C.
Pragmatics.
1. Pragmatics 2. Languages – Philosophy
I. Title
401   P99.4.P72

ISBN 0 521 29414 2 paperback

CONTENTS

Preface   ix
Acknowledgements   xiv
Notation conventions   xv

1   **The scope of pragmatics**   1
1.1   The origin and historical vagaries of the term
      pragmatics   1
1.2   Defining pragmatics   5
1.3   Current interest in pragmatics   35
1.4   Computing context: an example   47

2   **Deixis**   54
2.0   Introduction   54
2.1   Philosophical approaches   55
2.2   Descriptive approaches   61
2.2.1 *Person deixis*   68
2.2.2 *Time deixis*   73
2.2.3 *Place deixis*   79
2.2.4 *Discourse deixis*   85
2.2.5 *Social deixis*   89
2.3   Conclusions   94

3   **Conversational implicature**   97
3.0   Introduction   97
3.1   Grice's theory of implicature   100
3.2   Revisions, problems and applications   118
3.2.1 *Tests for implicature*   118
3.2.2 *Implicature and logical form*   122
3.2.3 *Kinds of implicature*   126
3.2.4 *Generalized Quantity implicatures*   132
3.2.5 *Metaphor : a case of maxim exploitation*   147
3.2.6 *Implicatum and language structure*   162

Contents

4 **Presupposition** 167
4.0 Introduction 167
4.1 Historical background 169
4.2 The phenomena: initial observations 177
4.3 The problematic properties 185
4.3.1 *Defeasibility* 186
4.3.2 *The projection problem* 191
4.4 Kinds of explanation 199
4.4.1 *Semantic presupposition* 199
4.4.2 *Pragmatic theories of presupposition* 204
4.5 Conclusions 225

5 **Speech acts** 226
5.0 Introduction 226
5.1 Philosophical background 227
5.2 Thesis: speech acts are irreducible to matters of truth and falsity 243
5.3 Antithesis: the reduction of illocutionary force to ordinary syntax and semantics 246
5.4 Collapse of Antithesis 251
5.4.1 *Semantic problems* 251
5.4.2 *Syntactic problems* 260
5.5 Indirect speech acts: a problem for Thesis and Antithesis 263
5.6 The context-change theory of speech acts 276
5.7 Beyond theories of speech acts 278

6 **Conversational structure** 284
6.0 Introduction 284
6.1 Discourse analysis versus conversation analysis 286
6.2 Conversation analysis 294
6.2.1 *Some basic findings* 296
6.2.1.1 *Turn-taking* 296
6.2.1.2 *Adjacency pairs* 303
6.2.1.3 *Overall organization* 308
6.2.2 *Some remarks on methodology* 318
6.2.3 *Some applications* 326
6.3 Preference organization 332
6.3.1 *Preferred second turns* 332
6.3.2 *Preferred sequences* 339
6.4 Pre-sequences 345
6.4.1 *General remarks* 345
6.4.2 *Pre-announcements* 349
6.4.3 *Pre-requests: a re-analysis of indirect speech acts* 356
6.5 Conclusions 364

Contents

6.5.1 *Conversation analysis and linguistics*   364
6.5.2 *Some remaining questions*   367
       Appendix: transcription conventions   369

7   **Conclusions**   371
7.0   Introduction   371
7.1   Pragmatics and 'core' linguistics   372
7.2   Pragmatics, sociolinguistics and psycholinguistics 374
7.3   Applied pragmatics: pragmatics and other fields 376

       Bibliography   379
       Subject index   397
       Index of names   417

To Nicholas' grandparents

PREFACE

To squeeze all that goes under the rubric of **pragmatics** within the confines of a linguistics textbook would be neither possible nor desirable. Consequently this book is quite conservative in scope and approach, and considers the main topics in a particular tradition of work. This is the largely Anglo-American linguistic and philosophical tradition that builds directly, for the most part, on philosophical approaches to language of both the logical and 'ordinary language' variety (an exception is the set of topics treated in Chapter 6, which has a sociological origin). In contrast, the continental tradition is altogether broader, and would include much that also goes under the rubric of *sociolinguistics*. But even within this much narrower field, this book is in some ways restricted, since its main aim is to provide an introduction and background to those topics that, perhaps largely for historical reasons, are central to the Anglo-American tradition of work in pragmatics. The would-be pragmaticist must understand these issues in depth, if he or she is to understand the background to a great deal of current research in both linguistics and philosophy.

One major way in which this book is perhaps innovative is the inclusion in Chapter 6 of a brief review of work in conversation analysis. Apart from its demonstrable importance for theories of language usage, work in conversation analysis contributes directly to many of the same issues that have preoccupied philosophers of language, and thence linguists, while employing a startlingly different methodology. So both despite and because of the fact that conversation analysis springs from a quite different tradition from the other topics reviewed, a summary of findings is included here. In the Chapter, I have presented explicitly a re-analysis of some issues in the philosophical theory of speech acts along conversation analytic lines, but the reader should be able to spot a number of further re-analyses of material dealt with differently elsewhere in the book.

Nevertheless, the omission of certain topics from coverage in this book does warrant explanation. In the first place, a relatively narrow range of contextual factors and their linguistic correlates are considered here: **context** in this book includes only some of the basic parameters of the context of utterance, including participants' identity, role and location, assumptions about what participants know or take for granted, the place of an utterance within a sequence of turns at talking, and so on. We know in fact that there are a number of additional contextual parameters that are systematically related to linguistic organization, particularly principles of social interaction of various sorts of both a culture-specific (see e.g. Keenan, 1976b) and universal kind (see e.g. Brown & Levinson, 1978). Such omissions reflect the primary aim of the book, namely to provide an introduction to the philosophico-linguistic tradition, rather than to attempt an exhaustive coverage of all the contextual co-ordinates of linguistic organization.

Secondly, there are two particular topics omitted that are generally admitted to belong within a fairly narrow view of what constitutes pragmatics. One is the **topic/comment** (or **theme/rheme**) distinction. Terminological profusion and confusion, and underlying conceptual vagueness, plague the relevant literature to a point where little may be salvageable (but see e.g. Gundel, 1977). For example, whereas we may be told how to identify a topic in a simplex declarative sentence, we are never told how to identify the topics of a sentence of arbitrary complexity (i.e. we are never offered a projection principle). In addition there is reason to think that the whole area may be reducible to a number of different factors: to matters of presupposition and implicature on the one hand, and to the discourse functions of utterance-initial (and other) positions on the other. The other major omission is less defensible, namely the absence of systematic remarks on prosody, and intonation and stress in particular. The fact is that, given the clear importance of prosodic factors in pragmatics, the area is grossly understudied. There is disagreement even about the fundamentals of how such factors should be described, whether as discrete elements or variable ones, wholes (e.g. tonal contours) or parts (e.g. 'levels'), evidenced by quite different approaches on either side of the Atlantic. But if the way in which the phenomena are to be recorded is unsettled, the pragmatic functions of prosodic patterns are really quite unexplored (see, though, e.g. Brazil, Coulthard & Johns, 1980). Future textbook writers will hopefully find themselves in a happier position. Meanwhile the omission should be recorded.

The reader may also be disappointed to find little reference to languages other than English (Chapter 2 is a partial exception). The problem here is that other languages, and especially non-Indo-European ones, have simply not been subjected to the same kind of analysis. This is the more regrettable because, from those investigations that have been done (e.g. Fillmore, 1975; Anderson & Keenan, in press; Sadock & Zwicky, in press), it seems likely that pragmatic organization is subject to very interesting cross-linguistic variation. But until we have much more information in hand, we can only guess at the universal application (or otherwise) of those categories of analysis that have been developed. In this respect, we can hope for significant advances in the next decade or so.

The book also contains no systematic observation and theory about the relations between pragmatics and syntax. There are, of course, theorists who hold, by theoretical *fiat*, that no such relations exist (Lightfoot, 1979: 43–4). The fact remains that there are clear interactions between the organization of syntactic elements in a clause and pragmatic constraints of various sorts (see e.g. Green, 1978a, 1978b; Givon, 1979a; Gazdar, 1980a). Two general issues arise here. One is how such interactions are to be described in models of grammar: should we think in terms of a syntax that can refer to pragmatic constraints (see e.g. Ross, 1975), or rather should we let the syntax generate pragmatic anomalies, which some pragmatic component can later filter out (see e.g. Gazdar & Klein, 1977)? Although current thinking would tend to prefer the latter solution, there have been few concrete proposals for such a pragmatic filtering device, and no serious assessment of the degree to which such a device would simply duplicate syntactic machinery. A second general issue that arises is whether these observable interactions have any systematic basis: can a pragmatic theory accurately predict just what kind of pragmatic constraints on what kinds of syntactic processes are likely to occur? That would certainly be a reasonable expectation, but at the moment we can only list an apparently heterogeneous collection of such constraints, of many different kinds. The present lack of interesting answers to either of these questions motivates the light treatment of these issues in this book, although possible interactions between pragmatics and syntax will be noted in passing.

The acquisition of pragmatic aspects of language by children is also excluded from consideration here, partly on the grounds that the early work in this area (e.g. Bates, 1976) was derivative from, rather than contributory to, the basic concepts reviewed in this book. Recently, though, acquisition studies have begun to contribute directly to theoretical issues in pragmatics (see e.g. Ochs & Schieffelin, 1979) and a review of this work would be valuable in a volume of larger dimensions.

Finally, those whose linguistic sights extend back beyond 1957 may find the lack of reference to Malinowski, Firth and other 'proto-pragmaticists' peculiar. And of course, within the history of linguistics, pragmatics is a remedial discipline born, or re-born, of the starkly limited scope of Chomskyan linguistics (while in philosophy, the interest in language use can in part be attributed to reaction against the extremes of logical positivism and 'language reformism'). Pragmatics prior to 1957, it could be argued, was practised (if in an informal way) without being preached. By way of extenuation for this historical myopia, it could be said that this book is at least in line with the attitudes of most of the current practitioners in the field.

With these limitations recognized, this book will, I hope, be of use to advanced undergraduates, as well as more advanced researchers, in linguistics, literary studies, psychology, anthropology and other disciplines with an interest in language use, as a crystallization of issues presupposed, but rarely explicated in full, elsewhere. Even philosophers should find interesting the distortion of many philosophical ideas in a linguistic mirror.

A note on how to use this book

There is a logical progression through the Chapters in the sense that each presupposes concepts explained in earlier ones. However, the reliance on concepts introduced earlier varies: Chapters 2, 3 and 5 are relatively self-contained, and 6 could almost stand alone. But Chapter 4 will make little sense without having previously read Chapter 3. Deft use of the Subject index to clarify concepts previously introduced should allow most of the Chapters to be read alone.

Finally, the introductory Chapter constantly refers to Chapters ahead – it is hard not to presuppose many pragmatic concepts in discussing the scope and nature of the field. Indeed, if readers find the introduction hard going, they should read just the last section, then plunge into the body of the book, and return to Chapter 1 when puzzles arise about the general nature of the field.

Although I have tried to make this book self-contained, there is no doubt that readers will get more out of it if they already have some grounding in semantics in particular. Here two other books in this series should be helpful, viz. *Semantic Theory* and *Logic in Linguistics*. Where further reading on any topic is required, the many references will provide a guide, but two works especially will be of general use, namely Lyons, 1977a and Gazdar, 1979a. The most useful collections of primary sources are Cole & Morgan, 1975; Rogers, Wall & Murphy, 1977; Cole, 1978; Schenkein, 1978; Oh & Dinneen, 1979; and Cole, 1981. The bibliography by Gazdar, Klein & Pullum (1978) has listings for various pragmatic topics, and there is an annotated bibliography of pragmatics by Verschueren (1978). Articles on pragmatics now appear in most of the major linguistic journals, but the *Journal of Pragmatics* and the series *Pragmatics and Beyond* may be of special interest.

ACKNOWLEDGEMENTS

Textbook writers must in general be intellectual sponges and spongers. Those whose brains have been drained include so many friends, colleagues and students, that to acknowledge them all here, let alone at every relevant place, would be impossible. I hope they will forgive me if they find an idea or expression of their own borrowed without particular acknowledgement. But I must offer specific thanks to Penny Brown, Paul Drew, John Haviland, John Heritage, Peter Matthews, Marion Owen, Alan Rumsey, Jerrold Sadock and Deirdre Wilson who gave me very helpful comments on parts of the draft, and especially to Jay Atlas, Gerald Gazdar and my extraordinarily diligent editor John Lyons who provided extremely detailed comments on the whole. The book has been improved immeasurably by their care. I have not always taken their advice, and where faults and infelicities remain, they are almost certainly my own. I should also record a debt to my original mentors in pragmatics, Charles Fillmore, John Gumperz, George Lakoff, Robin Lakoff, Emanuel Schegloff and John Trim. As an experiment, this book has been printed with the aid of computer files supplied by the author: however, without Colin Duly's re-organization of those files, it would be a heap of gibberish, and without John Haviland's help in converting the files from a Cambridge to a Canberra installation and back again, non-existent. Penny Carter, and other officers of the Press, were patient enough to see the process through. Finally, my thanks to the Department of Anthropology, Research School of Pacific Studies, at the Australian National University, for providing the facilities where this book was finished in congenial and stimulating company. If readers get anything out of this book, my thanks and theirs to the named and nameless here acknowledged.

NOTATION CONVENTIONS

(For elementary explications of logical symbolism see Allwood, Andersson & Dahl, 1977; for transcription conventions, used mostly in Chapter 6, see the Appendix to that Chapter.)

A, B, C	sentential variables (esp. Chapter 4)
p, q, r	sentential variables
$A(e_1)$	ad hoc notation for a sentential variable that indicates the occurrence of an expression e_1 in a sentence A
F, G	predicate constants, as in $F(x)$; also predicate variables in section 3.2.6
a, b, c	individual constants; also persons in expressions like 'a knows that p'
x, y, z	individual variables
∨	inclusive disjunction
V	exclusive disjunction
~	negation
→	material conditional
↔	biconditional
=	identity
≠	negative identity
∀	universal quantifier
∃	existential quantifier
∈	is an element of a set
{ }	sets
⟨ ⟩	ordered sets or n-tuples
‖-	entailment
⟩⟩	presupposes
+⟩	implicates
K	speaker knows that; thus Kp = speaker knows that p

P   epistemic possibility for speaker; thus $Pp = p$ is compatible
             with all that the speaker knows

$\square$ necessary; e.g. $\square p =$ it is necessary that p

$\diamond$ possible; e.g. $\diamond p =$ it is possible that p

λ lambda-operator (Chapter 4)

γ gamma-operator (Chapter 4)

I

The scope of pragmatics

The purpose of this Chapter is to provide some indication of the scope of linguistic pragmatics. First, the historical origin of the term **pragmatics** will be briefly summarized, in order to indicate some usages of the term that are divergent from the usage in this book. Secondly, we will review some definitions of the field, which, while being less than fully satisfactory, will at least serve to indicate the rough scope of linguistic pragmatics. Thirdly, some reasons for the current interest in the field will be explained, while a final section illustrates some basic kinds of pragmatic phenomena. In passing, some analytical notions that are useful background will be introduced.

1.1 The origin and historical vagaries of the term pragmatics

The modern usage of the term **pragmatics** is attributable to the philosopher Charles Morris (1938), who was concerned to outline (after Locke and Peirce)[1] the general shape of a science of signs, or **semiotics** (or **semiotic** as Morris preferred). Within semiotics, Morris distinguished three distinct branches of inquiry: **syntactics** (or **syntax**), being the study of "the formal relation of signs to one another", **semantics**, the study of "the relations of signs to the objects to which the signs are applicable" (their designata), and **pragmatics**, the study of "the relation of signs to interpreters" (1938: 6). Within each branch of semiotics, one could make the distinction between **pure** studies, concerned with the

---

[1] Apart from this connection, there is only the slightest historical relation between pragmatics and the philosophical doctrines of **pragmatism** (see Morris, 1938 (1971: 43); Lyons, 1977a: 119). There have been recent attempts, however, to recast Morris's trichotomy in a Peircean (or pragmatist) mould, which are not covered in this book: see Silverstein, 1976; Bean, 1978.

elaboration of the relevant metalanguage, and **descriptive** studies which applied the metalanguage to the description of specific signs and their usages (1938 (1971: 24)).

As instances of usage governed by **pragmatical rule**, Morris noted that "interjections such as *Oh!*, commands such as *Come here!*, ... expressions such as *Good morning!* and various rhetorical and poetical devices, occur only under certain definite conditions in the users of the language" (1938 (1971: 48)). Such matters would still today be given a treatment within linguistic pragmatics. But Morris went on to expand the scope of pragmatics in accord with his particular behaviouristic theory of semiotics (Black, 1947): "It is a sufficiently accurate characterization of pragmatics to say that it deals with the biotic aspects of semiosis, that is, with all the psychological, biological, and sociological phenomena which occur in the functioning of signs" (1938: 108). Such a scope is very much wider than the work that currently goes on under the rubric of linguistic pragmatics, for it would include what is now known as psycholinguistics, sociolinguistics, neurolinguistics and much besides.

Since Morris's introduction of the trichotomy syntax, semantics and pragmatics, the latter term has come to be used in two very distinct ways. On the one hand, the very broad use intended by Morris has been retained, and this explains the usage of the term *pragmatics* in the titles of books that deal, for example, with matters as diverse as the psychopathology of communication (in the manner of G. Bateson and R. D. Laing – see Watzlawick, Beavin & Jackson, 1967) and the evolution of symbol systems (see Cherry, 1974). Even here though, there has been a tendency to use *pragmatics* exclusively as a division of *linguistic* semiotics, rather than as pertaining to sign systems in general. This broad usage of the term, covering sociolinguistics, psycholinguistics and more, is still the one generally used on the Continent (see e.g. the collection in Wunderlich, 1972, and issues of the *Journal of Pragmatics*).

On the other hand, and especially within analytical philosophy, the term *pragmatics* was subject to a successive narrowing of scope. Here the philosopher and logician Carnap was particularly influential. After an initial Morrisian usage (Carnap, 1938: 2), he adopted the following version of the trichotomy:

> If in an investigation explicit reference is made to the speaker, or to put it in more general terms, to the user of the language,

then we assign it [the investigation] to the field of pragmatics
... If we abstract from the user of the language and analyze only
the expressions and their designata, we are in the field of
semantics. And, finally, if we abstract from the designata also
and analyze only the relations between the expressions, we are
in (logical) syntax.

Unfortunately Carnap's usage of the term *pragmatics* was confused
by his adoption of Morris's further distinction between pure and
descriptive studies, and he came to equate pragmatics with descriptive
semiotics in general, and thus with the study of natural (as opposed
to logical) languages (Carnap, 1959: 13; see the useful clarification
in Lieb, 1971). But Carnap was not even consistent here: he also held
(Carnap, 1956) that there was room for a **pure pragmatics** which
would be concerned with concepts like *belief*, *utterance*, and *intension*
and their logical inter-relation. This latter usage, now more or less
defunct, explains the use of the term in, for example, the title of a
book by Martin (1959). Thus at least four quite different senses of
the term can be found in Carnap's works, but it was the definition
quoted above that was finally influential.

Incidentally, already in Morris's and Carnap's usages there can be
found a systematic three-way ambiguity: the term *pragmatics* was
applied not only to branches of inquiry (as in the contrast between
pragmatics and semantics), but also to features of the object language
(or language under investigation), so that one could talk of, say, the
pragmatic particle *Oh!* in English, and to features of the metalanguage
(or technical description), so that one could talk of, say, a pragmatic,
versus a semantic, description of the particle *Oh!*. Such an ambiguity
merely seems to parallel the way in which the sister terms *semantics*
and *syntax* are used, and to introduce little confusion (but cf.
Sayward, 1974).

The idea that pragmatics was the study of aspects of language that
required reference to the users of the language then led to a very
natural, further restriction of the term in analytical philosophy. For
there is one aspect of natural languages that indubitably requires such
reference, namely the study of **deictic** or **indexical** words like the
pronouns *I* and *you* (see Chapter 2). The philosophical, and especially
logical, interest in these terms is simply that they account for the
potential failure of generally valid schemes of reasoning. For example,
"I am Greta Garbo, Greta Garbo is a woman, therefore I am a

3

woman", is only necessarily true if in addition to the first two premises being true, the speaker of the conclusion is the same speaker as the speaker of the first premise. Bar-Hillel (1954) therefore took the view that pragmatics is the study of languages, both natural and artificial, that contain indexical or deictic terms, and this usage was explicitly adopted by Kalish (1967), and most influentially by Montague (1968). Such a usage has little to offer linguists, since all natural languages have deictic terms, and it would follow, as Gazdar (1979a: 2) points out, that natural languages would have no semantics but only a syntax and a pragmatics. If the trichotomy is to do some work within linguistics, some less restricted scope for pragmatics must be found.

In fact, in the late 1960s, an implicit version of Carnap's definition – investigations requiring reference to the users of a language – was adopted within linguistics, and specifically within the movement known as **generative semantics**. The history of that movement awaits a historian of ideas (but see Newmeyer, 1980), but its association with pragmatics can be explained by the resurgence of the interest in meaning which the movement represented. Such an interest inevitably involves pragmatics, as we shall see. Moreover this interest in meaning in a wide sense proved to be one of the best directions from which generative semantics could assail Chomsky's (1965) **standard theory**. At the same time, there was a keen interest shown by linguists in philosophers' attempts to grapple with problems of meaning, sometimes from the point of view of the 'users of the language'. For a period, at least, linguists and philosophers seemed to be on a common path, and this commonality of interest crystallized many of the issues with which this book is concerned. During this period, the scope of pragmatics was implicitly restricted. Carnap's 'investigations making reference to users of the language' is at once too narrow and too broad for linguistic interests. It is too broad because it admits studies as non-linguistic as Freud's investigations of 'slips of the tongue' or Jung's studies of word associations. So studies in linguistic pragmatics need to be restricted to investigations that have at least potential linguistic implications. On the other hand, Carnap's definition is too narrow in that, on a simple inter-pretation, it excludes parallel phenomena.[2] For example, just as the

---

[2] On another interpretation, all pragmatic parameters refer to users of the language, if only because such parameters must, in order to be relevant, be known or believed by participants.

interpretation of the words *I* and *you* relies on the identification of particular participants (or 'users') and their role in the speech event, so the words *here* and *now* rely for their interpretation on the place and time of the speech event. Therefore Carnap's definition might be amended to something like: 'those linguistic investigations that make necessary reference to aspects of the context', where the term **context** is understood to cover the identities of participants, the temporal and spatial parameters of the speech event, and (as we shall see) the beliefs, knowledge and intentions of the participants in that speech event, and no doubt much besides.

To summarize, a number of distinct usages of the term *pragmatics* have sprung from Morris's original division of semiotics: the study of the huge range of psychological and sociological phenomena involved in sign systems in general or in language in particular (the Continental sense of the term); or the study of certain abstract concepts that make reference to agents (one of Carnap's senses); or the study of indexicals or deictic terms (Montague's sense); or finally the recent usage within Anglo-American linguistics and philosophy. This book is concerned exclusively with the last sense of the term, and it is to an explication of this particular usage that we should now turn.

1.2 Defining pragmatics

The relatively restricted sense of the term *pragmatics* in Anglo-American philosophy and linguistics, and correspondingly in this book, deserves some attempt at definition. Such a definition is, however, by no means easy to provide, and we shall play with a number of possibilities each of which will do little more than sketch a range of possible scopes for the field. This diversity of possible definitions and lack of clear boundaries may be disconcerting, but it is by no means unusual: since academic fields are congeries of preferred methods, implicit assumptions, and focal problems or subject matters, attempts to define them are rarely wholly satisfactory. And indeed, in one sense there is no problem of definition at all: just as, traditionally, syntax is taken to be the study of the combinatorial properties of words and their parts, and semantics to be the study of meaning, so pragmatics is the study of language usage. Such a definition is just as good (and bad) as the parallel definitions of the sister terms, but it will hardly suffice to indicate what the practioners

5

of pragmatics actually do; to find that out, as in any discipline, one must go and take a look.

Nevertheless, there are reasons for attempting at least some indication of the scope of pragmatics. In the first place, it is simply a sufficiently unfamiliar term. In the second place, it is not so easy to just 'go and take a look' at what workers in pragmatics do: there are (at the time of writing) no available textbooks, only one specialist journal (*Journal of Pragmatics*) and that covering the broader Continental usage of the term, only a handful of monographs and a few collections of papers. Nevertheless, there is much work scattered throughout the various journals of linguistics and philosophy. Thirdly, some authors seem to suggest that there is no coherent field at all; thus Lyons (1977a: 117) states that "the applicability [of the distinction between syntax, semantics and pragmatics] to the description of natural languages, in contrast to the description or construction of logical calculi, is, to say the least, uncertain", while Searle, Kiefer & Bierwisch (1980: viii) suggest that "*Pragmatics* is one of those words (*societal* and *cognitive* are others) that give the impression that something quite specific and technical is being talked about when often in fact it has no clear meaning." The pragmaticist is thus challenged to show that, at least within the linguistic and philosophical tradition that is the concern of this book, the term does have clear application.

Let us therefore consider a set of possible definitions of pragmatics. We shall find that each of them has deficiencies or difficulties of a sort that would equally hinder definitions of other fields, but at least in this way, by assaults from all flanks, a good sketch of the general topography can be obtained.

Let us start with some definitions that are in fact less than satisfactory. One possible definition might go as follows: pragmatics is the study of those principles that will account for why a certain set of sentences are anomalous, or not possible utterances. That set might include:[3]

---

[3] We shall use the symbol ?? at the beginning of example sentences to indicate that they are (at least putatively) pragmatically anomalous, reserving * for sentences that are syntactically ill-formed or semantically anomalous; a single initial ? indicates anomaly on at least one of these three levels, but is non-committal about the nature of the anomaly.

(1)   ??Come there please!
(2)   ??Aristotle was Greek, but I don't believe it
(3)   ??Fred's children are hippies, and he has no children
(4)   ??Fred's children are hippies, and he has children
(5)   ??I order you not to obey this order
(6)   ??I hereby sing
(7)   ??As everyone knows, the earth please revolves around the sun

The explanation of the anomalies exhibited by these sentences might be provided by pointing out that there are no, or at least no ordinary, contexts in which they could be appropriately used.[4] Although an approach of this sort may be quite a good way of illustrating the kind of principles that pragmatics is concerned with, it will hardly do as an explicit definition of the field – for the simple reason that the set of pragmatic (as opposed to semantic, syntactic or sociolinguistic) anomalies are presupposed, rather than explained.[5]

Another kind of definition that might be offered would be that pragmatics is the study of language from a **functional** perspective, that is, that it attempts to explain facets of linguistic structure by reference to non-linguistic pressures and causes. But such a definition, or scope, for pragmatics would fail to distinguish linguistic pragmatics from many other disciplines interested in functional approaches to language, including psycholinguistics and sociolinguistics. Moreover, it may be plausibly argued that to adopt a definition of this sort is to confuse the *motives* for studying pragmatics, with the *goals* or general shape of a theory (about which more later).

One quite restricted scope for pragmatics that has been proposed is that pragmatics should be concerned solely with principles of language usage, and have nothing to do with the description of linguistic structure. Or, to invoke Chomsky's distinction between **competence** and **performance**, pragmatics is concerned solely with performance principles of language use. Thus, Katz & Fodor (1963) suggested that a theory of pragmatics (or a theory of **setting**

---

[4] This line of argument relies on the distinction between **use** and **mention**, or between 'ordinary' usage and metalinguistic usage, for which see Lyons, 1977a: 5ff and references therein. In the sense of this distinction, sentences like (1)–(7) can be mentioned, but they cannot easily be used.

[5] Another problem is that it is often in fact possible to imagine contexts in which the alleged anomalies are after all quite usable – the reader can try with the examples above. This problem will recur when we consider the concept of appropriateness of an utterance, discussed below.

selection as they then called it) would essentially be concerned with the disambiguation of sentences by the contexts in which they were uttered. In fact it is clear that contexts do a lot more than merely select between available semantic readings of sentences – for example, irony, understatement and the like are kinds of use that actually create new interpretations in contexts. Still, one could claim that grammar (in the broad sense inclusive of phonology, syntax and semantics) is concerned with the context-free assignment of meaning to linguistic forms, while pragmatics is concerned with the further interpretation of those forms in a context:

> [Grammars] are theories about the structure of sentence types ... Pragmatic theories, in contrast, do nothing to explicate the structure of linguistic constructions or grammatical properties and relations ... They explicate the reasoning of speakers and hearers in working out the correlation in a context of a sentence token with a proposition. In this respect, a pragmatic theory is part of performance. (Katz, 1977: 19)

This position has a number of adherents (Kempson, 1975, 1977; Smith & Wilson, 1979), but it has a serious difficulty. The problem is that aspects of linguistic structure sometimes directly encode (or otherwise interact with) features of the context. It then becomes impossible to draw a neat boundary between context-independent grammar (competence) and context-dependent interpretation (performance). This problem is unwittingly illustrated by Katz's explication of this boundary: he points out that the pairs *rabbit* and *bunny*, or *dog* and *doggie* differ in that the second member of each pair is appropriately used either by or to children. Since the distinction is one relating to the appropriate users of the terms in a context, the distinction would not be part of a linguistic description of English, which would merely note that the members of each pair are synonymous. However, it is clear that the distinction is built into the language, in just the same way that in many languages degrees of respect between participants are encoded in lexis and morphology. Katz suggests that in order to ascertain whether a linguistic feature is context-dependent or context-independent, we imagine the feature occurring on an anonymous postcard (as an approximation to the empty or **null context**).[6] But if we apply this criterion we see that

---

[6] Here contrast Searle (1979b: 117): "There is no such thing as the zero or null context for the interpretation of sentences ... we understand the meaning

the implication or inference that speaker or addressee is a child is as available when *bunny* is written on an anonymous postcard as it is when said in some concrete appropriate context (Gazdar, 1979a: 3). And that of course is because the kind of appropriate speaker or addressee is encoded by the term *bunny*.

Here we come to the heart of the definitional problem: the term *pragmatics* covers both context-dependent aspects of language structure and principles of language usage and understanding that have nothing or little to do with linguistic structure. It is difficult to forge a definition that will happily cover both aspects. But this should not be taken to imply that pragmatics is a hodge-podge, concerned with quite disparate and unrelated aspects of language; rather, pragmaticists are specifically interested in the inter-relation of language structure and principles of language usage. Let us now consider some potential definitions that are more plausible candidates.

We may begin with a definition that is specifically aimed at capturing the concern of pragmatics with features of language structure. The definition might go as follows:

(8)   Pragmatics is the study of those relations between language and context that are **grammaticalized**, or encoded in the structure of a language[7]

Or, putting it another way, one could say that pragmatics is the study of just those aspects of the relationship between language and context that are relevant to the writing of grammars. Such a definition restricts pragmatics to the study of certain aspects of linguistic structure, and stands in strong contrast to Katz's proposal, outlined above, that would restrict pragmatics to the study of grammatically irrelevant aspects of language usage. Such a scope for pragmatics would include the study of **deixis**, including honorifics and the like, and probably the study of **presupposition** and **speech acts**, i.e. much of the present book. It would exclude the study of principles of language usage that could not be shown to have repercussions on the grammar of languages, and this could be an embarrassment,

of such sentences only against a set of background assumptions about the contexts in which the sentence could be appropriately uttered."

[7] The term *grammaticalization* is used throughout this book in the broad sense covering the encoding of meaning distinctions – again in a wide sense – in the lexicon, morphology, syntax and phonology of languages.

because, at least at first sight, the extremely important implications called **conversational implicatures** would lie outside the purview of a pragmatic theory. On the other hand, such a scope for pragmatics has the possible advantage that it would effectively delimit the field, and exclude neighbouring fields like sociolinguistics and psycho-linguistics – in short it would bound Morris's and Carnap's definitions in a way that guaranteed linguistic relevance.

Now, any definition of pragmatics that excludes one of its presumed focal phenomena, namely conversational implicature, is unlikely to be attractive. Nevertheless, its adherents might appeal to the plausi-bility of the following general principle: any systematic principle of language usage is ultimately likely to have an impact on language structure. There is perhaps some basis for such an assumption (see e.g. Brown & Levinson, 1978: 26off). And in fact conversational implicatures, which are inferences that arise on the basis of some general rules or maxims of conversational behaviour, can indeed be shown to have repercussions on linguistic structure (see Chapter 3 below). So the definition may in fact be much less restrictive than it appears at first sight.

Other problems concern the notions of context and gram-maticalization that the definition rests on. Arguably, though, it is a strength of this approach that it is not required to give a prior characterization of the notion of context. For, assuming that we have a clear idea of the limits of semantics, then pragmatics studies all the non-semantic features that are encoded in languages, and these features are aspects of the context. What aspects of the gross physical, social and interactional aspects of the situation of utterance are linguistically relevant is thus an empirical question, and we can study the world's languages to find out what they are. Of course, we would need to make an important distinction here between **universal pragmatics**, the general theory of what aspects of context get encoded and how, and the **language-specific pragmatics** of individual languages; for example, the pragmatics of English might have relatively little to say about social status (beyond what we need to describe the appropriate contexts for the use of *sir*, *your honour* and the like), while in contrast the pragmatics of Japanese would be greatly concerned with the grammaticalization of the relative social ranks of participants and referents.

On the other hand, the notion of grammaticalization, or linguistic encoding, is thorny. To be effective, we need to be able to distinguish mere correlation between linguistic form and context from incorporation of contextual significance into the associated linguistic form. There is little doubt that there are clear cases of the one and the other: for example, the slurred speech associated with drunkenness may be mere correlation, while the association of intimacy or solidarity with the French pronoun *tu* is a grammaticalized feature of context. But there are many borderline cases. To make the distinction, perhaps the following criteria might be suggested: for a feature of the context to be linguistically encoded, (a) it must be intentionally communicated, (b) it must be conventionally associated with the linguistic form in question, (c) the encoding form must be a member of a contrast set, the other members of which encode different features, (d) the linguistic form must be subject to regular grammatical processes. On these grounds one might hope to exclude, say, the association of a particular dialect with a speaker from a particular area – such an association, perhaps, not being normally intentionally conveyed, not being associated with the linguistic features by arbitrary convention but by historical 'accident', and so on. On the other hand, features of 'baby talk', of which the lexical alternate *bunny* is a part, would presumably be considered to be encoded in English, because at least some of them seem to meet these criteria. However, it is unlikely that these criteria are sufficient to distinguish many borderline cases, and the notion would need further explication.[8]

In sum, the main strength of this definition of pragmatics is that it restricts the field to purely linguistic matters. Yet it is probably too restrictive to reflect accurately current usage. The most unfortunate restriction is the exclusion of those principles of language use and interpretation that explain how extra meaning (in a broad sense) is 'read into' utterances without actually being encoded in them. It is a definition, then, that handles the aspect of pragmatics concerned with linguistic structure, but not the side concerned with principles of language usage, or at least only indirectly as they impinge on linguistic organization.

In the definition above, the notion of encoding implies that pragmatics is concerned with certain aspects of meaning. One kind of definition that would make this central might run as follows:

---

[8] Consider e.g. the French *Je suis malheureuse*, which encodes that the speaker is female: in what sense would this be *intentionally* communicated?

(9)   Pragmatics is the study of all those aspects of meaning not captured in a semantic theory

Or, as Gazdar (1979a: 2) has put it, assuming that semantics is limited to the statement of truth conditions:

> Pragmatics has as its topic those aspects of the meaning of utterances which cannot be accounted for by straightforward reference to the truth conditions of the sentences uttered.[9] Put crudely: PRAGMATICS   =   MEANING – TRUTH CONDITIONS.

Such a definition is likely, at first, to cause puzzlement. Surely semantics is, by definition, the study of meaning in its entirety, so how can there be any residue to constitute the topic of pragmatics? But here we need to note that the definition of semantics as the study of meaning is just as simplistic as the definition of pragmatics as the study of language usage. First, we need to distinguish between some broad sense of the term *semantics* used in a more or less pre-theoretical way (see e.g. the coverage in Lyons, 1977a),[10] and a technical use of the term to cover a particular, deliberately restricted semantic theory in an overall theory of grammar, or language structure. Semantic theory in the latter sense is going to have a very much narrower scope than the study of meaning in its entirety, as we shall indicate immediately below. Secondly, the intended scope of the term *meaning* in the definition is extremely broad, in a way that will need explication. So the answer to the puzzle is that, from the point of view of an overall integrated linguistic theory, there will be a great deal of the general field of meaning left unaccounted for by a restricted semantic theory, and this could indeed constitute the domain of pragmatics.

One objection to such a definition could be that the scope of pragmatics would seem therefore to vary considerably according to the kind of semantic theory adopted – narrow semantic theories like those based on truth conditions will leave a large residue of 'meaning' to be studied in pragmatics; apparently broader semantic theories, like some of those based on components or features of meaning, may leave much less for pragmatics to deal with.[11] Certainly it has to be

---

[9] The "straightforward" qualification, Gazdar explains, is necessary because pragmatic implications often derive in part from the truth conditions of sentences uttered. See Chapter 3 below.

[10] A usage general in linguistics until the influence of formal semantics, practised by philosophers, was felt in the 1960s.

[11] Feature-based semantic theories are not of course *inherently* broader than truth-conditional ones. But feature-based theories are usually associated with

admitted that to some extent the nature of a pragmatic theory must depend crucially on the kind of semantic theory adopted, but that will be true for any definition of pragmatics that seeks an exclusive domain, complementary and non-overlapping with semantics. But it is important to see that this dependency is only partial, for we now know enough about the nature of meaning in the broad sense to make it likely that there are substantial areas that could not be accommodated within *any* single semantic theory built on homogeneous principles.

This knowledge is based on some substantial advances made in the last ten years or so, namely the discovery that there are at least half a dozen distinct and different kinds of meaning component or implication (or inference) that are involved in the meaning of natural language utterances. The distinctions are based on the fact that each of these kinds of inference behaves in different ways. In particular, they behave differently in **projection**, i.e. in the ways in which they are compounded when a complex sentence, whose parts produce the inferences in question, is built up. Some of these meaning components disappear under specific and distinctive conditions, namely particular linguistic constructions. In addition, some of these meaning components are **defeasible**, i.e. subject to cancellation by features of the context (a notion explained in Chapter 3 below). Such features interact with or arise from assumptions made by participants in the context, and are particularly inappropriate aspects of meaning to incorporate within a semantic theory. The dilemma that these multiple aspects of meaning pose for the semanticist can perhaps best be gauged from Table 1.1. Here we list seven such putative meaning components or inferential relations of an utterance, but it should be borne in mind that these particular aspects of meaning are subject to revision and addition: some may well collapse into others, while additional kinds of inference are undoubtedly waiting to be discovered (indeed, in the Chapters below, we shall be much concerned with how well each of these concepts is established).

The problem posed for the semantic theorist is how much to bite off – certainly no single coherent semantic theory can contain all these divergent aspects of meaning. If the theorist admits just the first kind of meaning component, the truth-conditional content, then at least (a) there are no conflicting principles for the inclusion or exclusion

a scope for semantics that would include all the conventional content of sentences, whereas (as we shall see) truth-conditional theories cannot have such a broad scope.

Table 1.1 *Elements of the communicational content of an utterance*

1. truth-conditions or entailments (Chapter 2 and passim)
2. conventional implicatures (Chapter 3)
3. presuppositions (Chapter 4)
4. felicity conditions (Chapter 5)
5. conversational implicature – generalized (Chapter 3)
6. conversational implicature – particularized (Chapter 3)
7. inferences based on conversational structure (Chapter 6)

Note: 1–2, and possibly also 3 and 4, are *conventional*; 3–7 are *defeasible* or context-dependent.

of phenomena and (b) semantic theory can be built on strictly homogeneous lines. Such a semantics will be narrow, and leave a great deal to pragmatics. On the other hand, if the theorist is determined that semantics should deal with all the conventional content of an utterance's significance (however exactly that is to be determined),[12] then semantic theory will deal with aspects 1 and 2, and quite likely 3 and possibly 4 as well. The inclusion of presupposition is awkward, however, for if presupposition is conventional, then it is also defeasible or context-dependent, and matters of context are best left for pragmatics. Thus, such a semantic theory (a) will contain conflicting principles for the inclusion (conventionality) and exclusion (defeasibility) of phenomena and (b) will have to be built on heterogeneous lines to include phenomena with quite different properties. Such difficulties might motivate a retreat to a semantic theory that deals only with aspects 1 and 2, i.e. conventional content that is non-defeasible, as an unhappy compromise.

In this book we shall assume, for working purposes, that a semantic

---

[12] The notion of conventional content is clearer intuitively than it is theoretically; for example, we would want to say that the term *genius* has the conventional content 'exceptional intellect' or the like, even though it may be predicated ironically, and thus convey the non-conventional meaning 'exceptional idiot'. Such a distinction would seem to rest on the distinction between content that is inherent or 'given' (cf. the Saussurean notion of the arbitrariness of the linguistic sign) and meaning that may be derived by general principles of inference taking contextual factors into account. See Lewis, 1969 for an important philosophical analysis of the concept of convention, which stresses the essentially arbitrary nature of any convention. See also Morgan, 1978; Searle, 1979b on the notion *literal meaning*.

theory is truth-conditional. Apart from the fact that it avoids the above dilemmas, by claiming only the narrowest scope for semantics, such a theory recommends itself to the pragmaticist for the following reasons. First, it is the only kind of theory now available that is precise and predictive enough to make investigable the nature of a semantics/pragmatics boundary, or the interaction between the two components. Secondly, it is arguable that most other theories, e.g. those based on semantic components, can be subsumed within it, in so far as they are built on consistent and logical lines. Thirdly, it is perhaps still the kind of theory with the most support in linguistic and philosophical circles, despite many dissenters and many unresolved problems. Finally, many of the issues in pragmatics have arisen historically from this particular vantage point, and to understand them one must at least at first approach from the same direction. But ultimately, the pragmaticist may do well to remain agnostic, whatever semantic theory is assumed for working purposes.

The point here, however, is that whatever kind of semantic theory is adopted, many aspects of meaning in a broad sense simply cannot be accommodated if the theory is to have an internal coherence and consistency. From what we now know about the nature of meaning, a hybrid or modular account seems inescapable: there remains the hope that with two components, a semantics and a pragmatics working in tandem, each can be built on relatively homogeneous and systematic lines. Such a hybrid theory will almost certainly be simpler and more principled than a single amorphous and heterogeneous theory of semantics.

So the notion that pragmatics might be the study of aspects of meaning not covered in semantics certainly has some cogency. But we need to know how the broad sense of meaning, on which the definition relies, is to be delimited. This broad sense should include the ironic, metaphoric and implicit communicative content of an utterance, and so it cannot be restricted to the conventional content of what is said. But does it include *all* the inferences that can be made from (a) what is said and (b) all the available facts about the world known to participants? Suppose that Moriarty says that his watch broke, and from this Sherlock Holmes infers that he perpetrated the crime: although the information may have been indirectly conveyed, we should be loath to say that Moriarty communicated it. For communication involves the notions of intention and agency, and only those inferences that are openly intended to be conveyed can properly be said to have been communicated. To help us draw a line between the incidental transfer of information, and communication proper, we may appeal to an important idea of the philosopher Grice (1957). Distinguishing between what he calls **natural meaning** (as in *Those black clouds mean rain*), and **non-natural meaning** or **meaning-nn** (equivalent to the notion of intentional communication), Grice gives the following characterization of meaning-nn:[13]

(10)   S *meant-nn* z by uttering U if and only if:
         (i) S intended U to cause some effect z in recipient H
         (ii) S intended (i) to be achieved simply by H recognizing that intention (i)

Here, S stands for speaker (in the case of spoken communication; for sender or communicator in other cases); H for hearer, or more accurately, the intended recipient; "uttering U" for utterance of a linguistic token, i.e. a sentence part, sentence, or string of sentences or sentence parts (or the production of non-linguistic communicative acts); and z for (roughly) some belief or volition invoked in H.

Such a definition is likely to be opaque at first reading, but what it essentially states is that communication consists of the 'sender' intending to cause the 'receiver' to think or do something, just by getting the 'receiver' to recognize that the 'sender' is trying to cause that thought or action. So communication is a complex kind of intention that is achieved or satisfied just by being recognized. In the process of communication, the 'sender's' communicative intention becomes **mutual knowledge** to 'sender' (S) and 'receiver' (H), i.e. S knows that H knows that S knows that H knows (and so ad infinitum) that S has this particular intention.[14] Attaining this state of mutual knowledge of a communicative intention is to have successfully communicated. A simple illustration may help to clarify the concept: it distinguishes between two kinds of 'boos', or

---

[13] There is a slight rephrasing of Grice's (1957) formulation here, legitimated, I hope, by Schiffer's (1972: 14) discussion.

[14] The concept of mutual knowledge is discussed in Lewis, 1969, and Schiffer, 1972: 30ff, and is of considerable potential importance to pragmatic theory; e.g. one may want to say that a speaker *presupposes* what speaker and addressee mutually know (although there are difficulties with this view – see Chapter 4 below). Schiffer (1972: 39) argues that the definition of *meaning-nn* should in fact make explicit reference to the concept of mutual knowledge. For a recent collection of papers on the subject see Smith, 1982.

attempts to frighten someone. Suppose I leap out from behind a tree, and by sheer surprise frighten you. I have caused an effect in you by 'natural' means. But now suppose that you know I am behind the tree, you are expecting me to leap out, and I know you know all that: I can still (maybe) frighten you by leaping out, just by getting you to realize that I intend to frighten you. Only the second is an instance of communication (meaning-nn) in Grice's sense. Grice intended his definition of communication to cover such non-verbal cases, but we will be concerned here (and henceforth) only with those cases where linguistic behaviour is part of the means whereby the communicative intention is recognized.

A puzzle that immediately arises is how this complex reflexive communicative intention is meant to be recognized by the recipient. Surely, one could argue, it can only be recognized by knowledge of some convention that U means *z*; but in that case we can do away with talk of complex intentions and construct an account of communication based directly on the notion of conventional signal. But this misses Grice's essential insight, namely that what the speaker means by U is not necessarily closely related to the meaning of U at all. Indeed U may have no conventional meaning, which allows for the creation of new terms, nonce expressions, and thus ultimately for some aspects of language change (for an explanation of how these communications may be understood, see Schiffer, 1972: Chapter V). But crucial for pragmatics, Grice's theory explains how there can be interesting discrepancies between **speaker-meaning** (Grice's meaning-nn) and **sentence-meaning**.[15] For example, *Linguistics is fascinating* said ironically may be intended by the speaker to communicate 'Linguistics is deadly boring'. Further, there appear to be general conventions about the use of language that require (or, perhaps, merely recommend) a certain degree of implicitness in

---

[15] This distinction is sometimes talked about in terms of **conveyed meaning** vs. **literal meaning**. In this book, instead of the notion literal meaning, we shall prefer the terms **sentence-meaning** or **conventional content** (the latter to cover linguistic expressions that are not necessarily sentences), although it is hard to do without the adjectival uses of *literal*. The reader is warned that none of these concepts is entirely clear (see e.g. Gazdar, 1979a: 157ff; Searle, 1979b: Chapter 5). There is a possible distinction between the notions sentence-meaning and literal meaning, such that e.g. *kick the bucket* has two sentence-meanings (one idiomatic, the other compositional) but only one literal meaning (the compositional, non-idiomatic reading). But we shall not exploit this distinction below.

communication, with the consequence that it is virtually ensured that what the speaker means by any utterance U is not exhausted by the meaning of the linguistic form uttered (see Chapter 3 below). How then is the full communicative intention to be recognized? By taking into account, not only the meaning of U, but also the precise mechanisms (like irony, or general assumptions of a certain level of implicitness) which may cause a divergence between the meaning of U and what is communicated by the utterance of U in a particular context. Much of this book is concerned with spelling out these mechanisms which, like other aspects of linguistic knowledge, we use daily in an unconscious way.

If we now adopt Grice's *meaning-nn* as the scope of meaning in the definition of pragmatics in (9), we shall include most of the phenomena that we want to include, like the ironic, metaphoric and indirect implications of what we say (elements 5, 6 and 7 in Table 1.1), and exclude the unintended inferences that intuitively have no part to play in a theory of communication. It should be added that there are a number of philosophical problems with Grice's theory (see e.g. Schiffer, 1972), but they do not seem to vitiate the value of the central idea.

We now have some sketch of the scope of meaning that is referred to in the definition, namely all that can be said to have been communicated, in Grice's sense, by the use of a linguistic token in a context. But can we give as a definition of pragmatics nothing but the complement of, or the residue left by, semantics in the field of meaning? Is there no conceptual integrity to the scope of pragmatics itself? We might try to find such a conceptual unity by making the distinction between sentence-meaning and utterance-meaning, and hope then to be able to equate semantics with the study of sentence-meaning and pragmatics with the study of utterance-meaning.

The distinction between **sentence** and **utterance** is of fundamental importance to both semantics and pragmatics. Essentially, we want to say that a sentence is an abstract theoretical entity defined within a theory of grammar, while an utterance is the issuance of a sentence, a sentence-analogue, or sentence-fragment, in an actual context. Empirically, the relation between an utterance and a corresponding sentence may be quite obscure (e.g. the utterance may be elliptical, or contain sentence-fragments or 'false-starts'), but it is customary (after Bar-Hillel) to think of an utterance as the pairing of a sentence and a context, namely the context in which the sentence was uttered. It is important, but in practice exceedingly difficult, to maintain this distinction at all times in the study of meaning. As an index of the difficulty, one may note that linguists frequently oscillate between assigning notions like *presupposition, illocutionary force, truth condition* to sentences or utterances, although important theoretical consequences follow from the choice. One may claim that the confusion here results from the need for yet further distinctions: thus Lyons (1977a) advocates distinctions between text-sentences and system-sentences, sentence-types and sentence-tokens, utterance-types and utterance-tokens, and utterance-acts and utterance-products. It is unlikely, though, that we can handle all these if we cannot make the first distinction systematically (and the alert reader can no doubt find mistakes of this sort within this book). For expositional reasons, we shall need to use the word *utterance* in various ways in this book, but where it is used to contrast with *sentence* it should be taken in the sense advocated by Bar-Hillel, as a sentence (or sometimes string of sentences) paired with a context.[16] And this is the sense relevant to the proposal that semantics is concerned with sentence-meaning, and pragmatics with utterance-meaning.

Many authors accept this equation implicitly, but there are a number of problems with it. In the first place, in the (rare) cases where sentence-meaning exhausts utterance-meaning (i.e. where the speaker meant exactly what he said, no more, no less), the same content would be assigned both to semantics and pragmatics. In other words, we would need to restrict the notion of utterance-meaning in such a way that we subtract sentence-meaning, and in that case we are back to a definition of pragmatics by residue. But there are other problems: for there are aspects of sentence-meaning which, at least on truth-conditional or other narrow semantic theories, cannot be accounted for within semantic theory. Such aspects are conventional but non-truth-conditional elements of sentence-meaning, e.g. what we shall call *conventional implicatures* and (at least on many theories)

---

[16] Here the simplifying assumption is made that what speakers produce – Lyons's *utterance-products* – are equivalent to sentences, Lyons's *system-sentences* or theoretical entities. The limitations of such an assumption will be made clear in Chapter 6. The other main way in which the term *utterance* will be used is as a pre-theoretical term to label "any stretch of talk, by one person, before and after which there is silence on behalf of that person" (Harris, 1951: 14; adopted in Lyons, 1977a: 26).

presuppositions, and perhaps even aspects of *illocutionary force* (concepts expounded in the Chapters below). On the assumption of a truth-conditional semantics, such aspects of sentence-meaning would have to be dealt with in pragmatics, and so there can be no direct equation of sentence-meaning and semantics. On the same assumption, there is another overwhelming problem for the proposal: for it is not sentences but rather utterances that make definite statements, and thus can sensibly be assigned truth conditions (as philosophers have long noted; see e.g. Strawson, 1950; Stalnaker, 1972). The argument rests in part on the pervasive nature of deixis (see Chapter 2 below) in natural languages, for sentences like (11) are true or false only relative to contextual parameters, thanks to the fact that *I*, *now* and the tense of *am* are variables given specific values only on particular occasions of utterance (i.e. (11) is true only when spoken by certain speakers, those who are sixty-three, or true of individuals only at certain times, when they are sixty-three):

(11)   I am now sixty-three years old

These facts seem to establish that truth conditions must be assigned to utterances, i.e. sentences with their associated contexts of utterance, not to sentences alone (or, if one likes, truth conditions include context conditions). So again, it makes no sense to equate semantics with the study of sentence-meaning.

There is another formulation of essentially the same proposal: semantics should be concerned with meaning out of context, or non-context-dependent meaning, and pragmatics with meaning in context. The strong version of this, apparently held by Katz (1977), assumes that there is some given, natural level of context-independent meaning, and that sentence-meaning can be described independently and prior to utterance-meaning. But as we have argued, and will illustrate below, this does not seem to be the case. For, if one accepts a truth-conditional semantics then one is forced to state truth conditions on sentences-in-contexts, or if one prefers (as Katz would) that semantics is concerned with aspects of meaning assigned by convention to linguistic forms, then one includes context-dependent aspects of meaning within semantics. A weaker version of the same proposal would be to consider that semantics is an abstraction away from context-dependent utterances, in so far as this is possible (as suggested by Carnap, 1959: 13; Lyons, 1977a: 591). In any case, it does not seem that the distinction between sentence-meaning and utterance-meaning can be relied upon to clarify the distinction between semantics and pragmatics.

We are left with the unrefined definition that pragmatics is concerned with the study of those aspects of meaning not covered in semantics. Despite many advantages, such a definition fails to draw attention to the unifying characteristics of pragmatic phenomena. Let us turn to another definition that would give the context-dependent nature of such phenomena more centrality:

(12)   Pragmatics is the study of the relations between language and context that are basic to an account of language understanding

Here the term **language understanding** is used in the way favoured by workers in artificial intelligence to draw attention to the fact that understanding an utterance involves a great deal more than knowing the meanings of the words uttered and the grammatical relations between them. Above all, understanding an utterance involves the making of *inferences* that will connect what is said to what is mutually assumed or what has been said before.

The strengths of such a definition are as follows. It recognizes that pragmatics is essentially concerned with inference (Thomason, 1977): given a linguistic form uttered in a context, a pragmatic theory must account for the inference of presuppositions, implicatures, illocutionary force and other pragmatic implications. Secondly, unlike the definition in (8), it does not make the distinction between semantics and pragmatics along the encoded/unencoded line; this is important because, as we shall see, there is still controversy over whether such pragmatic implications as presuppositions or illocutionary force are or are not encoded or grammaticalized in linguistic forms. Thirdly, it includes most aspects of the study of principles of language usage, for there seems to be a general principle of the following kind: for each systematic set of constraints on the use of language, there will be a corresponding set of inference-procedures that will be applied to language understanding (see Levinson, 1979a).

The weaknesses are, unfortunately, equally clear. First, pragmatics will then include the study of the interaction between linguistic knowledge and the entirety of participants' knowledge of the world (or 'encylopaedic knowledge'). For example, in order to understand the little story in (13), one needs to know the following assorted facts: presents are usually bought with money; piggy-banks are used to hold money; piggy-banks are generally made of a dense material like metal or plastic; money inside a container of dense material will generally rattle, etc.

(13)   Jill wanted to get Bill a birthday present, so she went and found her piggy-bank; she shook it, but there was no noise; she would have to make Bill a present

This example comes from work in artificial intelligence (Charniak, 1972) which is concerned with the attempt to translate the significance of ordinary utterances into an explicit representation that might be used by a computer to produce 'intelligent' responses. The immense difficulties of such translations have served to emphasize just how great a role assumed knowledge plays in the understanding of utterances.

However, this interpretive dependence on background assumptions has been used as an argument against the possibility of any systematic study of language understanding: if the set of potentially relevant assumptions is coincident with the total set of facts and beliefs held by participants, then to study this interpretive process will be to study the total sum of human knowledge and beliefs (Katz & Fodor, 1963). The argument is clearly fallacious: just as rules of logical deduction can be stated which will apply to an indefinitely large set of propositions, so it is quite possible that the *principles* that underlie the interaction between utterances and assumptions (however particular they may be) can be simply and rigorously stated. Nevertheless, if pragmatics is to be considered a *component* within linguistic theory (a question to which we shall return), it may be that to include such principles is indeed to include too much. But little serious thought has been given to this problem.

Another difficulty facing this definition or scope for pragmatics, is that it calls for some explicit characterization of the notion of **context**. In an earlier definition, where pragmatics was restricted to encoded aspects of context, one could claim that the relevant aspects of context should not be specified in advance but rather discovered by a survey of the world's languages. Here though, unless one wants to claim that context is whatever (excluding semantics) produces inferences, some characterization of context seems required. What then might one mean by *context*? First, one needs to distinguish between actual situations of utterance in all their multiplicity of features, and the selection of just those features that are culturally and linguistically relevant to the production and interpretation of utterances (see e.g. Van Dijk, 1976: 29). The term *context*, of course, labels the latter (although **context-description** might have been a more appropriate term, as Bar-Hillel (1970: 80) suggests). But can we say in advance what such features are likely to be? Lyons boldly lists the following (1977a: 574), over and above universal principles of logic and language usage: (i) knowledge of *role* and *status* (where role covers both role in the speech event, as speaker or addressee, and social role, and status covers notions of relative social standing), (ii) knowledge of spatial and temporal *location*, (iii) knowledge of *formality level*, (iv) knowledge of the *medium* (roughly the code or style appropriate to a channel, like the distinction between written and spoken varieties of a language), (v) knowledge of appropriate *subject matter*, (vi) knowledge of appropriate *province* (or domain determining the *register* of a language). Ochs (1979c), in an extended discussion of the notion, notes "The scope of context is not easy to define ... one must consider the *social and psychological world in which the language user operates at any given time*" (p.1), "it includes minimally, language users' beliefs and assumptions about temporal, spatial, and social settings; prior, ongoing, and future actions (verbal, non-verbal), and the state of knowledge and attentiveness of those participating in the social interaction in hand" (p.5). Both Lyons and Ochs stress that context must not be understood to exclude linguistic features, since such features often invoke the relevant contextual assumptions (a point made nicely by Gumperz (1977) who calls such linguistic features *contextualization cues*). Certainly, in this book, we shall need to include participants' beliefs about most of the above parameters, including the place of the current utterance within the sequence of utterances that makes up the discourse. Other authors have been more coy: "I have left the central concept of this paper, namely *pragmatic context*, in rather thorough vagueness, and this for the simple reason that I see no clear way to reduce the vagueness at the moment" (Bar-Hillel, 1970: 80). Although, along the lines suggested by Lyons or Ochs, we may be able to reduce the vagueness by providing lists of relevant contextual features, we do not seem to have available any theory that will predict the relevance of all such features, and this is perhaps an embarrassment to a definition that seems to rely on the notion of context.[17]

[17] For particular purposes, pragmaticists are wont to restrict the nature of context in line with the problems in hand: thus in a work dealing mostly with presupposition and implicature, "contexts are sets of propositions

Another line of attack on a definition of this sort would start by questioning the notion of *language understanding*. How is this to be construed? A reasonable, and perhaps the only plausible, response would be to say that to understand an utterance is to decode or calculate all that might reasonably have been meant by the speaker of the utterance (cf. Strawson, 1964). Here the notion of speaker-meaning is best explicated, once again, by reference to Grice's concept of meaning-nn, for we are interested only in the inferences overtly and intentionally conveyed. So the definition really amounts to: pragmatics is the study of the role context plays in speaker- (or utterance-) meaning. But since we have failed to produce a clear notion of context, what we include in context is likely to be whatever we exclude from semantics in the way of meaning relations. And so we seem to be back to the idea that pragmatics concerns whatever aspects of meaning are not included in semantics. (In which case, it may be objected, the problematic concept of context has been gratuitously introduced.) Certainly the two definitions ((9) and (12)) are not far apart; but it might be claimed that at least the one that focuses on the nature of context makes clear that one of the goals of a pragmatic theory should be to explicate that nature.

Let us now turn to one of the definitions most favoured in the literature, albeit mostly in an implicit form. This definition would make central to pragmatics a notion of **appropriateness** or **felicity**:

(14)   Pragmatics is the study of the ability of language users to pair
         sentences with the contexts in which they would be appropriate

Such a definition should have a nice ring to it, from the point of view of those who wish to place pragmatics on a par with other aspects of linguistic inquiry. For if pragmatics is to be considered an aspect of linguistic competence in Chomsky's sense, then like other aspects it

constrained only by consistency ... The consistent sets of propositions that comprise contexts are to be interpreted as the unique speaker's own 'commitment slate' in the sense of Hamblin (1971: 136)" (Gazdar, 1979a: 130); while in a work concerned with literary interpretation, "a context is construed as a 'complex event', viz. as an ordered pair of events of which the first causes the second. The first event is – roughly – the production of an utterance by the speaker, the second the interpretation of the utterance by the hearer" (Van Dijk, 1976: 29). But clearly a general theory of aspects of context relevant to production and interpretation must be broader than either of these.

must consist of some abstract cognitive ability. Further, such a view provides a nice parallel with semantics: for just as a semantic theory is concerned, say, with the recursive assignment of truth conditions to well-formed formulae, so pragmatics is concerned with the recursive assignment of **appropriateness-conditions** to the same set of sentences with their semantic interpretations. In other words, a pragmatic theory should in principle predict for each and every well-formed sentence of a language, on a particular semantic reading, the set of contexts in which it would be appropriate.

Such a view enjoys much support, not only among linguists (see e.g. Van Dijk, 1976: 29; Allwood, Andersson & Dahl, 1977: 153; Lyons, 1977a: 574) but also among philosophers (originally Austin, 1962 and Searle, 1969). But unfortunately it is beset with many problems. First, as we shall see, most definitions of pragmatics will occasion overlap with the field of sociolinguistics, but this definition would have as a consequence exact identity with a sociolinguistics construed, in the manner of Hymes (1971), as the study of **communicative competence**. Secondly, it requires a fundamental idealization of a culturally homogeneous speech community or, alternatively, the construction of *n* pragmatic theories for each language, where *n* is the number of culturally distinct sub-communities. For example, in a village in South India, where there may be say twenty distinct castes, a single honorific particle may have just one meaning (e.g. speaker is inferior to addressee) but have twenty distinct rules for its *appropriate* usage: members of one caste may use it to their cross-cousins, others only to their affines, etc. (for the actual details see Levinson, 1977). Thirdly, speakers of a language do not always comport themselves in the manner recommended by the prevailing mores – they can be outrageous, and otherwise 'inappropriate'. So such a definition would make the data of pragmatics stand in quite an abstract relation to what is actually observable in language usage, whereas for many linguists one of the major contributions of pragmatics has been to direct attention once again to actual language usage. Fourthly, it seems to be a fact that pragmatic constraints are generally defeasible, or not invariable. So suppose we attempt, for example, to phrase accounts of the pragmatic notion of presupposition in terms of appropriateness conditions, we shall find that they wrongly predict conditions of usage. For instance, the verb *regret* seems to presuppose that its complement is true, and so we could try the following characterization: the sentence *John doesn't regret cheating* can only be used appropriately in contexts where it is known (or believed) that John cheated. But unfortunately we can then easily imagine a context in which that sentence might be appropriately used, in which it is *not* assumed that John cheated: for example, you thought he had cheated, asked me whether he now repents, but I tell you he never did, and persuade you accordingly, and then I say *So John doesn't regret cheating* (Gazdar, 1979a: 105). The problem is quite general: when the pragmatic implications of an utterance do not match the context, then in general the utterance is not treated as in any way infelicitous or inappropriate or bizarre – rather the pragmatic implications are simply assumed not to hold. But the use of the notion of appropriateness-conditions would in that case simply make the wrong predictions.

Finally, and decisively, there is another problem with the use of the notion of appropriateness as a primitive or basic concept in pragmatics. For, there is a widespread phenomenon that Grice has called **exploitation**: in general, if there is some communicative convention C that one does A in context Y, then suppose instead one does B in Y, or does A but in context Z, one will not normally be taken to have simply violated the convention C and produced nonsense. Rather, one will generally be taken to have exploited the conventions in order to communicate some further pertinent message. For example, if I normally doff my cap only to my superiors, but on an occasion doff my cap to an equal, then I can effectively communicate an ironic regard, with either a joking or a hostile intent (the non-linguistic example is intended to draw attention to the great generality of the phenomenon; for a study of a particular linguistic practice and the jokes thus made available, see the study of the openings of telephone calls by Schegloff (1979a)). Irony is a good example of this exploitation and the difficulties such usages pose for a pragmatic theory based on appropriateness, for ironies take their effect and their communicative import, and thus their appropriateness, precisely from their inappropriateness. So the problem is in general that, in being grossly inappropriate, one can nevertheless be supremely appropriate! True, one may need some notion of 'normal practice' (in preference perhaps to appropriateness) even to describe such phenomena, but it would be a mistake to limit pragmatics to the study of that normal practice or appropriateness. Pragmatics should be much concerned precisely with such mechanisms whereby a speaker can mean more than, or something quite different from, what he actually says, by inventively exploiting communicative conventions. We must conclude that, despite its initial attractions, the proposal that pragmatics be based on a notion of appropriateness should be discarded: language usage is too elastic to allow a pragmatic theory to be based on such a concept. If instead one accepts that the goal of a pragmatic theory is to predict the meaning, in the broad Gricean sense, of an utterance in a specified context, then none of these difficulties arises.

At this point, someone searching for a simple definition of pragmatics is likely to be exhausted. One possibility is to retreat to an *ostensive* or *extensional* definition, i.e. simply to provide a list of the phenomena for which a pragmatic theory must account (cf. Stalnaker, 1972). Such a definition might run as follows:

(15)   Pragmatics is the study of deixis (at least in part), implicature, presupposition, speech acts, and aspects of discourse structure

This list would certainly provide a reasonable indication of some central topics in pragmatics, but the definition scarcely helps those unfamiliar with these topics and has other more serious drawbacks. For in common with all extensional definitions, it provides no criteria for the inclusion or exclusion of further phenomena that may come to our attention; at best one can say that what warrants pragmatic treatment for some new topic is simply linguists' consensus based on intuitive 'family resemblance' to more familiar pragmatic topics. But surely such intuitive resemblance must be based on some underlying implicit common themes – our difficulty is that when we try to spell these out we arrive at the various problems experienced in our earlier attempts at definition.

At this point, we might step back and attempt some conceptual clarification from other angles. Katz & Fodor (1963) tried to delimit the scope of semantics by a boundary drawing exercise: the 'upper bound' of semantics was provided by the borders of syntax and phonology, and the 'lower bound' by a theory of pragmatics, understood as a theory of contextual disambiguation. Using the same strategy, we could say that the upper bound of pragmatics is provided by the borders of semantics, and the lower bound by sociolinguistics (and perhaps psycholinguistics too). Indirectly, we have already explored this way of thinking in our consideration of the proposal that pragmatics is 'meaning minus semantics', and the idea that some distinction from sociolinguistics is necessary was responsible for some of the dissatisfaction with a number of the definitions above. We have already seen the difficulties of drawing a neat dividing line between semantics and pragmatics; given the cross-cutting criteria of conventionality and non-defeasibility (see again Table 1.1), the best strategy seems to be to restrict semantics to truth-conditional content. Assuming that this is accepted (and many linguists would resist it), we can turn our consideration to the lower bound, the border between pragmatics and sociolinguistics. Here things are even more problematic. Let us take two paradigmatic kinds of sociolinguistic phenomenon, and ask how they fall with respect to two of our definitions of pragmatics, namely, the most restrictive and the broadest definitions. Consider **honorifics**, most simply exemplified by the polite singular pronoun of address in European languages (like *vous* vs. *tu* in French – let us call this the V vs. the T pronoun). There are a number of sociolinguistic investigations of such honorifics and their usage (e.g. Brown & Gilman, 1960; Lambert & Tucker, 1976). If we take the view that pragmatics is concerned only with grammatically encoded aspects of context (see definition (8) above), then we might propose a tidy division of labour between pragmatic and sociolinguistic accounts of honorifics: pragmatics would be concerned with the *meaning* of honorifics (e.g. with the specification that V encodes that the addressee is socially distant or superior), while sociolinguistics would be concerned with the detailed recipes for *usage* of such items (e.g. the specification that amongst some segment of the speech community, V is used to aunts, uncles, teachers and so on, or whatever the local facts are). Such studies would be exclusive but complementary. Now, however, consider what happens if we take pragmatics to be the study of the contribution of context to language understanding: suppose normally an aunt gives her nephew T, but on an occasion switches to V, then in order to predict the intended ironic or angry meaning, a pragmatic theory must have available the detailed recipe for usage that tells us that V is not the normal usage, and thus not to be taken at face value. So on this broader scope for pragmatics, the neat division of labour collapses – pragmatic accounts of language understanding will at least need access to sociolinguistic information.

Taking another paradigmatic kind of sociolinguistic phenomenon, namely the variable phonological realizations associated with social dialects (see e.g. Labov, 1972a), let us ask how our definitions of pragmatics treat such facts. On the most restrictive view, that pragmatics is concerned with linguistically encoded aspects of context, such facts would seem to lie outside the purview of pragmatics. Such an exclusion would rely on the restricted sense of *encoding* that required, *inter alia*, that the significances in question are (a) intentionally conveyed (and we can now say, meant-nn) and (b) conventionally associated with the relevant linguistic forms. For, as we noted, the association of particular accents (realized by proportions of phonological variables) with particular social or geographical communities is generally not part of an intentional message (Labov (1972a) argues that such variables are only very partially under conscious control), nor are such social significances associated with linguistic forms by arbitrary synchronic convention so much as by regular historical and social process. However, if we take the broader scope of pragmatics represented by the definition that relates context to language understanding, there may well be cases where sociolinguistic variables would be of relevance to language understanding. Gumperz (1977), for example, has argued that such variables can be used to invoke domains of interpretation, e.g. to mark transitions from chat to business. Or, consider the case of a comedian telling a joke about a Scotsman, an Irishman and an Englishman – he may well rely on mimicked features of accent to track which protagonist is talking. In short, drawing a boundary between sociolinguistic and pragmatic phenomena is likely to be an exceedingly difficult enterprise. In part this can be attributed to the diverse scopes that have been claimed for sociolinguistics (see Trudgill, 1978: Introduction), but in part it comes about because sociolinguists are interested in inter-relations between language and society however these are manifested in grammatical systems: sociolinguistics is not a component or level of a grammar in the way that syntax, semantics, phonology and, quite plausibly, pragmatics are.

Another angle from which we might attempt conceptual clarification of the issues is to ask: what are the **goals** of a pragmatic theory? The term *goal* is used here in the special way current in linguistic theorizing, and is to be distinguished from the ultimate goals or motivations that might prompt interest in a theory. Those ultimate motivations will be the subject of the next section, but here we are interested in exactly what it is that we expect a pragmatic theory to do. One abstract way of thinking about this is to think of a pragmatic theory as a 'black box' (an as yet unexplicated mechanism), and to ask: what should be the input to such a theory, and what should be the output (or: what is the theory meant to predict, given what particular information)? We can then think of a theory as a *function* in the mathematical sense, which assigns one set of entities (the *domain*) to another set of entities (the *range*), and the question is, what are these sets of entities? Thinking the same way about syntax, we can say that a given set of rules (a syntactic analysis) is a function whose domain is the set of possible combinations of morphemes in the language L, and whose range has just two elements, denoting the grammatical and the ungrammatical in L;[18] or thinking about semantics, we might say that a semantic analysis of L has as its domain the set of well-formed sentences of L, and as its range the set of semantic representations or propositions representing the meaning of each of those sentences. It is by no means so obvious what the input and output of a pragmatic theory should be.

Two authors, at least, have been explicit on this subject. Katz (1977: 19) suggests that the input should be the full grammatical (including semantical) description of a sentence, together with information about the context in which it was uttered, while the output is a set of representations (or propositions) which capture the full meaning of the utterance in the context specified. Since a sentence plus its context of use can be called an utterance, Katz's suggestion amounts to the idea that a pragmatic theory is a function whose domain is the set of utterances and whose range is the set of propositions. Or symbolically, if we let S be the set of sentences in language L, C the set of possible contexts, P the set of propositions, and U the cartesian product of $S \times C$ – i.e. the set of possible combinations of members of S with members of C, and we let the corresponding lower case letters stand for elements or members of each of those sets (i.e. $s \in S$, $c \in C$, $p \in P$, $u \in U$):

(16) $f(u) = p$ (or: $f(s, c) = p$)

[18] Or, in alternative parlance, a function *from* the set of morpheme combinations *to* the well- vs. ill-formed sentences, or a function that *maps* the set of morpheme combinations *into* the well- vs. ill-formed sentences. See Allwood, Andersson & Dahl (1977: 9ff) for elementary exposition.

i.e. f is a function that assigns to utterances the propositions that
express their full meaning in context

Gazdar (1979a: 4–5), on the other hand, wishes to capture the ways
in which utterances *change* the context in which they are uttered; he
shows that Katz's formulation is incompatible with that goal, and
therefore suggests instead:

(17) $f(u) = c$ (or: $f(s, c) = c$)
         i.e. f is a function from utterances to contexts, namely the
         contexts brought about by each utterance (or: f assigns to each
         sentence plus the context prior to its utterance, a second context
         caused by its utterance)

The idea here is that the shift from the context prior to an utterance
to the context post utterance itself constitutes the communicational
content of the utterance. It suggests that pragmatic theory as a whole
should be based on the notion of context change (see some applications
in Chapters 4 and 5 below).

Both these formulations are consistent with the definitions of
pragmatics as 'meaning minus semantics' or as the contribution of
context to language understanding. Our other definitions might
require slightly different formulations. For example, where pragmatics
is construed as the study of grammatically encoded aspects of context,
we might want to say:

(18) $f(s) = c$
         where C is the set of contexts potentially encoded by elements
         of S
         i.e. f is a theory that 'computes out' of sentences the
         contexts which they encode

Or, alternatively, where pragmatics is defined as the study of constraints on the appropriateness of utterances, we could say:

(19) $f(u) = a$
         where A has just two elements, denoting the *appropriate* vs. the
         inappropriate utterances
         i.e. f is a theory that selects just those felicitous or appropriate
         pairings of sentences and contexts – or identifies the set of
         appropriate utterances

Or, where pragmatics is defined ostensively as a list of topics, we could
say:

(20) $f(u) = b$
         where each element of B is a combination of a speech act, a

set of presuppositions, a set of conversational implicatures, etc.

i.e. f is a theory that assigns to each utterance the speech act it performs, the propositions it presupposes, the propositions it conversationally implicates, etc.

Clearly, there are other possibilities, and it is far from obvious, at this stage of the development of the subject, just which of the many possible formulations is the best. But as the subject develops we can expect researchers to be more explicit about exactly how they expect a pragmatic theory to be formulated.

Let us sum up the discussion so far. We have considered a number of rather different delimitations of the field. Some of these seem deficient: for example, the restriction of pragmatics to grammatically encoded aspects of context, or the notion that pragmatics should be built on the concept of appropriateness. The most promising are the definitions that equate pragmatics with 'meaning minus semantics', or with a theory of language understanding that takes context into account, in order to complement the contribution that semantics makes to meaning. They are not, however, without their difficulties, as we have noted. To some extent, other conceptions of pragmatics may ultimately be consistent with these. For example, as we noted, the definition of pragmatics as concerned with encoded aspects of context may be less restrictive than it seems at first sight; for if in general (a) principles of language usage have as corollaries principles of interpretation, and (b) principles of language usage are likely in the long run to impinge on grammar (and some empirical support can be found for both propositions), then theories about pragmatic aspects of meaning will be closely related to theories about the grammaticalization of aspects of context. So the multiplicity of alternative definitions may well seem greater than it really is.

In any case, we embarked on this definitional enterprise with the warning that satisfactory definitions of academic fields are rarely available, and the purpose was simply to sketch the sorts of concerns, and the sorts of boundary issues, with which pragmaticists are implicitly concerned. As was suggested at the outset, if one really wants to know what a particular field is concerned with at any particular time, one must simply observe what practitioners do. The rest of this book will largely be concerned with an overview of some of the central tasks that pragmaticists wrestle with.

Before proceeding to a discussion of the motivations that lie behind the growth of the field in recent years, it would be as well to clarify the role that pragmatics might be seen to play within linguistic theory as a whole. There is no doubt that some workers see pragmatics as a running commentary on current linguistic methods and concerns, and its role as the juxtaposition of actual language usage with the highly idealized data on which much current theorizing is based. Viewed in this way, attempts to delimit pragmatics in the ways explored above would make little sense; pragmatics would not be a component or level of linguistic theory but a way of looking afresh at the data and methods of linguistics. In that case, pragmatics would be a field more akin to sociolinguistics than semantics. It is therefore worthwhile seeing that, whatever the merits of this view, there is a need for a kind of pragmatic theory that can take its place beside syntax, semantics and phonology within an overall theory of grammar.

The need for a pragmatic component in an integrated theory of linguistic ability can be argued for in various ways. One way is to consider the relation of the pragmatics-semantics-syntax trichotomy to the competence-performance dichotomy advanced by Chomsky (see Kempson, 1975: Chapter 9). In Chomsky's view, grammars are models of competence, where competence is knowledge of a language idealized away from (especially) irregularity or error and variation; to this, Katz influentially added idealization away from context (see Lyons, 1977a: 585–91, for discussion of kinds of idealization). On such a view, insofar as pragmatics is concerned with context, it can be claimed that by definition pragmatics is not part of competence, and thus not within the scope of grammatical descriptions. But suppose now we require that adequate grammatical descriptions include specifications of the meaning of every word in a language, and such a requirement has normally been assumed, then we find words whose meaning-specifications can only be given by reference to contexts of usage. For example, the meaning of words like *well*, *oh* and *anyway* in English cannot be explicated simply by statements of context-independent content: rather one has to refer to pragmatic concepts like relevance, implicature, or discourse structure (this claim will be substantiated in the Chapters below). So either grammars (models of competence) must make reference to pragmatic information, or they cannot include full lexical descriptions of a language. But if the lexicon is not complete, then neither is the syntax, semantics or phonology likely to be. There are other arguments that have been made along the same general lines, to the effect that to capture regular processes (e.g. syntactic regularities) one must refer to pragmatic concepts (see e.g. Ross, 1975), arguments that will arise from time to time in the Chapters below.

Another more powerful kind of argument goes as follows. In order to construct an integrated theory of linguistic competence, it is essential to discover the logical ordering of components or levels. For example, Chomsky has elegantly argued that syntax is logically prior to phonology, in that phonological description requires reference to syntactic categories, but not vice versa; syntax is thus **autonomous** with respect to phonology, and phonology (non-autonomous with respect to syntax) can be envisaged as taking a syntactic input, on the basis of which phonological representations can be built up. Accepting for a moment this kind of argument, the question is, is it possible to argue that there is some accepted component of grammar that is non-autonomous with respect to pragmatics (i.e. some component requiring pragmatic input)? If so, pragmatics must be logically prior to that component, and so must be included in an overall theory of linguistic competence.

It seems fairly clear that it is possible to make this argument in a convincing way. For example, we have already noted the argument (and see Chapter 2 below) that if semantics is to be truth-conditional, then the truth conditions can only be assigned to utterances, not sentences – in other words, contextual specifications are a necessary input to a semantic component, and thus pragmatics is (at least in this respect)[19] prior to semantics. Gazdar (1979a: 164–8) assembles a number of detailed arguments to this effect (and philosophers have long noted further such arguments – see e.g. Donnellan, 1966; Stalnaker, 1972; Kaplan, 1978; etc.). One of these, due to Wilson (1975: 151), will have to suffice here, and holds not just for truth-conditional semantics but for virtually any semantic theory independent of pragmatics. Consider the following sentence:

[19] There are also simple arguments that pragmatics requires semantic input: for example, an ironic interpretation of an utterance can only be calculated if the semantic (or 'literal') reading is already available. So the two kinds of arguments together seem to show that neither semantics nor pragmatics is autonomous with respect to each other – information provided by the one component must be available to the other.

(21)   Getting married and having a child is better than having a child and getting married

Good arguments will be given in Chapter 3 to suggest that the word *and* of itself does not mean (have the semantic content) 'and then', but is neutral with respect to a temporal dimension. So, there is no difference in *semantic* content between *p and q* and *q and p*, or between 'getting married and having a child' and 'having a child and getting married'. How then are we to explain that (22) does not mean the same as (21)?

(22)   Having a child and getting married is better than getting married and having a child

We have to provide a pragmatic account, along the following lines. The 'and then' reading of both *and*s in the first sentence can be shown to be systematically 'read in' to conjoined reports of events by a pragmatic principle governing the reporting of events: tell them in the order in which they will or have occurred. If this is accepted, then the semantic content of (21) (and identically for (22)) would only allow the interpretation that A is better than A (where A is composed of *p and q* or *q and p*, neutral with respect to ordering). But such a reading is either necessarily false or meaningless, and in any case semantically anomalous. The sentence can only be assigned the right truth conditions, or alternatively be given the correct semantic representation, if the pragmatic significance of *and* in this sentential context (namely the 'and then' interpretation) is taken into account before doing the semantics. This amounts to a concise argument that semantics is not autonomous with respect to pragmatics, and that pragmatics provides part of the necessary input to a semantic theory. But if pragmatics is, on occasions, logically prior to semantics, a general linguistic theory simply must incorporate pragmatics as a component or level in the overall integrated theory.

1.3   Current interest in pragmatics

There are a number of convergent reasons for the growth of interest in pragmatics in recent years. Some of these are essentially historical: the interest developed in part as a reaction or antidote to Chomsky's treatment of language as an abstract device, or mental ability, dissociable from the uses, users and functions of language (an abstraction that Chomsky in part drew from the post-Bloomfieldian structuralism that predominated immediately before transformational generative grammar). In looking for the means to undermine Chomsky's position, *generative semanticists* were then attracted to a considerable body of philosophical thought devoted to showing the importance of the uses of language to an understanding of its nature (work by Austin, Strawson, Grice and Searle in particular). To this day, most of the important concepts in pragmatics are drawn directly from philosophy of language. Once this broader scope for mainstream American linguistics was established,[20] pragmatics soon took on a life of its own, for the issues raised are interesting and important in their own right.

But there have also been powerful motivations of a different kind. In the first place, as knowledge of the syntax, phonology and semantics of various languages has increased, it has become clear that there are specific phenomena that can only naturally be described by recourse to contextual concepts. On the one hand, various syntactic rules seem to be properly constrained only if one refers to pragmatic conditions; and similarly for matters of stress and intonation.[21] It is possible, in response to these apparent counter-examples to a context-independent notion of linguistic competence, simply to retreat: the rules can be left unconstrained and allowed to generate unacceptable sentences, and a performance theory of pragmatics assigned the job of filtering out the acceptable sentences. Such a move is less than entirely satisfactory because the relationship between the theory of competence and the data on which it is based (ultimately intuitions about acceptability) becomes abstract to a point where counter-examples to the theory may be explained away on an *ad hoc* basis, *unless* a systematic pragmatics has already been developed.

Alternatively, pragmatics and other linguistic components or levels can be allowed to interact. Arguments between these two positions have never been fully articulated, and because of their highly theory-dependent nature are dealt with, in this book, only in passing.

---

[20] It is worth noting that many other schools of linguistic thought had always taken for granted such a broader scope, e.g. the Prague school, the so-called London school, and even the glossematicians. For a treatment of the historical developments in America, see Newmeyer, 1980.

[21] A useful general list of pragmatic constraints on linguistic form can be found in Gazdar, 1980a (see also Green, 1978a).

(But see Gordon & Lakoff, 1975; Ross, 1975; Gazdar & Klein, 1977; Lightfoot, 1979: 43–4.)

On the other hand, concurrent developments in semantics have isolated intractable phenomena of a parallel kind: presuppositions, speech acts and other context-dependent implications, together with troublesome phenomena like honorifics and discourse particles that had long been given short shrift in the work of generative grammarians. Further, thought about the nature of the lexicon, and how one might construct a predictive concept of 'possible lexical item', has revealed the importance of pragmatic constraints (see Horn, 1972; McCawley, 1978; Gazdar, 1979a: 68ff). It is these issues, arising from the study of meaning, with which this book is centrally concerned.

In addition to these particular problems that seem to require pragmatic solutions, there are also a number of general motivations for the development of pragmatic theory. One of the most important of these is the possibility that pragmatics can effect a radical simplification of semantics.[22] The hope is based on the fact that pragmatic principles of language usage can be shown systematically to 'read in' to utterances more than they conventionally or literally mean. Such regularly superimposed implications can then become quite hard to disentangle from sentence or literal meaning; in order to prise them apart, the theorist has to construct or observe contexts in which the usual pragmatic implications do not hold. For example, it seems perfectly natural to claim that the quantifier *some* in (23) means 'some and not all':

(23)   Some ten cent pieces are rejected by this vending machine

and that would be the basis of the natural interpretation of a notice with this message, attached to the machine. But suppose I am trying to use the machine, and I try coin after coin unsuccessfully, and I utter (23); I might then very well communicate:

(24)   Some, and perhaps all, ten cent pieces are rejected by this vending machine

and indeed I could say this without contradiction. Faced with these facts the semanticist must either hold that *some* is ambiguous between the readings 'some and not all', and 'some and perhaps all', or allow a pragmatic account of the different interpretations. (Parallel

---

[22] Hence the term *radical pragmatics*, as in the title of Cole, 1981, although the term *radical semantics* might be more appropriate.

arguments can be made for the word *all*, and indeed most of the lexical items in a language.) This pragmatic account would explain how principles of language usage allow addressees to 'read in' the 'not all' implication. Since such a pragmatic account is available, as will be seen in Chapter 3, we can let the semantics just provide a reading compatible with 'some and perhaps all'. Not only will such a division of labour approximately halve the size of the lexicon (by accounting for different interpretations of words by a general external principle), it will also immeasurably simplify the logical base of semantics – the word *some* can be equated directly with the existential quantifier in predicate logic (while the reading 'some and not all' taken as basic leads to serious internal contradictions: see Horn, 1973 and Chapter 3 below). In this way, by unburdening semantics of phenomena that are resistant to semantic treatment but tractable to pragmatic explanation, there is considerable hope that pragmatics can simplify semantic theories.

Another powerful and general motivation for the interest in pragmatics is the growing realization that there is a very substantial gap between current linguistic theories of language and accounts of linguistic communication. When linguists talk of the goal of linguistic theory as being the construction of an account of a sound-meaning correspondence for the infinite set of sentences in any language, one might perhaps infer that such a grand theory would *eo ipso* give an account of at least the essentials of how we communicate using language. But if the term *meaning* in this correspondence is restricted to the output of a semantic component, those interested in a theory of linguistic communication are likely to be greatly disappointed. For it is becoming increasingly clear that a semantic theory alone can give us only a proportion, and perhaps only a small if essential proportion, of a general account of language understanding. The substantial gap that remains to be bridged between a semantic theory (together with a syntactic and phonological theory) and a complete theory of linguistic communication will be demonstrated throughout this book. Where are we to account for the hints, implicit purposes, assumptions, social attitudes and so on that are effectively communicated by the use of language, not to mention the figures of speech (e.g. metaphor, irony, rhetorical questions, understatement) that have preoccupied theorists of rhetoric and literature? These communicated inferences can be quite diverse in kind. Consider, for example, the following extracts from recorded conversations,[23] where the responses to an utterance indicate that for participants the utterance carried the implications (or something like them) indicated in brackets:

(25)   A: I could eat the whole of that cake [implication: 'I compliment
         you on the cake']
         B: Oh thanks
(26)   A: Do you have coffee to go?[24] [implication: 'Sell me coffee
         to go if you can']
         B: Cream and sugar? ((starts to pour))
(27)   B: Hi John
         A: How're you doing?
         B: Say, what're you doing [implication: 'I've got a suggestion
         about what we might do together']
         A: Well, we're going out. Why?
         B: Oh I was just going to say come out ...

There are also cases where the location of a verbal exchange in a particular kind of activity seems to warrant specific inferences:

(28)   (*In a classroom*)
         Teacher: Johnnie, how do you spell *Ann*?
         Johnnie: A, N, N
                    ((intervening material))
         Teacher: Okay, Isobel, do you see a name on that page you
         know?
         Isobel: Ann
         Teacher: That's the one that Johnnie just named [implication:
         'That doesn't count']
(29)   (*Beginning of a telephone conversation*)
         Caller: ((rings))
         Receiver: Hello
         Caller: Hello [implication: 'I know who you are, and you
         can tell from my voice who I am']
         Receiver: Oh hi [implication: 'Yes, I know who you are']

Each of these, or examples like them, will be treated in the pages below, together with more familiar examples of pragmatic implication. The point here, though, is that the existence of a great range of such implications, some of which have only the most tenuous relationship

---

[23] Drawn, with orthographic simplifications, from the following sources: (25), author's transcript; (26) from Merritt, 1976; (27) from Atkinson & Drew, 1979: 143; (28) from Gumperz & Herasimchuk, 1975: 109ff; (29) from Schegloff, 1979a. Double parentheses enclose descriptions that are not part of the verbal record; further conventions are developed in Chapter 6.

[24] American idiom for 'coffee to take away, rather than drink on premises'.

to the semantic content of what is said, emphasizes the need for a theory or theories that will complement semantics in order to give a relatively full account of how we use language to communicate.

Finally, another very important general motivation for the recent interest in pragmatics is the possibility that significant **functional** explanations can be offered for linguistic facts. Most recent linguistic explanations have tended to be internal to linguistic theory: that is to say, some linguistic feature is explained by reference to other linguistic features, or to aspects of the theory itself. But there is another possible kind of explanation, often more powerful, in which some linguistic feature is motivated by principles outside the scope of linguistic theory: for example, it seems possible that the syntactic processes known as *island constraints* (Ross, 1967) can be explained on the grounds of general psychological principles (see e.g. Grosu, 1972). This mode of explanation, by reference to external factors (especially causes and functions), is often called **functionalism** (see e.g. Grossman, San & Vance, 1975). Now the possibility exists that language structure is not independent (contrary to Chomsky's well-known views) of the uses to which it is put. That is to say, it may be possible to give powerful functionalist explanations of linguistic phenomena by reference to pragmatic principles. Indeed, to many thinkers such explanations seem to be obviously of the right kind (cf. Searle, 1974; Givon, 1979a, 1979b). For example, one might observe the fact that nearly all the world's languages have the three basic sentence-types: imperative, interrogative and declarative (Sadock & Zwicky, in press). On the grounds that these seem to be used paradigmatically for ordering, questioning and asserting, respectively, one might argue that it is pointless to search for internal linguistic motivations for these three sentence-types: they recur in the languages of the world because humans are, perhaps, specifically concerned with three functions of language in particular – the organizing of other persons' actions, the eliciting of information, and the conveying of information. (Such an explanation is of course suspiciously *post hoc*: we would need independent evidence that these three activities are indeed predominant in social life.) Or one might note that most languages have some, and many languages have elaborate, ways of encoding relative social status between participants: again, a functional explanation in terms of universal (or near universal) principles of social organization seems called for (see e.g. Brown & Levinson,

1978). Indeed, one might hope for still more in the way of functional explanation: much of the syntactic machinery of a language seems to be concerned with the linear re-organization of material in sentences (as in passive or topicalized constructions), a re-organization which does not seem substantially to affect the (truth-conditional) semantic content. What, then, is the purpose of such elaborate derivational machinery? It may be that it exists essentially for the purpose of meshing sentence-construction with pragmatic principles: for example, for 'foregrounding' and 'backgrounding' informational content[25] (or, in the terms preferred in this book, for eliciting certain pragmatic implications).

One of the motivations for research in pragmatics might then be to establish the effects of the uses of language on language structure. But such research requires a fundamental clarification of the *explicans*, i.e. the functional matrix that is to produce explanations of linguistic structure. Unfortunately, many recent examples of such work have utilized explanatory principles that have been left quite vague (see M. Atkinson, 1982). It is important, therefore, that there be sufficiently well-defined pragmatic principles and structures to make such functional explanations precise and testable.

How, therefore, should we think of the uses of language, in a way that could provide functional accounts of linguistic structure? We might turn to traditional approaches to the 'functions of speech' (see the summary in Lyons, 1977a: 50–6). Perhaps the most thoughtful of these is Jakobson's (1960) modification of earlier schemes (see especially Bühler, 1934). He suggests that the functions of speech can be to focus on any of the six basic components of the communicational event: thus the **referential** function focuses on the referential content of the message, the **emotive** function on the speaker's state, the **conative** function on the speaker's wishes that the addressee do or think such-and-such, the **metalinguistic** function on the code being used, the **phatic** function on the channel (establishment and maintainance of contact), and the **poetic** function on the way in which the message is encoded. Any such scheme, though, is of dubious utility to the pragmaticist in search of functional principles: the categories are of vague application, they do not have direct empirical motivation, and there are many other rival schemes built upon

---

[25] See Givon, 1979a; Foley & Van Valin, in press.

slightly different lines. Perhaps the only clear utility is to remind us that, contrary to the preoccupations of many philosophers and a great many semanticists, language is used to convey more than the propositional content of what is said. Certainly, very few linguists have produced analyses of linguistic facts that make use of gross functional categories of this sort (but cf. Halliday, 1973). A very similar sort of enterprise has been engaged in by philosophers interested in the notion of **speech act** (addressed in Chapter 5): either by examining a special set of verbs called **performative verbs**, or by more abstract conceptual analysis, they arrive at classifications of the basic purposes for which language can be used (see e.g. Searle, 1976). Again, such schemes seem to be far too broad to relate to detailed aspects of linguistic structure.

How else, then, might we proceed? One possibility, which has scarcely been explored, would be to take some large sample of the world's languages and ask what basic pragmatic distinctions are needed to describe their grammatical structures. (The procedure requires, of course, acceptance of the view that not all encoded features of meaning are semantic simply by definition.) We would note that many languages have, in addition to the three basic sentence-types mentioned above, others that appear to be similarly circumscribed in use: **exclamatives** that are used paradigmatically to express surprise, **imprecatives** to curse, **optatives** to express a wish, and so on (again, see Sadock & Zwicky, in press).[26] Some languages would motivate distinctions that, from the point of view of European languages, are quite exotic. For example, to describe the lexicon, morphology and syntax of Javanese one would need to distinguish three levels of respect to addressees and two levels of respect to referents (Geertz, 1960; Comrie, 1976b); to describe the particles of a number of South American Indian languages one would need to distinguish between sentences that are central versus those that are peripheral to the telling of a story (Longacre, 1976a); to describe the third person pronouns of Tunica one would need to distinguish not only the sex of the referent, but also the sex of the addressee (so there would be two words for 'she' depending on whether one is speaking to a man or a woman; Haas, 1964), while in

---

[26] But caution is necessary here – e.g. what are traditionally called optatives in Sanskrit and Greek do not necessarily, or perhaps even primarily, express wishes.

some Australian languages the pronouns encode the moiety or section (kinship division) of the referent, or the kinship relation between referents (e.g. there are sometimes two words one of which means 'you-dual of the same moiety' and another 'you-dual in different moieties from each other'; Dixon, 1980: 2–3; Heath et al. 1982); to describe the Quileute demonstratives one needs to make a distinction between objects visible and not visible to the speaker (Anderson & Keenan, in press); and so on.

From this profusion of language-specific material one then might be able to build up some idea of just which aspects of the context of utterance are likely in general to exert functional pressures on language. Further, taking features that are directly and simply encoded in one language, one may well be able to find the same features encoded in more subtle and less visible ways in either the structure or the use of other languages. For example, although we do not have in English the grammaticalization of the levels of respect that exist in Javanese, we do have means of expressing degrees of respect, largely by choices in the use of expressions: thus (31) would generally be a more polite request than (30):

(30)   I want to see you for a moment
(31)   I wondered if I could possibly see you for a moment

So by taking at first just the grammaticalized or encoded features of context in the world's languages, we would have both something like a 'discovery procedure' for relevant functions of language, and a constraint on the relatively vacuous theorizing that often attends speculation about the 'functions of speech'. We can then go on to ask how in other languages without such grammatical means, the same functions are achieved (if indeed they are). Such a way of proceeding has much to recommend it, but scant progress has been made in that direction.

To all such approaches to the uses of speech, a strong objection might be made along the following lines: rather than look for a series of static functions or contextual parameters, one should attend directly to the single most important dynamic context of language use, namely conversation, or face-to-face interaction. The centrality of this functional matrix for language use hardly needs arguing: face-to-face interaction is not only the context for language acquisition, but the only significant kind of language use in many of the world's communities, and indeed until relatively recently in all of them. Those interested in functional explanations of linguistic phenomena ought then to have a considerable interest in the systematics of face-to-face interaction. The question is how best to approach the study of such interaction. There are perhaps two basic lines of attack: straightforward empirical analysis, and analysis-by-synthesis.

It is the first kind of approach that has so far yielded the most insight, but it is worth considering the possibility of the analysis of interaction by synthesis. Interaction, in the abstract sense intended here, can be understood as the sustained production of chains of mutually-dependent acts, constructed by two or more agents each monitoring and building on the actions of the other (in this sense the mathematical theory of games studies one kind of interaction; see Luce & Raiffa, 1957). Such an approach might begin by adopting Goffman's (1976) distinction between **systems-constraints** and **ritual-constraints**, where the first labels the ingredients essential to sustaining any kind of systematic interweaving of actions by more than one party, and the second those ingredients that, while not essential to the maintaining of interaction, are nevertheless typical of it – they are, if one likes, the social dimensions of interaction. Concentrating on systems-constraints, one may then ask what necessary and jointly sufficient conditions must be met in order for that highly co-ordinated kind of inter-dependent behaviour that we call interaction to 'come off'. Suppose, for example, we had as our task the programming of two robots in such a way that they could systematically aid one another in an open range of tasks: what properties beyond the specific abilities required for the tasks would they need to have? (It may be helpful to think in terms of some specific co-operative task, like the production of a building or a machine.) First, it is clear that they would need to be mutually oriented; they would each need to be aware of what the other was doing at any time. Secondly, they would need to be aware of the interactional domain (e.g. their scope for movement, and the properties of objects around them), and be constantly updating this as it was affected by their actions. Thirdly, they would need, in some sense, to be rational – to have an effective means-ends reasoning that told them how to implement each desired goal. Fourthly, each would need to be able to produce acts conditional on the other producing acts, thus securing the chains of inter-dependent acts typical of interaction. This would seem to require the ability to reconstruct from each other's behaviour the probable goal that the behaviour was intended to achieve (otherwise, the inter-dependent actions would not be likely to culminate in the achievement of the joint task). Fifthly, there would need to be some specific relation between their overall goals (if interaction is agonistic, or in the terminology of the theory of games, *zero-sum*, then their goals must be inversely related; if interaction is co-operative then there must be some specific shared goals). Sixthly, each robot would have to know that the other had these properties, and know that each knew that, otherwise they could hardly rationally plan actions dependent on the other's plans. It is just possible that these properties would be sufficient, together with the abilities required by specific tasks, to engender a co-ordinated interdigitation of actions that would (remotely) resemble human interaction. The purpose of this thought-experiment is to draw attention to the fact that a number of pragmatic phenomena can be explicated by reference to just these sorts of features: for example, as we shall see, deixis can be thought of as based on the assumption of mutual orientation, presupposition on the assumption of shared knowledge of a domain and its updating, speech acts on the making explicit, for other participants, of one's interactional goals, conversational implicature on the assumption of interactional co-operation, and so on. Thus, if such an approach were developed, one might hope that all the essential concepts for the analysis of pragmatic phenomena would be traceable to the fundamentals of interaction (for an actual computer simulation of conversation along these lines see Power, 1979).

In fact, though, such an approach is still likely to be much too abstract to provide systematic functional accounts of the minutiae of linguistic structures. For a start, it would need to be complemented by the study of *ritual-constraints*, the social and cultural constraints on interaction. Amongst these, there are cross-situational constraints enjoining appropriate social decorum, while there are others appropriate just to specific interactional moments or specific kinds of cultural events. It might be thought that such social constraints would be likely, simply by being social, to be culturally variable, and thus of no great interest to a general (or universal) pragmatic theory. However, this does not seem necessarily to be the case. For example, there are clear pan-cultural principles governing the production of 'polite' or socially appropriate interaction, and these can be shown to have systematic effects on the linguistic structure of many languages (Brown & Levinson, 1978; Leech, 1980). It is also clear that there are highly specific ritual constraints of a universal, or near universal nature: for example, nearly all cultures seem to have greeting and parting routines (see Ferguson, 1976). More speculatively, it is also likely that in all cultures there are social events demarcated as *formal events* (Irvine, 1979; J. M. Atkinson, 1982), and that some aspects of formality have universal linguistic realizations. Here again there has been very little systematic exploration, although such universal features of the organization of interaction are good candidates for potentially important functional pressures on linguistic structure. Whatever the attractions of universal features of interaction for the explanation of universal pragmatic phenomena, there are also clear language-specific pragmatic phenomena, as in the domain of **social deixis** and elsewhere, where functional accounts of language structure would need to relate these to culture-specific aspects of interaction. Finally, where there are important divisions between kinds of culture and society, one might well expect systematic differences between the associated languages – for example, it is likely that literacy has systematic effects on the lexical, syntactic and semantic structure of languages, even if these have never been spelt out (see Goody, 1977). Here it is evident that an interest in language usage motivated by functionalist approaches to linguistics would take us well beyond the confines of pragmatics (as sketched in the definitions above) into the domain of sociolinguistics and beyond. However, in so far as such social features are part of the meaning of utterances, they ought also to be treated in pragmatics; yet within pragmatics, these social constraints on language usage and their systematic effects on language structure, have been very much understudied, perhaps as a result of the philosophical and linguistic bias (no doubt reflected in this book) towards what Bühler (1934) called the *representational*, and Jakobson (1960) the *referential*, function of language.

The other more promising line of investigation is to explore directly the nature of conversational interaction. The basic concepts of conversation analysis, as employed in a branch of **ethnomethodology**, are the subject of Chapter 6. Here it will suffice to note that this kind of investigation, employing techniques quite alien to the dominant tradition in linguistics, has revealed that conversational interaction has an elaborate and detailed structure of which we have very little conscious awareness. In this area, at least, the would-be functionalist is offered the kind of rich and intricate structure that may match the detailed organization of linguistic structure, and so can be claimed plausibly to stand in a causal relation to it. For example, the probable universal existence of tag-questions (under a functional definition) can perhaps be related to the universal operation of rules of turn-taking that allow as one option the ending of current speaker's turn by a selection of a next speaker. But, as yet, few linguists have applied the insights from conversation analysis to functionalist studies of linguistic structure.

Finally, there is another kind of empirical approach to the study of interaction, and its effects on linguistic structure, that might be claimed to have a distinct advantage. This is the study of the acquisition of language by children. During the early stages of acquisition, children establish an interactional matrix for language learning, and then slowly learn to utilize linguistic means for promoting interaction. We are thus enabled to distinguish more easily the would-be functionalist's *explicans* (interactional structure) from the *explicandum* (language). A second advantage is that children's 'errors' or incompetences reveal to us what adult competences in verbal interaction must involve. Thirdly, just as cross-linguistic comparisons can reveal general functions of language by contrasts between what is encoded in one language and not in another, so comparisons across stages of acquisition can be revealing in the same way (Ochs, 1979a). There has been much recent work by psychologists and linguists on these early stages of acquisition that has direct relevance to pragmatics, but is not reviewed in this book (see e.g. Ervin-Tripp & Mitchell-Kernan, 1977; Snow & Ferguson, 1977; Ochs & Schieffelin, 1979; and the critical account of such work in M. Atkinson, 1982).

1.4 Computing context: an example

Abstract discussions about the scope of pragmatics like those we have reviewed above, may well leave the reader with little feeling for the nature of pragmatic phenomena. Here an extended example may help to clarify the kinds of facts with which pragmatic theories are concerned.[27] Let us take a simple three-sentence exchange

[27] The mode of explication, and a number of the points, are derived from Fillmore, 1973.

47

between two parties, and ask what information it provides us with above and beyond what might be given by the semantic content of the component sentences. More specifically, we can ask what implications are carried by the sentences about the contexts in which they are being used. The example is constructed – the reader is warned because good reasons for preferring naturally occurring conversational data will be given in Chapter 6. Here is the exchange:

(32)   (i)   A: So can you please come over here again right now
        (ii) B: Well, I have to go to Edinburgh today sir
        (iii) A: Hmm. How about this Thursday?

It is not difficult to see that in understanding such an exchange we make a great number of detailed (pragmatic) inferences about the nature of the context in which (32) can be assumed to be taking place.[28] For example, we infer the facts in (33):

(33)   1. It is not the end of the conversation (nor the beginning)
        2. A is requesting B to come to A at (or soon after) the time of speaking; B implies he can't (or would rather not) comply; A repeats the request for some other time
        3. In requesting, A must (a) want B to come now, (b) think it possible that B can come, (c) think B is not already there, (d) think B was not about to come anyway, (e) expect that B will respond with an acceptance or rejection, and if B accepts, then A will also expect B to come, (f) think that his (A's) asking may be a possible motive for B to come, (g) not be, or be pretending not to be, in a position to order B to come
        4. A assumes that B knows where A is; A and B are not in the same place; neither A nor B are in Edinburgh; A thinks B has been to A's place before
        5. The day on which the exchange is taking place is not Thursday, nor Wednesday (or, at least, so A believes)
        6. A is male (or so B believes); A is acknowledged by B to have a higher social status than B (or to be playing the role of a superior)

[28] There may perhaps be some equivocation here between inferences that participants, i.e. A and B, might make, and inferences that observers or analysts – or readers of (32) – might make. For example, since A and B may well *presume* the facts in 4, 5, and 6, we might want to say that they didn't infer them; yet, from the fact that participants would be expected to correct errors in such presumptions, we can conclude that they must nevertheless make the inferences to check that their presumptions hold. Even the inference that the conversation is not about to terminate is, as we shall see

48

Obvious to the point of tediousness though some of these inferences may be,[29] they are not, on a reasonable circumscription of semantic theory, part of the semantic content of the three sentences. Rather, they reflect our ability to compute out of utterances in sequence the contextual assumptions they imply: the facts about the spatial, temporal and social relationships between participants, and their requisite beliefs and intentions in undertaking certain verbal exchanges. But if the inferences are not (or not all) part of the 'literal' meaning or conventional content of what is said, from what sources do they arise? One possibility is that the sentences simply invoke mental associations, in the way that hearing, say, the word *prognosis* might make one think of hospitals. But here that does not seem to be the case. The inferences are systematic, they are decodable by different interpreters in the same way, and without most of them the exchange cannot be understood; most of them must therefore be part of what is communicated, in Grice's strict sense of meant-nn. But above all, we can trace each of these inferences to the facts that trigger them, namely, aspects of the form and juxtaposition of the utterances themselves, and we can go on to specify the regular principles that, given such aspects of utterances, produce the inferences in question. The Chapters below will each be concerned with particular principles of this kind, but let us here just identify the aspects of the utterances that trigger each of the inferences.

First, we know ((33) 1) that it is not the end of the conversation because utterance (iii) is not a possible closing utterance: for one thing, it requires a response from B, and for another it is not a token of one of the regular closing forms that persons use in conversation (*Okay, see you later* or the like). That is, some turns at talking come in pairs, such that one part of the pair requires the second part in response, while conversations have overall structures with well-bounded beginnings and endings. In short we have strong expectations about the structure of conversation which warrant many different kinds of inference (see Chapter 6). We also incidentally know that it is not the beginning (although that, being known in advance by

in Chapter 5, potentially a constant consideration for participants. So at least most of these inferences are ones that A and B must calculate.

[29] Actually, all these inferences need further qualification of a rather tedious sort: e.g. the inference 6 in (33) that A is male, or at least that B believes that A is male, should have the additional qualification 'or at least, B is acting as if he or she thinks A is male', etc.

participants, is not part of what is communicated), because there is no token of a conversational opening (like *hello*), and the particle *so* with which utterance (i) begins has the function of tying the present utterance back to prior utterances.

We know the facts in (33) 2 in a rather more complicated way. Whereas the interrogative form of the first utterance might be claimed to encode a question, that is not all that is intended: it would be strikingly unco-operative if B were to say *yes* (meaning just 'yes I am able to come') and then not go to A. Somehow, the interrogative form can also convey a request, and this interpretation is strongly reinforced here by the presence of the word *please* (see Chapter 5). Much more difficult is to see how B's response in (ii) can be understood as a request refusal, for there is no overt relation at all between its semantic content and that function. The implication relies on some very general expectation of interactional co-operation, which allows one to assume that if one utterance calls for a response (and the request in (i) does so), then one may assume (other things being equal) that a following utterance is a relevant response (see Chapters 3 and 6). Such an assumption is strong enough that when one comes across a response that is apparently irrelevant (as (ii) overtly appears to be), an inference is triggered that would preserve the assumption of relevance. Here, in (ii), the utterance provides the clue: B has to go to Edinburgh; thus if A and B are both far from Edinburgh (and mutually know this), so that it will take the rest of the day to travel and do things there, then B is busy today; so B is indirectly producing a reason why he or she can't easily come to see A, and in so doing can be understood to be refusing A's request. In actual fact there is just one overt trigger for this inference: the particle *well* in English serves to warn the recipient that some inferencing must be done to preserve the assumption of relevance. It can be plausibly claimed that, like *so* and many other words, *well* has no semantic content, only pragmatic specifications for usage. (See Chapter 3; an alternative account of this inference and the role of *well* can be constructed using the notion of **dispreferred** response in Chapter 6.)

In (33) 2 we also have the inference that utterance (iii) counts as a repeat request. To account for this, we would need first of all to explain how the form *how about VERBing* is more or less restricted to usages in suggestions (again, this looks like a linguistic form that has pragmatic rather than semantic content, a problem discussed in Chapter 5). So A is suggesting that someone do something on

Thursday. Again, in order to preserve the assumption of relevance, an inference must be made about who is to do what: since the last mention of someone doing something involved B going to A, that is presumably what A intends, and may thus be taken to have meant. Here we seem to be implicitly relying on a further assumption, namely an assumption of topical coherence: if a second utterance can be interpreted as following on a first utterance, in the sense that they can be 'heard' as being concerned with the same topic, then such an interpretation of the second utterance is warranted unless there are overt indications to the contrary (again, see Chapters 3 and 6). Finally, the particle *hmm* is not dismissable as just a 'performance error' or a 'filled pause'; it has specific interactional functions, best explicated in terms of the system for taking turns at speaking in conversation, where it can be seen to be (amongst other things) a turn-holding device (see Chapter 6).

We come now to the inferences in (33) 3. What are the sources for these? We have already seen that indirectly the question in utterance (i) must be understood as a request. Now it simply follows that, if A is requesting B to come, and A is behaving rationally and sincerely, we may assume all the facts in (a)–(g). Why? Partly because if we explicate the concept of requesting, it will be found to be constituted of the very speaker beliefs and wishes listed in part in (a)–(g) (see Chapter 5). But of course it would be possible to go through the behavioural motions of requesting without having any of the requisite beliefs and intentions. Therefore one is warranted in making the inference from the behaviour to the beliefs and intentions of the speaker only by a general assumption of sincerity, or co-operativeness (see Chapter 3). If A knows in advance that B can't come, then he is being deceptive; but if he knows that B knows that he knows that B can't come, then he cannot be interpreted as requesting at all (utterance (i) might then be a joke, or if B is in an incapacitated (say, inebriated) state, perhaps a gibe).

The inferences in (33) 4 are easier to account for. The word *here* denotes the (pragmatically bounded) place where the speaker (A) is at the time of speaking; if B does not know (or cannot find out) where A is, *here* is uninterpretable in the sense that B cannot comply with the request to go there. So A would be less than fully co-operative or rational if he did not think that B knew (or could find out) where he was. We also know that A and B are not in the same place (or at least are at some distance from one another). We know this because the word *come* (at least with the tense and aspect in (i)) denotes either motion towards the speaker at the time of speaking (as in *Come to breakfast, Johnny*) or motion towards the addressee's location at the time of speaking (as in *I'm coming, Mummy*). Note that as with *here*, the meaning of *come* can only be explicated by reference to pragmatic or contextual parameters (speakers, addressees, times and places of speaking). In utterance (i), *come* cannot denote movement towards the addressee, because the subject of *come* is *you*, and the addressee can hardly move to where the addressee already is. So it must denote movement towards the speaker; but again, the addressee can hardly move towards the speaker if there is no significant distance between them; therefore A and B are not in the same place. Here we might note that they are also not in Edinburgh: we know this for B because B claims to have to *go* to Edinburgh, and *go* here means movement away from the place of the speaker at the time of speaking; we know it for A also, because if A is in Edinburgh, then B's having to go to Edinburgh can hardly be an excuse for B not going to A today. We make all these inferences on the basis of the deictic words, *come*, *go* and *here* (not to mention *now*), together with reasonings about the nature of our physical world (see Chapter 2). A natural interpretation (by an observer or analyst) of this deictic set-up is that A and B are talking on the telephone. Finally, we know that (A believes that) B has been to A's present location before because of the word *again*: this can be claimed to be a pragmatic rather than a semantic implication just because, unlike semantic implications, those associated with *again* are not normally negated by the negation of the main verb. We are inclined therefore to say that *again* **presupposes**, rather than semantically entails, that some event referred to happened before as well (see Chapter 4).

The implication (33) 5, that the day of speaking is other than Wednesday or Thursday, is also due to deixis (explained in Chapter 2), for the word *Thursday* in utterance (iii) is used in a deictic way that invokes pragmatic parameters (there are other usages that do not, e.g. *Pay day is Thursday*). Here the modifier *this* picks out a particular Thursday in relation to the speaker's location in the week: *this Thursday* means the Thursday of the week in which the speaker is speaking.[30] But on Thursday, the Thursday of this week cannot, by pragmatic convention, be referred to as *this Thursday*; we must

---

[30] Or the Thursday in some week otherwise pragmatically identified, e.g. by gesture at a calendar.

instead say *today*. By the same token, we cannot say *this Thursday* on Wednesday, because we ought to say *tomorrow*. So the exchange in (32) takes place neither on Wednesday nor on Thursday. (There may be some different restrictions on usage here in different varieties of English, and there are also some interesting ambiguities; see Chapter 2 below and Fillmore, 1975.)

Finally, we have the inferences in (33) 6 that A is male, and of apparently higher social status than B. These are based most soundly on the vocative item *sir*, for that is what that word seems to mean. Again, on a truth-conditional theory of semantics, those meanings cannot be captured – we would not want to say that B's assertion in (ii) was false if B had simply misidentified A and assumed mistakenly that A was a male superior (that would make truths relative to whomsoever they are addressed).[31] Further, in an intuitive way, the meanings of *sir* here are not part of the content of what is asserted; they are background assumptions about the context, specifically the kind of person B is addressing. We may therefore say that *sir* **conventionally implicates** that the addressee is male and socially higher in rank than the speaker (see Chapter 3).

There are no doubt many other pragmatic inferences that can be wrung from an exchange as short and insignificant as this. But these will serve to indicate the general nature of the phenomena that pragmatics is concerned with. The point is that we can compute out of sequences of utterances, taken together with background assumptions about language usage, highly detailed inferences about the nature of the assumptions participants are making, and the purposes for which utterances are being used. In order to participate in ordinary language usage, one must be able to make such calculations, both in production and interpretation. This ability is independent of idiosyncratic beliefs, feelings and usages (although it may refer to those shared by participants), and is based for the most part on quite regular and relatively abstract principles. Pragmatics can be taken to be the description of this ability, as it operates both for particular languages and language in general. Such a description must certainly play a role in any general theory of linguistics.

---

[31] But some assertions, e.g. those with *you* as argument of a predicate, do indeed have just such a relativity. The point here rests on the fact that the vocative item *sir* is not such an argument (e.g. subject or object of a verb); thus the meaning of *sir* seems not to be part of the proposition expressed by (ii), and thus not part of the truth conditions.

2

Deixis

2.0 Introduction

The single most obvious way in which the relationship between language and context is reflected in the structures of languages themselves, is through the phenomenon of **deixis**. The term is borrowed from the Greek word for pointing or indicating, and has as prototypical or focal exemplars the use of demonstratives, first and second person pronouns, tense, specific time and place adverbs like *now* and *here*, and a variety of other grammatical features tied directly to the circumstances of utterance.

Essentially deixis concerns the ways in which languages encode or grammaticalize features of the **context of utterance** or **speech event**, and thus also concerns ways in which the interpretation of utterances depends on the analysis of that context of utterance. Thus the pronoun *this* does not name or refer to any particular entity on all occasions of use; rather it is a variable or place-holder for some particular entity given by the context (e.g. by a gesture). The facts of deixis should act as a constant reminder to theoretical linguists of the simple but immensely important fact that natural languages are primarily designed, so to speak, for use in face-to-face interaction, and thus there are limits to the extent to which they can be analysed without taking this into account (Lyons, 1977a: 589ff).

The importance of deictic information for the interpretation of utterances is perhaps best illustrated by what happens when such information is lacking (Fillmore, 1975: 38–9). Consider, for example, finding the following notice on someone's office door:

(1)   I'll be back in an hour

Because we don't know *when* it was written, we cannot know when the writer will return. Or, imagine that the lights go out as Harry has just begun saying:

(2)   Listen, I'm not disagreeing with *you* but with *you*, and not about *this* but about *this*

Or, suppose we find a bottle in the sea, and inside it a message which reads:

(3)   Meet me here a week from now with a stick about this big

We do not know *who* to meet, *where* or *when* to meet him or her, or *how big* a stick to bring.

The many facets of deixis are so pervasive in natural languages, and so deeply grammaticalized, that it is hard to think of them as anything other than an essential part of semantics. If semantics is taken to include all conventional aspects of meaning, then perhaps most deictic phenomena are properly considered semantic. However, by at least some of the views that we reviewed in Chapter 1, deixis belongs within the domain of pragmatics, because it directly concerns the relationship between the structure of languages and the contexts in which they are used. But all such categorizations are theory-dependent, and on the view that we have adopted for convenience, namely that pragmatics concerns those aspects of meaning and language-structure that cannot be captured in a truth-conditional semantics, the grammatical category of deixis will probably be found to straddle the semantics/pragmatics border.

The important point, wherever the pragmatics/semantics boundary is drawn, is that deixis concerns the encoding of many different aspects of the circumstances surrounding the utterance, within the utterance itself. Natural language utterances are thus 'anchored' directly to aspects of the context.

2.1 Philosophical approaches

The topic of deixis, or as philosophers usually prefer, **indexical expressions** (or just **indexicals**), may be usefully approached by considering how truth-conditional semantics deals with certain natural language expressions. Suppose we identify the semantic content of a sentence with its truth conditions, then the semantic content of

(4)   Letizia de Ramolino was the mother of Napoleon

will amount to a specification of the circumstances under which it would be true, namely that the individual known as Letizia de Ramolino was in fact identical to the individual who was the mother of Napoleon. The truth of (4) in no way depends on who says it, but simply on the facts of history.[1] But now suppose we try to analyse:

(5)   I am the mother of Napoleon

We cannot assess the truth of this sentence without taking into account who the speaker is; for (5) is true just in case the person uttering the sentence is indeed identical to the individual who is the mother of Napoleon, and false otherwise. In which case, in order to assess the truth of (5) we need to know, in addition to the facts of history, certain details about the context in which it was uttered (here, the identity of the speaker). The expression *I* is not of course the only such troublesome feature of English; the following examples all present us with the same sort of problems (with the relevant deictic expression italicized, a convention followed throughout this Chapter):

(6)   *You* are the mother of Napoleon
(7)   *This* is an eighteenth-century man-trap
(8)   Mary is in love with *that* fellow over *there*
(9)   It is *now* 12.15

The sentences are true, respectively, just in case the addressee is indeed the mother of Napoleon, the object currently being indicated by the speaker is indeed an eighteenth-century man-trap, Mary is indeed in love with the fellow in the location indicated by the speaker, and at the time of speaking it is indeed 12.15. In each case the context-dependency can be traced to specific deictic expressions or indexicals. Sentences that contain such expressions, and whose truth values therefore depend on certain facts about the context of utterance (identity of speakers, addressees, indicated objects, places and times, etc.), are not of course in any way special or peculiar. For just about every utterance has this context-dependency, due in no small part (at least in many languages) to **tense**. For, roughly, the following utterance will be true

(10)   There *is* a man on Mars

just in case *at the time of speaking* there is a man on Mars, whereas

---

[1] The contrast here between context-independent and context-dependent modes of reference is not really quite so simple – ultimately, perhaps, many kinds of referential expressions rely on contextual information, a point raised below.

(11) will be true just in case at *some time prior to the time of speaking*
(10) would have been true:

(11)   There *was* a man on Mars

There has been considerable philosophical interest in expressions that
have this context-dependent property, like demonstratives, first and
second person pronouns, and morphemes indicating tense. It was
Peirce who first termed such expressions **indexical signs**, and
argued that they determined a referent by an existential relation
between sign and referent (see Burks, 1949). Peirce's category in fact
included rather more than the directly context-dependent expressions
that are now called deictic or indexical, and his particular system of
categories has not been put to much effective use in linguistic
pragmatics (but see e.g. Bean, 1978).

Part of the philosophical interest in this area arose from the
questions of whether (a) all indexical expressions can be reduced to
a single primary one, and thence (b) whether this final pragmatic
residue can be translated out into some eternal context-free artificial
language. Russell, for example, thought that the reduction in (a) was
possible, by translating all indexicals (or as he preferred, **egocentric
particulars**) into expressions containing *this*, where the latter referred
to a subjective experience. The pronoun *I* would thus be rendered
'the person who is experiencing this' (for severe difficulties with such
a view, see Gale, 1968). Reichenbach argued, also in support of (a)
and with an ultimate view to (b), that all indexicals involve an element
of **token-reflexivity**, i.e. refer to themselves, so that, for example,
I means 'the person who is uttering this token of the word *I*'. This
view may be initially attractive, but it has many difficulties (Gale,
1968). Further, while there are indeed token-reflexive or self-referring
expressions in natural languages, as in (12) and, arguably, in (13) (see
Chapter 5):

(12)   *This sentence* contains five words
(13)   I *hereby* apologize

these pose formidable problems for logical analysis, and nothing is
gained by assimilating indexicals to token-reflexives if this can
possibly be avoided.

From a linguistic point of view, the question in (b), whether
ultimately deictic expressions can be translated into context-

independent terms without loss of meaning, is perhaps a philosophical red-herring. Natural languages, after all, just do have indexicals, and it is the task of linguistic analysis to model these directly in order to capture the ways in which they are used. It is worth pointing out, however, that there are some good arguments to the effect that ultimate reduction is impossible (Bar-Hillel, 1970: 77–8; Lyons, 1977a: 639–46).

However, if it is intended, as part of a general programme of semantic analysis, to extend logical techniques to handle sentences containing indexicals, provision must somehow be made for their context-dependency. The syntax and semantics of classical logics (say, first order predicate calculus) make no such provision. How should indexicals be accommodated, so that the notion of **logical consequence**, as it applies for example to the inference from (14) to (15), can also be applied to the inference from (16) to (17) ?

(14)   John Henry McTavitty is six feet tall and weighs 200 pounds
(15)   John Henry McTavitty is six feet tall
(16)   I am six feet tall and weigh 200 pounds
(17)   I am six feet tall

Clearly, in order for (17) to be a valid inference from (16), the referent of *I* must somehow be fixed – the inference doesn't follow if (16) and (17) are said by different speakers. There are various different ways in which logics can be relativized to contexts of utterance in order to achieve this. Suppose, as is now common in logical semantics, we view a **proposition** as a function from possible worlds to truth values (i.e. as an abstract assignment of the value *true* to just those states of affairs which the proposition correctly describes – see Allwood, Andersson & Dahl, 1977: 20–3 for elementary exposition). Then one way in which we can accommodate context-relativity is to say that the proposition expressed by a sentence in a context is a function from possible worlds *and that context* to truth values. A context will here be a set of **pragmatic indices**, **co-ordinates** or **reference points** (as they are variously called) for speakers, addressees, times of utterance, places of utterance, indicated objects, and whatever else is needed. Sentences can therefore express different propositions on different occasions of use. Thus the inference from (16) to (17) will be valid only if the speaker index and the time index are held constant (see e.g. Montague, 1968; Scott, 1970; Lewis, 1972).

Another way of handling indexicals is to think of the specification of the content of an utterance as a two stage affair: the 'meaning' of an utterance is a function from contexts (sets of indices) to propositions, which are in turn functions from possible worlds to truth values (Montague, 1970; Stalnaker, 1972). On this view pragmatics (at least in part) is about how, given a sentence uttered in a context, that context plays a role in specifying what proposition the sentence expresses on this occasion of utterance. Semantics is then not concerned directly with natural language at all, but only with the abstract entities propositions, which sentences and contexts jointly pick out.

What this approach makes especially clear is that while we might want to say that the meaning of (17) remains constant across different occasions of utterance, the proposition that it expresses if Joe Bloggs utters it is different from the one it picks out if Sue Bloggs utters it. It also makes clear that sentences in the abstract do not in general express definite propositions at all; it is only utterances of them in specific contexts that express specific states of affairs, where the contexts achieve this by filling in the pragmatic parameters that indexicals are variables for. On this view, pragmatics is logically prior to semantics; that is, the output of the pragmatic component of the theory is the input to the semantic component. However, as we remarked in Chapter 1, to identify pragmatics wholly with the truth-conditional apparatus that will handle indexicals is to leave us with no term for all those aspects of natural language significance that are not in any way amenable to truth-conditional analysis. Where indexicals can be routinely treated truth-conditionally, we will therefore continue to think of the theory that handles them as part of semantics. However, it is clear that not all aspects of deixis can be treated truth-conditionally, as we shall see below, and there are considerable problems even for the apparently tractable cases. So we shall postpone consideration of just where the semantics/pragmatics borderline cuts across the field of deixis until 2.3 below.

Before leaving philosophical treatments of indexicals, we should just point to a subject of deep theoretical importance which lies well beyond the scope of this book – namely, the connection of indexical reference to the fundamentals of reference in general. Initially, philosophers interested in reference (with some notable exceptions) did not pay a great deal of attention to indexicals (Bar-Hillel, 1970: 76); then they began to treat them as very special kinds of expression requiring contextual co-ordinates or indices, as sketched above. Now they have begun to wonder whether many kinds of referring expressions are not in fact covertly indexical in at least some usages. Quine's (1960) views on ostension, and Strawson's (1950) treatment of referring expressions broached this issue (see Bar-Hillel, 1970: 84; Atlas, 1975b). Searle's (1969) treatment of reference as a particular species of *action* (rather than as some mysterious correspondence, however indirect, between words and sets of objects) also indirectly advanced the view that indexicals are closely linked to other kinds of reference. That children early in language acquisition produce isolated acts of reference, seems to support the view of reference as a **speech act** (see Chapter 5) that is prototypically 'demonstrative' (Lyons, 1975; Atkinson, 1979). Since demonstrative pronouns typically involve a gesture, it seems easy to assimilate such acts of reference to general theories of action; if one can then show that other kinds of referring expression are related to demonstratives, the case for viewing reference in general as a species of action is made plausible. In this connection, Lyons (1975) proposes that deictic reference is ontogenetically prior to other kinds of reference, and provides the basis for their acquisition (but see Tanz, 1980). However, it is only recently that the connection of reference in general to indexicals has begun to concern those philosophers with an investment in logical semantics. Donnellan (1966) began by noting a distinction between two usages of **definite descriptions** (*inter alia*, noun phrases in English with the determiner *the*):

(18)   *The man drinking champagne* is Lord Godolphin
(19)   *The man who can lift this stone* is stronger than an ox

The first would most naturally have a **referential** use, where the description might in fact be wrong (e.g. the man is actually drinking lemonade) but the reference succeed in any case; the second would most naturally have an **attributive** use where the speaker would not have any particular individual in mind (we could paraphrase (19) as 'whoever can lift this stone is stronger than an ox'). But in many cases an utterance is potentially ambiguous between these two usages. It is the speaker's intention and the addressee's successful location of the intended referent that matter in the first usage, not the exact aptness of the description, so that we could call this usage **speaker reference** (as opposed to **semantic reference**; Donnellan, 1978;

Kaplan, 1978). Indeed, just as with a demonstrative, so with the definite description in (18), the addressee is invited to look up and identify the referent. But then it is a small step to begin thinking of (18) as very similar to (20), and thus containing demonstrative or indexical elements:[2]

(20)   That man ((the speaker indicates the man drinking champagne)) is Lord Godolphin

And so it begins to look as if definite referring expressions may in general be used either in speaker reference or in semantic (or attributive) reference, and it is only the context of use that tells us which way to understand them (Donnellan, 1978; Kaplan, 1978). If this is so, then the role of pragmatics (in the indexical sense) in fixing the proposition that a sentence expresses, is greatly increased.

However, none of these philosophical approaches does justice to the complexity and variety of the deictic expressions that occur in natural languages, and we should now turn to consider linguistic approaches and findings.

2.2   Descriptive approaches

Given the undoubted importance of deixis to philosophical, psychological and linguistic approaches to the analysis of language, there has been surprisingly little work of a descriptive nature in the area, with a consequent lack of adequate theories and frameworks of analysis. In the absence of significant theories, in this section a series of tentative categories are advanced, together with some illustrations of their application. The most important of the earlier linguistic works in this area are Bühler, 1934: 79–148; Frei, 1944; Fillmore, 1966; Lyons, 1968; but much of this has been summarized and systematized in Lyons, 1977a, 1977b and Fillmore, 1971b, 1975, and it is to these latter works that most of what follows is directly indebted. There is also, though, a growing body of literature on the acquisition of deictic terms by children, most of which is referenced

---

[2] Linguists, too, have pointed out that there is a close relation between demonstrative pronouns on the one hand, and the definite article and third person pronouns on the other: in many of the Indo-European languages the latter derive diachronically from the former (Lyons, 1977a: 646–7); the conditions on usage are closely related (Hawkins, 1978); and, as mentioned above, early in language acquisition the two kinds of reference are not clearly differentiated (Lyons, 1975, 1977a: 648ff).

in Wales, 1979 and Tanz, 1980, while a useful collection of cross-linguistic observations can be found in Anderson & Keenan, in press.

The traditional categories of deixis are **person**, **place** and **time**. Briefly, as we shall devote a section to each below, these categories are understood in the following way. Person deixis concerns the encoding of the **role** of participants in the speech event in which the utterance in question is delivered: the category **first person** is the grammaticalization of the speaker's reference to himself, **second person** the encoding of the speaker's reference to one or more addressees, and **third person** the encoding of reference to persons and entities which are neither speakers nor addressees of the utterance in question. Familiar ways in which such participant-roles are encoded in language are of course the pronouns and their associated predicate agreements. Place deixis concerns the encoding of spatial locations *relative* to the location of the participants in the speech event. Probably most languages grammaticalize at least a distinction between **proximal** (or close to speaker) and **distal** (or non-proximal, sometimes close to addressee), but many make much more elaborate distinctions as we shall see. Such distinctions are commonly encoded in demonstratives (as in English *this* vs. *that*) and in deictic adverbs of place (like English *here* vs. *there*). Time deixis concerns the encoding of temporal points and spans *relative* to the time at which an utterance was spoken (or a written message inscribed). This time, following Fillmore (1971b), we shall call **coding time** or CT, which may be distinct from **receiving time** or RT, as example (1) made clear. Thus, just as place deixis encodes spatial locations on co-ordinates anchored to the place of utterance, so time deixis encodes times on co-ordinates anchored to the time of utterance. Time deixis is commonly grammaticalized in deictic adverbs of time (like English *now* and *then*, *yesterday* and *this year*), but above all in tense.

To these traditional categories, we should now add (following Lyons, 1968, 1977a, and Fillmore, 1971b, 1975) **discourse** (or **text**) **deixis** and **social deixis**. Discourse deixis has to do with the encoding of reference to portions of the unfolding discourse in which the utterance (which includes the text referring expression) is located.[3] Instances of discourse deixis are the use of *that* and *this* in the following:

[3] Token-reflexivity is thus a special sub-case of discourse deixis; both *that* in (21) and *this* in (22) are discourse deictic, but only the latter is token-reflexive.

(21)   Puff puff puff: *that* is what it sounded like
(22)   *This* is what phoneticians call creaky voice

Finally, social deixis concerns the encoding of social distinctions that are relative to participant-roles, particularly aspects of the social relationship holding between speaker and addressee(s) or speaker and some referent. In many languages, distinctions of fine gradation between the relative ranks of speaker and addressee are systematically encoded throughout, for example, the morphological system, in which case we talk of **honorifics**; but such distinctions are also regularly encoded in choices between pronouns, summons forms or vocatives, and titles of address in familiar languages.

Deictic systems in natural languages are not arbitrarily organized around the features of just any of the many different kinds of medium and context in which languages are used. Rather there is an essential assumption of that basic face-to-face conversational context in which all humans acquire language, or as Lyons (1977a: 637–8) has put it rather more precisely:

> The grammaticalization and lexicalization of deixis is best understood in relation to what may be termed the canonical situation of utterance: this involves one-one, or one-many, signalling in the phonic medium along the vocal-auditory channel, with all the participants present in the same actual situation able to see one another and to perceive the associated non-vocal paralinguistic features of their utterances, and each assuming the role of sender and receiver in turn ... There is much in the structure of languages that can only be explained on the assumption that they have developed for communication in face-to-face interaction. This is clearly so as far as deixis is concerned.[4]

Further, it is generally (but not invariably) true that deixis is organized in an egocentric way. That is, if (for the purposes of semantic or pragmatic interpretation) we think of deictic expressions as anchored to specific points in the communicative event, then the

---

[4] A direct illustration of this is provided by quite a number of languages of different stocks that encode a basic distinction between objects visible and non-visible to participants (see Anderson & Keenan, in press). This distinction is often subsumed under place deixis, as it tends to show up in demonstratives, but it is in fact an independent and parallel dimension of deictic organization that ought to be added to the major five categories of deixis considered in this Chapter.

unmarked anchorage points, constituting the **deictic centre**, are typically assumed to be as follows: (i) the central person is the speaker, (ii) the central time is the time at which the speaker produces the utterance, (iii) the central place is the speaker's location at utterance time or CT, (iv) the discourse centre is the point which the speaker is currently at in the production of his utterance, and (v) the social centre is the speaker's social status and rank, to which the status or rank of addressees or referents is relative. Now there are various exceptions to this: for example, some languages have demonstratives organized in part around the location of other participants than speakers. There are also various derivative usages, in which deictic expressions are used in ways that shift this deictic centre to other participants, or indeed to protagonists in narratives – Lyons (1977a: 579) calls this **deictic projection**, Fillmore (1975) shifts in **points of view**. The processes involved in such shifts are essential to an understanding of the diachronic development of various deictic words (see e.g. the remarks on *come* below) and to usages in non-conversational discourse (see Fillmore, 1981), but are beyond the scope of this Chapter.

It may help readers to visualize this unmarked deictic centre if they can imagine a four-dimensional space, composed of the three dimensions of space plus that of time, in which a speaker stands at the centre. Radiating out from the speaker are a number of concentric circles distinguishing different zones of spatial proximity; through the speaker passes a 'time line', on which events prior to his present utterance, and events prior to those, can be linearly arranged, and similarly events at points and spans in the future; while the discourse to which the speaker contributes unfolds along this same time line. To capture the social aspects of deixis, we would need to add at least one further dimension, say of relative rank, in which the speaker is socially higher, lower or equal to the addressee and other persons that might be referred to. Now when speaker and addressee switch participant-roles, the co-ordinates of this entire world switch to the space–time–social centre of the erstwhile addressee, now speaker. Such a picture makes the acquisition of deictic terms seem a miracle, and children do indeed have trouble with them (Tanz, 1980).

It is essential to distinguish different kinds of *usage* of deictic expression. Indeed by *deictic expression* we mean those linguistic units or morphemes that have a deictic usage as basic or central, for most such expressions have non-deictic usages. In addition to deictic vs. non-deictic usages of deictic expressions, we shall need to distinguish distinct kinds of deictic usage. Following Fillmore (1971b), let us first distinguish two kinds of deictic usage, namely **gestural usage** and **symbolic usage**. Terms used in a gestural deictic way can only be interpreted with reference to an audio–visual–tactile, and in general a physical, monitoring of the speech event. As a rough-and-ready guide, one can think of these gestural usages as requiring at least a video-tape of the speech event if the proper interpretation is to be available from a recording. Instances would be demonstrative pronouns used with a selecting gesture, as in:

(23)   *This* one's genuine, but *this* one is a fake

or second or third person pronouns used with some physical indication of the referent (e.g. direction of gaze), as in:

(24)   *He*'s not the Duke, *he* is. *He*'s the butler

There are usually a few words in a language that can only be used gesturally: for example there are presentatives like French *voici*, and toasts like British English *cheers*.[5] In contrast, symbolic usages of deictic terms require for their interpretation only knowledge of (in particular) the basic spatio-temporal parameters of the speech event (but also, on occasion, participant-role and discourse and social parameters). Thus it is sufficient to know the general location of the participants in order to interpret:

(25)   *This city* is really beautiful

and to know the set of potential addressees in the situation in order to interpret:

(26)   *You* can all come with me if you like

and to know when the interaction is taking place in order to know which calendar year is being referred to in

(27)   We can't afford a holiday *this year*

We could formulate the distinction thus: gestural usages require a moment by moment physical monitoring of the speech event for their interpretation, while symbolic usages make reference only to

---

[5] For a description of the increasing range of uses of this term see Trudgill, 1978: 8.

contextual co-ordinates available to participants antecedent to the utterance. It will then follow that the following are gestural usages, though the sense of gesture is here, of course, vocal:

(28)   Harvey can only speak about *this loud*
(29)   Don't do it *now*, but *NOW*!

These two kinds of deictic usage contrast with the non-deictic usage of the same words or morphemes. Some examples will help to make the three-way distinction clear; in the following the *a* cases are *gestural* usages, the *b* cases *symbolic* usages, and the *c* cases *non-deictic* usages:

(30)   a. *You, you,* but not *you,* are dismissed
          b. What did *you* say?
          c. *You* can never tell what sex they are nowadays
(31)   a. *This finger* hurts
          b. *This* city stinks
          c. I met *this* weird guy the other day
(32)   a. Push not *now,* but *now*
          b. Let's go *now* rather than tomorrow
          c. *Now,* that is not what I said
(33)   a. Not *that* one, idiot, *that* one
          b. *That*'s a beautiful view
          c. Oh, I did this and *that*
(34)   a. Move it from *there* to *there*
          b. Hello, is Harry *there*?
          c. *There* we go

(Note that, in most cases, the three kinds of sentences only favour the three kinds of interpretation.) Here are some further contrasts between just two of the usages, each labelled *a, b* or *c* as before:

(35)   a. ((In response to: "Who wants another?")) *I* do
          b. ((In response to: "Wilt thou have this woman to thy wedded wife?")) *I* will
(36)   b. I did it ten years *ago*
          c. Harry had done it ten years *ago*
(37)   b. John lives *opposite*
          c. John lives *opposite* Bill
(38)   b. We can't see the chimp because it's *behind* the tree
          c. When Harry's front axle buckled, he was *behind* a truck

A few brief comments on each of these: in (35a) the pronoun *I* is used gesturally to self-nominate from a group, in (35b) it just has the symbolic usage; in (36b) the word *ago* places the time at which the action occurred relative to the time of speaking, in (36c) the time is relative to the time at which the events in the narrative occurred. In (37b) *opposite* (and equally *nearby*, *around the corner*, etc.) is understood as relative to the place of utterance, in (37c) it is relative to Bill's location. In (38b) *behind* locates the chimp on the opposite side of the tree from the participants, in (38c) it locates Harry at the rear end of the truck.

These are perhaps the most important distinctions in the use of deictic terms, but they are not the only ones. As we shall see when we consider discourse deixis, within non-deictic usages we shall need to distinguish **anaphoric** from **non-anaphoric** usages.[6] All the *c* cases above are, in their most natural interpretations, non-deictic but also non-anaphoric usages. An anaphoric usage is where some term picks out as referent the same entity (or class of objects) that some prior term in the discourse picked out. Thus, in the following, *he* can naturally be interpreted as referring to whoever it is that *John* refers to:

(39)   John came in and he lit a fire

We will return to anaphora, but just note here that it is perfectly possible, as Lyons (1977a: 676) points out, for a deictic term to be used *both* anaphorically and deictically. For example, in:

(40)   I was born in *London* and have lived *there* ever since

there refers back to whatever place *London* refers to, but simultaneously contrasts with *here* on the deictic dimension of space, locating the utterance outside London. Note that it is also quite possible for the gestural usage to combine with the non-deictic anaphoric usage too:

(41)   I cut a finger: *this one*

Here *this one* refers to whatever *a finger* refers to, but simultaneously must be accompanied by a presentation of the relevant finger.

Clearly the proliferation of different kinds of usage of deictic terms is a source of considerable potential confusion to the analyst. The following summary of distinctions may help to keep them clear:

[6] One way of thinking about these non-deictic usages is to think of the deictic terms as being relativized to the text instead of to the situation of utterance. In that way, anaphoric usages can be seen to be related to various non-anaphoric non-deictic usages, e.g. to shifts in deictic interpretation due to indirect discourse. See Anderson & Keenan, in press; also Fillmore, 1981.

(42)   *Different usages of deictic terms*
      1. *deictic*:   a. gestural
                       b. symbolic
      2. *non-deictic*:   c. non-anaphoric
                       d. anaphoric

These difficulties are compounded when the phenomenon of **deictic projection**, or shifts from the egocentric centre, are taken into account; and they are further multiplied by the interaction of the semantics of non-deictic categorizations of (especially) space and time with deictic modifiers. We shall now take up each of the five major categories of deixis in turn: person, time, place, discourse and social deixis, in order to illustrate the complexities that arise. An appreciation of these complexities will indicate how involved and unexplored the phenomenon of deixis really is and how the philosophical approaches to indexicals can handle only a small proportion of these problems.

2.2.1   *Person deixis*

As speakers switch, so the deictic centre, on which the rest of the deictic system hangs, is itself abruptly moved from participant to participant. The difficulties that a Martian or child might have with such a system are neatly illustrated in the following Yiddish story:

> A melamed [Hebrew teacher] discovering that he had left his comfortable slippers back in the house, sent a student after them with a note for his wife. The note read: "Send me your slippers with this boy". When the student asked why he had written "your" slippers, the melamed answered: "Yold! If I wrote 'my' slippers, she would read 'my' slippers and would send her slippers. What could I do with her slippers? So I wrote 'your' slippers, she'll read 'your' slippers and send me mine". (Rosten, 1968: 443–4)

Although person deixis is reflected directly in the grammatical categories of person, it may be argued that we need to develop an independent pragmatic framework of possible **participant-roles**, so that we can then see how, and to what extent, these roles are grammaticalized in different languages. Such a framework would note that the speaker or **spokesman** can be distinct from the **source** of an utterance, the **recipient** distinct from the **target**, and hearers or **bystanders** distinct from addressees or targets, and that sometimes such distinctions are grammaticalized in non-obvious ways (see

Levinson, in prep.).[7] The Yiddish joke above depends, of course, on the distinction between source and speaker, which becomes immediately pertinent if one reads aloud.

However, the basic grammatical distinctions here are the categories of first, second and third person. If we were producing a componential analysis (for which see Lyons, 1968: 470–81) of pronominal systems, the features that we seem to need for the known systems would crucially include: for first person, speaker inclusion ($+S$); for second person, addressee inclusion ($+A$); and for third person, speaker and addressee exclusion ($-S$, $-A$) (see Burling, 1970: 14–17; Ingram, 1978). It is important to note that third person is quite unlike first or second person, in that it does not correspond to any specific participant-role in the speech event (Lyons, 1977a: 638).

Pronominal systems, which are the most obvious manifestations of person, generally exhibit this three-way distinction (Ingram, 1978). But some pronominal systems exhibit as many as fifteen basic pronouns (ignoring honorific alternates) by superimposing distinctions based on plurality (dual, trial and plural), gender and so on. Here it is important to see that the traditional category of plural is not symmetrically applied to first person in the way it is to third: *we* does not mean plural speakers in the same way that *they* means more than one third person entity (Lyons, 1968: 277). In addition, in many languages, there are two first person 'plural' pronouns, corresponding to 'we-inclusive-of-addressee' and 'we-exclusive-of-addressee'. This distinction is not manifested in English directly, but it is perhaps indirectly: for the contraction from *let us* to *let's* only seems felicitous if the *us* is understood inclusively, as illustrated below (Fillmore, 1971b):

(43)   Let's go to the cinema
(44)   ?Let's go to see you tomorrow

Other languages have pronominal systems much richer than the English one: in Japanese, pronouns are distinguished also with respect to sex of speaker, social status of referent and degree of intimacy with referent, so, for example, the second person pronoun

---

[7] Thus it can be argued that in English the sentence *Billie is to come in now* grammatically encodes (amongst other things) that the recipient is not the target (Billie is), in contrast to *Billy, come in now* where recipient and target are coincident. (The example comes from Gazdar, 1979a.) But see also example (50) below.

kimi can be glossed 'you, addressed by this intimate male speaker' (Uyeno, 1971: 16–17; Harada, 1976: 511); and village Tamil has up to six singular second person pronouns according to degree of relative rank between speaker and addressee (Brown & Levinson, 1978: 206).

We shall return to some of these facts below when we consider social deixis. Here we should simply note that these various distinctions are often encoded in verbal inflections in an isomorphic manner. Sometimes, though, morphological agreement can make further distinctions not overtly made by the pronouns themselves. A simple example of this occurs in languages that draw their polite second person singular pronoun from their plural one, where there will be no overt distinction between second person singular polite and second person plural pronouns. Here, finite verbs will agree in both cases with the superficially plural pronoun. But with nominal predicates the distinction is morphologically marked: such predicates agree with the real-world number of the referent (Comrie, 1975). So, in French, (45) is ambiguous as to whether there is one or more addressees, but (46) can only be addressed to a single addressee:

(45)   Vous parlez français?
(46)   Vous êtes le professeur?

In a similar sort of way, as Fillmore (1971b) notes, the editorial *we* of, for example, the *New Yorker* takes plural verb agreement (thus *we are* not *we am*), but in the reflexive the underlying singularity shows through in phrases like *as for ourself*. Finally, as we have noted, pronouns are often used non-deictically; but the actual variety of uses can be shown to be far greater than one would easily imagine (Watson, 1975; Sacks, 1976).

In addition to pronouns and agreeing predicates, person or participant-role is marked in various other ways. As is well known to anthropologists, kinship terms, and other kinds of title or proper name, often come in two quite distinct sets, one for use in address (as **vocatives** in second person usage) and the other for use in reference (i.e. referring to individuals in third person role). Even when the lexemes are the same, they may be *used* very differently in address and reference (see e.g. Beck, 1972: 290ff for Tamil usage), or only a sub-set of the reference terms may be used in address. The latter is the case with English kin terms – one can say both *Henry is my uncle* and *Henry is my cousin*, but only *Hello, Uncle!* not, in modern standard English, *Hello, Cousin!* Further, in some Australian languages there are up to four distinct sets of primary (as opposed to special supplementary) kin terms: (a) a set of vocative terms, (b) a set of terms which have an implicit first person possessive feature (i.e mean 'my mother's brother', etc.), (c) a set of terms which have a second person possessive feature (i.e. mean 'your mother's brother', etc.) and (d) a set of terms which have third person possessive features (i.e. mean 'his or her mother's brother', etc.). Some Australian languages even have 'triangular' kin terms, such that a term X denoting an individual x is only usable if x is (say) the speaker's father *and* the addressee's grandfather. Such suppletive sets of terms therefore encode person-deictic features in what are essentially terms for reference, not address (see Heath et al., 1982).

Vocatives in general are an interesting grammatical category, again underexplored. Vocatives are noun phrases that refer to the addressee, but are not syntactically or semantically incorporated as the arguments of a predicate; they are rather set apart prosodically from the body of a sentence that may accompany them. Vocatives can be divided into **calls**, or **summonses**, as in (47), and **addresses**, as in (48) (Zwicky, 1974):

(47)   *Hey you*, you just scratched my car with your frisbee
(48)   The truth is, *Madam*, nothing is as good nowadays

The distinction is precisely that between gestural and symbolic usages, applied in this domain. Summonses are naturally utterance-initial, indeed conversation-initial (see Schegloff, 1972a), and can be thought of as independent *speech acts* (see Chapter 5) in their own right. Addresses are parenthetical and can occur in the sorts of locations that other parentheticals can occupy. Not all summons forms can be used as addresses (e.g. *hey you* in (47) cannot occur in the slot occupied by *Madam* in (48)), although it may be that all addresses can be used as summonses (Zwicky, 1974: 791). Vocative forms in different languages appear to be highly idiosyncratic and complex. Note that greetings, partings and various 'ritual' formulae (e.g. *bless you* said after a sneeze) can be thought of as vocative in nature.

A further point to note in connection with person deixis, is that where face-to-face contact is lost, languages often enforce a distinct mode of, for instance, self-introduction. Thus, whereas in a face-to-face meeting I can say *I'm Joe Bloggs*, on the telephone I must say *This is Joe Bloggs* or *Joe Bloggs is speaking* with third person verb agreement (but see Schegloff, 1979a); in contrast in Tamil we would have to say on the telephone the equivalent of *Joe Bloggs am speaking*, with first person verb agreement.

In conclusion, it should be noted that the two basic participant roles, speaker and addressee, are not the only ones that can become involved in grammatical distinctions. Various languages (e.g. the Philippine language Samal) have demonstratives (discussed below) that specify location near other participants – in this case attending but not speaking parties, and present but non-participating parties. The Australian language Dyirbal has an entirely separate alternative vocabulary to be used in the presence of 'taboo' kinsmen, whether or not they are participants (Dixon, 1972: 32ff). Moreover it is common in many languages (e.g. German; Hymes, 1974: 56) for mother to say to father, in the presence of little Billie, something like:

(49)   Can Billie have an ice-cream, Daddy?

taking the point of view, for the purpose of vocative selection, of the audience. These distinctions make it important that we do not confuse, as is often done in the linguistic and philosophical literature, the categories of *addressee* and *hearer*. (Incidentally, note that as so often in the analysis of deixis, these various examples involve the overlapping organizations of the five basic categories of deixis: thus greetings usually involve temporal, person and discourse deixis; demonstratives both space and person; vocatives both person and social deixis; and so on.)

In addition to speaker, addressee and audience (third person, being, of course, definable in terms of the first two), there are a number of further distinctions in person deixis that probably need to be made. We know that, interactionally, important distinctions are often made between **overhearers**, **unratified** vs. **ratified participants**, those of the latter who are **addressees** and those who are **non-addressed participants**, and so on (see Goffman, 1976: 260; Goodwin, 1979a, 1981). Also, as we have noted, we sometimes need to distinguish speaker from source and addressee from target. Thus if the air-hostess announces

(50)   You are to fasten your seat-belts now

she is the speaker or spokesman, but not the source of the instructions, and this seems to be encoded in the use of the infinitive form. In Chinook, in formal ceremonies, neither the source (e.g. a chief) nor the target (e.g. the spirits) were necessarily present (Hymes, 1974: 56). In time many of these distinctions will perhaps be found reflected in the grammatical categories of some language or another (see Levinson, in prep.).

2.2.2   *Time deixis*

Both time and place deixis are greatly complicated by the interaction of deictic co-ordinates with the non-deictic conceptualization of time and space. To understand these aspects of deixis in depth it is first necessary to have a good understanding of the semantic organization of space and time in general, but these topics lie beyond the scope of this book (see though, Leech, 1969; Fillmore, 1975; Lyons, 1977a: Chapter 15). Briefly, though, the bases for systems of reckoning and measuring time in most languages seem to be the natural and prominent cycles of day and night, lunar months, seasons and years. Such units can either be used as **measures**, relative to some fixed point of interest (including, crucially, the deictic centre), or they can be used **calendrically** to locate events in 'absolute' time relative to some absolute *origo*, or at least to some part of each natural cycle designated as the beginning of that cycle (Fillmore, 1975). It is with these units, calendrical and non-calendrical, that time deixis interacts.

Like all aspects of deixis, time deixis makes ultimate reference to participant-role. Thus as a first approximation (but see below), *now* can be glossed as 'the time at which the speaker is producing the utterance containing *now*'. It is important to distinguish the moment of utterance (or inscription) or *coding time* (or CT) from the moment of reception or *receiving time* (or RT). As we noted, in the canonical situation of utterance, with the assumption of the unmarked deictic centre, RT can be assumed to be identical to CT (Lyons (1977a: 685) calls this assumption **deictic simultaneity**). Complexities arise in the usage of tense, time adverbs and other time-deictic morphemes wherever there is a departure from this assumption, e.g. in letter writing, or the pre-recording of media programmes. In that event, a decision has to be made about whether the deictic centre will remain on the speaker and CT, as in (51), or will be **projected** on the addressee and RT, as in (52) (Fillmore, 1975):

73

(51)   a. This programme is being recorded today, Wednesday April
           1st, to be relayed next Thursday
        b. I write this letter while chewing peyote
(52)   a. This programme was recorded last Wednesday, April 1st, to
           be relayed today
        b. I wrote this letter while chewing peyote

Linguistic conventions may often specify the proper usage in situations where RT is not coincident with CT. For example, the Latin 'epistolary tenses' used past tense for events including CT, pluperfect for events prior to CT – in other words the deictic centre was projected into the future, the recipients' RT (Lakoff, 1970: 847). But we shall have to skirt these issues here (see Fillmore, 1975).

There are a number of aspects of 'pure' time deixis, where there is no direct interaction with non-deictic methods of time reckoning. These include tense (to be discussed below), and the deictic time adverbs like English *now*, *then*, *soon*, *recently* and so on. We can improve on our previous gloss for *now*, by offering 'the pragmatically given span including CT', where that span may be the instant associated with the production of the morpheme itself, as in the gestural use in (53), or the perhaps interminable period indicated in (54):

(53)   Pull the trigger *now*!
(54)   I'm *now* working on a PhD

Now contrasts with *then*, and indeed *then* can be glossed as 'not now' to allow for its use in both past and future. *Then* is sometimes claimed to be necessarily anaphoric in nature, and to have no gestural deictic usage, but rather complex usages show this is not so - consider, for example, the following said pointing at a 1962 model Chevrolet (Nunberg, 1978: 33):

(55)   I was just a kid *then*

As an initial step towards seeing how time deixis interacts with cultural measurements of time in an absolute or non-deictic way, consider words like *today*, *tomorrow*, *yesterday*. Such terms presuppose a division of time into diurnal spans. Roughly, then, *today* glosses as 'the diurnal span including CT', *yesterday* as 'the diurnal span preceding the diurnal span that includes CT', and so on. However, as Fillmore (1975) notes, these have two kinds of referent: they can either refer to the entire span itself, as in (56), or to a point within the relevant span, as in (57):

(56)   *Tomorrow* is Wednesday
(57)   Dennis hit Murphy with a baseball bat *yesterday*

Note that the deictic words *yesterday*, *today* and *tomorrow* pre-empt the calendrical or absolute ways of referring to the relevant days. Thus the following, said on Thursday, can only be referring to next Thursday (or perhaps some more remote Thursday), otherwise the speaker should have said *today*:

(58)   I'll see you on *Thursday*

The same holds if it is said on Wednesday, due to pre-emptive *tomorrow*.[8] Languages differ in how many such deictic names of days there are: the Amerindian language Chinantec has four named days either side of today; Japanese names three days back from today, and two ahead; Hindi has the same word for yesterday and tomorrow (i.e. it glosses as 'the relevant day adjacent to the day including CT'); and so on (Fillmore, 1975).

Further aspects of the interaction of calendrical reckoning and time deixis arise when we consider complex time adverbials like *last Monday*, *next year*, or *this afternoon*. These consist of a deictic modifier, *this*, *next*, *last*, etc., together with a non-deictic name or measure word. Now, interpretation of such adverbials in English is systematically determined by (a) the calendrical vs. non-calendrical (and specifically deictic) modes of reckoning, and (b) the distinction between common noun units, like *weeks*, *months*, *years*, and proper name units, like *Monday*, *December*, and perhaps *afternoon*, which cannot be used as measures (Fillmore, 1975). Thus *this year* is ambiguous between the calendrical unit that runs from January 1 to January 1 and which includes CT,[9] and the measure of 365 days that begins on the day including CT. In general, the phrase *this X*, where

---

[8] Perhaps this pre-emptive nature of pure deictic words is a general tendency: it takes special conventions to make it appropriate for a speaker to refer to himself by name, and it would be strange to say *Do it at 10.36* instead of *Do it now*, when now is 10.36. Exceptions, though, are titles used instead of second person pronouns, as in *Your Honour should do as he wishes*, with full third person agreement; and one can say *London* instead of *here* if one is in London.

[9] There are other possibilities too, due to other kinds of calendrical fixed points, e.g. the tax year, the academic year, etc.

'X' ranges over the terms *week, month, year,* will refer to the unit X including CT, and will be ambiguous between the calendrical and non-calendrical interpretations.[10] Similarly, *next X* will refer to the unit X which follows the unit of the same order which includes CT, and so on. In contrast, *this Y,* where 'Y' is a proper name for a unit included in the larger calendrical span Z, will often mean 'that unit Y which is included in the larger span Z which includes CT'. Hence, *this August* does not necessarily mean the month that we are now in, in the way that *this week* ordinarily means the week that we are now in. Rather, *this August* means the August of the calendar year that includes CT; and *this morning* means the morning of the diurnal unit that includes CT. Thus I can say *this morning* either during the morning or the afternoon, and refer to the same span; whereas in Chinantec, I must use a different word for referring to the morning in the morning (i.e. when the span includes CT) from the one I use to refer to the morning in the afternoon (i.e. when the span referred to excludes CT, but is within the same larger diurnal span as CT – Fillmore, 1975: 47).

In the application of *next* to calendrical names of days, an ambiguity arises: *next Thursday* can refer either to the Thursday of the week that succeeds the week that includes CT, *or* that Thursday that first follows CT. Note that on a Friday or a Saturday, these will coincide; and given the rule that *today* and *tomorrow* pre-empt calendrical day names, on Wednesday and Thursday, *next Thursday* can only mean the Thursday of next week. It follows that, if one starts the week on Monday, *next Thursday* is ambiguous only on Monday and Tuesday (Fillmore, 1971b). The example nicely raises the issue of the degree to which a general linguistic theory is committed to giving an account of language understanding: for here we have a complex interaction between deictic words (clearly a linguistic problem) and a culture's temporal reckoning systems (not so clearly a linguistic problem), and the pre-emptive usage of deictic words (which lies somewhere in between). On the wider programme for pragmatics which we reviewed in Chapter 1, namely that pragmatics should provide (in connection with the rest of linguistic theory) a full account of language understanding, inferences like this must be fully explained.

Finally, we should turn briefly to **tense**, although the complexities

---

[10] Note that this use of *this* is perhaps borrowed from its proximal place deictic usage, here to indicate spans close to or including CT.

of this subject lie well beyond the scope of this book. In those languages that unequivocably exhibit it, tense is one of the main factors ensuring that nearly all sentences when uttered are deictically anchored to a context of utterance.[11] Confusion over whether some sentences like the following are tenseless or 'eternal' in part stems from a deep equivocation over the term *tense*.

(59)   Two and two is four
(60)   Iguanas eat ants

Let us, following Lyons (1977a: 682), distinguish the semantic or theoretical category of tense, which we may call metalinguistic tense or **M-tense** for short, from the verbal inflections that a traditional grammar of a particular language may call that language's tenses, which we may call **L-tenses**. M-tense can be given a purely deictic and strictly temporal interpretation, but it is an empirical question as to what extent L-tenses can also be treated in the same way. Then we may say that (59) and (60) are L-tensed, but M-tenseless and non-deictic (although they may be non-deictic in different ways; see Lyons, 1977a: 680). Now, we may investigate the properties of M-tense systems in isolation from their partial and imperfect realization in L-tense systems, as is done in tense logics (see Reichenbach, 1947; Prior, 1968). Obviously, though, if M-tense and L-tense get too far apart, M-tense may be of little use to the analysis of language. In an M-tense system we can easily distinguish *past* (events completed prior to CT), from *present* (events whose span includes CT), from *future* (events succeeding CT); we can further distinguish *points* from *spans* (Lyons, 1977a: 683); and we can also make first approximations to complex tenses like the *pluperfect*, by representing events that are prior to other events, which are themselves prior to CT (Reichenbach, 1947: 288ff; see also Allwood, Andersson & Dahl, 1977: 121ff). Thus (61) will be true, on this account, just in case there is some reference time (say, another event) prior to CT, such that at that reference time, (62) would have been true (while (62)

---

[11] But some languages require other forms of deictic anchoring in all sentences. Thus the North American Indian language Kwakwala requires virtually every noun phrase to be coded as either visible or non-visible to the speaker (Anderson & Keenan, in press, after Boas), while S.E. Asian languages like Korean and Japanese enforce the coding of social deixis, and other languages the encoding of discourse deixis (in the form of discourse topic), in almost every sentence.

is in turn true, just in case (63) would have been true at some point prior to the CT of (62)):

(61)   John *had seen* Mary
(62)   John *saw* Mary
(63)   John *sees* Mary

But such M-tenses do not match up simply with L-tenses, for L-tenses nearly always encode additional *aspectual* and *modal* features too (see Comrie, 1976a; Lyons, 1977a: 703ff, 809ff). For example, L-future-tenses probably invariably contain a modal element, and the nearest M-tense correlates of L-tenses are to be found in the distinction between past and non-past (Lyons, 1977a: 678). Any theorist who wants to claim that, for example, the English L-present and L-future coincide with the M-present and M-future, will find catalogues of insuperable odds in Huddleston, 1969; Lakoff, 1970; Lyons, 1977a: 809ff; and the references they cite. Nevertheless a pure deictic M-tense system seems to be an integral component, together with aspectual, modal and other notions, of most L-tense systems. Clearly, just what M-tense concepts are needed for linguistic description will differ from language to language. Further, we can expect interactions between pure deictic M-tense concepts and cultural divisions and measures of time to show up in L-tenses. Thus, in the Peruvian language Amahuacan, there is an L-tense affix (call it 'T') which means different things at different times of the day: *John kicked-T Bill* said in the afternoon means 'John kicked Bill in the morning', but said in the morning it means 'John kicked Bill yesterday'. In other words 'T' seems to mean that the event described took place in the largest unit of the daylight span that precedes the unit which contains CT, whether or not night intervenes. (For this, and other 'exotic' elements of time deixis, see Fillmore, 1975.)

It is sometimes claimed that there are languages without true tenses, for example Chinese or Yoruba, and this is correct in the sense that such languages may lack L-tenses morphologically marked in the verb, or indeed systematically elsewhere (Comrie, 1976a: 82ff; Lyons, 1977a: 678–9). But we can confidently assume that there are no languages where part of an M-tense system is not realized somewhere in time-adverbials or the like, not to mention the implicit assumption of M-present if no further specification is provided (Lyons, 1977a: 686).

Finally, we should mention that time deixis is relevant to various other deictic elements in a language. Thus *greetings* are usually time-restricted, so that

(64)   Good morning

can only be used in the morning, and so on. Curiously, while (64) can only be used as a greeting (at least in British English), (65) can only be used as a parting:

(65)   Good night

so that we have here an interaction of time and discourse deixis.

2.2.3   *Place deixis*

Place or space deixis concerns the specification of locations relative to anchorage points in the speech event. The importance of locational specifications in general can be gauged from the fact that there seem to be two basic ways of referring to objects – by describing or naming them on the one hand, and by locating them on the other (Lyons, 1977a: 648). Now, locations can be specified relative to other objects or fixed reference points, as in:

(66)   The station is two hundred yards from the cathedral
(67)   Kabul lies at latitude 34 degrees, longitude 70 degrees

Alternatively, they can be deictically specified relative to the location of participants at the time of speaking (CT), as in

(68)   It's two hundred yards *away*
(69)   Kabul is four hundred miles West of *here*

In either case it is likely that units of measurement, or descriptions of direction and location, will have to be used, and in that case place deixis comes to interact in complex ways with the non-deictic organization of space (see Leech, 1969; Fillmore, 1975: 16–28; Lyons, 1977a: 690ff; and references therein).

There are, though, some pure place-deictic words, notably in English the adverbs *here* and *there*, and the demonstrative pronouns *this* and *that*. The symbolic usage of *here*, as in (70), can be glossed as 'the pragmatically given unit of space that includes the location of the speaker at CT'.

(70)   I'm writing to say I'm having a marvellous time *here*

The gestural usage must be glossed a little differently, as 'the pragmatically given space, proximal to speaker's location at CT, that includes the point or location gesturally indicated'. Note that we cannot eradicate the modifier 'pragmatically given' in these definitions: an utterance of (71) may have quite different implications of precision if said to a crane operator in contrast to a fellow surgeon.

(71)   Place it *here*

Again, we have the interaction between 'encyclopaedic knowledge' and linguistic knowledge, which together determine the exact location in question. This is another point at which philosophical treatments of indexicals offer us no help. The proposition picked out by the utterance of (71), as with the referent of *next Thursday*, depends on complex interactions between deictic and non-deictic factors.

The adverbs *here* and *there* are often thought of as simple contrasts on a proximal/distal dimension, stretching away from the speaker's location, as in:

(72)   Bring *that here* and take *this there*

But this is only sometimes so, for although *there* basically means 'distal from speaker's location at CT', it can also be used to mean 'proximal to addressee at RT'. Thus, in non-anaphoric uses,

(73)   How are things *there*?

does not generally mean 'how are things at some place distant from the speaker', but rather 'how are things where the addressee is'. The gestural usage of *there* favours the first interpretation, the symbolic usage the second. There are also of course anaphoric usages of *there* (cf. (40) above), and this explains why there is no necessary pragmatic anomaly in:

(74)   We're *there*

where *there* refers to the place we previously mentioned as our goal (Fillmore, 1971b: 226).[12]

> [12] We seem also, though, to be able to say (74) if the referent of *there* is not actually mentioned but pragmatically given. Lyons (1977a: 672) draws attention to the fact that anaphoric references do not really require prior mention: it is sufficient if, for participants, the referent is situationally salient, and so already in the **domain of discourse**, the set of referents being talked about. The relation between domain of discourse and anaphora is taken up in 2.2.4 below.

The demonstrative pronouns are perhaps more clearly organized in a straightforward proximal–distal dimension, whereby *this* can mean 'the object in a pragmatically given area close to the speaker's location at CT', and *that* 'the object beyond the pragmatically given area close to the speaker's location at CT' (Lyons (1977a: 647) suggests the derivative glosses 'the one here', 'the one there', respectively). But the facts are complicated here by the shift from *that* to *this* to show empathy, and from *this* to *that* to show emotional distance (Lyons (1977a: 677) calls this **empathetic deixis**; see Fillmore, 1971b: 227 and R. Lakoff, 1974 for the intricacies of English usage). There is also a systematic neutralization of the proximal–distal dimension when it is not especially relevant, so that I can say, searching through a tin of needles for a number 9, either:

(75)   *This* is it!
(76)   *That*'s it!

Some languages have demonstratives with three and four way distinctions on the proximal–distal dimension, so that the North West American language Tlingit, for example, has demonstratives glossable as 'this one right here', 'this one nearby', 'that one over there', and 'that one way over there', while Malagasy has a six-way contrast on the same dimension (Frei, 1944: 115; Anderson & Keenan, in press). However, care must be exercised in the analysis of unfamiliar languages, as demonstratives are often organized with respect to contrasts between participant-roles rather than simply to distance in concentric circles from a fixed deictic centre (the speaker's location at CT). Thus in Latin, and correspondingly in Turkish, *hic* (Turkish *bu*) means 'close to speaker', *iste* (Turkish *şu*) means 'close to addressee', and *ille* (Turkish *o*) means 'remote from both speaker and addressee' (Lyons, 1968: 278–9; cf. Anderson & Keenan, in press). Similarly, in the Philippine language Samal, we have a four way distinction based on four kinds of participant role: (i) close to speaker, (ii) close to addressee, (iii) close to audience (other members of conversational group), (iv) close to persons present but outside the conversational group that consists of speaker, addressee(s) and audience. This system (specifically a switch from the demonstrative that encodes (ii) or (iii) to that encoding (iv)) provides nice ways of slighting people by cutting them, demonstratively, out of the conversation (Fillmore, 1975: 43). There are thus systems of demonstratives that are not organized primarily, or only, around the speaker's location. There are also systems (e.g. in Australian and New Guinea languages) that distinguish the three dimensions of space, having demonstratives that gloss as 'the one above the speaker', 'the one below the speaker', 'the one level with the speaker' as well as distinguishing relative distance from participants (see e.g. Dixon, 1972: 262ff re Dyirbal). Some systems combine additional 'exotic' deictic parameters like 'upriver/downriver from speaker' or 'visible/non-visible to speaker' to produce enormous arrays (up to thirty or more items) of demonstrative terms (see Anderson & Keenan, in press).

The demonstrative determiners combine with non-deictic terms for spatial organization to yield complex deictic descriptions of location. The non-deictic conceptual organization of space includes all those distinctions between surfaces, spaces, enclosures, containers and so on, and between fronts, backs, tops, sides, of objects, not to mention widths, lengths, heights, etc. Thus:

(77)   *This side* of the box

can mean 'the surface of the box that can be called a side which is nearest to the location of the speaker at CT', but:

(78)   *This side* of the tree

simply means 'that area of the tree visible from the point where the speaker is at CT (or the space between that area and that point)'. The difference between the glosses for (77) and (78) depends clearly on boxes, but not trees, having intrinsic sides (the difference is perhaps even clearer with an object like a car, which has an intrinsic orientation, so that its bottom remains its bottom even when the vehicle is turned over, and its front remains its front even when going backwards). The difference between (77) and (78) is not the same difficulty we met earlier, in the ambiguity of:

(79)   The cat is *behind* the car

where *behind* can have either a deictic usage (i.e. the car intervenes between the cat and the speaker's location), or a non-deictic usage (i.e. the cat is at the intrinsic rear-end of the car). But the ultimate source of the difficulty is the same: some objects have intrinsic orientations, with fronts, sides, etc., and these allow both the deictic selection of some oriented plane and the non-deictic reference to some such oriented plane. As a result the deictic/non-deictic ambiguity is very general, and plagues the recipients of expressions like:

(80)   Bob is the man to the left of Mark

where Bob may be to Mark's own left (non-deictic), or to the left from the speaker's point of view (deictic).

There are, as has been noted, fairly close connections between deictic determiners, third person pronouns, and the definite article (Lyons, 1968: 279, 1977a: 646ff; Hawkins, 1978). All three categories are **definite**, and **definiteness** may perhaps be an essentially deictic notion. Lyons suggests that *this x* retains a pronominal element, as well as containing an adverbial element similar to *here*. On this analysis, *the x* differs from *this x* and *that x* only in that *this x* is marked ' + proximal', *that x* is marked ' − proximal', and *the x* is unmarked for proximity, i.e. it is a neutral deictic term (Lyons, 1977a: 653–4).

Finally, let us consider some motion verbs that have built-in deictic components. English *come* vs. *go* makes some sort of distinction between the direction of motion relative to participants in the speech event (the exposition here follows Fillmore, 1966, 1975: 50ff). As a first approximation, we may note that

(81)   He's *coming*

seems to gloss as 'he is moving towards the speaker's location at CT', while

(82)   He's *going*

glosses as 'he is moving away from the speaker's location at CT'. The suggested gloss for *come* would in fact be roughly correct for Spanish *venir* or Japanese *kuru*, but it will not handle English usages like:

(83)   I'm *coming*

since this cannot mean 'the speaker is moving towards the location of the speaker', but rather means 'the speaker is moving towards the location of the *addressee* at CT'. (Such a usage may have diachronically arisen from a polite deictic shift to the addressee's point of view.) In Japanese one must here say the equivalent of *I go*. Taking this into account, we may suggest that English *come* glosses as 'movement towards either the location of the speaker, or towards the location of the addressee, at CT'. However this won't quite do either – one can say:

(84)   When I'm in the office, you can *come* to see me

where *come* glosses as 'movement towards the location of the speaker at the time of some other specified event' (let us call this time **reference time**). Such a usage is still ultimately deictic, in that it makes reference to participant-role, but it is not directly place-deictic (in that there is no anchorage to the location of the present speech event). In narrative, we sometimes dispense with even this last vestige of deictic content, using *come* relative to the locations of protagonists rather than participants, but this non-deictic usage we shall ignore. Our third approximation to a gloss for *come* is therefore: 'motion towards speaker's location, or addressee's location, at either CT, or reference time'.

Our analysis is still incomplete, however, as there is a deictic usage of *come* that is based not on participants' actual location, but on their normative location or **home-base**. Hence the possibility of saying, when neither speaker nor addressee is at home:

(85)   I *came* over several times to visit you, but you were never *there*

So we must append another clause to our gloss, namely: 'or motion towards the home-base maintained at CT by either speaker or addressee'. Very similar remarks throughout can be made for *go*, and also for verbs like *bring* and *take* (see Fillmore, 1975: 50ff).

A number of Amerindian languages encode reference to home-base in a more systematic way. Thus in Chinantec, there are four expressions to choose from if one wants to say 'Pedro moved to X', depending on the following criteria: (i) one verb form is used if the speaker S is at X at CT, and X is S's home-base; (ii) another is used if S is at X, but X is not S's home-base; (iii) a third is used if S is not at X, but X is S's home-base; (iv) a fourth is used if S is not at X, and X is not S's home-base (Fillmore, 1971b: 16).

Further complexities in place deixis arise if the speaker is in motion – it then becomes quite possible to use temporal terms in order to refer to deictic locations, as in:

(86)   I first heard that ominous rattle *ten miles ago*
(87)   There's a good fast food joint just *ten minutes from here*

This raises the issue about whether time deixis or place deixis is more basic. Lyons (1977a: 669) inclines to a view that, since place-deictic terms like *this* and *that* can be used in a temporal sense (especially to refer to proximal and distal parts of an unfolding discourse), place deixis is more fundamental than time deixis. Such a view is favourable to **localism**, the theory that attempts to reduce non-spatial to spatial expressions (Lyons, 1977a: 718ff). But the usage in (86) and (87) can be used to reverse the argument, and in general each domain (space and time) provides fertile ground for metaphors about the other (see Chapter 3 below). In addition, deictic locations always have to be specified with respect to the location of a participant *at coding time*, i.e. place deixis always incorporates a covert time deixis element, while the converse is not true.

2.2.4   *Discourse deixis*

Discourse, or text, deixis concerns the use of expressions within some utterance to refer to some portion of the discourse that contains that utterance (including the utterance itself). We may also include in discourse deixis a number of other ways in which an utterance signals its relation to surrounding text, e.g. utterance-initial *anyway* seems to indicate that the utterance that contains it is not addressed to the immediately preceding discourse, but to one or more steps back. (Such signals are deictic because they have the distinctive relativity of reference, being anchored to the discourse location of the current utterance.) The only detailed accounts of this area of deixis are, again, to be found in Fillmore, 1975 and Lyons, 1977a: 667ff. Since discourse unfolds in time, it seems natural that time-deictic words can be used to refer to portions of the discourse; thus analogously to *last week* and *next Thursday*, we have *in the last paragraph* and *in the next Chapter*. But we also have place-deictic terms re-used here, and especially the demonstratives *this* and *that*. Thus *this* can be used to refer to a forthcoming portion of the discourse, as in (88), and *that* to a preceding portion, as in (89):

(88)   I bet you haven't heard *this* story
(89)   *That* was the funniest story I've ever heard

Considerable confusion is likely to be caused here if we do not immediately make the distinction between *discourse deixis* and *ana-phora*. As we noted, anaphora concerns the use of (usually) a pronoun to refer to the same referent as some prior term, as in:

(90)   *Harry*'s a sweetheart; *he*'s so considerate

where *Harry* and *he* can be said to be **co-referential**, i.e. pick out the same referent. Anaphora can, of course, hold within sentences, across sentences, and across turns at speaking in a dialogue. Deictic or other definite referring expressions are often used to introduce a referent, and anaphoric pronouns used to refer to the same entity thereafter. It is important to remember, however, that deictic and anaphoric usages are not mutually exclusive, as was remarked in connection with example (40) above. Nevertheless, in principle the distinction is clear: where a pronoun refers to a linguistic expression (or chunk of discourse) itself, it is discourse-deictic; where a pronoun refers to the same entity as a prior linguistic expression refers to, it is anaphoric. It follows that there is a close, but quite unexplored, relation between discourse deixis and **mention** or quotation; thus in the following example (from Lyons, 1977a: 667):

(91)   A: That's a rhinoceros
         B: Spell *it* for me

it refers not to the referent, the beast itself, but to the word *rhinoceros*. Here, *it* is not doing duty for a use of *rhinoceros* but rather for a mention of it. Further, the property of **token reflexivity**, as in the following usage of *this*, is just a special case of intra-sentential discourse deixis:

(92)   *This* sentence is not true

Fillmore (1971b: 240) hopes that a theory of discourse deixis will resolve the well-known paradoxes associated with sentences like (92) (if it's false, it's true; and if it's true, it's false), and indeed with token reflexivity in general.

A number of significant problems for the distinction between anaphora and discourse deixis have been thrown up by the very considerable body of work on **pronominalization** (see Lyons, 1977b; Lyons, 1977a: 662ff for a review; and for recent work, see e.g. Heny & Schnelle, 1979). Firstly, there are the so-called **pronouns of laziness** (Geach, 1962: 125ff), as in Karttunen's well-known sentence (see Lyons, 1977a: 673ff):

(93)   The man who gave his paycheck to his wife was wiser than the
         man who gave *it* to his mistress

where *it* is not co-referential with *his paycheck*, but refers to what a repetition of that NP would have referred to (namely the paycheck of the man whose mistress got it) if it had occurred in place of *it*. One could perhaps say that the pronoun here refers successfully *via* a discourse-deictic reference to a prior NP. Secondly, in an exchange like the following (from Lyons, 1977a: 668):

(94)   A: I've never seen him
         B: *That*'s a lie

the pronoun *that* does not seem to be anaphoric (unless it is held that it refers to the same entity that A's utterance does, i.e. a proposition or a truth value); nor does it quite seem to be discourse-deictic (it refers not to the sentence but, perhaps, to the statement made by uttering that sentence). Rather, such a usage seems to fall in between: Lyons (1977a: 670) calls such usages **impure textual deixis**. Thirdly, Lyons points out that if one thinks of anaphora as reference to entities already established in the domain of discourse, then the ways in which they are referred to in anaphoric reference commonly make use of the order in which they were introduced by the discourse itself. For example, the Turkish translation of (95) might be glossed as (96), where the proximal demonstrative anaphorically refers to the first referent introduced, and the distal demonstrative to the second:

(95)   John and Mary came into the room: he was laughing but she was crying
(96)   John and Mary came into the room: *this* was laughing, but *that* was crying

In that case, there are good arguments for considering that anaphora ultimately rests on deictic notions (Lyons, 1977a: 671). Such a conclusion would have important repercussions for the philosophical worries about the deictic nature of reference which were sketched in section 2.1.

To return to straightforward issues in discourse deixis, there are many words and phrases in English, and no doubt most languages, that indicate the relationship between an utterance and the prior discourse. Examples are utterance-initial usages of *but, therefore, in conclusion, to the contrary, still, however, anyway, well, besides, actually, all in all, so, after all,* and so on. It is generally conceded that such words have at least a component of meaning that resists truth-conditional treatment (Grice, 1975; Wilson, 1975; Levinson, 1979b). What they seem to do is indicate, often in very complex ways, just how the utterance that contains them is a response to, or a continuation of, some portion of the prior discourse. We still await proper studies of these terms, but one kind of approach will be sketched in the next Chapter under the rubric of **conventional implicature,** another will be indicated in Chapter 6 in discussion of the conversational uses of *well* (see Owen, 1981), and a third may be found in Smith & Wilson (1979: 180), elaborated in Brockway (1981).

Some languages also have morphemes that mark such clearly discourse notions as **main story line**. For example, in the Amerindian language Cubeo, the main protagonists and their actions in a story are tagged by a particle in such a systematic way that a concise and accurate precis is obtained if just those sentences containing the particle are extracted (see Longacre, 1976a for many such cases in this and other Amerindian languages; and Anderson & Keenan, in press, re the so-called *fourth person* category in Algonquian languages, really a discourse-deictic category).

It is also well known that languages like Japanese and Tagalog have **topic** markers distinct from case markers. Thus the Japanese sentence

(97)   ano-hon-*wa* John-*ga* kat-ta
         That book-*topic* John-*subject* bought

means roughly 'as for that book (or, talking of that book), John bought it', where *wa* marks the topic, *ga* the grammatical subject (where topic and subject are identical, only *wa* is used; Gundel, 1977: 17). In some languages the grammatical encoding of topic is so prominent, that it is not clear that the notion of subject has the same purchase as it does in the analysis, for example, of Indo-European languages (Li & Thompson, 1976). A great deal of the discussion of such topic markers has been concerned with the sentence-internal organization of information as **given** (or the topic) vs. **new** (or comment about the topic – see Gundel, 1977 for a review). But it is clear that a major function of topic marking is precisely to relate the marked utterance to some specific topic raised in the prior discourse, i.e. to perform a discourse-deictic function.

The same function seems to be performed in English, and in other relatively fixed word-order languages, by word-order changes. Thus

left-dislocated sentences (Ross, 1967) like the following seem to mark the topic of the sentence by movement into initial position:[13]

(98)   That blouse, it's simply stunning
(99)   Vera, is she coming down then?

Studies of actual usage seem to show that items placed in this position really do correlate with discourse topic, or what the participants are talking 'about', although not always in simple ways (Duranti & Ochs, 1979). The issues that surround the topic/comment distinction are at present quite ill understood, and discussion has been confused by terminological chaos (see Gundel, 1977; Lyons, 1977a: 500ff), although the subject is clearly of considerable importance to pragmatic theory.

The remarks in this section only sketch out a province for which a proper theory of discourse deixis might provide an account. The scope, as indicated, may be very large, ranging from the borders of anaphora to issues of topic/comment structures.

2.2.5   *Social deixis*
            Social deixis concerns "that aspect of sentences which reflect or establish or are determined by certain realities of the social situation in which the speech act occurs" (Fillmore, 1975: 76). Fillmore, unfortunately, then proceeds to water down the concept of social deixis by including, for example, much of the theory of speech acts (see Chapter 5). Here we shall restrict the term to those aspects of language structure that encode the social identities of participants (properly, incumbents of participant-roles), or the social relationship between them, or between one of them and persons and entities referred to. There are of course many aspects of language usage that depend on these relations (see e.g. Brown & Levinson, 1978, 1979), but these usages are only relevant to the topic of social deixis in so far as they are grammaticalized. Obvious examples of such grammaticalizations are 'polite' pronouns and titles of address, but there are many other manifestations of social deixis (see Brown & Levinson, 1978: 183–92, 281–5; Levinson, 1977, 1979b).

---

[13] Ross proposed left-dislocation as a transformation, but there are in fact serious problems with such an analysis, and it seems better to treat such topic phrases as appositional NPs, not unlike vocatives, even though there is little theory about how to handle the syntax and semantics of these (see Gundel, 1977: 46ff).

There are two basic kinds of socially deictic information that seem to be encoded in languages around the world: **relational** and **absolute**. The relational variety is the most important, and the relations that typically get expressed are those between:

(i)   speaker and referent (e.g. referent honorifics)
(ii) speaker and addressee (e.g. addressee honorifics)
(iii) speaker and bystander (e.g. bystander or audience honorifics)
(iv) speaker and setting (e.g. formality levels)

We can talk of **honorifics** just where the relation in (i)–(iii) concerns relative rank or respect; but there are many other qualities of relationship that may be grammaticalized, e.g. kinship relations, totemic relations, clan membership, etc., as made available by the relevant social system. The first three kinds of honorific were clearly distinguished by Comrie (1976b), who pointed out that traditional descriptions have often confused (i) and (ii): the distinction is that in (i) respect can only be conveyed by referring to the 'target' of the respect, whereas in (ii) it can be conveyed without necessarily referring to the target. Thus the familiar *tu/vous* type of distinction in singular pronouns of address (which, following Brown & Gilman (1960), we shall call T/V pronouns) is really a **referent honorific** system, where the referent happens to be the addressee. In contrast, in many languages (notably the S. E. Asian languages, including Korean, Japanese and Javanese) it is possible to say some sentence glossing as 'The soup is hot' and by the choice of a linguistic alternate (e.g. for 'soup') encode respect to the addressee without referring to him, in which case we have an **addressee honorific** system. In general, in such languages, it is almost impossible to say anything at all which is not sociolinguistically marked as appropriate for certain kinds of addressees only. In practice, though, the elaborate 'speech levels' of the S. E. Asian languages are complex amalgams of referent and addressee honorifics (see Geertz, 1960 and Comrie, 1976b re Javanese; Kuno, 1973 and Harada, 1976 re Japanese).

The third kind of relational information, that between speaker and bystander, is more rarely encoded in **bystander honorifics**. (The term *bystander* here does duty as a cover term for participants in audience role and for non-participating overhearers.) Examples include the Dyirbal alternative vocabulary, referred to above, used in the presence of taboo relatives (see also Haviland, 1979 re Guugu

Yimidhirr), and certain features of Pacific languages, like aspects of the 'royal honorifics' in Ponapean (Garvin & Reisenberg, 1952: 203).

To these three kinds of relational information we may add a fourth, namely the relation between speaker (and perhaps other participants) and setting (or social activity). Although most languages are used differently in formal settings, in some the distinction formal/informal is firmly grammaticalized, for example in Japanese by so-called *mas-* style, and in Tamil by a high *diglossic variant* (see below). Note that while the first three kinds of information are relative strictly to the deictic centre, here specifically the social standing of the speaker, formality is perhaps best seen as involving a relation between all participant roles and situation (but see Irvine, 1979; J. M. Atkinson, 1982).[14]

The other main kind of socially deictic information that is often encoded is *absolute* rather than relational. There are, for example, forms reserved for certain speakers, in which case we may talk (after Fillmore, 1975) of **authorized speakers**. For example, in Thai the morpheme *khráb* is a polite particle that can only be used by male speakers, the corresponding form reserved for female speakers being *khá* (Haas, 1964). Similarly, there is a form of the first person pronoun specifically reserved for the use of the Japanese Emperor (Fillmore, 1971b: 6). There are also in many languages forms reserved for **authorized recipients**, including restrictions on most titles of address (*Your Honour, Mr President*, etc.); in Tunica there were pronouns that differed not only with sex of referent, but also with the sex of the addressee, so that there were, for example, two words for 'they', depending on whether one was speaking to a man or a woman (Haas, ibid.).

Having reviewed the main kinds of social-deictic information that are grammaticalized by different languages, we may now consider where in grammatical systems such distinctions are encoded. Note that only the first kind of relational information, i.e. that on the speaker–referent axis, imposes intrinsic limitations on the ways in which such information can be encoded – namely in referring expressions, and morphological agreements with them. For good sociological reasons, such referent honorifics are found for actors, their social

---

[14] The difference may be more apparent than real; there may well be honorific systems encoding relations between addressee and referent, and there are the Australian 'triangular' kin terms mentioned in section 2.2.1, so the role of the speaker may not always be so central to the first three kinds of social deixis either.

groups, their actions and belongings (see e.g. Geertz, 1960 and Horne, 1974: xxi re Javanese). We find, perhaps, pale shadows of these latter in the English 'elevated' terms *residence* (for 'home'), *dine* (for 'eat' or 'eat a meal'), *lady* (for 'woman'), *steed* (for 'horse') and so on. Expressions referring to the addressee, though, are particularly likely to encode speaker–referent relationships, due no doubt to the addressee's direct monitoring of the speaker's attitude to him or her. Hence the world-wide distribution through quite unrelated languages and cultures of the T/V distinction in second person singular pronouns (Head, 1978; Levinson, 1978; for the sociolinguistics, see Brown & Gilman, 1960 and Lambert & Tucker, 1976). The fact that the form of the polite or V pronoun is often borrowed from the second person plural, or third person singular or plural, pronouns, introduces considerable complexities into agreement systems (Comrie, 1975; Corbett, 1976; Levinson, 1979b). As we noted, nominal predicates tend to agree with *actual* number and person, finite verbs with the morphological person and number encoded in the polite form of the pronoun, with language-specific decisions on predicates of intermediate kind. The other way in which addressees are typically referred to, namely by titles of address, also causes agreement problems – a decision has to be made between second or third person agreement, and, where relevant, between which titles of address can co-occur with which degree of respect encoded in verbal agreements (Levinson, 1979b). In languages with honorifics, **honorific concord** can thus become an intricate aspect of morphology, which cannot always be treated formally without reference to the socially deictic values of particular morphemes. These are some of the most important, and most ignored, examples of the direct interaction between pragmatics and syntax. Finally, let us note that titles of address and all vocative forms seem invariably marked for speaker-referent relationship: there is no such thing, it seems, as a socially neutral summons or address (see Zwicky, 1974: 795 re English).

The other kinds of socially deictic information, however, can be encoded just about anywhere in the linguistic system. Addressee honorifics (including dishonorifics and intimacy markers), for example, turn up in lexical alternates or suppletive forms (in e.g. Javanese; Geertz, 1960), in morphology (in e.g. Japanese; Harada, 1976), in particles or affixes (in e.g. Tamil; Levinson, 1979b), in segmental phonology (in e.g. Basque; Corum, 1975: 96), in prosodics (in e.g. Tzeltal honorific falsetto; Brown & Levinson, 1978: 272), and in many cases a mixture of these (in e.g. Javanese, Japanese, Madurese, Korean). Similarly, bystander honorifics are encoded in Dyirbal and Guugu Yimidhirr by an entirely distinct vocabulary as we noted (Dixon, 1972: 32ff; Haviland, 1979), and in other languages by particles and morphology. Formality levels are encoded morphologically in Japanese, but in Tamil by differences across all the levels of the grammar, including phonology, morphology, syntax and lexicon. Cases like the latter are usually termed **diglossic variants** (Ferguson, 1964), although not everything so called has either the strict co-occurrence rules distinguishing levels or the restrictions in use that formal Tamil has. Some such levels are restricted to the medium, oral or written; but formal Tamil is used in both writing and formal address or speech making.

The linguist interested in delimiting the scope of an overall linguistic theory may be concerned that the description of social deixis will simply merge into sociolinguistics, and on this ground wish to exclude consideration of social deixis from formal descriptions of language altogether. This would be unfortunate. In the first place, as noted in section 1.2, a boundary can be drawn between deictic issues and wider sociolinguistic ones. For social deixis is concerned with the grammaticalization, or encoding in language structure, of social information, while sociolinguistics is also, and perhaps primarily, concerned with issues of language usage. Despite the fact that certain approaches seem to conflate the meaning and the use of social-deictic items (see e.g. Ervin-Tripp, 1972), the possibility of regular ironic usages of, for example, honorifics to children, argues for the existence of prior and well-established meanings independent of rules of usage. Social deixis is thus concerned with the meaning and grammar (e.g. the problems of honorific concord) of certain linguistic expressions, while sociolinguistics is also concerned, *inter alia*, with how these items are actually used in concrete social contexts classified with reference to the parameters of the relevant social system (Levinson, 1979b). Thus, social deixis can be systematically restricted to the study of facts that lie firmly within the scope of structural studies of linguistic systems, leaving the study of usage to another domain.

A second reason why grammarians should not simply ignore social deixis is that, while the study of English may suffer no obvious penalties for such neglect, there is scarcely a single sentence of, for example, Japanese, Javanese or Korean, that can be properly described from a strictly linguistic point of view without an analysis of social deixis. The neglect of the subject as a whole is no doubt simply due to the disproportionate amount of recent linguistic work that has been done on English or closely related languages.

2.3 **Conclusions**

This Chapter has been very largely concerned, first, with the presentation of some useful analytical distinctions, and, secondly, with a review of some of the many intricacies of deixis in familiar and less familiar languages. The lack of theoretical discussion reflects the present state of our understanding: we have, on the one hand, only the rather simple philosophical approaches to indexicals (covering just some aspects of person, time and place deixis), and, on the other hand, a mass of complicated linguistic facts, to which some preliminary order has been brought by the work of Fillmore and Lyons in particular.

A central question that remains, though, is whether the study of deixis belongs to semantics or to pragmatics. However, even if linguists could all agree on how the pragmatics/semantics boundary should be drawn, there would be no simple answer to this question. Montague (1974) held that the study of any language containing indexicals was, *eo ipso*, pragmatics. But this has the consequence, as we noted, that natural languages will only have a syntax and a pragmatics, and no semantics. So if the semantics/pragmatics distinction is to do any work at all, we can try and shift the study of indexicals into semantics. And since at least some aspects of deixis make a difference to truth conditions, we may hope that this shift will coincide with the decision to restrict semantics to the truth-conditional aspects of meaning.

However, we shall be disappointed, for there are aspects of deixis that are clearly not truth-conditional. The semantics/pragmatics border will then cut across what is, from the point of view adopted in section 2.2, a unified linguistic field. But if we proceed to draw the line, where exactly will it fall? As we saw in section 2.1, we cannot state the truth conditions of sentences with indexicals without reference to the deictic function of indexicals; but if we allow truth conditions to be relativized to speakers, addressees, times, places, indicated objects, etc., then it looks as if many aspects of deixis can be accommodated within truth-conditional semantics. It is a version of truth-conditional semantics, though, in which not sentences, but only utterances in context, can be assigned the propositions they express. Without such a move, the current attempts to define the notion of logical consequence more or less directly on fragments of natural language (as initiated by Montague, 1974) would make little sense as a general semantic programme.

There are, though, many obstacles to the accommodation of deixis within semantics by simply providing a list of indices or contextual points of reference relative to which truth conditions can be stated. For example, no attempt has been made to deal with the distinctions between gestural, non-gestural, and the various non-deictic usages of deictic words. For gestural usages, we seem to need, not just a list of abstract co-ordinates, but a complete monitoring of the physical properties of the speech event. For example, it will be insufficient to have merely a single deictic index for time of utterance, yet how many time indices we need seems to depend on the utterance itself:

(100)   Don't shoot now, but now, now and now!

The possibility of an indefinitely long list of necessary indices or co-ordinates thus has to be faced. In answer to this, Cresswell (1973: 111ff) produces, by a technical sleight of hand, a formulation which avoids specifying the necessary indices in advance. But this hardly solves the problem of knowing how to obtain the relevant indices just when we need them. A second problem is that utterances like

(101)   Harry can only speak this loud

are *token-reflexive* to the physical properties of the utterance itself, so that not only do the enormous technical problems of dealing with token-reflexives in a logical manner have to be solved, but all the physical properties of an utterance will also have to be available as indices (requiring, again, an indefinite number of indices). These problems alone would not make the prospects for the straightforward treatment of deictic sentences within truth-conditional semantics look very hopeful. It may be more helpful to admit that what we are dealing with here are very complex pragmatic ways in which a sentence and a context of utterance interact to pick out a proposition, by reference to the audio-visual monitoring of the speech event as it unfolds.

95

But whatever is ultimately decided about where person, place and time deixis belong, there is little doubt that most aspects of discourse deixis and social deixis will lie outside the scope of a truth-conditional semantics. The reason for this is quite simply that these aspects of deixis mostly make no difference to truth conditions. If I say either of the following,

(102)   Vous êtes Napoléon
(103)   Tu es Napoléon

the conditions under which they will be true will be identical. The utterer of the first may pragmatically presume that the addressee is socially superior or socially distant, but (102) does not entail that. If what (102) entailed was:

(104)   You are Napoleon and you are socially superior to (or socially distant from) me, the speaker

Then (105) would have to have one reading under which it meant (106), which it clearly does not have:

(105)   Vous n'êtes pas Napoléon
(106)   You are Napoleon, and you are not socially superior to (or socially distant from) me, the speaker

Exactly the same, and additional, arguments can be shown to hold for the complex honorifics of 'exotic' languages. Such aspects of language have conventional but non-truth-conditional meanings.

Similarly, it is generally agreed that the discourse-deictic words like *moreover, besides, anyway, well*, etc., in utterance-initial position, do not make any difference to truth conditions (Grice, 1961, 1975; Wilson, 1975). Here again, then, it seems that there are linguistic items that have conventional meanings, but no (or only partial) truth-conditional content. If we subscribe to a truth-conditional semantics, we shall therefore be forced to find a place for such meanings in pragmatic theory. Attempts have been made to assimilate such meanings to various pragmatic concepts, for example **pragmatic presupposition** (Keenan, 1971), or, as we shall find in the next Chapter, **conventional implicature**. But the general conclusion must be that most aspects of discourse deixis, and perhaps all aspects of social deixis, lie beyond the scope of a truth-conditional semantics. Deixis is therefore not reducible in its entirety, and perhaps hardly at all, to matters of truth-conditional semantics.

3
Conversational implicature

3.0 Introduction

The notion of **conversational implicature** is one of the single most important ideas in pragmatics (we shall often refer to the notion simply as **implicature** as a shorthand, although distinctions between this and other kinds of implicature will be introduced below). The salience of the concept in recent work in pragmatics is due to a number of sources. First, implicature stands as a paradigmatic example of the nature and power of pragmatic explanations of linguistic phenomena. The sources of this species of pragmatic inference can be shown to lie outside the organization of language, in some general principles for co-operative interaction, and yet these principles have a pervasive effect upon the structure of language. The concept of implicature, therefore, seems to offer some significant functional explanations of linguistic facts.

A second important contribution made by the notion of implicature is that it provides some explicit account of how it is possible to mean (in some general sense) more than what is actually 'said' (i.e. more than what is literally expressed by the conventional sense of the linguistic expressions uttered).[1] Consider, for example:

(1)   A: Can you tell me the time?
        B: Well, the milkman has come

All that we can reasonably expect a semantic theory to tell us about this minimal exchange is that there is at least one reading that we might paraphrase as follows:

---

[1] Grice uses the phrase *what is said* as a technical term for the truth-conditional content of an expression, which may in fact be somewhat less than the full conventional content.

(2)   A: Do you have the ability to tell me the time?
        B: [pragmatically interpreted particle][2] the milkman came at
        some time prior to the time of speaking

Yet it is clear to native speakers that what would ordinarily be
communicated by such an exchange involves considerably more,
along the lines of the italicized material in (3):

(3)   A: Do you have the ability to tell me the time *of the present
        moment, as standardly indicated on a watch, and if so please
        do so tell me*
        B: *No I don't know the exact time of the present moment, but I
        can provide some information from which you may be able to
        deduce the approximate time, namely* the milkman has come

(see R. Lakoff, 1973a; Smith & Wilson, 1979:172ff for a discussion
of such examples). Clearly the whole *point* of the exchange, namely
a request for specific information and an attempt to provide as much
of that information as possible, is not directly expressed in (2) at all;
so the gap between what is literally *said* in (2) and what is conveyed
in (3) is so substantial that we cannot expect a semantic theory to
provide more than a small part of an account of how we communicate
using language. The notion of implicature promises to bridge the gap,
by giving some account of how at least large portions of the italicized
material in (3) are effectively conveyed.

Thirdly, the notion of implicature seems likely to effect substantial
simplifications in both the structure and the content of semantic
descriptions. For example, consider:

(4)   The lone ranger jumped on his horse and rode into the sunset
(5)   The capital of France is Paris and the capital of England is
        London
(6)   ??The lone ranger rode into the sunset and jumped on his
        horse[3]
(7)   The capital of England is London and the capital of France is
        Paris

The sense of *and* in (4) and (5) seems to be rather different: in (4)
it seems to mean 'and then' and thus (6) is strange in that it is hard
to imagine the reverse ordering of the two events. But in (5) there

---

[2] The meaning of *well* is discussed in 3.2.6 below.
[3] As noted, the symbol ?? indicates pragmatic anomaly, * indicates semantic
or syntactic anomaly, while ? is non-committal about the nature of the
anomaly.

is no 'and then' sense; *and* here seems to mean just what the standard truth table for & would have it mean − namely that the whole is true just in case both conjuncts are true; hence the reversal of the conjuncts in (7) does not affect the conceptual import at all. Faced with examples like this, the semanticist has traditionally taken one of two tacks: he can either hold that there are two distinct senses of the word *and*, which is thus simply ambiguous, or he can claim that the meanings of words are in general vague and protean and are influenced by collocational environments. If the semanticist takes the first tack, he soon finds himself in the business of adducing an apparently endless proliferation of senses of the simplest looking words. He might for example be led by (8) and (9) to suggest that *white* is ambiguous, for in (8) it seems to mean 'only or wholly white' while in (9) it can only mean 'partially white':

(8)   The flag is white
(9)   The flag is white, red and blue

The semanticist who takes the other tack, that natural language senses are protean, sloppy and variable, is hardly in a better position: how do hearers then know (which they certainly do) just which variable value of *white* is involved in (8)? Nor will it do just to ignore the problem, for if one does one soon finds that one's semantics is self-contradictory. For example, (10) certainly seems to mean (11); but if we then build the 'uncertainty' interpretation in (11) into the meaning of *possible*, (12) should be an outright contradiction. But it is not.

(10)   It's possible that there's life on Mars
(11)   It's possible that there's life on Mars and it's possible that there is no life on Mars
(12)   It's possible that there's life on Mars, and in fact it is now certain that there is

Now from this set of dilemmas the notion of implicature offers a way out, for it allows one to claim that natural language expressions do tend to have simple, stable and unitary senses (in many cases anyway), but that this stable semantic core often has an unstable, context-specific pragmatic overlay − namely a set of implicatures. As long as some specific predictive content can be given to the notion of implicature, this is a genuine and substantial solution to the sorts of problems we have just illustrated.

An important point to note is that this simplification of semantics is not just a reduction of problems in the lexicon; it also makes possible the adoption of a semantics built on simple logical principles. It does this by demonstrating that once pragmatic implications of the sort we shall call implicature are taken into account, the apparently radical differences between logic and natural language seem to fade away. We shall explore this below when we come to consider the 'logical' words in English, *and*, *or*, *if ... then*, *not*, the quantifiers and the modals.

Fourthly, implicature, or at least some closely related concept, seems to be simply essential if various basic facts about language are to be accounted for properly. For example, particles like *well*, *anyway*, *by the way* require some meaning specification in a theory of meaning just like all the other words in English; but when we come to consider what their meaning is, we shall find ourselves referring to the pragmatic mechanisms that produce implicatures. We shall also see that certain syntactic rules appear at least to be sensitive to implicature, and that implicature puts interesting constraints on what can be a possible lexical item in natural languages.

Finally, the principles that generate implicatures have a very general explanatory power: a few basic principles provide explanations for a large array of apparently unrelated facts. For example, explanations will be offered below for why English has no lexical item *nall* meaning 'not all', for why Aristotle got his logics wrong, for 'Moore's paradox', for why obvious tautologies like *War is war* can convey any conceptual import, for how metaphors work and many other phenomena besides.

3.1 Grice's theory of implicature

Unlike many other topics in pragmatics, implicature does not have an extended history.[4] The key ideas were proposed by Grice in the William James lectures delivered at Harvard in 1967 and still only partially published (Grice, 1975, 1978). The proposals were relatively brief and only suggestive of how future work might proceed.

Before we review Grice's suggestions it would be as well to make

---

[4] There was, though, considerable speculation within philosophy about the utility of a notion of pragmatic implication, and some proto-Gricean ideas can be found in e.g. Fogelin, 1967.

clear that the other major theory associated with Grice, namely his theory of meaning-nn discussed above in Chapter 1, is not generally treated as having any connection with his theory of implicature (cf. Walker, 1975). In fact there is a connection of an important kind. If, as we indicated, Grice's theory of meaning-nn is construed as a theory of communication, it has the interesting consequence that it gives an account of how communication might be achieved in the absence of any conventional means for expressing the intended message. A corollary is that it provides an account of how more can be communicated, in his rather strict sense of non-naturally meant, than what is actually said. Obviously we can, given an utterance, often derive a number of inferences from it; but not all those inferences may have been communicative in Grice's sense, i.e. intended to be recognized as having been intended. The kind of inferences that are called implicatures are always of this special intended kind, and the theory of implicature sketches one way in which such inferences, of a non-conventional sort, can be conveyed while meeting the criterion of communicated messages sketched in Grice's theory of meaning-nn.

Grice's second theory, in which he develops the concept of implicature, is essentially a theory about how people *use* language. Grice's suggestion is that there is a set of over-arching assumptions guiding the conduct of conversation. These arise, it seems, from basic rational considerations and may be formulated as guidelines for the efficient and effective use of language in conversation to further co-operative ends. Grice identifies as guidelines of this sort four basic **maxims of conversation** or general principles underlying the efficient co-operative use of language, which jointly express a general **co-operative principle**. These principles are expressed as follows:

(13)   *The co-operative principle*
make your contribution such as is required, at the stage at which it occurs, by the accepted purpose or direction of the talk exchange in which you are engaged

(14)   *The maxim of Quality*
try to make your contribution one that is true, specifically:
(i)   do not say what you believe to be false
(ii) do not say that for which you lack adequate evidence

(15)   *The maxim of Quantity*
(i)   make your contribution as informative as is required for the current purposes of the exchange
(ii) do not make your contribution more informative than is required

(16)   *The maxim of Relevance*
         make your contributions relevant
(17)   *The maxim of Manner*
         be perspicuous, and specifically:
         (i)   avoid obscurity
         (ii)   avoid ambiguity
         (iii) be brief
         (iv)   be orderly

In short, these maxims specify what participants have to do in order to converse in a maximally efficient, rational, co-operative way: they should speak sincerely, relevantly and clearly, while providing sufficient information.

To this view of the nature of communication there is an immediate objection: the view may describe a philosopher's paradise, but no one actually speaks like that the whole time! But Grice's point is subtly different. It is not the case, he will readily admit, that people follow these guidelines to the letter. Rather, in most ordinary kinds of talk these principles are oriented to, such that when talk does not proceed according to their specifications, hearers assume that, contrary to appearances, the principles are nevertheless being adhered to at some deeper level. An example should make this clear:

(18)   A: Where's Bill?
         B: There's a yellow VW outside Sue's house

Here B's contribution, taken literally, fails to answer A's question, and thus seems to violate at least the maxims of Quantity and Relevance. We might therefore expect B's utterance to be interpreted as a non-co-operative response, a brushing aside of A's concerns with a change of topic. Yet it is clear that despite this *apparent* failure of co-operation, we try to interpret B's utterance as nevertheless co-operative at some deeper (non-superficial) level. We do this by assuming that it is in fact co-operative, and then asking ourselves what possible connection there could be between the location of Bill and the location of a yellow VW, and thus arrive at the suggestion (which B effectively conveys) that, if Bill has a yellow VW, he may be in Sue's house.

In cases of this sort, inferences arise to preserve the assumption of co-operation; it is only by making the assumption contrary to superficial indications that the inferences arise in the first place. It is this kind of inference that Grice dubs an *implicature*, or more properly a *conversational implicature*. So Grice's point is not that we always adhere to these maxims on a superficial level but rather that, wherever possible, people will interpret what we say as conforming to the maxims on at least some level.

But what is the source of these maxims of conversational behaviour? Are they conventional rules that we learn as we learn, say, table manners? Grice suggests that the maxims are in fact not arbitrary conventions, but rather describe rational means for conducting co-operative exchanges. If this is so, we would expect them to govern aspects of non-linguistic behaviour too, and indeed they seem to do so. Consider, for example, a situation in which A and B are fixing a car. If the maxim of Quality is interpreted as the injunction to produce non-spurious or sincere acts (a move we need to make anyway to extend the maxim to questions, promises, invitations, etc.), B would fail to comply with this if, when asked for brake fluid, he knowingly passes A the oil, or when asked to tighten up the bolts on the steering column he merely pretends to do so. Similarly, A would fail to observe the maxim of Quantity, the injunction to make one's contribution in the right proportion, if, when B needs three bolts, he purposely passes him only one, or alternatively passes him 300. Likewise with Relevance: if B wants three bolts, he wants them *now* not half an hour later. Finally, B would fail to comply with the maxim of Manner, enjoining clarity of purpose, if, when A needs a bolt of size 8, B passes him the bolt in a box that usually contains bolts of size 10. In each of these cases the behaviour falls short of some natural notion of full co-operation, because it violates one or another of the non-verbal analogues of the maxims of conversation. This suggests that the maxims do indeed derive from general considerations of rationality applicable to all kinds of co-operative exchanges, and if so they ought in addition to have universal application, at least to the extent that other, culture-specific, constraints on interaction allow. Broadly, this too seems to be so.

However, the reason for linguistic interest in the maxims is that they generate inferences beyond the semantic content of the sentences uttered. Such inferences are, by definition, conversational implicatures, where the term *implicature* is intended to contrast with terms like *logical implication*, *entailment* and *logical consequence* which are generally used to refer to inferences that are derived solely from logical or semantic content.[5] For implicatures are not semantic inferences, but rather inferences based on both the content of what has been said and some specific assumptions about the co-operative nature of ordinary verbal interaction.

These inferences come about in at least two distinct ways, depending on the relation that the speaker is taken to have towards the maxims. If the speaker is **observing** the maxims in a fairly direct way, he may nevertheless rely on the addressee to amplify what he says by some straightforward inferences based on the assumption that the speaker is following the maxims. For example, consider the following exchange:

(19)   A (to passer by): I've just run out of petrol
         B: Oh; there's a garage just around the corner

Here B's utterance may be taken to implicate that A may obtain petrol there, and he would certainly be being less than fully co-operative if he knew the garage was closed or was sold out of petrol (hence the inference). Let us call these inferences that arise from observing the maxims **standard implicatures** (the term is not Grice's, although he introduces the term **generalized implicature** for a subset of these implicatures which do not require particular contextual conditions in order to be inferred).[6]

Another way in which inferences may be generated by the maxims is where the speaker deliberately and ostentatiously breaches or (as Grice puts it) **flouts** the maxims. Consider for example:

(20)   A: Let's get the kids something
         B: Okay, but I veto I-C-E C-R-E-A-M-S

where B ostentatiously infringes the maxim of Manner (be perspicuous) by spelling out the word *ice-creams*, and thereby conveys to A

---

[5] To maintain the contrast, Grice is careful to restrict the use of the term **implicate** so that, primarily, it is speakers that implicate, while it is sentences, statements or propositions that enter into logical relations. However, taking an utterance to be a pairing of a sentence and a context, we may derivatively talk of utterances having implicatures, and here we shall adopt this practice, current in linguistics.

[6] I have also supplied the term *observing* the maxims (for the behaviour that gives rise to the standard implicatures), to contrast with Grice's term *flouting*. The lack of terminology here presumably derives from the erroneous assumption that all standard implicatures are generalized ones. See 3.2.3 below.

that B would rather not have ice-cream mentioned directly in the presence of the children, in case they are thereby prompted to demand some.

Both kinds of implicature are of great interest. Some further examples of each kind, organized under the maxims that give rise to them, may help to make the distinction clear. Let us start with examples of implicatures that arise directly from the assumption that the speaker is observing the maxims, and which simply amplify the communicated content in restricted ways (the symbol $+\rangle$ may stand for 'the uttering of the prior sentence will generally implicate the following').

Quality
(21)   John has two PhDs
          $+\rangle$ I believe he has, and have adequate evidence that he has
(22)   Does your farm contain 400 acres?
          $+\rangle$ I don't know that it does, and I want to know if it does

The first of these provides an explanation for 'Moore's paradox', namely the unacceptability of utterances like (23):[7]

(23)   ??John has two PhDs but I don't believe he has

This sentence is pragmatically anomalous because it contradicts the standard Quality implicature that one believes what one asserts. The example in (22) simply extends the scope of Quality by viewing *truth* as a special sub-case of sincerity applied to assertions; when one asks a question, one may standardly be taken to be asking sincerely and hence to be indeed lacking and requiring the requested information. (As we shall see when we come to consider **speech acts** in Chapter 5, these kinds of inferences are often talked about as **felicity conditions** as if they had no connection to implicature at all.) Normally then, in co-operative circumstances, when one asserts something one implicates that one believes it, when one asks a

---

[7] Grice (1978: 114) indicates that he actually wishes to withhold the term implicature from the inference in (21), on the ground that it only expresses the maxim of Quality itself. Another problem with viewing this inference as an implicature is that implicatures (as we shall see) are deniable, and this would suggest that (23) should not in fact be anomalous. One explanation for this might be that in addition to a general maxim of Quality holding for assertoric and non-assertoric speech acts, there is an additional convention that if one asserts p, one should believe and know p (cf. Gazdar, 1979a: 46–8).

question one implicates that one sincerely desires an answer and, by extension, when one promises to do x, one implicates that one sincerely intends to do x, and so on. Any other use of such utterances is likely to be a spurious or counterfeit one, and thus liable to violate the maxim of Quality.

Quantity

This maxim provides some of the most interesting of the standard implicatures. Suppose I say:

(24)   Nigel has fourteen children

I shall implicate that Nigel has only fourteen children, although it would be compatible with the truth of (24) that Nigel in fact has twenty children. I shall be taken to implicate that he has only fourteen and no more because had he had twenty, then by the maxim of Quantity ('say as much as is required') I should have said so. Since I haven't, I must intend to convey that Nigel only has fourteen. Similarly, reconsider the example introduced as (8) above:

(25)   The flag is white

Since I have given no further information about other colours the flag may contain, which might indeed be highly relevant to the proceedings, I may be taken to implicate that the flag has no other colours and is thus wholly white. Or again suppose we overhear the following exchange:

(26)   A: How did Harry fare in court the other day?
        B: Oh he got a fine

If it later transpires that Harry got a life sentence too, then B (if he knew this all along) would certainly be guilty of misleading A, for he has failed to provide all the information that might reasonably be required in the situation.

All these examples involve the first sub-maxim of Quantity, which appears to be the important one, in which the provision of full information is enjoined. The effect of the maxim is to add to most utterances a pragmatic inference to the effect that the statement presented is the strongest, or most informative, that can be made in the situation;[8] in many cases the implicatures can be glossed by

---

[8] I.e. the strongest statement that can be *relevantly* made. Such implicit appeals to the maxim of Relevance have prompted Wilson & Sperber (1981) to claim that the maxim of Relevance in fact subsumes the other maxims.

adding *only* to the propositional content of the sentence, e.g. 'Nigel has only fourteen children', 'the flag is only white', 'Harry only got a fine'.

Relevance
This maxim is also responsible for producing a large range of standard implicatures. For example, where possible imperatives will be interpreted as relevant to the present interaction, and thus as requests to implement some action at the present time. Hence:

(27)   Pass the salt
         +⟩ pass the salt now

Or reconsider example (1) repeated here:

(28)   A: Can you tell me the time?
         B: Well, the milkman has come

It is only on the basis of assuming the relevance of B's response that we can understand it as providing a partial answer to A's question. The inference seems to work roughly like this: assume B's utterance is relevant; if it's relevant then given that A asked a question, B should be providing an answer; the only way one can reconcile the assumption that B is co-operatively answering A's question with the content of B's utterance is to assume that B is not in a position to provide the full information, but thinks that the milkman's coming might provide A with the means of deriving a partial answer. Hence A may infer that B intends to convey that the time is at least after whenever the milkman normally calls. Exactly similar inferences can be made in cases like example (18), and it is clear that such inferences are fundamental to our sense of coherence in discourse: if the implicatures were not constructed on the basis of the assumption of relevance, many adjacent utterances in conversation would appear quite unconnected.

Manner
Finally, a number of different kinds of inference arise from the assumption that the maxim of Manner is being observed. For example, by the third sub-maxim of Manner ('be brief'), wherever I avoid some simple expression in favour of some more complex paraphrase, it may be assumed that I do not do so wantonly, but because the details are somehow relevant to the present enterprise.

If, instead of (29), I say (30), then I direct you to pay particular attention and care to each of the operations involved in doing (29), this being an implicature of the use of the longer expression:

(29)   Open the door
(30)   Walk up to the door, turn the door handle clockwise as far as it will go, and then pull gently towards you

But perhaps the most important of the sub-maxims of Manner is the fourth, 'be orderly'. For this can be used to explain the oddity of (6) above, repeated here:

(31)   ??The lone ranger rode into the sunset and jumped on his horse

This violates our expectation that events are recounted in the order in which they happened. But it is just because participants in conversation may be expected to observe the sub-maxim 'be orderly' that we have that expectation. Presented with (32), we therefore read it as a sequence of two events that occurred in that order:

(32)   Alfred went to the store and bought some whisky

We now see how the semanticist armed with the notion of implicature can extricate himself from the dilemmas raised above in connection with examples (4)–(7). He need not claim that there are two words *and* in English, one meaning simply that both conjuncts are true, the other having the same meaning plus a notion of sequentiality. For the sequentiality, the 'and then' sense of *and* in sentences like (32), is simply a standard implicature due to the fourth sub-maxim of Manner, which provides a pragmatic overlay on the semantic content of *and* wherever descriptions of two events, which might be sequentially ordered, are conjoined.[9]

Implicatures that are 'triggered' in this unostentatious way, simply by the assumption that the maxims are being observed, have so far been of the greater interest to linguists. This is because such inferences often arise wherever features of the context do not actually block them, with the result that they can be easily confused with the permanent aspects of the semantics of the expressions involved. Consequently, a semantic theory can become plagued by a proliferation

---

[9] For some difficulties here see Schmerling (1975), who argues that not all cases of asymmetric *and* are reducible in the Gricean way; for some extensions of the maxim of Manner to domains other than temporal ordering see e.g. Harnish, 1976.

of hypothetical senses and internal contradictions in ways we shall spell out below. Before returning to these implicatures in the next section, let us first illustrate the other major kind of implicatures that Grice had in mind.

The second kind of implicatures come about by overtly and blatantly *not* following some maxim, in order to exploit it for communicative purposes. Grice calls such usages **floutings** or **exploitations** of the maxims, and they can be seen to give rise to many of the traditional 'figures of speech'. These inferences are based on the remarkable robustness of the assumption of co-operation: if someone drastically and dramatically deviates from maxim-type behaviour, then his utterances are still read as underlyingly co-operative if this is at all possible. Thus by overtly infringing some maxim, the speaker can force the hearer to do extensive inferencing to some set of propositions, such that if the speaker can be assumed to be conveying these then at least the over-arching co-operative principle would be sustained. Some examples follow.

Quality
This maxim might be flouted in the following exchange:

(33)   A: What if the USSR blockades the Gulf and all the oil?
          B: Oh come now, Britain rules the seas!

Any reasonably informed participant will know that B's utterance is blatantly false. That being so, B cannot be trying to deceive A. The only way in which the assumption that B is co-operating can be maintained is if we take B to mean something rather different from what he has actually said. Searching around for a related but co-operative proposition that B might be intending to convey, we arrive at the opposite, or negation, of what B has stated – namely that Britain doesn't rule the seas, and thus by way of Relevance to the prior utterance, the suggestion that there is nothing that Britain could do. Hence, Grice claims, ironies arise and are successfully decoded. If there was no underlying assumption of co-operation, recipients of ironies ought simply to be nonplussed; no inferences could be drawn.[10]

---

[10] For a more detailed account, see Sperber & Wilson, 1981. They argue that ironies consist of sentences *mentioned* rather than *used* – much as if they were in implicit quotation marks – from which recipients calculate implicatures by reference to Relevance rather than Quality.

Similar remarks can be made for at least some examples of metaphor. For example, if I say (34) I express a categorial falsehood (i.e. a semantic category, or selectional, violation). Either therefore I am being non-co-operative or I intend to convey something rather different:

(34)   Queen Victoria was made of iron

The straightforward interpretation is that since Queen Victoria in fact lacked the definitional properties of iron, she merely had some of the incidental properties like hardness, resilience, non-flexibility or durability. Which particular set of such properties are attributed to her by the utterance of (34) are at least in part dependent on the contexts of utterance: said by an admirer it may be a commendation, conveying the properties of toughness and resilience; said by a detractor it may be taken as a denigration, conveying her lack of flexibility, emotional impassivity or belligerence.

Other Quality floutings include the uttering of patent falsehoods as in (35):

(35)   A: Teheran's in Turkey isn't it, teacher?
         B: And London's in Armenia I suppose

where B's utterance serves to suggest that A's is absurdly incorrect. Or consider rhetorical questions like (36):

(36)   Was Mussolini going to be moderate?

which if the participants believe that whatever Mussolini was, he was not moderate, is likely to convey (37):

(37)   Mussolini was definitely not going to be moderate

Here, by overtly violating the sincerity of a question, once again an implicature is generated by a flouting of the maxim of Quality.

Quantity

The uttering of simple and obvious tautologies should, in principle, have absolutely no communicative import.[11] However, utterances of (38)–(40) and the like can in fact convey a great deal:

[11] Exceptions, of course, will be tautologies that are not obvious to addressees, as in the didactic use of definitions, or those that point out non-obvious logical consequences.

(38)   War is war
(39)   Either John will come or he won't
(40)   If he does it, he does it

Note that these, by virtue of their logical forms (respectively: $\forall x$ $(W(x) \rightarrow W(x)); p \lor \sim p; p \rightarrow p)$ are necessarily true; ergo they share the same truth conditions, and the differences we feel to lie between them, as well as their communicative import, must be almost entirely due to their pragmatic implications. An account of how they come to have communicative significance, and different communicative significances, can be given in terms of the flouting of the maxim of Quantity. Since this requires that speakers be informative, the asserting of tautologies blatantly violates it. Therefore, if the assumption that the speaker is actually co-operating is to be preserved, some informative inference must be made. Thus in the case of (38) it might be 'terrible things always happen in war, that's its nature and it's no good lamenting that particular disaster'; in the case of (39) it might be 'calm down, there's no point in worrying about whether he's going to come because there's nothing we can do about it'; and in the case of (40) it might be 'it's no concern of ours'. Clearly these share a dismissive or topic-closing quality, but the details of what is implicated will depend upon the particular context of utterance. (Incidentally, exactly how the appropriate implicatures in these cases are to be predicted remains quite unclear, although the maxim of Relevance would presumably play a crucial role.)

Relevance
Exploitations of this maxim are, as Grice notes, a little harder to find, if only because it is hard to construct responses that *must* be interpreted as irrelevant. But Grice provides an example like the following:

(41)   A: I do think Mrs Jenkins is an old windbag, don't you?
         B: Huh, lovely weather for March, isn't it?

where B's utterance might implicate in the appropriate circumstances 'hey, watch out, her nephew is standing right behind you'. More naturally, consider (42):

(42)   Johnny: Hey Sally let's play marbles
         Mother: How is your homework getting along Johnny?

whereby Johnny's mother can remind him that he may not yet be free to play.

Manner

One example of the exploitation of this maxim will suffice here. Suppose we find in a review of a musical performance something like (43) where we might have expected (44):

(43)   Miss Singer produced a series of sounds corresponding closely to the score of an aria from *Rigoletto*
(44)   Miss Singer sang an aria from *Rigoletto*

By the flagrant avoidance of the simple (44) in favour of the prolix (43) (and the consequent violation of the sub-maxim 'be brief'), the reviewer implicates that there was in fact some considerable difference between Miss Singer's performance and those to which the term *singing* is usually applied.

Unhappily, in this book we shall have to pass over most of these figures of speech (although section 3.2.5 below is devoted to metaphor). Since Aristotle, much has been written about each of them from a rhetorical, philosophical and literary point of view, but until Grice's brief remarks there had been few attempts to explicate the inferential mechanisms that must be involved in interpreting figures of speech, or to explain how such mechanisms might be reconciled with any kind of standard semantic theory. Grice's work at least suggests ways in which these important communicative mechanisms can be brought within the scope of a pragmatic theory, although (as we shall see when we come to consider metaphor) much mystery still remains. (Indeed, there are authors who think that Grice's treatment of tropes is fundamentally incorrect – see e.g. Sperber & Wilson, 1981; Wilson & Sperber, 1981.)

One general point that these exploitations of the maxims raise is that there is a fundamental way in which a full account of the communicative power of language can never be reduced to a set of conventions for the use of language. The reason is that wherever some convention or expectation about the use of language arises, there will also therewith arise the possibility of the non-conventional *exploitation* of that convention or expectation. It follows that a purely conventional or rule-based account of natural language usage can never be complete, and that what can be communicated always exceeds the communicative power provided by the conventions of the language and its use. There thus remains a fundamental need for some theory or notion of communication which is not based on the concept of conventional meaning, as sketched by Grice (1957) in his theory of meaning-nn.

So far we have only roughly indicated how implicatures actually come about. Grice tries to tighten up the notion along the following lines. First he proposes a definition of implicature which we may state as follows:[12]

(45)   S's saying that *p* conversationally implicates *q* iff:
        (i)   S is presumed to be observing the maxims, or at least (in the case of floutings) the co-operative principle
        (ii) in order to maintain this assumption it must be supposed that S thinks that *q*
        (iii) S thinks that both S and the addressee H mutually know that H can work out that to preserve the assumption in (i), *q* is in fact required

Then he points out that, for the addressee H to be able to calculate the implicature *q*, H must know, or believe that he knows, the facts in (46):

(46)   (i)   the conventional content of the sentence (P) uttered
        (ii) the co-operative principle and its maxims
        (iii) the context of P (e.g. its relevance)
        (iv) certain bits of background information (e.g. P is blatantly false)
        (v)   that (i)–(v) are mutual knowledge shared by speaker and addressee

From all this a general pattern for working out an implicature may be adduced:[13]

(47)   (i)   S has said that *p*
        (ii) there's no reason to think S is not observing the maxims, or at least the co-operative principle
        (iii) in order for S to say that *p* and be indeed observing the maxims or the co-operative principle, S must think that *q*

---

[12] This phrasing, which is not exactly Grice's, makes explicit the relation of the notion of implicature to the concept of *mutual knowledge*, as explored in Lewis, 1969, and Schiffer, 1972. As we noted in 1.2, we can say that S and H *mutually know p* iff S knows *p*, H knows *p*, S knows that H knows *p*, H knows that S knows that H knows *p*, and so on, ad infinitum. Many other pragmatic concepts, e.g. *presupposition, meaning-nn, felicity condition*, etc., may rely implicitly on such a concept (see Smith, 1982).

[13] A more precise formulation will be found in (125) below.

(iv) S must know that it is mutual knowledge that q must be supposed if S is to be taken to be co-operating

(v) S has done nothing to stop me, the addressee, thinking that q

(vi) therefore S intends me to think that q, and in saying that p has implicated q

From the ways in which implicatures are calculated, Grice suggests that the essential properties of implicatures are largely predictable. He isolates five characteristic properties of which the first, and perhaps the most important, is that they are **cancellable**, or more exactly **defeasible**.[14] The notion of defeasibility is crucial in pragmatics as most pragmatic inferences, of various different kinds, exhibit this property. An inference is defeasible if it is possible to cancel it by adding some additional premises to the original ones. **Deductive** or logical inferences are thus not defeasible. For example, given some logical argument like that in (48), it is not possible to defeat the argument simply by adding premises no matter what they be:

(48)   i. If Socrates is a man, he is mortal
           ii. Socrates is a man

           iii. Therefore, Socrates is mortal

If the two premises i and ii are true, then whatever else is true or false, iii is true.

In contrast, **inductive** arguments are defeasible. Take for example (49):

(49)   i. I have dug up 1001 carrots
           ii. Every one of the 1001 carrots is orange

           iii. Therefore, all carrots are orange

Suppose we now dig up a green carrot: if we add the additional premiss iii to the argument, it fails and the conclusion is invalidated:

(50)   i. I have dug up 1001 carrots
           ii. Every one of the 1001 carrots is orange

---

[14] Grice (1975) in fact lists six properties: *calculability* on p. 50, the rest on pp. 57–8. The additional property is that implicatures (unlike perhaps entailments) are not inferences carried by sentences, but by utterances, a general point already made above.

iii. The 1002nd carrot is green

---

iv. *Invalid :* Therefore, all carrots are orange

In this respect implicatures are more like inductive inferences than they are like deductive ones, for implicatures too are inferences easily defeasible (Grice, 1973). Consider for example (51) and its straightforward Quantity implicature (52):

(51)   John has three cows
(52)   John has only three cows and no more

Notice too that (51) entails (53):

(53)   John has two cows

Now we can immediately see that implicatures are suspendable by mention in an *if* clause:[15]

(54)   John has three cows, if not more

which does not have the implicature in (52). Note here that entailments, being non-defeasible, cannot be suspended in this way:

(55)   ?John has three cows, if not two

More importantly, implicatures are directly and overtly deniable without a sense of contradiction:

(56)   John has three cows, in fact ten
(57)   John has three cows and maybe more

Again, one cannot deny entailments in this way, as illustrated in (58) and (59):

(58)   *John has three cows, in fact none
(59)   *John has three cows and maybe none

Further, and most importantly, implicatures can just disappear when it is clear from the context of utterance that such an inference could not have been intended as part of the utterance's full communicative import. For example, suppose that in order to get the lavish subsidy

[15] Horn (1972) makes a distinction between two kinds of defeasibility of implicatures (and presuppositions): **suspension**, where the speaker is not committed to the truth or falsity of the implicature, and **cancellation**, where the speaker is committed to the falsity of the implicature. The distinction is useful descriptively, but both kinds of defeasibility can be accounted for by the same general kind of mechanism – see e.g. Gazdar, 1979a, and discussion below.

under the EEC Hill Cow Subsidy Scheme one must have three cows, and the inspector asks John's neighbour the following question:

(60) I: Has John really got the requisite number of cows?
      N: Oh sure, he's got three cows all right

then N's reply does not commit him to the implicature ordinarily associated with (51), namely (52), because it is clear from the context that all the information that is required is whether John's herd passes the threshold for subsidy payment, not the exact number of cows he might in fact have.

So implicatures are defeasible, and can drop out in certain linguistic or non-linguistic contexts. In that respect they appear to be quite unlike logical inferences, and cannot directly be modelled in terms of some semantic relation like entailment (for the contrary opinion see G. Lakoff, 1975; Sperber & Wilson, forthcoming).

The second important property of implicatures is that (with the exception of those due to the maxim of Manner) they are, as Grice puts it, **non-detachable**. By this Grice means that the implicature is attached to the semantic content of what is said, not to linguistic form, and therefore implicatures cannot be detached from an utterance simply by changing the words of the utterance for synonyms. There at least appear to be other kinds of pragmatic implication that are attached to the form rather than the meaning of what is said; for example, (61) seems to pragmatically imply (or **presuppose** as will be suggested in Chapter 4) (62); but (63), which seems at least to be semantically and truth-conditionally equivalent to (61) (Karttunen & Peters, 1979), lacks the inference to (62):

(61) John didn't manage to reach the summit
(62) John tried to reach the summit
(63) John didn't reach the summit

So in contrast to implicatures, this particular brand of pragmatic inference (**presupposition**) does seem to be detachable; that is, it does seem to be possible to find another way of saying the same thing that happens to lack the inference in question (e.g. by saying (63) instead of (61) one can avoid conveying (62)). In contrast, take some implicature like the ironic interpretation (65) of (64):

(64) John's a genius
(65) John's an idiot

Suppose instead we say any of the sentences in (66) in a context in which it is mutually known that (64) is very definitely false:

(66)   John's a mental prodigy
         John's an exceptionally clever human being
         John's an enormous intellect
         John's a big brain

Then the ironic reading will be shared by all the different ways of expressing the proposition that gives rise to it. So implicatures are standardly non-detachable, with the exception of those arising under the maxim of Manner that are specifically linked to the form of the utterance. And this property may serve to distinguish conversational implicatures from other kinds of pragmatic inferences like *presupposition* (see Chapter 4) and *conventional implicatures* (see 3.2.3).

The third distinguishing feature of implicatures is that they are **calculable**. That is to say, for every putative implicature it should be possible to construct an argument of the type in (47) above, showing how from the literal meaning or the sense of the utterance on the one hand, and the co-operative principle and the maxims on the other, it follows that an addressee would make the inference in question to preserve the assumption of co-operation.

Fourthly, implicatures are **non-conventional**, that is, not part of the conventional meaning of linguistic expressions. Some reasons for believing this have already been adduced under cancellability (or defeasibility) and non-detachability. But in addition, if Grice is right about the manner in which implicatures come about, then since you need to know the literal meaning or sense of a sentence *before* you can calculate its implicatures in a context, the implicatures cannot be part of that meaning. In addition we can show that an utterance can be true while its implicature is false, and vice versa, as in:

(67)   Herb hit Sally

which by Quantity would implicate

(68)   Herb didn't kill Sally by hitting her

(since if Herb had killed Sally, the speaker would, in saying just (67), be withholding information in a non-co-operative way); but a speaker might say (67) nevertheless, attempting to mislead, in a situation where (67) is true, but (68) is false.

Finally, and importantly, an expression with a single meaning can give rise to different implicatures on different occasions, and indeed on any one occasion the set of associated implicatures may not be exactly determinable.[16] Consider for example:

(69)   John's a machine

This could convey that John is cold, or efficient, or never stops working, or puffs and blows, or has little in the way of grey matter, or indeed any and all of these. So implicatures can have a certain indeterminacy in at least some cases, incompatible with the stable determinate senses usually assumed in semantic theories.

This section has presented a straightforward review of Grice's theory of implicature. We now turn to consider linguistic reformulations and extensions of these ideas, and their impact on linguistic theory.

3.2   **Revisions, problems and applications**

Grice has provided little more than a sketch of the large area and the numerous separate issues that might be illumined by a fully worked out theory of conversational implicature. So if use is to be made of these ideas in a systematic way within linguistic theory, much has to be done to tighten up the concepts employed and to work out exactly how they apply to particular cases.

The theory though is of such broad scope, with ramifications in so many areas, that here we can do no more than take up a selection of some of the issues raised. We shall start with some general problems concerning the identification of, semantic input to and typology of implicatures, then proceed, first, to a detailed analysis of standard (non-flouted) Quantity implicatures, then secondly, to a consideration of metaphor as deriving from the flouting of the maxim of Quality, and finally to a general assessment of the possible relations between implicature and language structure.

3.2.1   *Tests for implicature*

If conversational implicature is to play a principled role in linguistic theory, it is crucial that we understand its properties and

---

[16] This is claimed by Wilson & Sperber (1981) to be true only of implicatures due to exploitations of the maxims, and thus to indicate that such exploitations involve quite different inferential mechanisms.

thus have some sound ways of distinguishing implicatures from other kinds of semantic and pragmatic inferences.

Grice suggested, as we saw, that implicatures exhibit the following four major distinguishing properties:

(i) cancellability (or defeasibility)
(ii) non-detachability (or inference based on meaning rather -than form)
(iii) calculability
(iv) non-conventionality

Now as Grice was aware, and Sadock (1978) has made doubly clear, none of these is as unproblematic as it might seem. Suppose, for example, we claim that (70) implicates (71), this being proved by the fact that we can *cancel* (71) as in (72):

(70) Joe taunted Ralph and Ralph hit him
(71) First Joe taunted Ralph and then Ralph hit him
(72) Joe taunted Ralph and Ralph hit him, but not necessarily in that order

To this the sceptic can reply: (70) is just *ambiguous* between two senses of *an l*, one equivalent to logical &, the other to 'and then'; all (72) does is disambiguate the *and* in this particular case by indicating that ɪn 'and then' reading is not intended. The attack has some force because, as we noted in 3.0, one of the attractions of implicature is that it would rule out or make unnecessary ambiguity claims of this sort.

Similarly *non-detachability*, as a defining property of implicatures, has its problems. As Sadock points out, to test for non-detachability you have to have a set of synonymous expressions, which should share the same implicatures. But suppose the alleged implicature is actually part of the semantic content of each member of that set: then it will be 'non-detachable' but hardly because it is in fact an implicature! Worse, even in the clearest examples of implicature, problems arise; for example, consider (73) which is usually claimed (as we shall see in detail in 3.2.4) to implicate (74) and to *mean* (have the same truth conditions as) something like (75):

(73) Some of the boys went to the soccer match
(74) Not all of the boys went to the soccer match
(75) Some and perhaps all of the boys went to the soccer match

So (73) and (75), being equivalent in meaning, should share the same implicatures. But they don't, since only (73) implicates (74).

Many problems of this sort in fact evaporate if the properties (i) to (iv) above are taken together (with some additional criteria to be discussed) as necessary conditions which are only jointly sufficient for an inference to be considered an implicature. Thus the fact that in (70) we can also show that the inference is calculable from the maxim of Manner, that it is not detachable when *but* or paratactic conjunction (or sheer adjacency) is substituted for *and*, and so on, argues for a rejection of the ambiguity claim. Other problems, like those associated with (73) and (75), yield to particular counter-arguments. For example, Gazdar suggests that some designated implicatures can cancel others. Thus in (75) there is an additional implicature due to the phrase *perhaps all*, namely:

(76)   Perhaps not all

which cancels the implicature (74) due to the quantifier *some* (see Gazdar, 1979a: 139 for details).

In addition we may hope that, as work proceeds, further properties of implicature will come to light. For example, Sadock notes that implicatures seem to be the only kinds of pragmatic or semantic inferences that are freely **reinforceable**, i.e. can be conjoined with an overt statement of their content without a sense of anomalous redundancy.[17] Compare for example:

(77)   Some of the boys went to the soccer match but not all
(78)   ?Some of the boys went to the soccer match but not none

A further important feature of generalized conversational implicatures is that we would expect them to be *universal*. That is, we would expect that in every language in which (79) or (80) is directly expressible, the utterance of the equivalents of (79) and (80) should carry the standard implicatures (81) and (82), respectively:

[17] Presuppositions (Chapter 5), and even perhaps entailments, may also allow 'reinforcing', but only if the reinforcing phrase contains heavy stress, e.g. *John realized it was raining and it WAS raining*. Here, it may be argued, the exceptions prove the rule, for the stress seems to produce an additional implicature (of the sort 'and boy! was it raining', i.e. it was raining very hard), so explaining how the reinforcing phrase is not entirely redundant, and thus pragmatically acceptable. See Grice, 1978: 121ff.

(79)   That man has two children
(80)   The cloth is white
(81)   That man has no more than two children
(82)   The cloth is wholly white

Universality follows from the theory: if the maxims are derivable from considerations of rational co-operation, we should expect them to be universal in application, at least in co-operative kinds of interaction.[18] This feature has not yet been put to extensive use but may turn out to be one of the clearest indications of the presence of a conversational implicature. Note that without a theory of implicature the many cross-linguistic generalizations of the sort illustrated by (79)'s implicating (81) and (80)'s implicating (82) in (presumably) all languages would be entirely unaccounted for.

Another prediction from the theory is also empirically verifiable, and may yield a test for implicatures. Recollect that implicatures are said to arise from the assumption of underlying co-operation in conversation. But suppose we can find kinds of talk where a systematic and avowed non-co-operation is assumed, except for some minimum essential to maintain talk. Then the implicatures normally associated with what is said should not routinely go through. And in fact this seems to be the case; for example, in cross-examination in a court of law (at least in England or the United States, where there are adversarial systems) one finds exchanges like:

(83)   C: On many occasions?
          W: Not many
          C: Some?
          W: Yes, a few

Here legal counsel C is cross-examining defendant W. It is C's job to extract damaging admissions from W, and W's job to resist that, this being the accepted convention in an adversarial legal process. Hence W is not expected to co-operate with C beyond the demands required by sticking to the truth (the maxim of Quality, it is hoped, stays in force). So the maxim of Quantity is in abeyance; it follows that W's first utterance in (83) cannot be assumed to commit him to the proposition that he did do the action in question on at least some occasions, despite the fact that it would standardly implicate that (*not*

---

[18] For apparent counter-evidence see Keenan, 1976b; and for a counter-argument to that see Brown & Levinson, 1978: 298–9.

many implicating 'some' by Quantity – see below). This being the case counsel cannot take *not many* to commit W to 'some' (it would after all be strictly compatible with 'none'). C therefore has to question W explicitly as to whether W did in fact do the action in question on some previous occasions, such explicit questioning giving cross-examination some of its distinctive (and to the layman, unpleasant) flavour (see Levinson, 1979a for some further examples). Again, there would be no such prediction of a failure of the inference from *not many* to 'some' just in non-co-operative circumstances, without the theory of implicature. But given the theory we can predict, for example, that if some inference is genuinely a generalized Quantity implicature it should be possible to find cases where it is implicitly cancelled simply by virtue of a non-co-operative context, whether this is antagonistic, as in legal cross-examination, or playfully unco-operative, as in games like 'twenty questions' or the posing of riddles.

There is every reason for confidence, then, that the sorts of problems raised by Sadock (1978) are capable of detailed solutions. Another kind of attack that has been made on the notion of implicature is that the maxims are so broad that they allow the derivation of just about any proposition as an alleged implicature, and thus that the whole theory is vacuous (see e.g. Kroch, 1972 and Kiefer, 1979 and replies in, respectively, Gazdar, 1979a: 53 and Gazdar, 1980b). However this kind of attack would only have force if it were in principle impossible to predict implicatures on a rigorous basis. But as we shall demonstrate in section 3.2.4, a firm start has in fact already been made in the direction of formalization, and there is no reason to think that further progress cannot be made.

3.2.2   *Implicature and logical form*
We have seen that implicatures are derived from (a) what is said, and (b) the assumption that at least the co-operative principle is being maintained. But exactly what aspect of 'what is said' is relevant? More precisely, what linguistic level or levels must be referred to in the derivation of an implicature? Are implicatures derived from, for example, the surface structure, the semantic representation or the truth conditions?

Some quite detailed arguments can be given to show that all but the Manner implicatures must be read from the level of **semantic**

representation, including some specification of **logical form**. They cannot be read off from uninterpreted surface structures, nor can they be inferred simply from the truth conditions of the sentence uttered.

First let us show that implicatures cannot sensibly be derived from uninterpreted surface structures. There are many utterances that differ in surface structure but which share the same implicatures. For example the utterance of any of the sentences in (84), where P is any declarative sentence expressing the proposition p, will share the implicature in (85) (providing of course the implicature is not cancelled):

(84)   perhaps P
          maybe P
          possibly P
          potentially P
(85)   possibly not p

Thus (86) will implicate (87):

(86)   There may be life on Mars
(87)   There may not be life on Mars

because, by Quantity, if one knew that there must be life on Mars one should have said so (again, see section 3.2.4 for the details). The problem here is that there is no way to relate the expressions in (84) simply on surface structure grounds, although they share the implicature in (85). So we should miss the basic generalization that all expressions with the same semantic content seem to have the same implicatures (see Gazdar, 1979a: 56ff for further argument).

Secondly, as we shall show in section 3.2.4, an utterance of the form *Not all of the As are B* has the generalized conversational implicature 'some As are B' (the former does not entail the latter because the former could be true even if the latter were false). Now consider:

(88)   All of the arrows didn't hit the target

This exhibits a well-known type of ambiguity (a so–called **scope-ambiguity**) between the two senses expressible by the following logical forms:

(89) $\sim (\forall x \, (A(x) \rightarrow \text{Hit}(x, \text{ the target})))$
          i.e. it is not the case that for all x, if x is an arrow, then x hit the target
(90) $\forall x \, (A(x) \rightarrow \sim (\text{Hit}(x, \text{ the target})))$

123

> i.e. for all x, if x is an arrow, then it is not the case that x hit
> the target

Here (90) expresses the sense 'None of the arrows hit the target'.
But (89) on the other hand is an expression of the form *Not all As
are B*; it therefore implicates 'Some As are B', or, instantiating:

(91)   Some of the arrows hit the target

Therefore only one of the two readings of (88), namely (89), has the
implicature (91). Therefore, implicatures must be derived not from
uninterpreted surface structures like (88) but from some semantic
representation of a particular reading, in this case from some representation with at least the structure in (89).

We can now go on to show that, while implicatures are derived from
a level of semantic representation, they often cannot be calculated
from the truth conditions alone. Consider any expressions of the form
(92) or (93):

(92) p
(93) p and if p then p

Clearly these will share the same truth conditions: whenever p is true,
so also (93) is true, and vice versa. But now compare the instantiations
in (94) and (95):

(94)   It's done
(95)   It's done and if it's done, it's done

The latter alone has a distinctive implicature, roughly that in (96):

(96)   It's no good regretting what has already happened

So at least some implicatures are derived from the semantic or logical
structure of what is said and not just from the truth conditions,
although the latter will of course also be relevant.

Further evidence for the need to refer to semantic representation
and not just truth conditions comes from a consideration of tautologies.
Compare, for example, (97) and (98):

(97)   A square has four sides
(98)   Boys are boys

Since these are both necessarily true, they must share the same truth
conditions. So if implicatures were read off truth conditions alone,
they should share the same implicatures. But clearly only the second

could implicate something like 'that's the kind of unruly behaviour you would expect from boys'.

In general, therefore, the linguistic levels that must be referred to in the calculation of implicatures include the semantic representation or logical form of the sentences uttered, together with the attendant truth conditions. The sensitivity to logical form will explain why, for example, the readings (89) and (90) are associated with different implicatures. The fact that utterances with identical truth conditions but different logical forms (as in (92) and (93)) can give rise to different implicatures is important: it raises the possibility that various near-synonyms, like (99) and (100), might have their slight meaning differences accounted for in terms of different implicatures generated by different logical forms (as, on a first approximation, in (101) and (102) respectively) sharing the same or similar truth conditions:[19]

(99)   John kissed the girl
(100)   It was John who kissed the girl
(101) $K(j, g)$
(102) $\exists x\, (K(x, g)\, \&\, (x = j))$

The different usages of 'stylistic options' with the same truth conditions might thereby be explicated (see Atlas & Levinson, 1981 for a variant of such an account; but see also Chapter 4 for a *presuppositional* account of the difference between (99) and (100)).

Finally it should be noted that there is one obvious but important exception to the claim that implicatures make reference to semantic representation and truth conditions but not to surface structure. The exceptions are those implicatures due to two of the sub-maxims of Manner, namely 'avoid obscurity' and 'avoid ambiguity', which make essential reference to the surface form of utterances. (The other two sub-maxims of Manner, 'be brief' and 'be orderly', can at least in part be interpreted equally as applying to the level of semantic representation.)[20]

[19] In fact, (100) requires a more complex logical form than (102), and it can also be claimed that (99) and (100) have slightly different truth conditions; here compare the accounts in Halvorsen, 1978 and Atlas & Levinson, 1981. See also 4.4.2 below.

[20] Here a unitary level of interpreted surface structure would avoid the embarrassment of reading some implicatures off truth conditions, others off logical form, and yet others (some of the Manner implicatures) off surface structure. Such a level, consisting essentially of surface structure trees annotated with the meanings of their constituents, is made available in recent work by e.g. Gazdar (1982).

3.2.3   *Kinds of implicature*

In our account of Grice's theory of implicature (section 3.1), we stressed a dichotomy between those implicatures (which we called **standard**) that are derived from a simple assumption that the speaker is *observing* the maxims and those derived in more complex ways on the basis of the speaker *flouting* or exploiting a maxim. The distinction underlies the common view that there is some special class of utterances that are 'figures of speech' or exploitations of more straightforward ways of talking.[21] But Grice also distinguished between kinds of conversational implicature on another dimension: **generalized** conversational implicatures are those that arise without any particular context or special scenario being necessary, in contrast to **particularized** implicatures which do require such specific contexts. As an example, Grice notes that in general whenever I say (103) I shall be taken to implicate (104):

(103)   I walked into a house
(104)   The house was not my house

So there seems to be a *generalized* conversational implicature from the expression *an F* to the assumption that the mentioned F is not closely related to the speaker. In contrast (105) will only implicate (106) if (105) occurs in the particular sort of setting illustrated in (107):

(105)   The dog is looking very happy
(106)   Perhaps the dog has eaten the roast beef
(107)   A: What on earth has happened to the roast beef?
         B: The dog is looking very happy

The implicature in (106) is thus *particularized* (see Smith & Wilson, 1979: 171ff for an account of how implicatures like this might be calculated).

Now most of the floutings or exploitations of the maxims are particularized, in that, for example, ironies require particular background assumptions to rule out the literal interpretations. But it could

---

[21] Indeed, Sperber & Wilson (forthcoming) insist that the distinction is so fundamental that two quite different kinds of reasoning are employed, both of which cannot be subsumed within a single theory of implicature. While claiming that the standard implicatures are deductions from a single maxim of Relevance, background assumptions and what is said, they suggest that 'figures of speech' typically invoke images and associations of a quite different kind.

perhaps be claimed that metaphors like (108) or tautologies like (109) convey what they convey in a relatively context-independent way:

(108)   England is a sinking ship
(109)   War is war

In any case, it is clear that the two dimensions cross-cut: for example, all implicatures that arise from observing the maxim of Relevance are particularized, since utterances are relevant only with respect to the particular topic or issue at hand. Thus B's response in (107) implicates (106) by virtue of its juxtaposition to A's question in (107).

But the important point here is that those implicatures that are both derived from observing the maxims and are generalized have a special importance for linguistic theory. For it is these in particular which will be hard to distinguish from the *semantic* content of linguistic expressions, because such implicatures will be routinely associated with the relevant expressions in all ordinary contexts.

We have been using the term *implicature* loosely to refer to what Grice was careful to designate *conversational implicature* (and we shall continue to use the shorthand where no misunderstanding will result). But Grice in fact intended the term *implicature* to be a general cover term, to stand in contrast to what is *said* or expressed by the truth conditions of expressions, and to include all the kinds of pragmatic (non-truth-conditional) inference discernible. In addition then to *conversational* implicatures, i.e. those calculated on the basis of the maxims, Grice envisaged an entirely different kind of non-truth-conditional inferences, namely **conventional implicatures**. Conventional implicatures are non-truth-conditional inferences that are *not* derived from superordinate pragmatic principles like the maxims, but are simply attached by convention to particular lexical items or expressions. Grice provides just two examples: the word *but* has the same truth-conditional (or truth-functional) content as the word *and*, with an additional conventional implicature to the effect that there is some contrast between the conjuncts (Grice, 1961); the other example is the word *therefore* which Grice holds contributes nothing to the truth conditions of the expressions it occurs within (Grice, 1975: 44). Other examples that have been suggested are the meanings of *even* (Kempson, 1975; Karttunen & Peters, 1979) and *yet* (Wilson, 1975).

Conventional implicatures can be expected to contrast with

conversational ones on all the distinctive properties we have outlined for the latter. For example, conventional implicatures will be *non-cancellable* because they do not rely on defeasible assumptions about the nature of the context; they will be *detachable* because they depend on the particular linguistic items used (e.g. if you substitute *and* for *but* you lose the conventional implicature but retain the same truth conditions); they will not be *calculated* using pragmatic principles and contextual knowledge, but rather given by convention (e.g. there is no way that given the truth conditions of *but* you can derive or calculate that there is a contrast between the two conjuncts); they may be expected therefore to have a relatively *determinate* content or meaning; and there will be no expectation of a *universal* tendency for languages to associate the same conventional implicatures with expressions with certain truth conditions.

In a sense conventional implicature is not a very interesting concept – it is rather an admission of the failure of truth-conditional semantics to capture all the conventional content or meaning of natural language words and expressions. It is natural, therefore, that the acceptance of the notion has been resisted (see e.g. Kempson, 1975), and that attempts have been made to reduce alleged cases to matters of entailment, conversational implicature or presupposition. Grice's few examples of conventional implicature encourage the would-be reductionist: indeed Kempson (1975) claims that there are only several candidates for the category anyway. But this is an error, for a very large number of deictic expressions of the sort described in Chapter 2 seem to have conventional implicatures as a central meaning component. This is especially true of discourse-deictic items as in (110),[22] and socially deictic items as in (111) (when used in address):

(110) however, moreover, besides, anyway, well, still, furthermore, although, oh, so

(111) sir, madam, mate, your honour, sonny, hey, oi

Take, for example, T/V pronouns, like *tu/vous* in French: what a choice of (112) over (113) conveys (as we argued in Chapter 2) is not

---

[22] In section 3.2.6, it will be argued that the meaning of such items often involves reference to processes of *conversational* implicature. But the way in which such meanings are encoded, it is here being argued, is by *conventional* implicature.

any difference in truth conditions but just a difference in the expressed social relationship between speaker and addressee:

(112)   Tu es le professeur
(113)   Vous êtes le professeur

Thus *vous*, when used to a singular addressee, conventionally but non-truth-conditionally indicates that the addressee is socially distant from, or socially superior to, the speaker. The whole vast range of honorifics in, for example, the S.E. Asian languages, like Korean and Japanese, are similarly encoded as conventional implicatures.

Or take the discourse particle *oh* in English. As Heritage (in press) shows, *oh* as an utterance-initial particle is generally produced (at least in one distinctive usage) by one speaker just after another has announced some news. It is the conventional signal in English for indicating that news has been received and recognized, but in itself it has no propositional content that could be analysed truth-conditionally. (See also Owen, 1981, 1982, on related particles.)

Note that discourse-deictic items, as in (110), and address forms, as in (111), exhibit the properties Grice expects of conventional implicatures. For example, they are non-cancellable – you cannot add a conjoined phrase, for instance, that effectively denies the implication. Compare:

(114)   The Duke of Norfolk has three mansions, and in fact more
(115)   ??The Duke of Norfolk has three mansions, but only one car, and there is in fact no contrast between these two facts

In (114), the implicature 'no more than three' is effectively cancelled by the conjoined phrase; but in (115) a similar conjoined phrase denying the conventional implicature of *but* does not seem to lift the force of *but* at all, and indeed seems anomalous (here cf. Grice, 1961). Just as conventional implicatures are non-cancellable, so they are detachable (in contrast to conversational implicatures), as illustrated by the switch from *tu* to *vous*; nor are they calculated (no one has to calculate why *vous* might be more polite than *tu*); and they do not seem to have radically different interpretations in different contexts (consider, for example, the meaning of the items in (110)).

Various important issues about the organization of a grammar are raised by the concept of conventional implicature. On the account suggested here, lexical items will often have non-truth-conditional but nevertheless conventional features of meaning: so a lexicon for a natural language will contain reference to pragmatic components of meaning. Secondly, syntactic rules seem to be sensitive to such elements of meaning. Consider again, for example, (112) and (113) above: *tu* takes the singular form of the verb, *vous* the plural form, but *vous* does not take a plural noun phrase after the verb *être* if it is being used to refer to a singular addressee. Consequently, as we noted in 2.2.5, there is a morphologically encoded distinction between the *vous* that is genuinely plural and the *vous* that actually refers to a singular referent, which appears just with nominal predicates (see Comrie, 1975 for cross-linguistic data here). Now in some languages which have additional honorific devices, the morphology requires that all items referring to a particular person be at the same honorific level. Thus most Tamil speakers would find (116) ill-formed or unacceptable because the honorific level in the subject does not agree with the honorific level in the predicate:

(116)   ??talaivar colraanka
          headman-honorific says-super-honorific

Such honorific levels are not always encoded by regular morphological elements or otherwise in the form of the linguistic items. So rules of morphological agreement have to refer to the conventional implicatures that specify the degree of respect offered by the speaker to the hearer or the referent. But in that case syntax is not autonomous with respect to pragmatics, a claim that most linguists would resist. The only way to escape such a conclusion is to generate sentences with, for example, unacceptable collocations of honorifics, and then have an additional set of pragmatic *filtering* rules that ape standard morphological processes. The machinery for such a solution has been explored by Gazdar & Klein (1977). It is not an elegant solution in that such pragmatic filters would do a tremendous amount of work in a language rich in honorifics, of a sort that would normally be thought of as standardly morphological or syntactic (for the magnitude of the problem see e.g. Harada, 1976, on Japanese). The issue is important because the inter-relation between conventional implicature and syntax is one of the clearest areas where pragmatics impinges deeply on grammatical processes. In fact little thought has yet been given to the implications that such inter-relations have for the overall organization of a theory of grammar.

Recently a new and different interpretation of the nature of conventional implicature, and the linguistic phenomena that fall within its scope, has been put forward by Karttunen & Peters (1975, 1979). Essentially they suggest that the core examples of the phenomenon usually described as *presupposition* are really best treated as conventional implicatures, and they outline a formal treatment within the framework of Montague grammar. The theory is discussed extensively in Chapter 4, and we note its existence here to minimize terminological confusion. In fact the phenomena they describe have quite different properties from the conventional implicatures of items like those in (110) and (111) (see Levinson, 1979b) and in this book the term will be retained, as Grice intended, for the inferences associated with such items.

We have described the kinds of implicature central to the literature, but, as anticipated by Grice, there do seem to be additional non-conventional kinds of inference produced by different maxims or principles of language usage. For example, we shall see below that there is a *principle of informativeness* that produces implicatures sometimes in conflict with those due to the maxim of Quantity (Atlas & Levinson, 1981), and there are principles of politeness that produce

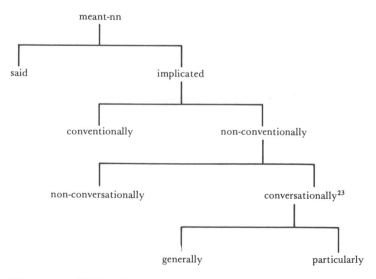

Figure 3.1 *Kinds of communicational content*

[23] I.e. implicated by the maxims of conversation.

systematic inferences of intriguing complexity (Brown & Levinson, 1978). Indeed, there may well be a general principle here: for every kind of mutually assumed constraint on language usage, there will be a corresponding set of potential inferences that come about either from the speaker observing or flouting the constraint. If this is so, there are many kinds of implicature yet to be discovered.

The proliferation of species of implicature reminds us of the point made in Chapter 1, namely that recent developments in pragmatics have as a consequence a 'hybrid' view of the nature of meaning. The total signification or communicative content of an utterance may be divided, according to Grice (1975), along the lines indicated in Figure 3.1. Here we see that the truth-conditional content of an utterance (what, in Grice's special sense, is *said*) may be only a small part of its total meaning, and as we explore other topics in pragmatics we shall continue to add further kinds of pragmatic inference to this inventory.

3.2.4 *Generalized Quantity implicatures*

One of the great attractions of the notion of conversational implicature, as was indicated in 3.0, is that it promises to simplify semantics substantially. For instance, the proliferation of senses of lexical items can be avoided by noting that implicatures often account for different interpretations of the same item in different contexts; thus, as we have seen, the 'and then' interpretation of *and* can be attributed to the maxim of Manner.

But to demonstrate how far-reaching the contributions from Grice's theory can be in this regard, we shall need to express more rigorously our understanding of how the maxims work, so that we can accurately predict some range of implicatures, show how these could be mistaken for aspects of the *sense* of the linguistic expressions involved, and demonstrate the substantial benefits that accrue to semantics if these mistakes are not made and the systematic effects of implicature are taken into account.

Here we shall concentrate on some generalized Quantity implicatures, as these seem at present to be the best understood (thanks especially to the work of Horn, 1972, 1973 and Gazdar, 1979a). Following Gazdar (1979a), we shall consider two specific and important sub-cases: **scalar** Quantity implicatures, and **clausal** Quantity implicatures.

A linguistic **scale** consists of a set of linguistic alternates, or contrastive expressions of the same grammatical category, which can be arranged in a linear order by degree of *informativeness* or semantic strength. Such a scale will have the general form of an ordered set (indicated by angled brackets) of linguistic expressions or **scalar predicates**, e_1, e_2, e_3 ... e_n, as in:

(117) $\langle e_1, e_2, e_3, \ldots e_n \rangle$

where if we substitute e_1, or e_2 etc., in a sentential frame A we obtain the well-formed sentences $A(e_1)$, $A(e_2)$, etc.; and where $A(e_1)$ entails $A(e_2)$, $A(e_2)$ entails $A(e_3)$, etc, but not vice versa. For example, take the English quantifiers *all* and *some*. These form an implicational scale $\langle all, some \rangle$, because any sentence like (118) *entails* (119) (i.e. whenever (118) is true (119) is true also) but not vice versa:

(118)   All of the boys went to the party
(119)   Some of the boys went to the party

Now, given any such scale, there is a general predictive rule for deriving a set of Quantity implicatures, namely if a speaker asserts that a lower or weaker point (i.e. a rightwards item in the ordered set of alternates) on a scale obtains, then he implicates that a higher or stronger point (leftwards in the ordered set) does *not* obtain. Thus if one asserts (119) one conversationally implicates that not all the boys went to the party; this is so even though it is quite compatible with the truth of (119) that (118) is also true, as shown by the non-contradictoriness of (120):

(120)   Some of the boys went to the party, in fact all

We may formulate this generally as a rule for deriving **scalar implicatures** from scalar predicates:

(121)   *Scalar implicatures*: Given any scale of the form $\langle e_1, e_2, e_3, \ldots e_n \rangle$, if a speaker asserts $A(e_2)$, then he implicates $\sim A(e_1)$, if he asserts $A(e_3)$, then he implicates $\sim A(e_2)$ and $\sim A(e_1)$, and in general, if he asserts $A(e_n)$, then he implicates $\sim (A(e_n-1))$, $\sim (A(e_n-2))$ and so on, up to $\sim (A(e_1))$

For the scalar implicature to be actually inferred, the expression that gives rise to it must be entailed by any complex sentence of which it is a part. Thus the utterance of

(122)   John says that some of the boys went

does not commit the speaker to knowing 'Not all of them went', because *some* occurs in a complement clause that is not entailed by the matrix clause. For this reason, and because of defeasibility in general, it is useful to make the distinction between **potential** and **actual** implicatures (as in Gazdar, 1979a); rule (121) (and similarly rule (126) below) generates potential, not necessarily actual, implicatures.

Such a rule embodies a claim that the semantic content of lower items on a scale is compatible with the truth of higher items obtaining, and the inference that higher items do not in fact obtain is merely an implicature. Thus *some* is compatible with *all*, and it therefore does not include as part of its semantic content 'not all', the latter being a scalar implicature regularly associated with *some* (but cancellable as implicatures always potentially are). If readers now apply the rule in (121) to the following scales (from Horn, 1972), they may check the rule-derived implicatures against their intuitions:

(123)   ⟨all, most, many, some, few⟩
          ⟨and, or⟩
          ⟨n, ... 5, 4, 3, 2, 1⟩
          ⟨excellent, good⟩
          ⟨hot, warm⟩
          ⟨always, often, sometimes⟩
          ⟨succeed in *V*ing, try to *V*, want to *V*⟩
          ⟨necessarily *p*, *p*, possibly *p*⟩
          ⟨certain that *p*, probable that *p*, possible that *p*⟩
          ⟨must, should, may⟩
          ⟨cold, cool⟩
          ⟨love, like⟩
          ⟨none, not all⟩[24]

To show that these regular scalar inferences are indeed implicatures we need now to produce a Gricean argument deriving the inference, for example, that (118) is not the case, from the utterance of (119) in co-operative circumstances. A short version of such an argument might go as follows:

(124)   The speaker S has said $A(e_2)$; if S was in a position to state that a stronger item on the scale holds – i.e. to assert $A(e_1)$ – then

---

[24] The implicature here, from *not all* to 'not none', i.e. 'some', is the source of one interpretation of example (88) discussed above.

he would be in breach of the first maxim of Quantity if he asserted $A(e_2)$. Since I the addressee assume that S is co-operating, and therefore will not violate the maxim of Quantity without warning, I take it that S wishes to convey that he is *not* in a position to state that the stronger item e_1 on the scale holds, and indeed knows that it does not hold

More generally, and somewhat more explicitly:

(125)   (i)   S has said p

         (ii) There is an expression q, more informative than p (and thus q entails p), which might be desirable as a contribution to the current purposes of the exchange (and here there is perhaps an implicit reference to the maxim of Relevance)

       (iii) q is of roughly equal brevity to p; so S did not say p rather than q simply in order to be brief (i.e. to conform to the maxim of Manner)

       (iv) Since if S knew that q holds but nevertheless uttered p he would be in breach of the injunction to make his contribution as informative as is required, S must mean me, the addressee, to infer that S knows that q is not the case (K $\sim q$), or at least that he does not know that q is the case ($\sim Kq$)

The important feature of such arguments to note is that they derive an implicature by reference to what has *not* been said: the absence of a statement $A(e_1)$, in the presence of a weaker one, legitimates the inference that it is not the case that $A(e_1)$, via the maxim of Quantity. Another feature to note is that the inference is implicitly or explicitly **epistemically modified**; that is to say that from the utterance of $A(e_2)$ one actually infers 'speaker knows that not $A(e_1)$', (symbolically, K $\sim A(e_1)$), rather than just $\sim A(e_1)$. Hence what is conveyed is the speaker's commitment to his knowing that $\sim A(e_1)$. This makes clear the pragmatic nature of the implication (referring to participants' knowledge states), and has important implications for formalization. Following Hintikka (1962) we may represent 'S knows that p' as Kp, and 'S doesn't know whether p' (or 'it is epistemically possible that p') as Pp. The two concepts K and P are then related just like the modal notions *necessary* and *possible* (see Allwood, Andersson & Dahl, 1977: 110), i.e. K$p \leftrightarrow \sim P \sim p$ (S knows that p iff it is epistemically impossible, given what S knows, that not p). A final and related point to note about this Gricean argument is that it equivocates (and we here use the epistemic notation to good effect) between the inference $\sim K(A(e_1))$ and K $\sim (A(e_1))$, i.e. between 'S does not know that

A(e_1)' and 'S knows that not A(e_1)'. Now empirically the inference from, for example, (119) is to the stronger 'S knows that not (118)', and this is a general fact about the scalar implicatures. Other kinds of Quantity implicature seem generally to license only the weaker form of the inference, to the effect that the speaker is not aware that some stronger statement obtains. Why this should be remains one of the many mysteries in this area (see Atlas & Levinson, 1981 for discussion).

We now turn to **clausal implicatures**. Gazdar's (1979a) formulation is (with slight simplification) as follows:

(126)   *Clausal implicatures*: If S asserts some complex expression *p* which (i) contains an embedded sentence *q*, and (ii) *p* neither entails nor presupposes *q* and (iii) there's an alternative expression *r* of roughly equal brevity which contains *q* such that *r does* entail or presuppose *q*; *then*, by asserting *p* rather than *r*, S implicates that he doesn't know whether *q* is true or false, i.e. he implicates Pq & P $\sim q$.

The underlying intuition is this: if I use some linguistic expression that fails to commit me to some embedded proposition, in preference to another available stronger expression that would so commit me, then I may be taken to implicate that I am not in the (epistemic) position to make the stronger statement. Thus if I say (127) instead of (128),

(127)   I believe John is away
(128)   I know John is away

I implicate that it is possible, for all I know, that John is in fact not away. Or if I say,

(129)   The Russians or the Americans have just landed on Mars

it is entailed that one or the other party has landed on Mars, but I implicate that it is possible that it is the Russians, and it is possible that it is not the Russians, for all I know. This is because I have chosen to utter (129) in preference, for example, to (130), the saying of which would commit me (*inter alia*) to the Russians landing:

(130)   The Russians and the Americans have landed on Mars

Thus the uttering of a disjunction implicates that one does not know which disjunct is true, because the choice of a disjunction has the consequence that neither of the embedded sentences is entailed (or presupposed) by the whole. Since one could have chosen a stronger expression that did entail one or both of the disjuncts, one can be taken not to be in a position to utter the stronger expression. Hence a statement of the form p *or* q generates the set of implicatures: $\{Pp,$ $P \sim p, Pq, P \sim q\}$ i.e. it is epistemically possible that p, also that not p, also that q, also that not q.

A sentence of the form p *or* q has these implicatures by reference to the availability of other sentences like p *and* q or simply p or q which are stronger or more informative because they do entail p or q or both. Similar pairs of 'stronger' and 'weaker' constructions are illustrated in (131):

(131)	(a) *stronger form*	(b) *weaker form*	(c) *implicatures of (b)*
	'p and q'	'p or q'	$\{Pp, P \sim p, Pq, P \sim q\}$
	'since p, q'	'if p then q'	$\{Pp, P \sim p, Pq, P \sim q\}$
	'a knows p'	'a believes p'	$\{Pp, P \sim p\}$
	'a realized p'	'a thought p'	$\{Pp, P \sim p\}$
	'a revealed p'	'a said p'	$\{Pp, P \sim p\}$
	'necessarily p'	'possibly p'	$\{Pp, P \sim p\}$

Note that items that occurred in the list of scales in (121) with the appropriate scalar implicatures could reappear here with additional and slightly different clausal implicatures. For example, the utterance of *possibly* p carries the scalar implicature 'not necessarily p'; but since *possibly* p in contrast to *necessarily* p does not entail p, there will also be a clausal implicature from the utterance of *possibly* p to the effect that the speaker does not know whether p is or is not the case (i.e. the set of implicatures $\{Pp, P \sim p\}$ will arise). Or again, utterances of the form p *or* q will have the scalar implicature $K \sim (p \& q)$ and the clausal implicatures $\{Pp, P \sim p, Pq, P \sim q\}$. So under rules (121) and (126) even the more simple complex sentences may give rise to multiple Quantity implicatures.

We are now in a position to show how the recognition of such generalized Quantity implicatures can help us to simplify semantics. At the beginning of the Chapter we outlined a pervasive problem in semantics: a large number of words seem to behave as if they either had a single sense that is protean (i.e. may change from context to context), or alternatively had a very large number of distinct but closely related senses. Neither conclusion is very palatable. Implicature offers a more attractive solution: words may often have one single central sense which is augmentable in a context-sensitive and thus defeasible way by systematic implicatures of various sorts.

For example, faced with the English words *hot* and *warm*, the semanticist might be tempted to claim that each covers a distinct and different (if approximate) span on some range of heat. It follows that it ought to be contradictory to say:

(132)   This soup is warm, in fact hot

just as it would be to say

(133)   *This book is short, in fact long

But of course it isn't. The semanticist might then either claim that the meanings of natural language terms like *warm* are simply too vague or loose to engender contradictions, or he might suggest that *warm* is in fact ambiguous between a 'neither cold nor hot' sense (clearly not possible in (132)), and a 'not cold' or 'at least warm' sense (the reading relevant for (132)). But the theorist who utilizes implicature has another kind of response: the scale of heat is not divided into discrete, labelled spans, but rather organized so that what is hot is a special sub-case of what is warm; thus a sentence of the form *X is hot* entails 'X is warm'. Consequently the terms form a scale ⟨hot, warm⟩, as in (121), and this predicts that to say *X is warm* conversationally implicates 'X is not hot'. But the implicature, like all implicatures, is defeasible and thus is cancelled by the assertion in (132) that X is in fact hot. Such an account can become a general claim about the meaning of items in linguistic scales: in general such items (when embedded in statements) *entail* their lower bounds (*warm* in a sentence will entail 'at least warm') but merely *implicate* their upper bounds (*warm* implicates 'not hot').

The recognition of such scalar implicatures not only aids the understanding of the semantics of the general vocabulary in a language, but it also plays a crucial role in understanding the 'logical' expressions in natural language, specifically the connectives, the quantifiers and the modals. The correct analysis of such terms is of course crucial to any semantic theory, but especially to those based on logical principles. Nevertheless understanding in this area was seriously hampered until the development of a theory of implicature.

For example, it has long been noted that in many natural languages, disjunction appears to be ambiguous between an **exclusive** reading as in (134) where it seems to be asserted that only one disjunct is true, and an **inclusive** reading as in (135) where both disjuncts can be true:

(134)   Mirabelle's in the kitchen or the bedroom
(135)   The book is red or crimson

Thus the two hypothetical senses would be: one and only one of the disjuncts is true (exclusive, symbolically $\vee$); one or both of the disjuncts are true (inclusive, symbolically $\vee$). On this account the addition of *or both* in (136) would serve to 'disambiguate' the sentence:

(136)   Ronald is a movie star or a politician, or both

However Gazdar (1979a: 82) argues that the ambiguity theory cannot be correct. For by standard logical equivalences the following correspondences can be established:

(137) $\sim (p \vee q) \leftrightarrow (\sim p) \,\&\, (\sim q)$
(138) $\sim (p \veebar q) \leftrightarrow ((\sim p) \,\&\, (\sim q)) \vee (p \,\&\, q)$

Now given (138) we would predict that there ought to be a reading of (139) as (140):

(139)   Ronald isn't a movie star or a politician
(140)   Either Ronald's not a movie star and he's not a politician, or he's both

But there does not seem to be such a reading, where what is asserted is that either both conjuncts are false or both are true.[25] So the ambiguity view seems to provide the wrong predictions.

But there's an alternative to the ambiguity claim, namely an implicatural account. For the scalar mechanism in (121) straightforwardly predicts that *p or q* will standardly get interpreted as '*p* $\veebar$ *q*' (i.e. exclusively) as follows. There is a scale ⟨*and, or*⟩ where the sense of *and* may be equated with logical & and the sense of *or* with logical $\vee$ (i.e. inclusive disjunction). Hence to say *p or q* will implicate that the stronger item on the scale does not hold, i.e. $\sim (p \,\&\, q)$. But if we then conjoin the sense of *p or q* with the scalar implicature we

---

[25] Although with heavy stress on *or* it is possible to interpret (139) as conveying just the second disjunct of (140), as shown by the possibility of saying: *Ronald isn't a movie star OR a politician, he's BOTH*. This might seem to argue that *or* cannot be equated with logical $\vee$, because $\sim (p \vee q) \,\&\, (p \,\&\, q)$ is a contradiction. However, this special interaction between stress and negation is quite general – thus one can say *Harry doesn't LIKE Martha, he LOVES her*, although not liking someone entails not loving them. The principle here seems to be that given a scale ⟨e_1, e_2⟩, if one asserts $\sim A(e_2)$ with heavy stress on e_2, one can mean $A(e_1)$. It could be claimed that e_2 is here not *used* but rather *mentioned*. For further remarks, see Grice, 1978 and Horn, 1978.

obtain the exclusive reading: $(p \vee q) \& \sim (p \& q) \leftrightarrow p \vee q$. The sense of *or* in English, and perhaps in natural language generally, can thus be considered *univocal*, and *inclusive*, the exclusive interpretation being due to a generalized type of implicature (see Gazdar, 1979a: 78–83).

The modals provide another crucial logical domain where implicature provides essential insights. Over many centuries of logical thought, as Horn (1973) has nicely documented, there has been considerable confusion about the proper interpretation of the relation between the sentential operators *necessary* and *possible* and the related modals *must* and *may*, etc. The problems arise in this way. Consider (141); this seems to imply (142):

(141)   The gorilla may in fact be a member of the genus *homo*
(142)   The gorilla may not in fact be a member of the genus *homo*

We might thus be led, as Aristotle was on occasion, to take the following as a basic axiom (where $\Box$ = necessarily, $\Diamond$ = possibly):

(143) $\Diamond p \rightarrow \Diamond \sim p$
         i.e. if p is possible, then it is possible that not p

But we will also want to allow that whatever is necessary must also be possible, and thus we will also adopt the axiom in (144):

(144) $\Box p \rightarrow \Diamond p$
         i.e. if p is necessary, then it is possible

And as a matter of definition:

(145) $\Box p \rightarrow \sim \Diamond \sim p$
         i.e. if p is necessary, then it is not
         possible that not p

But putting these three axioms together we arrive immediately at the absurdity that, if p is necessary, then it is not necessary:

(146)   (i) $\Box p \rightarrow \Diamond p$ (by (144))
         (ii) $\Diamond p \rightarrow \Diamond \sim p$ (by (143))
         (iii) $\Diamond \sim p \rightarrow \sim \Box p$ (by contraposition from (145) with suppression of double negations)
         (iv) therefore, $\Box p \rightarrow \sim \Box p$

Clearly we cannot hold onto both axioms, and logicians have mostly had the good sense to reject (143). But what leads us to think that (143) might be a valid inference? The answer is a scalar implicature: $\Box$ and $\Diamond$ form a scale $\langle \Box, \Diamond \rangle$, so to assert the weaker element,

$\Diamond p$, will be to implicate that (the speaker knows that) the stronger does not hold, i.e. $\sim \Box p$ (or, strictly, K $\sim \Box p$). But, by logical equivalence, if p is not necessary, then it is possibly not the case, i.e. $\sim \Box p \rightarrow \Diamond \sim p$. So (143) is a legitimate inference in natural language, if it is viewed as an implicature rather than a logical inference. Let us rephrase it therefore as:

(147)   an utterance of the form $\Diamond p$ conversationally implicates $\sim \Box p$, and thus by logical equivalence, $\Diamond \sim p$

A considerable amount of confusion in early attempts to formalize modal logic might have been avoided if the distinction between logical consequence and conversational inference had been available (see Horn, 1973).

Turning now to clausal implicatures, note that *p or q* has the following implicatures:

(148)   *Implicatures of 'p or q'*
scalar: K $\sim (p \& q)$
clausal: $\{Pp, P \sim p, Pq, P \sim q\}$

The clausal implicature explains the intuition that it would be extremely misleading to utter (149) if one knew that Claude was in the dining room:

(149)   Claude's either in the dining room or in the study

for by (148) the utterance of (149) has the clausal implicature that for all the speaker knows he may be in either room. Thus if one knows that p, one does not co-operatively convey that by stating *p or q*; the use of the disjunction rather conveys that one has grounds for believing one or the other disjunct but does not know which. By accounting for the fact that the utterance of a disjunction thus effectively conveys much more than its logical sense, the theory of implicature once again makes it possible to retain the simple logical analysis of *or* as inclusive disjunction while accounting for the divergence from that analysis in actual use.

Similar remarks can be made about conditionals. Whatever the correct *semantic* analysis of conditionals is (and there is now good reason to think that natural language *if ... then* cannot be equated with logical $\rightarrow$, the material conditional – see Gazdar, 1979a: 83–7), a number of particularly troublesome features can be accounted for by means of implicature. By our rule (126) we can predict (150):

(150)   *Clausal implicatures of 'if p then q'*
          $\{Pp, P \sim p, Pq, P \sim q\}$

Therefore to say (151) is to implicate that one does not have any reason to think that Chuck has actually already got a scholarship or to think that he will definitely give up medicine:

(151)   If Chuck has got a scholarship, he'll give up medicine

Some have thought that the hypothetical implications associated with the use of *if ... then* should be built into the meaning of the conditional. But the problem is that such implications – like all the others we have discussed in this section – are defeasible. Thus if we embed (151) in the discourse context indicated in (152), the clausal implicatures evaporate:

(152)   A: I've just heard that Chuck has got a scholarship
          B: Oh dear. If Chuck has got a scholarship, he'll give up
             medicine

Hence consistently associated but nevertheless defeasible aspects of the meaning of the conditional can be explained by implicature. If such hypothetical implications were built into the semantics of the conditional, the usage in (152) would force us into yet another ambiguity claim.

The existence of a number of different kinds of Quantity implicature, including scalar and clausal, gives rise to a **projection problem** for implicatures, i.e. the implicatures of complex expressions may not be equivalent to the simple sum of the implicatures of all the parts. Consider, for example, the fact, discussed in 3.1, that implicatures can be suspended by explicit mention in *if*-clauses, as in:

(153)   Some, if not all, of the workers went on strike

Here there should be a scalar implicature (154) due to *some* (by rule (121) above):

(154) $K \sim$ (all the workers went on strike)
          i.e. S knows that not all the workers went on strike

But there should also be the clausal implicature (155) due to the phrase *if not all* (see the prediction in (150)):

(155)   P(all the workers went on strike)
          i.e. it is possible, for all S knows, that all of the workers went
          on strike

Now the two implicatures (154) and (155) are inconsistent, and it seems intuitively clear that the clausal implicature (155) effectively *cancels* the scalar implicature (154). On the basis of such observations, Gazdar (1979a) sets up a projection (or cancellation) mechanism designed to model implicature cancellation, as follows.[26] Let the communicative content of an utterance U be assessed by adding the distinct semantic and pragmatic inferences of U sequentially to the context C, where C is understood to be the set of beliefs that the speaker is committed to at the point when U is uttered. On the utterance of U, first the *entailments* (or semantic content) of U are added to the context (here we might add: only if they are themselves consistent with all the propositions in C; otherwise participants will analyse U as a Quality flout and expect an appropriate implicature). Next, all the *clausal* implicatures are added that are *consistent* with the content of C (now augmented with the entailments of U), inconsistent clausal implicatures simply being rejected and not added to the set of propositions in context C. Only now can *scalar* implicatures be added, just in case they in turn are consistent with the context as already incremented by the entailments and clausal implicatures of U. This mechanism will correctly predict that the scalar implicature (154), being assessed after the clausal implicature (155) has been added to the context C, will be rejected as inconsistent with what has already been accepted. Thus on Gazdar's account *defeasibility* is captured by making implicatures acceptable only if they are consistent with entailments and other implicatures that have priority. Note that this mechanism also explains why implicatures may be overtly denied as in (156):

(156)   Some of my best friends are drug-addicts, in fact probably all

for the entailments of the second clause, being added to the context first, will cancel the implicature due to *some*.

Gazdar's mechanism appears to be perfectly general and to operate on sentences of arbitrary complexity. For example consider (157):

---

[26] Gazdar's model is a model of what individual speakers are committed to, and the way in which this cancels implicatures. It does not capture interactive aspects of what may be mutually taken for granted as conversation proceeds. It also makes the wrong predictions with respect to tropes or exploitations of the maxims, where implicatures often cancel entailments. But it seems to operate well within the limited, but important, domain of generalized conversational implicatures.

(157)   Some of the Elgin Marbles are fakes, and either the rest of them are too, or they're inferior originals

(158)   (i)   K $\sim$ (all of the Elgin Marbles are fakes)

           (ii) P(the rest of the Elgin Marbles are fakes too)

           (iii) P $\sim$ (the rest of the Elgin Marbles are fakes too)

           (iv) P(the rest of the Elgin Marbles are inferior originals)

           (v) P $\sim$ (the rest of the Elgin Marbles are inferior originals)

Here (i) is a scalar implicature due to *some*, and the rest of the implicatures are clausal ones due to the disjunction in the second conjunct of (157). Note that implicatures (i) and (ii) are inconsistent, so the scalar implicature (i) will be cancelled, and the sentence as a whole will have just the implicatures (ii)–(v).

We also now have some account of the problem raised by Sadock (1978: 291) and discussed above in connection with example (75). Implicatures are said to be *non-detachable* and therefore not defeasible simply by substituting a synonymous expression for the expression that gives rise to them. But consider that the meaning of rightmost scalar items like *some* is consistent with leftmost items like *all* in such scales. It follows that *some* has the semantic content paraphrasable as 'at least some' or 'some if not all'. Therefore (159) and (160) should be synonymous, and *ergo* by the principle of non-detachability they should share the same implicatures. But they don't. However, we now have a perfectly general mechanism that explains this: by introducing the additional clause in (160) we have introduced an additional clausal implicature which cancels the scalar implicature due to *some*. Similarly, if we take (161) to be the paraphrase of the semantic content of (159), we introduce an additional clause, and in this case an additional entailment which cancels the scalar implicature due to *some*:

(159)   Some academics are lazy

(160)   Some if not all academics are lazy

(161)   Some and perhaps all academics are lazy

So we simply need to refine our understanding of non-detachability: implicatures will be preserved by the substitution of synonymous expressions provided that the substitutes carry no additional implicatures or entailments inconsistent with the original expressions (and which happen to have priority in the incremental mechanism outlined).

The analyses sketched here provide some substantial insights into the interaction between the *sense* and the *use* of some crucial expressions in natural language. Such insights, we hope to have shown, promise to simplify semantics in two basic ways:

(a) In the area of general vocabulary an implicatural analysis can help to avoid the proliferation of hypothetical senses promoted by apparent ambiguities, together with the attendant inconsistencies and difficulties posed by the selective defeasibility of aspects of meaning (see McCawley, 1978).

(b) In the crucial area of logical vocabulary, implicature can allow the semanticist to maintain relatively simple logical analyses supplemented by implicature, whereas in the absence of such an analysis the linguistic relevance of the entire body of logical machinery built up over two millennia of thought about linguistic and philosophical problems would be seriously in doubt.

A hybrid theory of meaning in which both semantics and pragmatics play a part therefore has the cardinal attraction of shifting some of the most problematic aspects of meaning out of the domain of semantics proper into a different component where the difficult properties of defeasibility and context-sensitivity can be systematically handled.

It would be misleading, though, to give the impression that all the problems are solved, even in this quite limited area of two specific kinds of Quantity implicature. It is quite unlikely, for example, that the projection mechanism for Quantity implicatures is as simple as Gazdar's rule that clausal implicatures take precedence over scalar ones – and it should be noted that we do not have any *explanation* for this observable regularity. There are other kinds of Quantity implicature, and other kinds of pragmatic inference that are sometimes in conflict with clausal and scalar implicatures. Some of these latter, whose origin is not understood, actually take precedence over our two kinds of Quantity implicature. Consider, for example:

(162)   If you give me a bite of your ice-cream, you can have a bite of mine

which clearly seems to 'invite' the inference (163) (see Geiss & Zwicky, 1971):

(163)   If and only if you give me a bite of your ice-cream, can you have a bite of mine

There is thus a clear inference from *q if p* to '*q* if and only if *p*'. However, these connectives form a scale, namely ⟨*if and only if, if*⟩, where the stronger biconditional implies the simple conditional. Therefore by principle (121) above there ought to be a scalar implicature from (162) to the effect that *not* (163). But the implicature works in precisely the reverse direction: *q if p* invites the inference '*q* if and only if *p*'. So we have here an inference that is working in the opposite direction from ordinary Quantity inferences: normally by Quantity if I say a weaker statement where a stronger one would have been relevant, I implicate that I am not in a position to make the stronger one. Here on the other hand by making the weaker statement (162) I implicate the stronger one (163).

In fact the phenomenon is widespread. Consider the normal interpretations of:

(164)   He turned on the switch and the motor started

We read this in a way that is as 'strong' (informationally rich) as the world allows – and thus read in the following relations between two conjoined clauses wherever possible:

(165)   Given *p and q*, try interpreting it as:
         (i)   '*p* and then *q*'; if successful try:
         (ii) '*p* and therefore *q*'; if successful try also:
         (iii) '*p*, and *p* is the cause of *q*'

We have already given an account of the inference in (i) by appeal to the maxim of Manner; but this will not help us with the inference in (iii) to a causal connection between the two events (of course we could invent *ad hoc* new maxims – see e.g. Harnish, 1976 – but this would soon water down the notion of implicature).

The problem here is that by the maxim of Quantity the inference from (164) to (165)(iii) should be specifically banned. For if I had meant the informationally richer (165)(iii) I should have said so; having not said so, I implicate that as far as I know (165)(iii) does not obtain. But that of course is the wrong prediction. There therefore seems to be an independent principle or maxim, which we may call the **principle of informativeness**, that in just some circumstances allows us to read into an utterance *more* information than it actually contains – in contrast to Quantity, which only allows the additional inference that (as far as the speaker knows) no stronger statement could be made. The problem that now besets the analyst is to provide a principled account of how in just some cases this additional principle ('read as much into an utterance as is consistent with what you know about the world') takes precedence over the maxim of Quantity, while in other circumstances (e.g. most of the examples in this Chapter) the reverse precedence holds (see here Atlas & Levinson, 1981). Thus note that in (166) Quantity prevails, licensing only the inference to (167); but in (168) the additional principle appears to license the inference (169) against Quantity's strict limitation of what one can mean by saying something:

(166)   Gilbert wrote *The Mikado*
(167)   Gilbert and he alone wrote *The Mikado*
(168)   Gilbert and Sullivan wrote *The Mikado*
(169)   Gilbert and Sullivan jointly wrote *The Mikado* (rather than independently inventing the same work)

(see Harnish, 1976 and Atlas & Levinson, 1981 for discussion of these and related examples). In addition, then, to the important insights the theory of implicature has provided, substantial problems remain concerning how different kinds of implicature and pragmatic inferences interact. Nevertheless enough progress has been made to show that the various attacks that have been made on the theory of implicature, usually on the grounds that the concepts involved are too vacuous to be formalizable or testable (see e.g. Cohen, 1971; Kroch, 1972), are quite ill-founded.

3.2.5   *Metaphor: a case of maxim exploitation*
We turn now to the other major kind of implicatures suggested by Grice, those arising from the exploitation or flouting of the maxims; and we shall consider here to what extent the theory of implicature actually contributes to the study of metaphor. The subject of metaphor, and its relations to other classical tropes or figures of speech, has of course been the focus of much thought since at least Aristotle's *Rhetoric*. Fundamental issues about the nature of language, and indeed the nature of thought, are raised by the subject: metaphor is not only central to poetry, and indeed to a very large proportion of ordinary language usage, but also to realms as diverse as the interpretation of dreams and the nature of models in scientific thought (see e.g. the collection in Ortony, 1979a for the wide scope of the issues raised). Here, however, we can only try to establish the need for a pragmatic approach to metaphor, and sketch the directions in which such a pragmatic account might contribute to the study of metaphor.

Any discussion of metaphor, or the tropes in general, is plagued by divergent classifications and terminologies (see e.g. Levin, 1977: 8off). For example, is the following a metonym, a synecdoche or a metaphor? Different classificatory schemes yield different answers.

(170)   Britain rules the waves

Here we shall simply take a very broad view of what metaphor is, accepting examples like the following as paradigm cases:

(171)   The tree wept in the wind
(172)   Iago is an eel
(173)   These stones have drunk a thousand years

It should be pointed out immediately that there is a long and respectable tradition that views metaphor as a central *semantic* process and not a problem in pragmatics at all. Indeed the two traditional theories (or classes of theory) whose central tenets are laid out in (174) and (175) are both usually construed as *semantic* theories of metaphor:

(174)   *The comparison theory*:
          Metaphors are similes with suppressed or deleted predications of similarity. Thus (172) is semantically equivalent to *Iago is like an eel*
(175)   *The interaction theory*:
          Metaphors are special uses of linguistic expressions where one 'metaphorical' expression (or *focus*) is embedded in another 'literal' expression (or *frame*), such that the meaning of the focus interacts with and *changes* the meaning of the *frame*, and vice versa

To establish the need for a pragmatic approach to metaphor, we shall need to show, at some length, how such semantic approaches fail to yield adequate accounts of the phenomena. To see how such semantic theories of metaphor can be given some plausibility, let us take a particular instantiation of each and examine its achievements and shortcomings. One particular version of the *interaction* theory can be formalized (or at least given some precision) using the framework of *semantic features* as utilized by, for example, Katz & Fodor (1963) or componential analysts (see Lyons, 1968: 407ff). On such a semantic theory, the meanings of lexical items are specified by a set of features, each of which is an atomic concept or irreducible semantic prime drawn from a larger but restricted set, the members of the latter being in principle sufficient to jointly define all the complex senses of actually occurring lexical items. Thus the noun *stone* might have the following set of semantic features associated with it, which jointly define its sense:

(176)   *physical object*
          natural
          non-living
          mineral
          concreted

and the verb *die* might be represented as a set of features related in particular ways, as indicated:

(177)   *process* with *result*, namely, that some *living entity x ceases to be living*

Now consider the interpretation of:

(178)   The stone died

(this argument is drawn directly from Levin, 1977: Chapter III; see also Cohen, 1979). It is clear that the sentence is not straightforwardly interpretable because the reading for *stone* in (176) has the feature *non-living*, while the reading for *die* in (177) requires that its subject be living. In such cases, the argument goes, an additional set of 'construal rules' are brought into play in order to interpret the sentence. Essentially what such rules will do is map features from one lexical item on to another: the additional features may be conjoined or disjoined from the existing ones, or they may replace them. Applying such rules to (178) we obtain (*inter alia*) the reading

(179)   The stone ceased to be

where the feature *non-living* is added disjunctively to the verb's specification for a living subject and the specification *living* simply dropped from *cease to be living*, to yield *cease to be*. In short, the verb's meaning has changed to become neutral to living and non-living subjects. Or alternatively, the reading:

(180)   The living natural mineral concreted thing died

can be obtained, by replacing the feature *non-living* in the specification for *stone* with the feature *living* transferred from the verb, so that *stone* might here refer to some rather solid human individual. Such analyses can be 'formalized' in feature frameworks (as has been done by Weinreich, 1966; Van Dijk, 1972; Levin, 1977; etc.).

149

The main attraction of such theories is that they attempt to bring within the fold of standard semantics interpretive processes like metaphor which are not always clearly distinct from ordinary processes of language understanding. Consider the range of examples in (181) below: where does literal interpretation cease and metaphorical interpretation take over?

(181)   John came hurriedly down the stairs
          John ran down the stairs
          John rushed down the stairs
          John hustled down the stairs
          John shot down the stairs
          John whistled down the stairs

Some have claimed in fact (see e.g. Wilks, 1975; Carling & Moore, 1982) that natural language semantics has an inbuilt 'elasticity' that allows such interaction between the senses of words to take place in standard processes of semantic interpretation, and not just in metaphors.

However, there are numerous problems for any such account of metaphor, of which a few will suffice here. First, it seems fairly clear that the supposed readings of metaphors thus provided are not good paraphrases: the feature-mapping process is both too limited and too determinate to capture the metaphorical force of the expressions. Secondly, and relatedly, many aspects of that force have more to do with the *contingent*, factual (real-world) attributes of the referents of the metaphorical *focus* than with the semantic features that can be claimed to express its meaning. For example, if I say (172) I may effectively convey that Iago is slimy, eats offal (and thus perhaps, metaphorically at second remove, stoops to dirty deeds), and has the ability to wriggle off hooks (and thus out of difficult situations). But none of these associations is a *semantic* feature by any reasonable stretch of theory or imagination: an unslimy, non-offal-eating, non-wriggling eel would still be an eel. An important part of the force of any metaphor thus seems to involve what might be called the 'connotational penumbra' of the expressions involved, the *incidental* rather than the defining characteristics of words, and knowledge of the factual properties of referents and hence knowledge of the world in general. All of these matters are beyond the scope of a semantic theory, as generally understood within linguistics (although some semantic metaphor theorists find themselves pushed by these arguments to deny any distinction between semantics and the totality of knowledge in a speech community – see e.g. Cohen, 1979).

A final and crucial argument against the feature-transfer variety of semantic theories of metaphor is that there are metaphors, intuitively part and parcel of the same phenomenon, which do not involve the initial semantic anomaly within the sentence required to trigger the 'construal rules' (rules for feature-transfer). Suppose, for example, playing chess, I say to my opponent:

(182)   Your defence is an impregnable castle

This may be understood in a number of ways: literally, providing the defence in question is constituted by a rook; or metaphorically if the defensive position is in general impregnable; or, interestingly, both at once. But in no case is there any semantic anomaly in (182) itself. Indeed metaphors are closely linked to parables and proverbs – if I say (183) I generally mean it to apply metaphorically to the situation in hand:

(183)   A stitch in time saves nine

Whatever explains the understanding of these sorts of utterances is likely to explain metaphor, and it will not be a semantic theory however construed.

We turn now to the so-called *comparison* theory of metaphor. The essential claim is that metaphors are derived from explicit similes. Thus one could hold that (184) is equivalent to (185), and that therefore there is no outstanding problem of metaphor at all beyond the problems of the semantics of similes.

(184)   Universities are compost heaps
(185)   Universities are like compost heaps

One should note that there are various possible *linguistic* positions here: one could maintain that (184) shares the underlying *syntactic* structure of (185), or alternatively, whatever the underlying structure of (184), that (184) shares the *semantic* interpretation of (185). In any case, by relating (184) and (185) the claim can be made that the problem of understanding metaphors is not really distinct from the problem of understanding some specific kinds of 'literal' uses of language, namely those in similes.

A relatively sophisticated version of this position is held by Miller (1979) (although he eschews any specific *syntactic* or *semantic* claims and presents a version of comparison theory as a *psychological* theory of how metaphors are comprehended). The claim is that in order to comprehend metaphors they must be converted into a complex simile-like form – complex because there are always a number of extra implicit predicates or variables which have to be reconstructed by the listener. Rules are proposed that will convert metaphors into their complex simile-like form for understanding. The rules rely on a tripartite classification of metaphors. First, we have **nominal metaphors** : metaphors like (172) (*Iago is an eel*) have the form BE(x, y); to understand them the recipient must construct a corresponding simile in line with the following rule (where $+\rangle$ should be understood as 'is interpreted as'):

(186)   BE(x, y) $+\rangle$ ∃F ∃G (SIMILAR(F(x), G(y)))
         i.e. metaphors of the *x is a y* kind are interpreted as: 'There are two properties F and G such that x having property F is like y having property G'[27]

The claim then is that a metaphor of the *x is y* variety is not actually a comparison between two *objects* x and y but between two *propositions* (x being F, y being G). The job for the listener is to infer what these two similar properties are: thus (172) might be decoded as 'Iago's ability to get out of difficult situations is like an eel's ability to wriggle off hooks'.

The second kind of metaphors are **predicative metaphors** : metaphors like (187) have the conceptual form G(x) or G(x, y):

(187)   Mrs Gandhi steamed ahead

To understand them the recipient must construct a corresponding complex simile in accordance with the following rule:

---

[27] The relation BE is presumably predicative rather than an identity relation. It is not clear that identity statements can be used alone to construct metaphors – it is more natural to say *The professor is a Stalin* (where the indefinite article makes it clear *is a Stalin* is a predicate) than *The professor is Stalin*. On the other hand, if the professor's department has already been likened to Russia in the 1940s, and the correspondence is now being spelt out, the latter seems quite natural: cf. *The department is like Russia in the 1940s, and the professor is Stalin.* Incidentally, although we follow Miller's notation, one should note that F and G are here predicate *variables*, not predicate *constants*, in a second-order predicate logic and should properly be distinguished, e.g. by Greek capital letters (see Allwood, Andersson & Dahl, 1977: 148ff).

(188) $G(x) +\rangle \exists F \exists y$ (SIMILAR $(F(x), (G(y)))$
i.e. metaphors of the x Gs kind (i.e. with metaphorical predicates)
are interpreted as: 'There is a property F and an entity y such
that x Fing is like y Ging'

The interpreter here has to reconstruct another predicate and another
entity so that once again two propositions may be found to be
compared. Thus for (187) the rule will produce a simile like (189) and
thus more specifically something like (190):

(189)   Mrs Gandhi is doing something which is like something
steaming ahead
(190)   Mrs Gandhi's progress in the elections is like a ship steaming
ahead

The third kind of metaphors are **sentential metaphors**: some
metaphors, like B's remark in (191), are not categorically false (in the
way in which Iago cannot really be an eel, or Mrs Gandhi cannot
really steam ahead); rather they are identified by being *irrelevant* to
the surrounding discourse when literally construed:

(191)   A: What kind of mood did you find the boss in?
B: The lion roared

Here a sentence of the conceptual form $G(y)$ is interpreted utilizing
the following rule:

(192) $G(y) +\rangle \exists F \exists x$ (SIMILAR $(F(x), G(y)))$
i.e. given an irrelevant proposition y Gs interpret it as: 'There
is another property F and another entity x such that the
proposition 'x Fs' is similar to 'y Gs' (and 'x Fs' *is* relevant
to the discourse)'

Thus for (191)B we have the interpretation (193), and thus more
specifically in the context, (194):

(193)   The lion's roaring is like something doing something
(194)   The lion's roaring is like the boss displaying anger

On this general scheme there are thus three rules for converting
metaphors into simile form: (186), (188) and (192). The central
problem then becomes how each of the *unknowns* in each formula is
given a value: for example, how does the interpreter move from the
vacuous (189) to the specific (190), and similarly from (193) to (194)?
Miller has little to offer here, although he notes that a partial solution
can be given for metaphors like (187): given a predicate like *steam*

ahead applied metaphorically, one reconstructs the missing argument by going to the most general type of argument the predicate can take (and thus to *ship* rather than, say, *Mississippi paddle steamer*). That still leaves a missing predicate unresolved, and the other kinds of metaphor entirely unexplained. But obtaining a specific interpretation for a metaphor *is* the heart of the problem, so most of the mysteries still remain.

However Miller's theory is not, in the version he puts forward, a *semantic* theory of metaphor, which is what we are here concerned with. It might though form the basis of one. Suppose now (in contrast to Miller) we take the strong line that the comparison theory is a syntactico-semantic theory of metaphor: we would then identify (185) as the underlying syntactic structure of (184), deriving the latter from the former by the elliptical deletion of *like*. We would then claim that the normal semantic processes involved in the interpretation of (185) are involved directly in the interpretation of (184).

An initial problem for this position is that not every metaphor can be simply derived from a simile by deletion of the predicate of similarity (*is like, is similar to*, etc.). For example:

(195)   The government is going the wrong way down a one-way street

Here to derive the related simile we need to reconstruct much more than a deleted *like* or *as if* (no well-formed sentence results from the insertion of such items) – namely we need a structure like the output of Miller's rule (188), which specifies an additional implicit predicate and implicit argument of the sort indicated by italicization below:

(196)   The government is *pursuing policies* like *a car* going the wrong way down a one-way street

Since it seems unlikely that any motivated syntactic machinery could ever derive (195) from (196), let us retreat to a weaker position: whatever the syntactic relation between the pairs (184) and (185), or (195) and (196), the first sentence in each pair has the *semantic representation* made most explicit in the second. The claim is therefore that the members of such pairs share semantic representations. The question now is whether such a view is tenable, and if so whether it is at all enlightening.

The crucial issue here is how we are to interpret *like* or the underlying concept SIMILAR in, for example, (188). Now many authors are agreed that there is a contrast between *comparisons* and *similes.* Thus (197) is a comparison, (198) a simile (from Ortony, 1979b: 191):

(197)   Encylopaedias are like dictionaries
(198)   Encyclopaedias are like gold mines

The first is true, the second, arguably, is literally false; the first admits of empirical verification, the second, arguably, does not (at least when read as a simile); the first draws attention to certain key attributes shared by both kinds of volumes (e.g. they are both reference books, and both alphabetically organized), the second to less salient and very abstract shared attributes (e.g. value, labyrinthine nature, etc.). In short, the similarity in (197) is a literal one, the similarity in (198) is *figurative*. And of course it is not to comparisons like (197) that metaphor is closely related, but to similes like (198). Thus we see immediately that if we relate (198) to the metaphor (199), we are no more clear about how (198) is actually interpreted than we are about how metaphors like (199) are understood.

(199)   Encyclopaedias are gold mines

To interpret both (198) and (199) we seem to have to infer some analogy of the sort:

(200)   *knowledge* : *value* : encyclopaedias :: *gold* : *value* : gold mines

where the italicized terms are implicit. And even then we have only pushed the problem back a step, for how we understand that analogy is still mysterious. We therefore appear to have gained little or nothing by considering that the semantic representation of metaphors should be identical to the representations of the corresponding similes.

Even if there were some advantage in the claim, it is far from clear that it is actually tenable. Searle (1979a), for example, produces a number of difficulties for the view. First, take Miller's rules (186), (188) and (192): these assert the existence of the objects or relations mentioned or implicit, but there is in fact no such requirement on successful metaphor, as (201) illustrates:

(201)   The President is a Martian

Secondly, there are some metaphors that do not seem to be based on similarity: Searle instances (202) and notes that when it is converted to simile form as in (203) the metaphor is still quite unreduced, residing now in the term *coldness*.

(202)   Sally is a block of ice
(203)   Sally has an emotional makeup similar to the coldness of a block of ice

There is, concludes Searle, simply *no* relation of similarity between Sally and a block of ice, or indeed unemotional natures and coldness (literally construed). Thirdly, it is not clear that the simile counterparts of metaphors produce paraphrases that are intuitively correct at all – compare, for example, the following:

(204)   The interviewer hammered the senator
(205)   What the interviewer did to the senator was like someone hammering a nail

There are enough difficulties then with any view that claims that metaphors are syntactically or semantically (or both) implicit similes to make that theoretical path quite unattractive.

We have found substantial problems for both of the two main semantic approaches to metaphor, and it is reasonable to see what a pragmatic approach to metaphor has to offer in contrast. A pragmatic approach will be based on the assumption that the metaphorical content of utterances will not be derived by principles of semantic interpretation; rather the semantics will just provide a characterization of the literal meaning or conventional content of the expressions involved, and from this, together with details of the context, the pragmatics will have to provide the metaphorical interpretation. There have been many objections to a move of this sort on the grounds that a line is drawn between 'literal' and 'figurative' usages of linguistic expressions, and that consequently poetry and other highly valued uses of language find themselves treated as somehow bizarre or different from the rest of language usage. The objections are misplaced: all that is being suggested is that the full meaning of most of the sentences we utter is best captured by a technical division of labour between a semantic component and a pragmatic one. To claim that metaphor is in part pragmatic in nature is not to denigrate or isolate it, but merely to place it firmly among the other more straightforward usages of language that we have described throughout this book.

As an initial step we may revert to Grice's suggestion, noted in 3.1, that metaphors are exploitations or floutings of the maxim of Quality. However we have already come far enough to see that this is not always true – Miller's sentential metaphors are not necessarily false, and are not categorial falsehoods like (184) and the other sorts of examples Grice had in mind. Thus (182) could be true and metaphorical at the same time, as we indicated, and similarly (206) could be both literally true and metaphorical, if said of a place where it was both the case that Freud lived there and also the case that his theories were kept alive there after his death:

(206)   Freud lived here

So we shall have to say rather that metaphors taken literally either violate the maxim of Quality or are conversationally inadequate in other ways, especially with reference to the maxim of Relevance (cf. (191) above; and see Sperber & Wilson, forthcoming).

A second problem with Grice's suggestion that then immediately emerges is that such a characterization of itself offers little insight into the nature of metaphor. All it does is offer us a partial criterion for the recognition of metaphor – only partial because all the other kinds of implicature due to maxim exploitation (e.g. rhetorical questions, understatements, etc.) share the same property of being generated by an overt flouting of a conversational maxim – and how we get from the *recognition* to the *interpretation* remains entirely unclear.

Indeed it may be helpful to reformulate Grice's general account of how an implicature is worked out, in terms of a two stage process (where speaker S says p to addressee H and thereby implicates q):

(207)   *Stage 1 : locating a trigger*
          i.e. identifying the need for inference. There are two kinds of triggers:
          (a) In saying that p S has generally observed the maxims, but p is nevertheless conversationally inadequate in some degree, requiring that p be 'amplified' or 'repaired' with the additional assumption q
          (b) In saying that p, S has flouted the maxims, and whatever he means he cannot mean p; to preserve the Co-operative Principle, S must substitute some proposition q for p
          Stage 2 : inferring q
          In the case of (a), H can use the reckoning involved in standard implicatures, as, e.g., in (125). In the case of (b), H must (i) determine what kind of trope p is, (ii) apply the reasoning characteristic of that trope, (iii) select among competing values

for *q* on the basis of their conversational adequacy vis–à-vis the maxims

What the reformulation makes clear is that Grice's account of metaphor only takes us as far as stage 1 (although the maxims play a role in the final stage of stage 2). What is further required is an account of (i) how metaphors are distinguished from other tropes, and crucially (ii) how, once recognized, they are interpreted. Searle (1979a) has here, within this sort of framework, offered some suggestions, especially for problem (ii). He suggests that once a conversational inadequacy is recognized, an utterance is matched to a series of pragmatic construal rules or principles of interpretation (and presumably the best match selected as the speaker's intended message). Thus given (208) and one of the rules for metaphoric interpretation in (209), the recipient may derive (210):

(208) Sam is a giant
(209) Given an utterance of the form *x is F* where this entails '*x* is G' and G is a salient feature of things that are F, then interpret the utterance as '*x* is G'
(210) Sam is big

Searle lists seven such principles, of which the search for a relation of similarity is only one, which can be stated roughly as follows:

(211) Given an utterance U of the form *x is F* look for some G or H which is a salient property of F things; then, if such is found, interpret U as '*x* is G', rejecting the interpretation '*x* is H' if H is less obviously predicable of *x*

This is intended to handle examples like (172) and (184). However, even if we grant that many kinds of metaphor have nothing to do with relations of similarity (and that may be as much a matter of definition as of fact), (211) tells us precious little about what is, at the very least, a central kind of metaphor. Moreover, it leaves obscure the motivation for, and the expressive power of, metaphors.

More concrete suggestions for a pragmatic theory of metaphor simply do not, at the time of writing, exist. Sperber & Wilson (forthcoming), experiencing the same sort of difficulties with other figures of speech, conclude that the theory of implicature does little to explain how such utterances are decoded, and indeed that the problems lie largely beyond pragmatics in an essentially psychological theory of rhetoric. This is, however, to undervalue the role that the maxims play in the location and recognition of tropes, and in the selection of interpretations relevant to the context. It may be conceded, though, that the theory of implicature alone cannot produce or predict such interpretations. One important consideration with respect to metaphor is that it is, perhaps, too much to ask of a pragmatic theory that it should actually give us an account of what is clearly a perfectly general and crucial psychological capacity that operates in many domains of human life, namely the ability to think *analogically*. Such an ability is basic not only to language usage but also to model-building of all sorts, from map-making to the construction of theories (see e.g. Black, 1979; Kuhn, 1979), and metaphors, frozen and unfrozen, are perhaps best thought of as the impingement of this sort of reasoning on the pragmatics of natural language. Taking such a view, there is much in the existing literature on metaphor that could be drawn upon to give an account of metaphor. Crucial, for example, seems to be the way in which what is involved in metaphor is the mapping of one whole cognitive domain into another, allowing the tracing out of multiple correspondences. For example, as Lakoff & Johnson (1980) have pointed out, two domains or conceptual fields like *politics* and *war*, once put into correspondence, productively produce all those familiar metaphors, dead and alive, of the sort:[28]

(212)   The Conservatives routed the Labour Party at the elections, and Labour has been in retreat ever since

(213)   Under Mrs Gandhi's generalship, the forces of the Congress Party were rapidly marshalled for a spirited counter-attack on the flanks of the disorderly rabble that constituted the Janata faction

Or, consider the way in which the domains of the future and the weather are often superimposed as in:

(214)   Britain's economy, apart from the sunny prospects of continued finds in the North Sea oilfields, is as bleak as ever; the future of education and the arts is clouded, and only the outlook for the electronics industry is bright

It thus happens, as Black (1962, 1979) has argued, that a single metaphor reverberates through two entire conceptual fields. The weakness of any paraphrase of a metaphor is much more than any

---

[28] For an interesting and involved correspondence of this sort between kinds of people and species of animal, see Leach, 1964.

mere omission of the literal semantic content of the term used metaphorically (*pace* Searle, 1979a: 123); such a paraphrase is talk within a single domain, while a metaphor links two domains in potentially elaborate parallelisms of indefinite depth. Sperber & Wilson (forthcoming), argue that the interpretations of tropes are fundamentally *non-propositional*, and one way of construing this claim is precisely in terms of such domain correspondence. The correspondence theory helps explain why good metaphors usually substitute 'concrete' terms for (metaphorically implied) 'abstract' ones – as made clear by a comparison of the relative success of the following two metaphors:

(215)   Love is a flame
(216)   A flame is love

For if a metaphor is like a model, or a map, or an analogue, of a domain, then just like models, maps and analogues in general, if they are to be useful and successful, metaphors had better be simpler, idealized, more easily grasped than the complex domains that they model. The correspondence theory also helps to explain the basis for other failed metaphors. For example, Morgan (1979) points out that Miller's simile schema for nominal metaphors should allow (217) to be used as a metaphor just in case my father (who is not called Herbert) is a machinist, to convey that Herbert is also a machinist:[29]

(217)   Herbert is my father

The account would proceed in terms of the failure of the attempted metaphor to set up any proper correspondence between the two domains of which *fathers* and *machinists* are parts: not just any domain is a possible model for any other.

The correspondence theory of metaphors therefore has the virtue of accounting for various well-known properties of metaphors: the 'non-propositional' nature, or relative indeterminacy of a metaphor's import, the tendency for the substitution of concrete for abstract terms, and the different degrees to which metaphors can be successful.

Let us now, in summary, consider the broad outlines of a pragmatic

[29] It might be argued that (217) fails as a metaphor because it is an identity statement, and Miller implicitly ruled these out. But *Herbert is a father* or *Herbert is fatherly* will not work either.

account of metaphor. First, we need an account of how any trope or non-literal use of language is recognized; and here Grice's maxims, or some reworking of them, may be expected to play a central role. Then we need to know how metaphors are distinguished from other tropes, and here the search for a possible corresponding domain, relevant to the conversation in hand, may be a crucial element; another heuristic may be the absence of all the features associated with other tropes like irony or understatement (e.g. ironies seem typically used to make criticisms). Once recognized, the interpretation of metaphor must rely on features of our general ability to reason analogically. If we had an account of this very general cognitive ability, we might expect it to apply directly to the interpretation of linguistic expressions used metaphorically. It is possible, though there is no real evidence for it, that such processing would involve the conversion of metaphors into the complex simile form proposed by Miller. In any event it could be claimed that linguistic pragmatics alone should not be expected to provide such a general theory of analogy, without considerable help from psychological theory. If there is to be a division of labour the psychologists' task might be to provide the general theory of analogy, while the pragmaticists' job should be to locate the kinds of utterances that are subject to such interpretation, provide an account of how they are recognized and constructed, and of the conditions under which they are used. In addition we would require an account of the way in which contexts constrain the interpretive search for correspondences, as the following examples suggest:

(218)   A: Oh what a beautiful house
           B: Yes, my wife's the curator
(219)   A: Oh what a dingy old office
           B: Yes, Bill's the curator

In short, just as the theory of implicature itself reflects the impingement of general properties of co-operative interaction (not in any way specific to language behaviour) on language structure and use, so a theory of metaphor will crucially involve the impingement of a very general cognitive ability, the capacity to reason analogically, on language structure and use. Just as we may look to empirical studies of interaction to refine our understanding of implicature and pragmatic inference, so we may look to psychological studies of analogical reasoning (including Artificial Intelligence theories of pattern matching and extraction) to provide the basic understanding of metaphorical processing that we currently lack. In both cases pragmatics is centrally concerned with the interaction between a linguistic and an essentially independent domain of human experience.

3.2.6   *Implicature and language structure*

The theory of conversational implicature is a theory of language *use*; nevertheless it can be shown to have considerable implications for the study of language *structure*, that is to say for language viewed as a self-contained system of rules. To show this is, of course, to show that there are interesting relations between structure and function of a sort that many current theories of grammar do not envisage, or at least consider beyond the purview of linguistic theory.

It is fairly simple to show that the linguistic description of morphemes and lexical items must at times refer to the notion of conversational implicature (or at least to something like it). Consider for example the English discourse particles *well, oh, ah, so, anyway, actually, still, after all*, and the like: these might be described as 'maxim hedges' that indicate for recipients just how the utterance so prefaced matches up to co-operative expectations (Brown & Levinson, 1978: 169ff). For example, R. Lakoff (1973a) has pointed out that one might characterize at least one sense of *well* as follows: *well* serves notice that the speaker is aware that he is unable to meet the requirements of the maxim of Quantity in full. Hence the typical occurrence of *well* in partial answers like the following:

(220)   A: Where are my glasses?
          B: Well, they're not here

(there are in fact alternative treatments of *well* either in terms of relevance-hedging (see Brockway, 1981) or in terms of discourse-structural notions (see e.g. Owen, 1980: 68–78, 1981) but these all refer to conversational expectations, however expressed). Similarly, a term like *anyway* could be claimed to be a relevance-hedge in at least some usages, in that it seems to imply that an utterance prefaced with it is relevant to the proceedings in some more direct way than an immediately preceding utterance (Brockway, 1981; Owen, 1982), as illustrated below:

(221)   A: Oh I thought it was good
          B: Anyway, can we get back to the point?

(Again it may be that a better analysis can be given using the concepts of conversational analysis – see Chapter 6 – but the point remains valid: the description of certain lexical items requires reference to modes of conversational inference.) There is no shortage of such items in any language – one could add *by the way, now, all right, you know* to the above list for English (see also James, 1972, 1973), and other languages are sometimes exceptionally rich in them (see e.g. Longacre, 1976a; Brown & Levinson, 1978: 151ff). So we may take it as clear that the metalanguage for the description of the lexicon of a natural language must make reference to conversational function, and one way to formulate such functions is in terms of implicature.

Another connection between conversational implicature and the lexicon is of more theoretical interest. Conversational implicature can be shown to provide systematic constraints on what is a *possible lexical item* in a natural language (see especially Horn, 1972).[30] The basic constraint imposed is roughly as follows:

(222)   If the use of a lexical item w carries a generalized conversational implicature I, then *ceteris paribus* there will be no lexical item x that directly encodes I

In essence this is a redundancy constraint: if a concept is generally implicated by an existing term in a language, that concept will not be directly lexicalized. Consider for example the lexicalized incorporation of negatives in English as in *none, never, nor, impossible*, etc. There is in fact a systematic paradigm of possible (realized) and impossible (unrealized) incorporations of the negative:

(223) | *Negative phrase* | *Lexical incorporation* |
|---|---|
| not possible | impossible |
| not necessary | *innecessary |
| | |
| not some | none |
| not all | *nall |
| | |
| not sometimes | never |
| not always | *nalways |
| not or | nor |
| not and | *nand |

Now observe that the following are scales in the sense of (117) above:

---

[30] We shall here gloss over considerable difficulties concerning the definition of the concept *lexical item* (as opposed to *morpheme*, etc.) that would need to be clarified to make the following generalizations clearly testable.

(224)   ⟨necessary, possible⟩
             ⟨all, some⟩
             ⟨always, sometimes⟩
             ⟨and, or⟩

Hence to use the item on the right of each scale assertively will be to implicate that the stronger item does not apply – i.e. to implicate 'not necessary', 'not all', 'not always', 'not and' (by (121) above). But then by the constraint (222) they will not be lexicalized, hence the paradigm in (223).[31]

Together with additional principles, Gricean principles have been used by Gazdar & Pullum (1976) to give an account of what is, theoretically, a surprising economy in the lexicon, namely the very small set (two or three) of the crucial truth-functional connectives employed in natural languages, given the theoretically indefinite number that might exist. Thus, for example, it can confidently be predicted that no language will lexicalize a truth function that takes two sentences but yields a truth value that is determined solely by the truth or falsity of, say, the righthand conjunct. The reason is of course that such a connective would render its left conjunct always redundant – and hence it would force a consistent breach of the maxim of Relevance.

An interesting question is whether there are any pragmatic constraints on syntax that can be attributed to conversational implicature. There are a number of good candidates. For example, G. Lakoff (1974) has drawn attention to **syntactic amalgams** like (225), where one finds parts of one sentence within another:

(225)   John invited *you'll never guess how many people* to *you can't imagine what kind of a* party

Lakoff notes that this is closely related to:

(226)   John invited *a lot of people* to a *weird* party

Note that not just any sentence fragments can occur in the italicized slots:

(227)   ?John invited *Harry used to know how many people* to *you didn't imagine what kind of a* party

---

[31] An exception might appear to be *unnecessary*, but the negative prefix *un-* can be argued to be too productive and non-assimilating to be considered lexically incorporated (see Horn, 1972: 274).

The constraint appears to work roughly as follows: suppose we have a sentence like (228) which conversationally implicates (229); then one may replace the noun phrase *a lot of people* with the indirect question *you'll never guess how many people*, which stands in an implicating relationship to that noun phrase, as in (230):

(228)   *You'll never guess how many people* John invited to his party
(229)   John invited *a lot of people* to his party
(230)   John invited *you'll never guess how many people* to his party

(clearly there are a number of additional constraints – see G. Lakoff, 1974: 323). So here we appear to have a syntactic process constrained in a systematic way by conversational implicature.[32]

There are other candidates for constructions with implicatural constraints, including our familiar asymmetric conjunction, where two conjuncts must be ordered in the sequence in which the two events they report occurred if the maxim of Manner is not to be breached. In addition, it has been noted that non-restrictive relatives are conversationally constrained by relevance: the embedded clause must be less relevant to the current conversational topic than the matrix sentence (see Gazdar, 1980a). One may note too that ironies, metaphors and rhetorical questions can acquire conventional indicators and structural correlates (Brown & Levinson, 1978: 267ff). Thus Sadock (1974) notes that in English, rhetorical questions that presume a *no*-answer permit the occurrence of **negative polarity items**, i.e. linguistic expressions otherwise restricted to negative environments. A large number of possible further cases are raised by the analysis of *indirect speech acts* as implicatures (as we shall see in Chapter 5; see also G. Lakoff, 1974; Ross, 1975).

A final and neglected interaction between implicature and language structure lies in the domain of *language change*. It is well known that metaphor and the other tropes are in part responsible for the significant semantic shift that can take place in the meaning of words over time. Euphemisms, for example, begin as polite metaphors but soon acquire the sense they originally implicated. Similar remarks can be made about honorifics. Overstatement as in the English use of

---

[32] It may, in response, be claimed that strings like (230) are not in fact well-formed sentences, and that they should be handled by a (so far, non-existent) theory of **semi-sentences**, which is independently required to handle conversational ellipsis. In that case much of the entire syntactic machinery of a language will be duplicated in such a pragmatic theory of semi-sentences – see Morgan, 1973.

frightfully, awfully, terribly can induce new senses: thus the term *starve* meant in Middle English just 'to die', but through uses parallel to (231) has of course come to mean 'suffer from severe hunger' in most dialects of English (we have now to specify 'starve to death' if that is what we mean; see Samuels, 1972: 53 from which these examples are taken; see also Ullman, 1962).

(231)   I'm dying to see you

Although the process is well documented, we do not know exactly how it works: is there a point at which implicatures suddenly become conventional senses, or is there some gradual process of conventionalization (and if so, how does this accord with our concept of the lexicon)? In some limited domains one seems to be able to find a series of stages in the linguistic change: e.g. from particularized to generalized conversational implicature, then to conventional implicature, in the case of some conventionally encoded honorifics in Asian languages (see Levinson, 1977: 47–60), not to mention second person polite pronouns in Indo-European languages (see Brown & Gilman, 1960, and references therein). Other questions arise: do the observable syntactic correlates of such semantic shifts (e.g. the acquisition of a *to*-complement for *die* in (231) above) follow the creation of a new sense, or do they cause it? We simply do not yet know much about the role of implicature in this process (but see Cole, 1975; Brown & Levinson, 1978: 263ff; Morgan, 1978 for comment and speculation).[33]

In any case it is clear that implicature plays a major role in language change, triggering both syntactic and semantic changes. Indeed it seems to be one of the single most important mechanisms whereby matters of language usage feed back into and affect matters of language structure. It is thus a major route for functional pressures to leave their imprint on the structure of a language.

[33] This is not to deny the existence of a rich literature on semantic change, but to suggest that the theory of implicature may provide interesting re-analyses of this material.

4

Presupposition

4.0 Introduction

In the previous Chapter we discussed conversational implicature as a special kind of pragmatic inference. Such inferences cannot be thought of as semantic (i.e. as pertaining to the meanings of words, phrases and sentences) because they are based squarely on certain contextual assumptions concerning the co-operativeness of participants in a conversation, rather than being built into the linguistic structure of the sentences that give rise to them. We turn in this Chapter to another kind of pragmatic inference, namely **presupposition**, that does seem at least to be based more closely on the actual linguistic structure of sentences; we shall conclude, however, that such inferences cannot be thought of as semantic in the narrow sense, because they are too sensitive to contextual factors in ways that this Chapter will be centrally concerned with.

The reader should be warned of two things at the outset. The first is that there is more literature on presupposition than on almost any other topic in pragmatics (excepting perhaps speech acts), and while much of this is of a technical and complex kind, a great deal is also obsolete and sterile. The volume of work is in part accounted for by a long tradition of philosophical interest which, because it is much referred to in the linguistic literature, will be briefly reviewed in 4.1. In addition presupposition was a focal area in linguistic theory during the period 1969–76, because it raised substantial problems for almost all kinds of (generative) linguistic theories then available. As a consequence of the large literature, the assiduous student will find just about every pronouncement in this Chapter contradicted somewhere in the literature; if the views expressed here seem partial, that is in part because they have the benefit of hindsight. Much that seemed confusing and mysterious has become clearer now that some basic distinctions and frameworks have been established (but see Oh & Dinneen, 1979 for a lively compendium of divergent modern views).

The second caveat concerns the distinction that has evolved between the ordinary usage of the word *presupposition* and its technical usage within linguistics. The technical concept accommodates only a small proportion of the usages associated with the ordinary language term, and the reader who hopes for a full explication of the latter within a single pragmatic concept is bound to find the rather narrow range of phenomena discussed below disappointing. The following examples illustrate some 'ordinary' senses of the term that are *not* dealt with within a theory of presupposition in pragmatics, although many of the cases have accounts within other branches of pragmatic theory:[1]

(1)   Effects presuppose causes
(2)   John wrote Harry a letter, presupposing he could read
(3)   John said "Harry is *so* competent", presupposing that we knew Harry had fouled things up – in fact we didn't know and so failed to realize that he was being ironic
(4)   Harry asked Bill to close the door, presupposing that Bill had left it open as usual; he hadn't so he threw a chair at Harry
(5)   Adolph addressed the butler as "sir", presupposing that he was the host Sir Ansel himself
(6)   The theory of evolution presupposes a vast time-scale
(7)   The article by Jackendoff presupposes Chomsky's theory of nominalizations

What these examples have in common is that they use the ordinary language notion of presupposition to describe any kind of background assumption against which an action, theory, expression or utterance makes sense or is rational. In contrast, the technical sense of presupposition is restricted to certain pragmatic inferences or assumptions that seem at least to be built into linguistic expressions and which can be isolated using specific linguistic tests (especially, traditionally, constancy under negation, as will be discussed below).

---

[1] For example, (3) would be given an explication in terms of the exploitation of a conversational maxim (see Chapter 3); (4) in terms of the notion of *felicity condition* employed within the theory of speech acts (Chapter 5); and (5) in terms of the notion of *conventional implicature* (Chapter 3).

4.1 Historical background

Once again concern with this topic in pragmatics originates with debates in philosophy, specifically debates about the nature of reference and referring expressions. Such problems lie at the heart of logical theory and arise from consideration of how referring expressions in natural language should be translated into the restricted logical languages.

The first philosopher in recent times to wrestle with such problems was Frege, the architect of modern logic. In elliptical discussion that allows considerable freedom of interpretation, he raised many of the issues that were later to become central to discussions of presupposition. For example, he said:

> If anything is asserted there is always an obvious presupposition[2] that the simple or compound proper names used have a reference. If one therefore asserts 'Kepler died in misery', there is a presupposition that the name 'Kepler' designates something. (Frege, 1892 (1952: 69))

And he went on immediately to say that it is not part of the meaning of *Kepler died in misery* that 'Kepler designates something'; if it was then *Kepler died in misery* would have the logical form 'Kepler died in misery & Kepler designates something', and thus the sentence *Kepler did not die in misery* would be equivalent to 'Kepler did not die in misery or the name Kepler has no reference'.[3] That he felt would be absurd. He adds:

> That the name 'Kepler' designates something is just as much a presupposition of the assertion 'Kepler died in misery', as for the contrary [i.e.negative] assertion. (ibid.)

Similarly he considers the special status of the meaning of temporal clauses:

> 'After the separation of Schleswig-Holstein from Denmark, Prussia and Austria quarrelled.' ... It is surely sufficiently clear that the sense is not to be taken as having as a part the thought that Schleswig-Holstein was once separated from Denmark, but that this is the necessary presupposition in order for the expression 'After the separation of Schleswig-Holstein from Denmark' to have any reference at all. (1892 (1952: 71))

[2] The German term that Frege used was *Voraussetzung*.
[3] This follows from the equivalence of $\sim (p \ \& \ q)$ to $\sim p \lor \sim q$, where p is 'Kepler died in misery' and q is 'The name Kepler refers'.

A Chinaman, he goes on, ignorant of the historical facts,

> will take our sentence ... to be neither true nor false but will deny it to have any reference, on the ground of absence of reference for its subordinate clause. This clause would only apparently determine a time. (ibid.)

Frege thus sketches a theory of presupposition with the following propositions:

(i) Referring phrases and temporal clauses (for example) carry presuppositions to the effect that they do in fact refer

(ii) A sentence and its negative counterpart share the same set of presuppositions

(iii) In order for an assertion (as he put in the Kepler case) or a sentence (as he put in the Schleswig-Holstein case) to be either true or false, its presuppositions must be true or satisfied

As is clear from (iii), Frege held more than one view of presupposition – sometimes he speaks of uses of sentences (assertions) as having presuppositions, sometimes of sentences themselves as having pre- suppositions, and elsewhere he even talks of speakers holding pre- suppositions (see Atlas, 1975a): "when we say 'the Moon' ... we presuppose a reference" (1892 (1952: 61)). Later these distinctions came to have importance. But it is clear that we have here in embryo the parameters that have guided much of the subsequent discussion of presupposition.

Now Russell, writing in 1905, thought that Frege's views were simply wrong. Struggling with the same problems in the theory of reference, he came to quite different conclusions. One problem was how to account for the fact that sentences that lacked proper referents, like (8), could be meaningful.

(8)   The King of France is wise

Frege had an answer provided by his distinction between sense and reference: such sentences retain their sense or meaning even if they lack referents and thus fail to have a truth value. But Russell argued that Frege's views led to anomalies, and he proposed instead his well-known **theory of descriptions**, which for forty-five years was to dominate such inquiries. He held that definite descriptions like *The so & so* have nothing like the simple logical translation that one might imagine. Whereas they occur in natural languages as subjects, as in

(8) above, in logical form they are not logical subjects at all but correspond instead to conjunctions of propositions. So instead of translating *The* F *is* G into the simple subject-predicate formula G(*The* F), he held it should be decomposed into the conjunction of the following three assertions:

(9)   There is some entity x, such that:

     (a) x has property F
     (b) there is no other entity y which is distinct from x and has property F
     (c) x has property G

Thus the logical form of (8) is not (10) but rather the complex (11) (where we will let 'King' stand for *King of France*):

(10)   Wise(the King)
(11) $\exists x\, (\text{King}(x)\ \&\ \sim \exists y\, ((y \neq x)\ \&\ \text{King}(y))\ \&\ \text{Wise}(x))$
     (Paraphrasable as 'There is a King of France and there's no one else who's King of France and he is wise')

Russell was able to show that this analysis handled the difficulties that arose on other views. For example, on this account (8) is meaningful because it is simply false; it is an assertion that, by virtue of the Russellian expansion of the phrase *The King of France*, also asserts the existence of that individual (by (9) above).

One particular advantage that Russell saw in his analysis was that it allowed what we today call **scope-ambiguities**. Thus the negative sentence:

(12)   The King of France is not wise

can be taken two ways: either it is presumed that there is a King of France and it is asserted that he is non-wise, or (less usually) what is denied is that it is true that there is both a King of France and that he is wise. The latter reading is the only one that can be involved in the following sentence:

(13)   The King of France is not wise – because there is no such person

Russell's formula in (11) allows (at least) two slots for negation to capture this ambiguity: negation either occurs with **wide scope** as in (14) or with **narrow scope** as in (15) below:

(14) $\sim (\exists x\, (\text{King}(x)\ \&\ \sim \exists y\, ((y \neq x)\ \&\ \text{King}(y))\ \&\ \text{Wise}\,(x)))$
     (Paraphrasable as 'It is not the case that: (a) there's a King of

France, and (b) there's no one else who's King, and (c) he's
wise')

(15) $\exists x \ (\text{King}(x) \ \& \sim \exists y \ ((y \neq x) \ \& \ \text{King}(y)) \ \& \sim \text{Wise}(x))$
(Paraphrasable as 'There is a King of France and there's no
one else who's King of France, and the King of France is not
wise')

The former wide-scope negation allows one to use (12) to deny that
the King of France exists, while the latter narrow-scope negation only
denies that the predicate applies to him.

Russell's analysis remained largely unchallenged until Strawson
(1950) proposed a quite different approach. Many of the puzzles arise,
argued Strawson, from a failure to distinguish sentences from *uses* of
sentences to make, for example, statements that are true or false.
Russell's conflation of the distinction led him to think that because
(8) is significant, and has a clear meaning, it must be either true or
false. But *sentences* aren't true or false; only *statements* are. Hence the
statement of (8) may well have been true in A.D. 1670 and false in
A.D. 1770, but in 1970 the statement cannot sensibly be said to be
either true or false: due to the non-existence of a King of France in
1970, the question of its truth or falsity does not even arise.

Strawson was therefore led to claim that there is a special kind of
relationship between (8) and (16):

(16)   There is a present King of France

namely, that (16) is a precondition for (8) being judgable as either true
or false. He called this relation **presupposition**, and he held that it
was a special species of (what would now be called) pragmatic
inference, distinct from logical implication or entailment, a species
which derives from conventions about the use of referring expressions.
These conventions, he held, are considerably more complex than can
be captured by the "jejune existential analysis" (as he termed
Russell's theory – Strawson (1952: 187)), and are bound up with
conventions about what it is to assert or state something. More
formally he held that a statement A presupposes a statement B iff B
is a precondition of the truth or falsity of A (Strawson 1952: 175).

One consequence of Strawson's disagreement with Russell, not
directly addressed, is that, in rejecting the complex logical form
underlying definite descriptions, he has lost a means of explaining
negative sentences like (13), where the presuppositions themselves

are cancelled. For normally, on Strawson's view (as on Frege's), a negative sentence, when uttered, will preserve its presuppositions. Russell could point to the two scopes or slots for negation provided by his complex logical forms. Strawson, had he faced up to this difficulty, would have had to claim that the word *not* is ambiguous: on one reading or sense it preserves presuppositions, on another it includes presuppositions within its scope and is thus compatible with denying them. What he actually contended, however, was that there was only one reading of (12), namely that in (15) where the predicate is negated, which of course leaves the denial of presuppositions in (13) quite unexplained.

Strawson and Frege thus held very similar views in opposition to Russell's approach to definite descriptions. Presuppositional theories of course have one signal attraction: they seem much more in line with our direct linguistic intuitions that, for example, when we utter (8) there is a foreground assertion, namely that a particular individual is wise; the implication that that individual exists is somehow a background assumption against which the assertion makes sense. Certainly Russell had no account of this.

By the time linguists became interested in the concept of presupposition (mostly after about 1969), a set of important distinctions and alternative approaches were thus well established in the philosophical literature. Foremost among these were:

(i)   the distinction between logical implication or entailment and presupposition (in the work of Frege and especially Strawson)

(ii) the contrast between assertion and presupposition (again, in the work of Frege and Strawson)

(iii) the issue of whether it was proper to think of presupposition as a relation between *sentences* (as Frege sometimes did), between *statements* (as Strawson held) or between *speakers* on the one hand and assumptions on the other (as Frege did on other occasions)

(iv) the issue of whether the apparent ambiguity of negation between a presupposition-denying sense and a presupposition-preserving sense is to be thought of as a *scope* distinction (a structural ambiguity) or a *lexical* ambiguity[4]

(v)   the possibility that apparently background assumptions, presuppositions, could in fact be viewed as assertions or

[4] This was not actually an explicit element in philosophical discussion, but it is an issue implicitly raised by Strawson's attack on Russell's views.

entailments, on a par with the rest of a sentence's meaning (Russell's approach)

In addition, a certain range of presuppositional phenomena had been adduced in the philosophical literature, including the presuppositions of:

(a) singular terms, e.g. definite descriptions, proper names
(b) quantified noun phrases, e.g. *All of John's children* can be claimed to presuppose 'John has children' (Strawson, 1952)
(c) temporal clauses (as in Frege's example quoted above)
(d) change-of-state verbs: e.g. *Bertrand has stopped beating his wife* can be claimed to presuppose 'Bertrand had been beating his wife' (Sellars, 1954)

When Strawson's notion of presupposition came to the attention of linguists, it seemed to open up a new and interesting possibility. Up till this point linguists had been operating with one crucial semantic relation in particular, namely **entailment** or **logical consequence**.[5] This relation can be defined in terms of valid rules of inference, or alternatively in terms of the assignment of truth and falsity ('semantically' as logicians say). **Semantic entailment** is thus definable as follows:

(17)   A *semantically entails* B (written A $\|$- B) iff every situation that makes A true, makes B true (or: in all worlds in which A is true, B is true)

Such a relation is basic to semantics. Not only does it capture logical truths, but all the other essential semantic relations (like equivalence, contradiction) can be directly defined in terms of it. The interesting possibility opened up by the notion of presupposition was that we might be able to add a new and distinct semantic relation to the inventory of the well-known ones. In doing so we would be bringing logical models more into line with natural language semantics. This programme, the creation of a new, well-defined semantic relation that would play a role within formal semantic theories, was realized within a number of theories of **semantic presupposition** (to be contrasted with pragmatic theories of presupposition below).

[5] Caveat: in just some logical systems (those with truth-value gaps or non-bivalence) one may wish to make a distinction between the notions of entailment and logical consequence, but logical terminology is not consistent here.

In order to achieve such a programme, it was necessary to make some subtle but important changes in Strawson's view. Strawson's concept of presupposition can be stated as follows:

(18)   A statement A presupposes another statement B iff:
         (a) if A is true, then B is true
         (b) if A is false, then B is true

The simplest view of semantic presupposition on the other hand would be based on the following definition:

(19)   A sentence A semantically presupposes another sentence B iff:
         (a) in all situations where A is true, B is true
         (b) in all situations where A is false, B is true

or equivalently, given our definition of entailment in (17) above (and assuming a definition of negation where if a sentence is neither true nor false, its negation is also neither true nor false):

(20)   A sentence A semantically presupposes a sentence B iff:
         (a) A ||- B
         (b) ~ A ||- B

The important and significant difference between (18), on the one hand, and (19) or (20), on the other, is that the first, Strawson's view, is a relation between statements (i.e. particular uses of sentences), whereas the second (semantic) view is a relation between sentences. It is clear that Strawson would not have approved of the shift.[6]

Now it becomes rapidly clear that the definition of semantic presupposition in (20) requires some fundamental changes in the kind of logic that can be used to model natural language semantics. To see this, consider the following argument, based on classical logical assumptions:

(21)   1. A presupposes B
         2. Therefore, by definition (20), A entails B and ~ A entails B
         3. (a) Every sentence A has a negation ~ A
            (b) A is true or A is false (Bivalence)
            (c) A is true or ~ A is true (Negation)
         4. B must always be true

---

[6] The general thrust of Strawson's views, firmly in the Oxford school of ordinary language philosophy, are summed up by the closing sentence of the (1950) article: "Neither Aristotelian nor Russellian rules give the exact logic of any expression in ordinary language; for ordinary language has no exact logic." See also Garner, 1971.

Suppose now A = *The King of France is bald*, and B = *There is a present King of France*. Then the conclusion of the argument above (which is valid on classical assumptions) is that the sentence *The King of France exists* is a tautology, or always true. Since the whole point of such presuppositional theories is to deal with presupposition failure and to explain the intuition that when their presuppositions fail sentences are neither true nor false, some of the classical logical assumptions must be abandoned to avert conclusions like that of (21). The simplest way to reconcile a definition of semantic presupposition like that in (20) with the bulk of accepted logical apparatus, is to abandon the assumption that there are only two truth values (the assumption of **bivalence**). Instead we can adopt three values, *true*, *false* and *neither-true-nor-false* (the latter for sentences whose presuppositions are false), and make just the modifications in the rest of the logical system that this change requires (notably, the abandoning of *modus tollens*, and bivalence).[7] It has been shown that perfectly well-behaved logics with three values can be constructed and it could be claimed that such logical systems are (by virtue of their ability to handle presuppositions) a notable advance in models of natural language semantics (see e.g. Keenan, 1972). It is also possible to retain what is formally a two-valued system by allowing **truth-value gaps** instead of a third value, and this would now be the preferred method. However, such systems have many of the same formal properties (e.g. the invalidity of *modus tollens*) and will prove just as inadequate as models of presupposition for the same reasons that we shall adduce against three-valued models. (Since students tend to find value-gap systems harder to conceptualize, they are not discussed here – but see Van Fraassen, 1971.)

The intellectual moves made here were congenial to the linguistic theory called *generative semantics* (which flourished 1968–75), for workers in this theory were concerned to expand and modify logical models of semantics to accommodate as many of the distinctive properties of natural language as possible. It thus became their aim to *reduce* pragmatic phenomena to the orderly domain of semantics (see especially G. Lakoff, 1972, 1975). However it soon became apparent that there are some presupposition-like phenomena that don't behave in quite the way that the concept of semantic pre-

---

[7] *Modus tollens* is the inference from $p \rightarrow q$ and $\sim q$ to $\sim p$ (see Allwood, Andersson & Dahl, 1977: 101).

supposition requires. For example, Keenan noted that the use of the pronoun *tu* in the French sentence (22) seems to presuppose that "the addressee is an animal, child, socially inferior to the speaker, or personally intimate with the speaker" (1971: 51):

(22)   Tu es Napoléon

But suppose I use (22) when none of these conditions obtains – it would be strange to say that what I said was neither true nor false: it is true just in case the addressee is indeed Napoleon and false otherwise. And the polite or formal (23) shares just the same truth conditions:

(23)   Vous êtes Napoléon

Thus the 'presuppositions' concerning the relationship holding between speaker and addressee, expressed by the use of *tu* or *vous*, simply do not affect truth conditions. Keenan (1971) therefore held that such examples form an independent and distinct class of pragmatic inferences which he called **pragmatic presuppositions**, which are best described as a relation between a speaker and the appropriateness of a sentence in a context.[8]

Other putative cases of presupposition that do not fit the definition of semantic presupposition soon emerged, cases where the inferences in question seem to be context-sensitive in a way that will occupy us below. Hence, for a while it was suggested that there are two distinct kinds of presupposition in natural languages, semantic presuppositions and pragmatic presuppositions, existing independently (see e.g. Keenan, 1971). But from 1973 onwards it became increasingly clear that there were so many problems with the notion of semantic presupposition that a theory of language (and specifically of semantics) would do better without it. The reasons for abandoning the notion of semantic presupposition rest firmly in the nature and properties of the phenomena when properly explored, a task to which we should now turn.

4.2   The phenomena: initial observations

Frege's and Strawson's claim that presuppositions are preserved in negative sentences or statements – a claim embodied in

---

[8] Note, though, that we have already argued that this kind of inference is in fact an aspect of social deixis (see 2.2.5) encoded as a conventional implicature (see 3.2.3).

Strawson's definition (18) above – provides us with an initial operational test for identifying presuppositions. We can simply take a sentence, negate it, and see what inferences survive – i.e. are shared by both the positive and the negative sentence. It should be noted that from now on we shall sometimes talk as if sentences are the objects that presuppose; this is a looseness adopted simply for purposes of exposition, and in fact it is a theory-relative matter as to whether it is sentences or utterances (sentence-context pairs) that presuppose, as we shall see.[9]

Let us start by taking the relatively simple sentence in (24):

(24)   John managed to stop in time

From this we can infer:

(25)   John stopped in time
(26)   John tried to stop in time

Now take the negation of (24) (note that 'the negation' here means the negation of the main verb or the topmost clause in a complex sentence):

(27)   John didn't manage to stop in time

From this we *cannot* infer (25) – in fact the main point of the utterance could be to deny (25). Yet the inference to (26) is preserved and thus shared by both (24) and its negation (27). Thus on the basis of the negation test (and the assumption of its sufficiency), (26) is a presupposition of both (24) and (27).

Note that whenever (24) is true, (25) must be true, but that when (27) is true, (25) need not be true. So, (24) entails (25), but (27) does not entail (25), by the definition of entailment in (17) above. Clearly, then, when we negate (24) to obtain (27), the entailments of (24) are no longer the entailments of (27). In short, negation alters a sentence's entailments, but it leaves the presuppositions untouched. Thus (25) is an entailment of (24) which constitutes at least part (and it has been claimed, all)[10] of the truth conditions of (24), while (26) is a

---

[9] In the linguistics literature, at any rate, the third possible notion of a speaker presupposing has played little important role in theorizing. However, those theories (discussed below) that seek to reduce presupposition to conversational implicature could be seen as built on this third notion.

[10] See e.g. Halvorsen, 1978; on the semantic view of presupposition the presupposition (26) would also be part, but a special part, of the truth conditions of (24).

presupposition of both (24) and (27). Behaviour under negation makes a basic distinction between presupposition and entailment.

Where does the presupposition in (24) come from? From the word *manage* of course. If we substitute the word *tried* in (24) the inference to (26) of course is the same, but this is now an entailment as is shown by considering the negative sentence (28):

(28)   John didn't try to stop in time

So presuppositions seem to be tied to particular *words* – or, as we shall see later, aspects of surface structure in general. We shall call such presupposition-generating linguistic items **presupposition-triggers**.

Let us now take a somewhat more complex example. Consider (29) and its negation (30):

(29)   John, who is a good friend of mine, regrets that he stopped doing linguistics before he left Cambridge
(30)   John, who is a good friend of mine, doesn't regret that he stopped doing linguistics before he left Cambridge

There are quite a large set of inferences that seem to hold good both for (29) and for its negation (30), for example:

(31)   There is someone uniquely identifiable to speaker and addressee as 'John'
(32)   John is a good friend of the speaker's
(33)   John stopped doing linguistics before he left Cambridge
(34)   John was doing linguistics before he left Cambridge
(35)   John left Cambridge

Since these are constant or invariant under negation, they are candidate presuppositions under the Frege/Strawson conception. Notice too that each of the inferences can be tied back to particular words or constructions that give rise to them. Thus (31) seems to be tied to, or arise from, the use of the proper name *John*; (32) seems to arise because relative clauses of this informative (non-restrictive) sort are not affected by the negation of a main verb outside the clause, and are thus preserved in their entirety under negation; and similarly for (35), which seems to arise from the fact that temporal clauses (initiated by *before, after, while, when*, etc.) are likewise unaffected by the negation of a main verb. The source of (33) is a little more opaque: it arises because (33) is the complement of a particular kind of verb (called **factive**), here *regret*; it appears that it simply makes no sense to talk about *X regretting Y*, or alternatively *X not regretting Y*, unless *Y* is an event that has happened or will definitely happen. So the complement *Y* is *presupposed* by both positive and negative sentences with main verbs in this class. The source of (34) is easier to locate: if one asserts that *X stopped Ving*, then one presupposes that *X* had been *Ving*, an inference shared by the assertion that *X has not stopped Ving*. So the verb *stop* is responsible for the pre-supposition (34).

These are fairly heterogeneous sources, and natural questions then arise of the sort: what are all the structures and lexemes that give rise to presuppositions?, do they have anything in common?, why do some linguistic items have such inferences built into them and not others? and so forth. But before we explore these, let us note that there is a way in which there is an intuitive unity to this set of inferences. For the basic intuition is that they are all in some important sense *background assumptions* against which the main import of the utterance of (29) is to be assessed. A useful analogy here is the notion of *figure* and *ground* in Gestalt psychology: in a picture a figure stands out only relative to a background, and there are well-known visual illusions or 'ambiguities' where figure and ground are reversible, demon-strating that the perception of each is relative to the perception of the other. The analogy is that the figure of an utterance is what is asserted or what is the main point of what is said, while the ground is the set of presuppositions against which the figure is assessed. (There are even some cases where figure and ground, i.e. assertion and pre-supposition, seem to get inverted like the classic Gestalt ambiguities; see Langendoen, 1971.) To see that the set of presuppositions really forms a set of background assumptions, and not just a set of inferences picked out by some technical definition of presupposition, consider what happens when we convert (29) into a question:

(36)   Does John, who is a good friend of mine, regret that he stopped doing linguistics before he left Cambridge?

Here the main point of an utterance of (36) will be to question whether John really does regret stopping doing linguistics, rather than to assert that he does (as in (29)) or to deny that he does (as in (30)). But (36) shares all the presuppositions listed above for (29) and (30). Thus the main point of an utterance may be to assert or to deny or to question some proposition, and yet the presuppositions can remain constant, or – to employ our analogy – the figure can vary within limits, and the ground remain the same. This is of course the intuition that lies behind the position taken by Frege and Strawson, and the way in which the technical notion of presupposition is intended to capture at least part of our pre-theoretical intuitions about what is presumed or (in the ordinary language sense) presupposed when we speak.

Let us now return to the questions that arose above. What sort of range of presuppositional phenomena is there? We may begin by listing some of the constructions that have been isolated by linguists as sources of presuppositions, i.e. by constructing a list of known **presupposition-triggers**. Karttunen (n.d.) has collected thirty-one kinds of such triggers, and the following list is a selection from these (the examples provide positive and negative versions separated by '/' to allow the reader to check the inferences; the presupposition-triggers themselves are italicized; the symbol $\rangle\rangle$ stands for 'presupposes'):

1.   *Definite descriptions* (see Strawson, 1950, 1952):
(37)   John saw/didn't see *the man with two heads*
     $\rangle\rangle$ there exists a man with two heads
2.   *Factive verbs* (see Kiparsky & Kiparsky, 1971):
(38)   Martha *regrets*/doesn't *regret* drinking John's home brew
     $\rangle\rangle$ Martha drank John's home brew
(39)   Frankenstein was/wasn't *aware* that Dracula was there
     $\rangle\rangle$ Dracula was there
(40)   John *realized*/didn't *realize* that he was in debt
     $\rangle\rangle$ John was in debt
(41)   It was *odd*/it wasn't *odd* how proud he was
     $\rangle\rangle$ he was proud
(42)   some further factive predicates: *know*; *be sorry that*; *be proud that*; *be indifferent that*; *be glad that*; *be sad that*
3.   *Implicative verbs* (Karttunen, 1971b):
(43)   John *managed*/didn't *manage* to open the door
     $\rangle\rangle$ John tried to open the door
(44)   John *forgot*/didn't *forget* to lock the door
     $\rangle\rangle$ John ought to have locked, or intended to lock, the door
(45)   some further implicative predicates: X *happened to* $V \rangle\rangle$ X didn't plan or intend to V; X *avoided* $Ving \rangle\rangle$ X was expected to, or usually did, or ought to V, etc.
4.   *Change of state verbs* (see Sellars, 1954; Karttunen, 1973):
(46)   John *stopped*/didn't *stop* beating his wife
     $\rangle\rangle$ John had been beating his wife

(47)   Joan *began*/didn't *begin* to beat her husband
>> Joan hadn't been beating her husband
(48)   Kissinger *continued*/didn't *continue* to rule the world
>> Kissinger had been ruling the world
(49)   some further change of state verbs: *start*; *finish*; *carry on*; *cease*;
         take (as in *X took Y from Z* >> Y was at/in/ with Z); *leave*;
         enter; *come*; *go*; *arrive*; etc.
5.   *Iteratives*:
(50)   The flying saucer came/didn't come *again*
>> The flying saucer came before
(51)   You can't get gobstoppers *anymore*[11]
>> You once could get gobstoppers
(52)   Carter *returned*/didn't *return* to power
>> Carter held power before
(53)   further iteratives: *another time*; *to come back*;
         restore; *repeat*; *for the nth time*
6.   *Verbs of judging* (see Fillmore, 1971a):
         This kind of implication is, arguably, not really presuppositional
         at all; for, unlike other presuppositions, the implications are not
         attributed to the speaker, so much as to the subject of the verb
         of judging (see Wilson, 1975).
(54)   Agatha *accused*/didn't *accuse* Ian of plagiarism
>> (Agatha thinks) plagiarism is bad
(55)   Ian *criticized*/didn't *criticize* Agatha for running away
>> (Ian thinks) Agatha ran away
7.   *Temporal clauses* (Frege, 1892 (1952); Heinämäki, 1972):
(56)   *Before* Strawson was even born, Frege noticed/didn't notice
         presuppositions
>> Strawson was born
(57)   *While* Chomsky was revolutionizing linguistics, the rest of
         social science was/wasn't asleep
>> Chomsky was revolutionizing linguistics
(58)   *Since* Churchill died, we've lacked/we haven't lacked a leader
>> Churchill died
(59)   further temporal clause constructors: *after*; *during*; *whenever*;
         as (as in *As John was getting up, he slipped*)
8.   *Cleft sentences* (see Halvorsen, 1978; Prince, 1978a; Atlas &
         Levinson, 1981):
         Sentence (60) exhibits what is known as the *cleft construction*
         (cf. unclefted *Henry kissed Rosie*), (61) what is known as the
         pseudo-cleft construction (cf. unclefted *John lost his wallet*).
         Both constructions seem to share approximately the same

---

[11] In British English *anymore* is a negative polarity item, i.e. can only generally
occur in negative declarative sentences, hence the lack of a positive exemplar
in (51).

presuppositions, and share in addition – it has been claimed (see Halvorsen, 1978) – a further presupposition that the focal element (*Henry* in (60) and *his wallet* in (61)) is the only element to which the predicate applies.

(60)   It was/wasn't Henry that kissed Rosie
    >> someone kissed Rosie
(61)   What John lost/didn't lose was his wallet
    >> John lost something
9.   *Implicit clefts with stressed constituents* (see Chomsky, 1972; Wilson & Sperber, 1979):

The particular presuppositions that seem to arise from the two cleft constructions seem also to be triggered simply by heavy stress on a constituent, as illustrated by the following examples where upper-case characters indicate contrastive stress:

(62)   Linguistics was/wasn't invented by CHOMSKY!
    >> someone invented linguistics
      (cf. It was/wasn't Chomsky that invented linguistics)
(63)   John did/didn't compete in the OLYMPICS
    >> John did compete somewhere (cf. It was/wasn't in the Olympics that John competed)
10.   *Comparisons and contrasts* (see G. Lakoff, 1971):

Comparisons and contrasts may be marked by stress (or by other prosodic means), by particles like *too, back, in return,* or by comparative constructions:

(64)   Marianne called Adolph a male chauvinist, and then HE insulted HER
    >> For Marianne to call Adolph a male chauvinist would be to insult him
(65)   Adolph called Marianne a Valkyrie, and she complimented him *back/in return/too*
    >> to call someone (or at least Marianne) a Valkyrie is to compliment them[12]
(66)   Carol is/isn't a *better linguist than Barbara*
    >> Barbara is a linguist
(67)   Jimmy is/isn't *as unpredictably gauche as Billy*
    >> Billy is unpredictably gauche
11.   *Non-restrictive relative clauses:*

Note that there are two major kinds of relative clause in English – those that restrict or delimit the noun phrase they modify (**restrictive** as in *Only the boys who are tall can reach the cupboard*) and those that provide additional parenthetical information (**non-restrictive** as in *Hillary, who climbed Everest*

---

[12] But perhaps the inference is more restricted: 'For someone (or at least Adolph) to call someone (or at least Marianne) a Valkyrie is to compliment them'. See the cautionary note re verbs of judging in 6 above.

in 1953, was the greatest explorer of our day). The latter kind is not affected by the negation of the main verb outside the relative clause and thus gives rise to presuppositions:

(68)　The Proto-Harrappans, who flourished 2800–2650 B.C., were/were not great temple builders

　　>> The Proto-Harrappans flourished 2800–2650 B.C.

12.　*Counterfactual conditionals*:

(69)　*If Hannibal had only had twelve more elephants*, the Romance languages would/would not this day exist

　　>> Hannibal didn't have twelve more elephants

(70)　*If the notice had only said 'mine-field' in English* as well as Welsh, we would/would never have lost poor Llewellyn

　　>> The notice didn't say mine-field in English

13.　*Questions* (see Katz, 1972: 201ff; Lyons, 1977a: 597, 762ff)

As noted in connection with (36) above, questions will generally share the presuppositions of their assertive counterparts. However, interrogative forms themselves introduce further presuppositions, of a rather different kind, which are what concern us here. It is necessary to distinguish different types of questions: **yes/no questions** will generally have vacuous presuppositions, being the disjunction of their possible answers, as in (71). These are the only kinds of presuppositions of questions that are invariant under negation. **Alternative questions**, as in (72), presuppose the disjunction of their answers, but in this case non-vacuously. **WH-questions** introduce the presuppositions obtained by replacing the WH-word by the appropriate existentially quantified variable, e.g. *who* by *someone*, *where* by *somewhere*, *how* by *somehow*, etc., as in (73). These presuppositions are *not* invariant to negation.

(71)　Is there a professor of linguistics at MIT?

　　>> Either there is a professor of linguistics at MIT or there isn't

(72)　Is Newcastle in England or is it in Australia?

　　>> Newcastle is in England or Newcastle is in Australia

(73)　Who is the professor of linguistics at MIT?

　　>> Someone is the professor of linguistics at MIT

The above list contains perhaps the core of the phenomena that are generally considered presuppositional.[13] However it is important to bear in mind that any such list is crucially dependent on one's definition of presupposition. For example, taking constancy under negation alone as the definitional criterion one would include phenomena like those immediately below, even though these would

---

[13] There are other good candidates, though, which happen to have received less attention. For example, adverbs, and especially manner adverbs, generally trigger presuppositions; thus *John ran/didn't run slowly* will presuppose 'John ran'.

probably be better accounted for under different aspects of pragmatic theory, as indicated by the rubrics in parentheses after each example (where $\rangle\rangle$? stands for 'putatively presupposes'):

(74)   Do/don't close the door
    $\rangle\rangle$? the door is open (*felicity condition on requests*)
(75)   Vous êtes/n'êtes pas le professeur
    $\rangle\rangle$? the addressee is socially superior to or non-familiar with the speaker (*conventional implicature*)
(76)   The planet Pluto is/isn't larger than Ceres
    $\rangle\rangle$? s the speaker believes the proposition expressed (*The maxim of Quality*, or alternatively, *sincerity condition on assertions*)

Or suppose instead we abandon constancy under negation as the acid test of presuppositionhood (as Karttunen (1973) advised), substituting behaviour in say *if... then* clauses (see below), then we might be led to claim that certain particles like *only, even, just* are presupposition-triggers. The grounds would be that, even though they do not yield inferences that survive negation, the inferences do survive in conditional contexts where entailments do not, as illustrated below:

(77)   If *only* Harry failed the exam, it must have been easy
    $\rangle\rangle$? Harry failed the exam
        (cf. If *only* Harry didn't fail the exam, it must have been easy
    $\rangle\rangle$? Harry didn't fail)
(78)   If *even* Harry didn't cheat, the exam must have been easy
    $\rangle\rangle$? Harry is the most likely person to cheat
        (cf. If *even* Harry cheated, the exam must have been easy
    $\rangle\rangle$? Harry is the least likely person to cheat)
(79)   If I *just* caught the train, it was because I ran
    $\rangle\rangle$? I almost didn't catch the train
        (cf. If I *just* didn't catch the train, it was because I ran
    $\rangle\rangle$? I almost did catch the train)

The isolation of the range of the phenomena thus depends crucially on the definition of presupposition adopted. But any theory of presupposition might reasonably be required to handle at least the majority of the cases listed in 1–13 above. We shall use this set of core phenomena to investigate some further basic properties that presuppositions exhibit.

4.3 The problematic properties

Constancy under negation is not in fact a rich enough definition to pick out a coherent, homogeneous set of inferences.

However, if we examine the core phenomena listed above we soon find that actually presuppositions do exhibit a further set of distinguishing characteristics. We shall find that presuppositions seem to have the following properties:

(i)   They are *defeasible*[14] in (a) certain discourse contexts, (b) certain intra-sentential contexts;
(ii) They are apparently tied to particular aspects of surface structure

The first property will prove to be the undoing of any possible semantic theory of presupposition, while the second property may serve to distinguish presuppositions from conversational implicatures, the other major form of pragmatic inference.

Defeasibility turns out to be one of the crucial properties of presuppositional behaviour, and one of the touchstones against which all theories of presupposition have to be assessed. In addition there is another problematic property of presuppositions, known as **the projection problem**, namely the behaviour of presuppositions in complex sentences. In part the problems raised here overlap with those raised under the rubric of defeasibility, but we shall deal with the problems one by one.

4.3.1   *Defeasibility*

One of the peculiar things about presuppositions is that they are liable to evaporate in certain contexts, either immediate linguistic context or the less immediate discourse context, or in circumstances where contrary assumptions are made. A simple example of this is provided by a certain asymmetry to do with the factive verb *know*. In sentences where *know* has second or third person subjects, the complement is presupposed to be true, as in (80). But where the subject is first person and the verb is negated, the presupposition clearly fails; thus (81) does not presuppose (82):

(80)   John doesn't know that Bill came
(81)   I don't know that Bill came
(82)   Bill came

The reason of course is that the presupposition that the speaker knows (82) is precisely what the sentence denies, and such denials override contradictory presuppositions (see Gazdar, 1979a: 142ff).

---

[14] See 3.1 above for explication of this term.

Similarly, when it is mutually known that certain facts do not obtain, we can use sentences that might otherwise presuppose those facts, with no consequent presuppositions arising. For example, if participants mutually know that John failed to get into a doctoral course, we can say:

(83)   At least John won't have to regret that he did a PhD

despite the fact that *regret* normally presupposes its complement. The presupposition is simply cancelled by prevailing assumptions. Note that in other contexts, e.g. where John has just finally got a job after finishing a PhD, the normal presupposition will hold.[15]

Consider another example. As noted above, propositions expressed by *before*-clauses are generally presupposed. Hence if I say (84) I shall – other things being equal – have communicated that I know (85):

(84)   Sue cried before she finished her thesis
(85)   Sue finished her thesis

But now compare (86):

(86)   Sue died before she finished her thesis

which certainly does not presuppose (85), but rather conveys that Sue never finished her thesis. Thus in (86) the presupposition seems to drop out. The reason for this seems to be the following: the statement of (86) asserts that the event of Sue's death precedes the (anticipated) event of her finishing her thesis; since we generally hold that people (and we assume Sue is a person) do not do things after they die, it follows that she could not have finished her thesis; this deduction from the entailments of the sentence together with background assumptions about mortals, clashes with the presupposition (85); the presupposition is therefore abandoned in this context, or set of background beliefs (see Heinämäki, 1972). Again, presuppositions prove to be defeasible.

This sensitivity to background assumptions about the world seems to be something quite general about presuppositions, and not some peculiar property of those due to *before*-clauses, as shown by the following examples (Karttunen, 1973):

(87)   If the Vice-Chancellor invites Simone de Beauvoir to dinner, he'll regret having invited a feminist to his table

---

[15] For another example of the same kind see (200) below.

(88)   If the Vice-Chancellor invites the U.S. President to dinner,
          he'll regret having invited a feminist to his table
(89)   The Vice-Chancellor has invited a feminist to his table

Now (88) here seems to presuppose (89) (assuming that the U.S. President is not a feminist). The presupposition is due, of course, to the factive verb *regret*, which presupposes its complement. But if we compare (87), we see that (87) does not seem to presuppose (89), despite the identical presence of *regret* and its complement. This, it is clear, is because if we know that Simone de Beauvoir is a well-known feminist, then we tend to interpret the phrase *a feminist* as anaphorically referring back to Simone de Beauvoir. But since the use of the conditional in (87) specifically indicates that the speaker does not know for certain that the Vice-Chancellor has invited Simone de Beauvoir,[16] the presupposition (89), where *a feminist* is assumed to refer to Beauvoir, is cancelled. The crucial point here is that the presupposition (89) is sensitive to our background assumptions: if we assume the U.S. President is not a feminist, then (88) will presuppose (89); if we assume Beauvoir is a feminist, then (87) will not presuppose (89). Again, then, a presupposition turns out to be defeasible in certain belief contexts.

Here is yet another example of the same kind (due to Karttunen, 1974). Consider (90):

(90)   Either Sue has never been a Mormon or she has stopped
          wearing holy underwear
(91)   Sue has stopped wearing holy underwear
(92)   Sue used to wear holy underwear

The presuppositions inferrable from (90) depend on one's beliefs about whether Mormons wear holy underwear. For the second disjunct or clause of (90) is (91), which as we have seen will presuppose (92) by virtue of the change of state verb *stop*. The whole sentence, (90), shares this presupposition (92) with (91) *unless* we assume that only Mormons habitually wear holy underwear.[17] In that

---

[16] The indication is due to the clausal implicatures of the conditional: *if p then q* implicates {Pp, $P \sim p$}, i.e. that the speaker doesn't know whether p is or is not the case, as discussed in 3.2.4.

[17] Actually, because there is a generalized conversational implicature from *p or q* to there being non-truth-functional connections between p and q (as discussed by Grice, 1967), we tend to favour this assumption. Perhaps a clearer case in which the presupposition (92) would generally survive would be *Either Sue has lengthened her dresses, or Sue has stopped wearing holy*

case, the first clause might be true (Sue has never been a Mormon) with the implication that Sue never did wear holy underwear; this implication is inconsistent with the presupposition (92), and the latter thereby evaporates.

Another kind of contextual defeasibility arises in certain kinds of discourse contexts. For example, recollect that a cleft sentence like (93) is held to presuppose (94):

(93)   It isn't Luke who will betray you
(94)   Someone will betray you

Now consider the following argument that proceeds by elimination (see Keenan, 1971; Wilson, 1975: 29ff):

(95)   You say that someone in this room will betray you. Well maybe so. But it won't be Luke who will betray you, it won't be Paul, it won't be Matthew, and it certainly won't be John. Therefore no one in this room is actually going to betray you

Here each of the cleft sentences (*It won't be Luke*, etc.) should presuppose that there will be someone who will betray the addressee. But the whole purpose of the utterance of (95) is, of course, to persuade the addressee that no one will betray him, as stated in the conclusion. So the presupposition is again defeated; it was adopted as a counterfactual assumption to argue to the untenability of such an assumption.

A slightly different kind of discourse context can also lead to the evaporation of presuppositions, namely where evidence for the truth of the presupposition is being weighed and rejected. For example, consider (96):

(96)   A: Well we've simply got to find out if Serge is a KGB infiltrator
         B: Who if anyone would know?
         C: The only person who would know for sure is Alexis; I've talked to him and he isn't aware that Serge is on the KGB payroll. So I think Serge can be trusted

The sentence (97) in the exchange in (96) should presuppose (98), for *be aware that* is a factive predicate which presupposes the truth of its complement (i.e. (98)).

underwear. The presupposition would then only be cancelled if we made the (unlikely) assumption 'All people who lengthen their dresses have never worn holy underwear'.

(97)   He isn't aware that Serge is on the KGB payroll
(98)   Serge is on the KGB payroll

However the point of C's utterance in (96) is to argue that since (97) is true, (98) is probably false. So once again a specific discourse context can override a presuppositional inference. There are a number of further kinds of discourse setting that can have similar effects.

So far we have shown that some of the core examples of presuppositional phenomena are subject to presupposition cancellation in certain kinds of context, namely:

(i)   Where it is common knowledge that the presupposition is false, the speaker is not assumed to be committed to the truth of the presupposition
(ii)   Where what is said, taken together with background assumptions, is inconsistent with what is presupposed, the presuppositions are cancelled, and are not assumed to be held by the speaker
(iii)   In certain kinds of discourse contexts, e.g. the construction of *reductio* arguments or the presentation of evidence against some possibility or assumption, presuppositions can systematically fail to survive

There are no doubt many other kinds of contextual defeasibility as well, but these examples are sufficient to establish that presuppositions are defeasible by virtue of contrary beliefs held in a context.

In addition to such cases, there are also many kinds of intra-sentential cancellation or suspension of presuppositions. For example, bearing in mind that (99) presupposes (100), note that when we embed or conjoin (99) in the range of sentences that follow, (100) cannot be a presupposition of the resulting complex sentences:

(99)   John didn't manage to pass his exams
(100)   John tried to pass his exams
(101)   John didn't manage to pass his exams, in fact he didn't even try
(102)   John didn't manage to pass his exams, if indeed he even tried
(103)   Either John never tried to pass his exams, or he tried but he never managed to pass them
(104)   John didn't *manage* to pass his exams; he got through without even trying

But the problems raised here are best dealt with in conjunction with the general problem of how presuppositions of component sentences behave when these components are part of complex and compound sentences, a problem to which we should now turn.[18]

4.3.2 *The projection problem*

Frege held that the meanings of sentences are compositional, i.e. that the meaning of the whole expression is a function of the meaning of the parts. It was originally suggested by Langendoen & Savin (1971) that this was true of presuppositions too, and moreover that the set of presuppositions of the complex whole is the simple sum of the presuppositions of the parts, i.e. if S_0 is a complex sentence containing sentences S_1, S_2, ... S_n as constituents, then the presuppositions of S_0 = the presuppositions of S_1 + the presuppositions of S_2 ... + the presuppositions of S_n. But such a simple solution to the presuppositions of complex sentences is far from correct, and it has proved in fact extremely difficult to formulate a theory that will predict correctly which presuppositions of component clauses will in fact be inherited by the complex whole. This compositional problem is known as the **projection problem** for presuppositions, and the particular behaviour of presuppositions in complex sentences turns out to be the really distinctive characteristic of presuppositions.

There are two sides to the projection problem. On the one hand, presuppositions survive in linguistic contexts where entailments cannot (i.e. the presuppositions of component sentences are inherited by the whole complex sentence where the entailments of those components would not be). On the other hand, presuppositions disappear in other contexts where one might expect them to survive, and where entailments would.

Let us start by considering the peculiar survival properties of presuppositions. The first and obvious kind of context in which presuppositions survive where entailments do not is, of course, under negation. One may, but need not, take this as a defining characteristic of presuppositions. Thus (105) could be held to presuppose (106) and entail (107):

[18] In traditional grammar, complex sentences are those formed by embedding (or subordinating) sentences within sentences, compound sentences those formed by sentences linked by conjunction (Lyons, 1968: 178, 266). Hereafter, we shall use the term complex sentence to subsume both, simply as a shorthand, reserving the term compound sentence for sentences containing clauses linked by any of the logical connectives (whether or not, for example, the conditional construction is thought of as subordinating).

(105)   The chief constable arrested three men
(106)   There is a chief constable
(107)   The chief constable arrested two men

If we now negate (105), as in (108), the entailment (107) does not survive; but the presupposition (106) does; this being of course the initial observation from which presuppositional theories sprang.

(108)   The chief constable didn't arrest three men

So much is obvious. But in a precisely similar way, presuppositions survive in other kinds of context in which entailments do not. One such is modal contexts, i.e. embedding under modal operators like *possible, there's a chance that* and so on. Thus (109) intuitively continues to presuppose (106):

(109)   It's possible that the chief constable arrested three men

But (109) certainly does not entail (107), because one cannot logically infer from the mere possibility of a state of affairs that any part of it is actual. This survival in modal contexts will turn out to be an extremely important fact, and it is worth while noting that the same behaviour occurs under, for example, deontic modalities like those expressed by *ought, should* and the like. Hence (110) presupposes (106) but does not entail (107), just like (109):

(110)   The chief constable ought to have arrested three men

Consider also a sentence like (111) which has several interpretations depending on how *could* is taken – e.g. in the permission sense, or the ability sense; but whichever interpretation is taken (111) presupposes (106) and fails to entail (107):

(111)   The chief constable could have arrested three men

A rather different set of contexts in which presuppositions distinguish themselves by the ability to survive, are the compound sentences formed by the connectives *and, or, if... then* and their equivalents.[19] Take for example (112):

---

[19] The logical connectives can always be expressed in various alternative ways: e.g. the conditional by *Given A, then B,* or *Suppose A, then B,* or *Assuming A, then B* and so on. The remarks throughout this Chapter concerning compound sentences formed from the connectives should carry over to all these equivalent or near-equivalent means of expressing the same logical relations.

(112)   The two thieves were caught again last night

which entails, *inter alia*, (113) and presupposes (114) by virtue of the iterative *again*:

(113)   A thief was caught last night
(114)   The two thieves had been caught before

Now embed (112) in the antecedent of a conditional as in (115):

(115)   If the two thieves were caught again last night, P.C. Katch will get an honourable mention

Here (113) is not an entailment of (115), but the presupposition (114) survives unscathed. Similarly, when (112) is embedded in a disjunction, its presuppositions but not its entailments survive:

(116)   Either the two thieves were caught again last night, or P.C. Katch will be losing his job

Presuppositions also have a habit of disappearing within such compound sentences formed with the connectives (as will be discussed below at length), but the circumstances are quite specific.

There are other environments in which it could be claimed presuppositions survive in a special way. Karttunen (1973), for example, lists a large set of complement-taking verbs or sentential operators, which he calls **holes** because they allow presuppositions to ascend to become presuppositions of the complex whole, where entailments would be blocked. The list includes the factive verbs, modal operators, negation and so on. It then becomes possible to define presuppositions not as inferences that merely happen to survive negation, but that also systematically survive in a range of other contexts where entailments do not. A problem here is that in many of these cases it can be reasonably claimed that the positive sentences constructed with *holes* in fact *entail* their alleged presuppositions, and it is only in negative, modal, disjunctive or conditional contexts that the uniquely presuppositional survival behaviour manifests itself.

Let us now turn to the second side of the projection problem, namely the way in which presuppositions of lower clauses sometimes fail to be inherited by the whole complex sentence. In other words, presuppositions are sometimes defeasible by virtue of intra-sentential context.

The most straightforward way in which such disappearances occur is where the presuppositions of a sentence are overtly **denied** in a co-ordinate sentence, as for example in:

(117)   John doesn't regret doing a useless PhD in linguistics because in fact he never did do one!

(118)   John didn't manage to pass his exams, in fact he didn't even try

(119)   Le Comte de Berry claims to be the King of France, but of course there isn't any such King anymore

Obviously, one can't do this with entailments on pain of direct contradiction:

(120)   *John doesn't regret doing a useless PhD because in fact he does regret doing a useless PhD

The possibility of denying one's own presuppositions is a fundamentally important property of presuppositional behaviour, which forces semantic theories of presupposition into special claims about the ambiguity of negation in ways which we shall describe below (see also Wilson, 1975: 32ff).

In connection with overt denials as in (117)–(119), it is important to note that at least in many cases they are not possible with positive sentences. Thus the following sentences seem in contrast quite unacceptable:

(121)   *John regrets doing a PhD because in fact he never did do one

(122)   *Florence has stopped beating her husband and in fact she never did beat him

(123)   *It was Luke who would betray him, because in fact no one would

A simple but important explanation of this is to claim that, at least in these cases, the affirmative sentences *entail* what we have hitherto called the presuppositions of each of them. Thus (121)–(123) are simply contradictions and thus semantically anomalous. This claim leaves it open whether in addition to being entailed the alleged presuppositions are also (redundantly) presupposed in the affirmative sentences, although most presuppositional theorists would claim that they are.[20] The asymmetries that thus show up between negative and

----

[20] But not those who seek to reduce presupposition to conversational implicature – see discussion in 4.4.2 below. Note that the entailment claim allows an essentially Russellian treatment of, for example, definite descriptions in the affirmative cases.

positive sentences with respect to overt denial of presuppositions argue strongly for the entailment analysis in positive sentences (see Wilson, 1975: 25–8; Gazdar, 1979a: 119–23 for further argument).

In addition to the overt denial of presuppositions there is the possibility of what Horn (1972) has called **suspension**. Here the use of a following *if*-clause can very naturally suspend the speaker's commitment to presuppositions as illustrated by:

(124)   John didn't cheat again, if indeed he ever did
(125)   Harry clearly doesn't regret being a CIA agent, if he actually ever was one

Such suspension behaviour is probably just part of the special ways in which presuppositions behave in conditionals, which we shall turn to immediately below.

Much more controversial is another kind of blocking of the presuppositions of constituent parts of complex sentences, which appears to take place under certain verbs of propositional attitude like *want, believe, imagine, dream* and all the verbs of saying like *say, tell, mumble, retort*, etc. Apparently clear cases are the following:

(126)   Loony old Harry believes he's the King of France
(127)   Nixon announced his regret that he did not know what his subordinates were up to
(128)   The teacher told the students that even he had once made a mistake in linear algebra

which do not seem to have, respectively, the expectable presuppositions:

(129)   There is a present King of France
(130)   Nixon did not know what his subordinates were up to
(131)   The teacher is the least likely person to make a mistake in linear algebra

In view of this behaviour, Karttunen (1973) has dubbed such verbs of propositional attitude and verbs of saying **plugs**, because, in contrast to *holes*, they block the presuppositions of lower sentences ascending to become presuppositions of the whole. However, it is far from clear that this is generally true. Consider for example:

(132)   a. The mechanic didn't tell me that my car would never run properly again
          b. My car used to run properly

195

(133) a. Churchill said that he would never regret being tough with Stalin
    b. Churchill was tough with Stalin

Here the *a* sentences continue to presuppose the *b* sentences despite the presence of *plugs*. So if one believes in the existence of *plugs* one is forced to account for these apparently presuppositional inferences in another way (Karttunen & Peters (1975) employ the notion of generalized conversational implicature). This is such an awkward solution – requiring non-presuppositional inferences to produce presupposition-mimicking inferences – that one has to conclude that the existence of *plugs* is very dubious indeed.

We come now to the most troublesome aspect of the projection problem, namely the behaviour of presuppositions in complex sentences formed using the connectives *and, or, if... then* and the related expressions that include *but, alternatively, suppose that* and many others. As we have already noticed, presuppositions tend to survive in disjunctions and conditionals where entailments do not, and one might therefore be tempted to claim that these constructions are *holes* that just let presuppositions through. That this is not the case is shown by examples like:

(134) If John does linguistics, he will regret doing it
(135) John will do linguistics

Here the consequent (second clause of the conditional) alone would presuppose (135), but the whole conditional does not – clearly because the presupposition is mentioned in the first clause and is thus made hypothetical. This turns out to be completely general. Now consider:

(136) Either John will not in the end do linguistics, or he will regret doing it

Here again the second clause alone presupposes (135), but the whole does not. The presupposition seems to be cancelled in this case because the alternative expressed in the first clause is the negation of the presupposition of the second clause. Once again this is a completely general phenomenon.

Because of this treatment of presuppositions in compounds formed by the connectives, Karttunen (1973) dubbed the connectives **filters**: they let some presuppositions through but not others. He stated the filtering conditions as follows:

(137) In a sentence of the form *if p then q*, (and also, perhaps, in a sentence of the form *p & q*) the presuppositions of the parts will be inherited by the whole *unless q* presupposes *r* and *p* entails *r*

(138) In a sentence of the form *p or q*, the presuppositions of the parts will be inherited by the whole *unless q* presupposes *r* and ~ *p* entails *r*

For those who think that presupposition and entailment are mutually exclusive, i.e. that a sentence cannot both presuppose and entail the same proposition, then it also makes sense to set up filtering conditions for conjunctions. Thus one might want to claim that (139) does not presuppose (135) but rather asserts or entails it:

(139) John is going to do linguistics and he is going to regret it

On this account, (139) fails to presuppose (135) because the first conjunct asserts what the second presupposes. It is not difficult to see that, viewed in this way, the filtering condition for conjunctions is identical to that for conditionals stated in (137) above. However, it is far from clear that this is a sensible way to view things: the doctrine of the mutual exclusivity of presupposition and entailment seems to be left over from the contrast in the philosophical literature between presupposition and assertion which has not proved of much use to linguistic analysis. In addition, as we showed above, a good case can be made for viewing many cases of alleged presuppositions in positive sentences as entailments, in which case either one will have systematically to block presuppositions in such simple positive sentences or simply accept that a sentence can both entail and presuppose the same proposition.

The filtering conditions stated in (137) and (138) above are to a large extent observationally adequate, and any would-be theory of presupposition that cannot predict this kind of behaviour cannot be taken very seriously. One way in which they are not quite adequate, though, was noted by Karttunen (1974) himself: we have to allow for the fact that the first clause may be taken together with background information and that these premises (in conditionals) or the negation of the first clause plus the background assumption (in disjunctions) may then filter out a presupposition of the second clause by entailing it. This is the explanation for the context-sensitivity of the presuppositions in (88) and (90) noted above.[21]

---

[21] Consider, for example, (90): if we take the first clause, *Sue has never been a Mormon*, and negate it, we obtain ' It's not the case that Sue has never been

We now have the essential delimitations of the projection problem. Any theory of how presuppositions are compositionally collected must be able to deal with the following basic facts:

> (i) Presuppositions may be overtly denied without contradiction or anomaly; and they may also be suspended by the use of *if*-clauses
> (ii) Presuppositions may be filtered in specifiable contexts when they arise from sentences that are part of compounds formed by the use of the connectives *or*, *if... then* and others
> (iii) Presuppositions survive in contexts where entailments cannot: in modal contexts, conditionals and disjunctions in particular

One influential way of talking about these projection properties, due to Karttunen (1973, 1974) is to talk of the contexts in (iii) as *holes*, and those in (ii) as *filters* – a terminology we introduced in passing. For Karttunen there is also the third important category of *plugs*, including the verbs of saying, which we have already shown to be a dubiously genuine property of the projection problem.

Although this discussion has introduced no great complexities, testing out potential solutions to the projection problem in fact involves considering how presuppositions behave in multiply-embedded sentences constructed out of such *filters*, *holes* and so on, up to a complexity that strains the intuitions. Readers may for example like to compare their intuitions with the predictions made by the filtering conditions, and other principles discussed above, on the following sentence:[22]

(140)   If after taking advice you determine to file form PF101, then either you have paid arrears and no deductions will be made from source or before PF101 is filed the Inland Revenue regrets that deductions will be made from source

---

a Mormon', i.e. 'Sue has been a Mormon'. If we now take the background assumption 'Mormons always wear holy underwear' together with 'Sue has been a Mormon', we can infer 'Sue has worn holy underwear'. This entails the presupposition (92) of the second clause, (91). Therefore, on the background assumption that Mormons wear holy underwear, the presupposition (92) will be filtered in line with the condition in (138).

[22] Hint: to work out the predictions from the filtering rules note that the logical form of the sentence is $p \rightarrow ((q \ \& \ r) \lor s)$, where s has, *inter alia*, two presuppositions, one entailed by $\sim r$ and the other (making certain assumptions) by p.

4.4   **Kinds of explanation**

The properties of presupposition that we have surveyed
are sufficiently intricate to narrow down the contending theories of
presupposition to a handful of current runners. To show this we shall
first of all demonstrate that no semantic theory of presupposition is
likely to be viable, and we shall then proceed to evaluate the three
main kinds of pragmatic theory that have been proposed.

4.4.1   *Semantic presupposition*

There are two main classes of semantic theories available
to linguists at the present time. One is the truth-conditional class of
theories, around which this book is primarily organized since it alone
makes clear predictions about what cannot be captured in semantics.
The other is the (not necessarily mutually exclusive) class that
assumes that all semantic relations are definable in terms of translations
of sentences into atomic concepts or semantic features. Attempts have
been made to formulate semantic theories of presupposition in both
frameworks; but both attempts, we shall argue, are misplaced. We
shall deal with the theories one by one.

In order to incorporate presupposition into truth-conditional
theories, presupposition has been characterized as a special species
of entailment, as in (19) and (20) above, namely one in which a logical
consequence relation can be defined in such a way that it is unaffected
by negation. Such theories, we noted, require a drastic re-organization
of the entire logical structure of a semantic theory. Such a re-
organization might be justified if the properties of presupposition
could thereby be captured, but it is not difficult to see that any such
theory cannot in principle succeed.

What dooms such semantic theories of presupposition are the two
cardinal properties of presuppositional behaviour we isolated above:
defeasibility and the peculiar nature of the projection problem. The
point about defeasibility is that presuppositions do not always survive
in certain discourse contexts, as we showed above in connection with
examples (93)–(98). It is often sufficient that contrary beliefs are held
in a context to cause presuppositions to evaporate, without any sense
of semantic or pragmatic anomaly. Now, the definition of semantic
presupposition in (20) is constructed using the notion of semantic
entailment; and the definition of semantic entailment in (17) specifies
that for a proposition p to semantically entail a proposition q it is

necessary that in *all worlds* in which p is true, q is true. The consequence is that semantic presupposition is a necessarily *invariant* relation: if p semantically presupposes q, then p *always* semantically presupposes q (providing that p is not embedded in a linguistic environment – other than negation – in which p fails to entail q). But the examples that we raised above under the rubric of defeasibility are not special linguistic contexts, they are specific extra-linguistic contexts where presuppositions drop out.

If we now turn to one side of the projection problem, namely the way in which presuppositions are defeasible or fail to project in specified linguistic environments, exactly the same problems emerge. Consider, for example, (141) and (142):

(141)   Either John is away or John's wife is away
(142)   Either John has no wife or John's wife is away
(143)   John has a wife

(141) straightforwardly presupposes (143) (although getting semantic presupposition to model even that may not be so easy, as we shall see immediately below). But (142) fails to presuppose (143) as of course predicted by the filter for disjunctions in (138) above. Again we are faced with the problem of cancelling presuppositions in some environments and not others, here just in case the first disjunct when negated entails the presupposition of the second disjunct. While it is easy to imagine that a semantic relation like semantic presupposition should be affected systematically by embedding in a disjunction, it is not easy to see how such an invariant relation could be sensitive to the content of another disjunct (but cf. Peters, 1979).

An exactly similar point can be made with respect to conditionals: on the semantic theory of presupposition (144) and (145) should have the same presuppositions, but in fact only (144) presupposes (146):

(144)   If Harry has children, he won't regret doing linguistics
(145)   If Harry does linguistics, he won't regret doing it
(146)   Harry is doing linguistics

In linguistic contexts like (145) (as generally described by (137) above) presuppositions are not invariant relations as semantic presupposition would require: they sometimes do and sometimes do not survive when the constructions that give rise to them are embedded in the consequent clause of a conditional.

We noticed also that it is possible to overtly deny a presupposition without causing anomaly, as in (147) and examples (117)–(119) above:

(147)   John doesn't regret having failed, because in fact he passed

Now clearly such examples pose severe problems for the semantic presuppositionalist, for by definition semantic presuppositions survive negation – but in that case (147) should amount to a contradiction: it both semantically presupposes (148) and entails by virtue of the *because*-clause that (148) is false:

(148)   John failed

Faced with examples like these, there is only one way out for the semantic presuppositionalist: he must claim that negation is ambiguous between a presupposition-preserving kind of negation and a kind in which both entailments and presuppositions get negated. These are sometimes called **internal** or **predicate** negation and **external** or **sentence** negation respectively, but here this terminology is misleading because the claim required to salvage semantic presupposition is not the Russellian claim that there are different scopes for negation, but rather that the negative morphemes are actually ambiguous (Wilson, 1975: 35). Further, the semantic presuppositionalist can point to the fact that his trivalent logic (or equivalent truth-value gaps) allows the definition of two distinct logical negations, thus making the ambiguity claim technically feasible (see Gazdar, 1979a: 65 for details).

The problem with this claim is that there is no evidence whatsoever that there is such an ambiguity in natural language negations, and considerable evidence that there is not. Linguistic tests for ambiguity do not confirm the claim (Atlas, 1977), and there appear to be no languages in which the two senses are lexically distinguished (Horn, 1978; Gazdar, 1979a), whereas the claim would lead one to expect that it was sheer coincidence that only one word exists for the two senses in English. (For sundry other arguments against the claim see e.g. Allwood, 1972; Kempson, 1975: 95–100.) Moreover the notion of a presupposition-destroying negation lands in technical difficulties as soon as iterations of such an operator are considered (see Atlas, 1980). The failure of the ambiguity claim means that semantic presuppositionalists have no account of sentences like (147), or rather the semantic theory makes the wrong predictions (here, that (147) should be drastically anomalous due to semantic contradiction).

Let us now turn to consider how semantic presupposition fares with the other side of the projection problem: namely accounting for how presuppositions survive in contexts where entailments don't. Such contexts we noted include modals of various sorts, as illustrated by (149), which when embedded in a modal context, as in (150), continues to presuppose (151):

(149)   John is sorry that he was rude
(150)   It's possible that John is sorry that he was rude
(151)   John was rude

When this was first noted, it was correctly pointed out that in order to maintain a presuppositional relation between (150) and (151) it would be necessary to change the definition of semantic presupposition, so that instead of reading as in (20) above it would read as in (152) below:

(152)   A semantically presupposes B iff:
          (a) $\Diamond$ A $\|$- B
          (b) $\Diamond$ ~ A $\|$- B

(see Karttunen, 1971a). The problem with this definition is that it has been proved that none of the standard logical systems can accommodate such a semantic relation.[23] The technical difficulties here militate strongly against the possibility of maintaining any coherent notion of semantic presupposition.

In addition, possibility is not the only modal operator presuppositions survive through – as pointed out above deontic modalities also let presuppositions through in a way that is quite irreconcilable with a relation based on entailment. Also, except under the special conditions noted above, presuppositions survive embedding in conditionals and disjunctions where entailments do not. If *p* entails *r*, and we embed *p* in *either p or q*, we can no longer infer *r*; but if *p* presupposes *s* then *either p or q* will presuppose *s* unless filtered under the condition in (138). Thus (153) below entails (154) and presupposes (155), but only (155) survives embedding in a disjunction as in (156):

[23] The proof is due to an unpublished note by Herzberger (1971); a further demonstration that such a relation can be accommodated in much more complex logical systems, namely two-dimensional four-valued modal logics, is due to Martin (1975, 1979), but there would need to be considerable independent justification for adopting such logical systems as models for natural language semantics.

(153)   The Duke of Westminster has four houses
(154)   The Duke of Westminster has three houses
(155)   There is a Duke of Westminster
(156)   Either the Duke of Westminster has four houses or he borrows other people's stationery

It is quite unclear how the definition of semantic presupposition could be modified to allow presuppositions to be preserved in such disjunctive contexts.

As a final problem, note that even if the definition of semantic presupposition could be altered to accommodate all these contexts in which presuppositions and not entailments survive,[24] the same problem that arose concerning the ambiguity of negation would plague such a definition with a vengeance. For wherever in such contexts it is possible to add an overt denial of the presuppositions of other clauses, one would have to claim that there was an ambiguity between presupposition-preserving and presupposition-destroying senses of the expressions involved (Wilson, 1975). Thus given that one can say (157) without anomaly, it would be necessary to claim that the possibility operator in (152) above is ambiguous in just the same way that negation is:

(157)   It's possible that Nixon regrets tampering with the tapes, although I don't believe he ever did

This assortment of problems is sufficient to rule out the possibility of an account of presupposition within a truth-conditional theory of semantics.

Let us now turn to the attempts to accommodate presupposition within a semantic theory based on atomic concepts or semantic primes or features. The properties of such semantic theories are much less well defined than logical models, and to a certain extent this makes them more adaptable to handling new kinds of supposed semantic relations. Thus Katz & Langendoen (1976) maintain that semantic presupposition is a perfectly viable concept, indeed the only viable one, when modelled within a feature-style semantics (see also Leech, 1974). In actual fact it has been shown that Katz & Langendoen's suggestions simply cannot handle the projection problem (see the critique in Gazdar, 1978). Given the informal nature of such semantic theories, it is open to Katz & Langendoen to make another attempt

---

[24] And note that these would include the verbs of saying if one does not subscribe to the view that these are *plugs*.

using quite different apparatus invented for the purpose, and it is therefore difficult to prove that no such attempt could be successful.

However it is not difficult to show that any such attempt, given the avowed goals of such semantic theories, is simply misplaced. For the aim of such theories is to tease apart our knowledge of the semantics of our language from our knowledge of the world, and to isolate the relatively small set of atomic concepts required for the description of the semantics alone (see e.g. Katz & Fodor, 1963). Semantics on this view is concerned with the context-independent, stable meanings of words and clauses, leaving to pragmatics those inferences that are special to certain contexts (see e.g. Katz, 1977: 19ff).

Given this much, it is clear that presupposition belongs in pragmatics and not in semantics. For presuppositions are not stable, context-independent aspects of meaning – that is shown conclusively by the examples discussed under defeasibility above, one of which is repeated here:

(158)   Sue cried before she finished her thesis
(159)   Sue died before she finished her thesis
(160)   Sue finished her thesis

where the presupposition due to the *before*-clause in (158) does not go through in (159). Why? Because our knowledge of the world, taken together with the truth of (159), is inconsistent with the assumption that (160) is true.

To sum up: semantic theories of presupposition are not viable for the simple reason that semantics is concerned with the specification of invariant stable meanings that can be associated with expressions. Presuppositions are not invariant and they are not stable, and they do not belong in any orderly semantics.

4.4.2   *Pragmatic theories of presupposition*

For the reasons adduced above, and others catalogued by Stalnaker (1974), Kempson (1975), Wilson (1975) and Boër & Lycan (1976), semantic theories of presupposition have largely been abandoned (but see Martin, 1979). In their place, various theories of **pragmatic presupposition** have been put forward. The earlier of these were programmatic, and offered little more than possible definitions of presupposition using pragmatic notions (a list of such definitions and a discussion of them can be found in Gazdar, 1979a: 103ff). These definitions, despite differing terminology, utilized two basic concepts in particular: **appropriateness** (or **felicity**) and

mutual knowledge (or **common ground**, or joint assumption) in the way indicated in the following definition:[25]

(161)   An utterance A *pragmatically presupposes* a proposition B iff A is *appropriate* only if B is *mutually known* by participants

The idea, then, was to suggest that there are pragmatic constraints on the use of sentences such that they can only be appropriately used if it is assumed in the context that the propositions indicated by the presupposition-triggers are true. So to utter a sentence whose presuppositions are, and are known to be, false, would merely be to produce an inappropriate utterance, rather than (on the semantic view) to have asserted a sentence that was neither true nor false.

Apart from the sketchiness of such proposals, there are objections to the utility of the notion of *appropriateness* which we raised in Chapter 1. In addition, as Sadock has pointed out (see Stalnaker, 1977: 145–6), the mutual knowledge condition is far too strong: I can very well say (162) in conditions where my addressee did not previously know the presupposition (163):

(162)   I'm sorry I'm late, I'm afraid my car broke down
(163)   The speaker has a car

It is sufficient, as Gazdar (1979a: 105ff) notes, that what I presuppose is *consistent with* the propositions assumed in the context. It is interesting to note that (164) is probably not appropriate in circumstances where it is not mutual knowledge that the presupposition (165) is true:

(164)   I'm sorry I'm late, my fire-engine broke down
(165)   The speaker has a fire-engine

presumably because it is not consistent with the average man's beliefs that an average man owns a fire-engine (but see Prince, 1978b for some more complex explanations).

Such problems indicate that definitions like (161) are at least in need of refinement. But in the long run what we are interested in is not a definition, but some model that will accurately predict presuppositional behaviour and capture in particular the problematic properties of defeasibility and projection reviewed above. In fact there are only two sophisticated formal models that get anywhere near accounting for the observable facts, and we shall now review these

[25] On the concepts of *mutual knowledge* and *appropriateness* see 1.2 above; on *felicity* see 5.1 below.

in detail, returning later to ask whether any other kinds of approach are available as alternatives.

We have established that presuppositional inferences cannot be thought of as semantic in the usual sense, and we have indicated above that presuppositions seem to be tied to the surface form of expressions. Thus it could be claimed, not necessarily correctly but nevertheless plausibly, that the following sentences all share the same truth conditions:

(166)   John didn't give Bill a book
(167)   It wasn't a book that John gave to Bill
(168)   It wasn't John who gave Bill a book

and differ only in that (167) has the additional presupposition (169), and (168) the additional presupposition (170):

(169)   John gave Bill something
(170)   Someone gave Bill a book

The presupposition of a cleft sentence (like those in (167) and (168)) can therefore be identified with a proposition formed by taking the material after the relative clause marker (*who*, *that*) and inserting a variable or indefinite existential expression like *somebody, something* that agrees in number, gender (and indeed grammatical category) with the item in focus position. There seems therefore to be a conventional association between the surface organization of constituents in a cleft construction and particular presuppositions.

The two theories we are about to review both assume that presuppositions are therefore part of the conventional meaning of expressions, even though they are not semantic inferences. This should serve to distinguish presuppositions from conversational implicatures, which otherwise share many of the same properties of defeasibility, for conversational implicatures are (as we noted in Chapter 3) *non-detachable*: i.e. it is not possible to find another way of conveying the same truth conditions that will lack the implicatures in question. On the other hand, there appears to be no problem in finding a way of expressing the same truth-conditional content as in (167) or (168), while avoiding conveying (169) or (170) respectively – for example by saying (166).[26]

[26] The detachability of presuppositions by paraphrase will in fact be questioned below; and it is not in fact clear that (166), (167) and (168) actually share truth conditions (see Atlas & Levinson, 1981).

The first such conventional theory we shall review has been developed by Karttunen & Peters (1975, 1979). The theory is expressed in the framework of **Montague grammar**, in which clauses are built up from their constituents from the bottom up rather than from the top down as in transformational generative grammar.[27] In such a theory, the semantic content of an expression is built up in tandem with the syntax, so that in the process of sentence generation semantic representations are constructed stage by stage in parallel to the construction of the surface natural language expression. Thus every word, clause or syntactic operation can have associated with it a semantic representation or **extension expression**, as Karttunen & Peters call it. Now the basic idea in Karttunen & Peters' theory is simply to add to the framework of Montague grammar an additional set of meaning expressions to be generated in the same sort of way as extension expressions, as sentences are built up from their constituent parts; these meaning expressions will, just like extension expressions, be associated with words, clauses, and constructions – but here just with what we have called presupposition-triggers. And unlike extension expressions these presuppositional expressions will not generally play any part in the specification of truth conditions, for their function is purely to represent the presuppositions of constituents. Thus, on this theory, the distinction between truth-conditional aspects of meaning and presuppositional inferences is captured by the generation of two quite separate kinds of meaning for each natural language expression.

Karttunen & Peters call the meaning expressions that capture presuppositions **implicature expressions** or **conventional implicatures**, and the terminology overtly identifies presuppositions with those pragmatic inferences that Grice (1975) isolated as being conventional, non-cancellable and yet not part of the truth conditions. For on Karttunen & Peters' theory, presuppositions (or, as they would have it, conventional implicatures) are in fact non-cancellable. But Karttunen is well aware of the defeasibility and projection properties of presuppositions – indeed he was the first to explore them in detail. How then can it be claimed that presuppositions are non-cancellable?

The answer lies in the details of Karttunen & Peters' system. The idea is that in addition to implicature expressions capturing the

---

[27] See Dowty, Peters & Wall, 1981 for an introduction to Montague grammar.

presuppositional content of each presupposition-triggering item, there will be associated with each constituent a **heritage expression** whose sole function will be to govern the projection of the presuppositions expressed in the implicature expressions. In this way, Karttunen's (1973) classification of embedding constructions into *plugs*, *filters* and *holes* can be incorporated into the Montague grammar framework: for example, where an embedding complement is a plug it will have a heritage expression that will block the presuppositions (expressed by the implicature expressions) from ascending to be presuppositions of the whole sentence. Thus (171) will not have the presupposition (172) because the word *claims* will have an associated heritage expression that will block it:

(171)   Nato claims that the nuclear deterrent is vital
(172)   There exists a nuclear deterrent

As we noted above, it is not clear that plugs are a useful category, but if they are, here is a coherent way of modelling them. Similarly with the class of filters: each connective will have associated with it a heritage expression that will block the presuppositions of the lower constituent sentences just in case the filtering conditions in (137) and (138) are met. For example, the heritage expression that captures the filtering condition for conditionals can be thought of as something like (173):

(173)   The conventional implicatures of *if p then q* (and also perhaps of *p and q*) are the conventional implicatures of *p* together with the expression 'if *p* then the conventional implicatures of *q*'

To see how this works apply it to a case like (174) where the presupposition, (175), of the consequent is filtered:

(174)   If John has children, all of John's children must be away
(175)   John has children

Here the presuppositions of the whole will be whatever the presuppositions of the antecedent are (e.g. John exists), plus the proposition that if John has children, then he has children. Since this proposition is tautologous, it is vacuous, and the speaker is specifically not committed to (175) even though the phrase *all of John's children* presupposes (or conventionally implicates, in the terminology of this theory) (175).

For *holes* Karttunen & Peters can obviously just let the heritage expression allow the implicature expressions to ascend to become the conventional implicatures of the whole.

Thus, on this theory, presuppositions are not actually cancelled, they are blocked during the derivation of the sentence and simply do not arise from the whole. In many ways this is a highly sophisticated and carefully constructed model that can be fully formalized within what is perhaps the most rigorous of contemporary linguistic theories.

Karttunen & Peters connect their theory to the earlier attempts to define pragmatic presupposition, along the following lines: co-operative participants have the obligation to "organize their contributions in such a way that the conventional implicata of the sentence uttered are already part of the common ground at the time of utterance" (1975: 269). As we have seen, this is too strong a constraint, and it will be sufficient to require that the so-called conventional implicata are consistent with the common ground.

There are a number of substantial problems for this theory. It is formulated specifically to deal with the problems of projection that we reviewed above, and the solutions offered are what we may call 'engineering solutions' – i.e. whatever is required in the way of formal apparatus is simply built into the compositional process of sentence construction. In order to handle the intricacies of the projection problem, therefore, the details of the engineering must become increasingly complicated. It is possible, for example, to show that the latest formulation does not in fact handle some of the more intractable cases. For example, the filtering rule for conditionals we sketched in (173) is identical to the rule for conjunctions, and so the rule for conjunctions incorrectly predicts that (176) has the presupposition (177) (this counter-example is drawn from the substantial set assembled in Gazdar, 1979a: 108–19):

(176)   It is possible that John has children and it is possible that his children are away

(177)   John has children

This happens because the filtering rule in (173) will predict that the presuppositions of (176) are (or at least include) those in (178):

(178)   John exists and if it is possible that John has children then John has children

But since the antecedent of the conditional in (178) is entailed by

(176), (176) plus the conditional entails (177). So it is predicted, incorrectly, that (176) will have (177) as a presupposition. Since the solutions are simply of an engineering sort, it remains open to Karttunen & Peters to try to re-tool the solutions to cope with the known counter-examples of this sort. Rather more troublesome is the evidence that the proposed filtering constraints are asymmetrical in the way that (137) is above – this makes it impossible to account for the filtering in (179) (drawn from Wilson, 1975) where the consequent entails what the antecedent presupposes, namely (180):

(179) If Nixon knows the war is over, the war is over
(180) The war is over

Again, though, it is possible that with sufficient ingenuity more complex filtering rules that will acount for (179) can be built into the apparatus.

Where the theory begins to get into the greatest difficulty is where it has to deal with some of the other aspects of contextual defeasibility that we have reviewed above. For example, to handle the simple examples of overt presupposition denial like (181) and (182), the conventional implicature theory is forced to adopt the view that the negative morphemes in natural languages are ambiguous between presupposition-preserving and presupposition-negating senses:

(181) John didn't manage to stop – he didn't even try
(182) John didn't regret losing the game, because in fact he won

Because presuppositions are, on this theory, really conventional implicata, they cannot be cancelled, and since they must ordinarily survive negation (and this has to be built into the heritage expressions for negative morphemes), the negation in (181) and (182) must be a different kind of negation, namely one which does not let conventional implicata survive. But this view runs into all the objections we raised above against the view that negation is ambiguous (and others: see Atlas, 1980).

But the main objection is that such a theory cannot handle contextual defeasibility of the sorts illustrated in examples (84)–(96). It cannot do this for the same reasons that semantic theories of presupposition cannot: there is no reference, in the calculation of the presuppositions of a sentence, to the assumptions that are made in the context. There is merely an additional pragmatic constraint that the speaker should not presuppose what is not already mutually assumed (which is too strong as we have noted). Therefore, if there are any ways in which contextual assumptions, modes of discourse, or the like serve to nullify presuppositions – which, we have argued, there are in abundance – such a theory is going to make the wrong predictions about what inferences participants make from sentences in context. It is also going to make the wrong predictions wherever the classification of linguistic items into *holes*, *plugs* and *filters* is itself subject to pragmatic re-classification. A number of relevant cases were brought up by Liberman (1973), who pointed out that two sentences like the following ought to behave quite differently under the filtering rule for conjunctions (as in (137)), and yet in fact both have the presuppositions of their second clauses filtered out:

(183)   Perhaps John has children but perhaps John's children are
         away
(184)   Perhaps John has no children, but perhaps John's children are
         away

Now we have already noted, in connection with (176) above, that the filtering theory makes the wrong predictions with sentences like (183): let us therefore assume, as a way of patching up the theory, that the presuppositions of modal sentences are calculated first on the basis of their non-modal subordinate sentences (this expedient will not, in the long run, work – see Gazdar, 1979a: 111–12). Then (183) will not presuppose that John has children, despite the potential presupposition due to the phrase *John's children*, for the first clause (ignoring the modal) will entail the presupposition, and the presupposition will therefore be filtered in accord with the filtering rule for conjunctions in (137) or (173). This seems the correct result, and is to be expected on the assumption that *but* has the logical properties of *and* (as argued in Chapter 3). However, now consider (184): intuitively this also fails to presuppose that John has children. But we cannot account for this in terms of the filtering rule for conjunctions, as readers may verify for themselves. However, we *could* account for it if *but* was here functioning like *or*, for then the filtering condition for disjunctions in (138) would correctly predict the loss of the presupposition. And, intuitively, this is the correct analysis: the most likely use of (183) is as a single speculation, but of (184) as two alternative or disjunctive speculations. So it is the use of an utterance in discourse for specific conversational purposes, rather than the logical properties of the particular connective, that seems to determine the appropriate filtering condition. Once again, presupposition proves contextually dependent.

In short, Karttunen & Peters' theory suffers from much of the inflexibility of theories of semantic presupposition, even though it differs from those theories by not including presuppositional inferences in the truth conditions of sentences.

The other sophisticated attempt to deal with the projection problem handles the problems of contextual defeasibility as well. In this theory, which is due to Gazdar (1979a, 1979b), presuppositions are assumed once again to be non-truth-conditional aspects of the meaning of linguistic expressions. As on the prior theory there is no way to predict the presuppositions of any linguistic expression simply given its truth-conditional characterization; instead presuppositions have to be arbitrarily associated with linguistic expressions, principally in the lexicon.

In contrast to the prior theory, in Gazdar's theory presuppositions are actually cancelled. First, all the **potential presuppositions** of a sentence are generated as a complete set, as in the original Langendoen & Savin (1971) suggestion. So at this stage, the presuppositions of any complex sentence will consist of all the presuppositions of each of its parts. Then a cancelling mechanism is brought into play which culls out of this total set of potential presuppositions all those that will survive to become **actual presuppositions** of a sentence uttered in a particular context. (Note that this distinction will allow us to talk sensibly about both sentences and utterances presupposing: sentences will be associated with potential presuppositions, utterances with actual presuppositions.)

The cancelling mechanism works in this way. The context here consists of a set of propositions that are mutually known by participants, or which would at least be accepted to be non-controversial. Participants therefore bring to a conversation or discourse some set of accepted propositions: e.g. 'France is a republic', 'the second world war ended in 1945', 'Joe Bloggs lives in Liverpool', or whatever. When they converse, participants augment the context by the addition of the propositions they express.[28] Crucial to Gazdar's theory is that this augmentation should proceed in a specific order:

---

[28] Actually, Gazdar's formulation is phrased only in terms of an individual speaker's commitment to what his utterances entail, implicate and presuppose, but there is a natural, though not necessarily simple, extension to what is jointly assumed by participants.

first the entailments of what are said are added to the context, then the conversational implicatures, and only finally the presuppositions. More precisely the order in which an utterance's inferences are added is that in (185):

(185)   1. the entailments of the uttered sentence S
         2. the *clausal* conversational implicatures of S
         3. the *scalar* conversational implicatures of S
         4. the presuppositions of S

The ordering is important because there is a crucial constraint put on the addition of new propositions to the context: at each step, the additional proposition may only be added if it is consistent with all the propositions already in the context. It is essential to the formalization of the theory, although it will not concern us here, that all potential implicatures and presuppositions are epistemically modified – i.e. what is implicated or presupposed as the proposition p on other theories, will here have the form 'the speaker knows that p' or symbolically, Kp.

Some examples will quickly demonstrate how cancellation of both conversational implicatures and presuppositions works. In Chapter 3 we showed that the conditional and the disjunction have the clausal implicatures indicated in (186):

(186)   A sentence of the form *if p then q* or *p or q* will clausally implicate $\{Pp, P \sim p, Pq, P \sim q\}$ (where Pp is to be read 'It is consistent with all the speaker knows that p')

We also showed that the assertion of a low point on a scale will implicate that a higher point on the scale does not hold, as in the examples in (187):

(187)   *some of the boys* implicates 'K(not all of the boys)'
         ten boys implicates 'K(not eleven or more)'
         the coffee was warm implicates 'K(the coffee was not hot)'

Now given the ordering in (185) and the consistency requirement, (189) will not have the same implicatures as (188) (as we noted in 3.2.4):

(188)   Some of the police, if not all of them, beat up the protester
(189)   Some of the police beat up the protester

Only (189) implicates (190), and this is accounted for by the fact that

(188) has the additional clausal implicature (due to the parenthetical conditional) (191) which is added to the context before the scalar implicature (190). But (190) is not consistent with (191), so when we come to add (190) to the context, we cannot, due to the fact that (191) has already been added. The implicature in (190) is therefore rejected.

(190)   The speaker knows that not all of the police beat up the protester

(191)   It is consistent with all the speaker knows that all of the police beat up the protester

Notice that if there had been an inconsistent entailment, as in (192), that also would block (190), which could not therefore be added to the context:

(192)   Some of the police, and in fact all of them, beat up the protester

If we now turn to presupposition cancellation, we see that the same mechanisms work. Thus, (193) potentially presupposes (194) due to the definite description in the consequent, but this is cancelled by the clausal implicature of the conditional construction, here (195):

(193)   If there is a King of France, the King of France doesn't any longer live in Versailles

(194)   The speaker knows that there exists a King of France

(195)   It is consistent with all the speaker knows that there is not a King of France

For (195) will be added to the context prior to the potential presupposition (194) and thus will block the addition of the latter, which is inconsistent with (195). The advantages of this mode of presupposition-blocking over the one utilized by Karttunen & Peters' theory become especially clear when one considers disjunctions and conditionals: on Karttunen & Peters' theory the filtering rules treat the clauses asymmetrically with the difficulties pointed out above in connection with (179), but Gazdar's theory makes the order of constituents irrelevant to the cancellation process.

Gazdar's theory also handles the cases of overt presupposition denial very straightforwardly. A sentence like (196) will entail (197), which will be added to the context prior to the potential presupposition (198) so ensuring that the latter is cancelled:

(196)   John doesn't regret failing, because in fact he passed

(197)   John passed
(198)   John failed

As a result this theory is the only extant presuppositional theory that
can handle sentences like (199):

(199)   The King of France doesn't exist

Other theories would commit their authors, given the truth of (199),
to the inconsistent propositions that there is a King of France and
there isn't.

In precisely the same way Gazdar's theory handles those cases like
(200), where a presupposition is cancelled simply by background
knowledge:

(200)   Kissinger ceased to be Secretary of State before the third world
          war started
(201)   The third world war started

For the presupposition (201) will simply not be added to the context
if it is inconsistent with what is already there. It is for this reason that
Gazdar can happily dispense with Karttunen's *plugs* – for example,
the presupposition due to *realize* in (202) will be rejected not because
it falls under a verb of saying but because we happen to know it is
not the case:

(202)   The student said that he hadn't realized that Wales was a
          republic

Similarly, for those sentences above like (84)–(96) where reference is
made to contextual assumptions in calculating the presuppositions of
a complex sentence, only Gazdar's theory allows such reference to
be made. Thus the presupposition of the *before*-clause in (203) is
cancelled just because it is inconsistent with what we already take for
granted (namely, that people without heads do not continue to do
things):

(203)   King Charles I had his head cut off half an hour before he
          finished filing through the bars

But the great strength of Gazdar's system is that while handling the
cases of contextual defeasibility, it predicts correctly the solutions to
the projection problem for sentences of arbitrary complexity. There
are relatively few counter-examples known (but see Gazdar 1979a:
156–7, and also Soames, 1979: 660). Given the complexities of the

projection problem, this suggests that there must at least be something correct about Gazdar's solution. It contrasts here with the Karttunen & Peters' solution using the categories of *plugs*, *filters* and *holes*, where no independent reasons for the existence of these categories can be advanced, and where the imperfect filtering conditions also have an unmotivated and *ad hoc* existence.

The two theories discussed above are the most developed theories of presupposition that deal with the projection problem in anything like an adequate way. However, they are by no means the only directions in which the best solutions may ultimately be found. In particular, both theories assume that each presupposition-trigger will have its own presupposition recorded in the lexicon or elsewhere. A theory that would be preferable, if it could be found, would not treat presuppositions item-by-item in this way, but rather would predict the presuppositions from the semantic content of presupposition-triggers, by means of general pragmatic principles. There are a number of indications that such a more powerful explanation will ultimately prove correct. First, there always seem to be intuitively close relations between the semantic content of presupposition-triggers and their corresponding presuppositions. In this way, presuppositions contrast with conventional implicatures, which often have no close relation to the semantic content of the linguistic items that give rise to them (e.g. in Javanese there is a word *pisang* that means 'banana', but conventionally implicates that the addressee is socially superior to the speaker). Secondly, the item-by-item treatment suggests that presuppositions are attached to presupposition-triggers merely by arbitrary convention. In that case, there would be no reason to expect presupposition-triggers in different languages to be parallel in any way; however, even in languages of quite different families, the linguistic items that give rise to presuppositions seem to be precisely parallel, in so far as the syntax and semantics of particular languages allow (see e.g. Annamalai & Levinson, in press). It seems reasonable, then, to hope that some theory of presupposition can be found that, given a trigger's semantic specification, will predict its presuppositions.

In order to show that alternative theories could be viable, it is useful to apply what we may call the *re-allocation programme*, a programme independent of any particular theory of presupposition and a sensible preliminary to any such theory. The first step is to assume that part of the difficulty of formulating adequate theories of presupposition arises from the fact that what is normally called *presupposition* is actually a heterogeneous collection of quite distinct and different phenomena, some perhaps semantic, others different varieties of pragmatic implication. The task then is to try to reduce presupposition to other kinds of inference, in particular to semantic entailment and matters of logical form on the one hand, and to conversational implicatures, conventional implicatures, felicity conditions and the like on the other. If this reductionist programme leaves no residue, then the notion *presupposition* would be successfully reduced to other more useful concepts. If, on the other hand, some clear cases of presuppositional phenomena remain unreducible, then we can formulate a theory of presupposition to handle just these cases.

Most theorists have assumed that at least some such re-allocation of the phenomena is due, and have argued accordingly (for different versions see e.g. Keenan, 1971; Kempson, 1975; Wilson, 1975; Karttunen & Peters, 1977, 1979). Karttunen & Peters have argued for total reduction, mostly to conventional implicature, but this is little more than a terminological switch, and displaces other phenomena that seem better thought of as conventional implicatures (see Chapter 3 above). In reality their concept of conventional implicature has largely been fashioned to deal precisely with the class of facts once called presuppositions. More genuine reductionism – in this case mostly to matters of entailment and conversational implicature – has been advocated independently by Atlas (1975b), Kempson (1975), Wilson (1975), Boër & Lycan (1976), and more recently by Wilson & Sperber (1979) and Atlas & Levinson (1981).

The attraction and initial plausibility of the reduction to matters of entailment and conversational implicature can be gauged best from some examples. If we take the cleft construction as in (204) and its associated presupposition as in (205):

(204)   It was his coat that John lost
(205)   John lost something

we can see immediately that in fact (204) entails (205) – in all worlds in which John loses his coat it will also be true that he loses something. It is therefore only necessary to invoke the notion of presupposition in the negative cases, as in (206):

(206)   It wasn't his coat that John lost

which still continues to pragmatically imply (205). But here we could say that the implication is in fact a conversational implicature, of the generalized variety. To show this, we must produce a Gricean argument of the standard sort that will show that in order to preserve the assumption of co-operation, a hearer of (206) must assume (205). The argument might go roughly as follows:

1.　The speaker has said (206), and not the simpler (207):

(207)　John didn't lose his coat

2.　The logical form of (206) might be roughly as in (208):

(208)　$\sim (\exists x \, (\text{Lost } (j, x) \, \& \, (x = jcoat)))$

3.　Like most negative sentences (208) is not very informative; therefore if the speaker is co-operating it is likely that he intended to convey more than what the relatively uninformative statement actually means

4.　The utterance (206) would be relatively informative if the speaker meant in fact to convey one of the following related propositions:

(209)　$\exists x \, (\sim \text{Lost } (j, x) \, \& \, (x = jcoat))$
(210)　$\exists x \, (\text{Lost } (j, x) \, \& \, (x \neq jcoat))$

But (209) is more directly expressed by (211),

(211)　It was his coat that John didn't lose

so if the speaker had meant that he should, by the maxim of Manner, have said it directly; since he didn't, (210) is left as the more informative reading of (206).

5.　To preserve the assumption of co-operation, the relatively uninformative sentence (206) should be read as (210), which entails the 'presupposition' (205); the speaker has done nothing to stop me so reasoning, so this is what he must intend to convey

An argument of this sort can be faulted in various ways. It is based in fact on the *principle of informativeness* (outlined in 3.2.4) rather than on Grice's maxims, and it fails to explain why the cleft sentence was used in the first place. Moreover such an approach to presupposition in general would be both *ad hoc* and piecemeal: for each kind of presupposition-trigger an argument of this sort will have to be made. An approach based on general principles that would apply to a large range of presuppositional phenomena would be preferable if it could be found. Here two recent suggestions deserve mention.

The first, advanced by Wilson & Sperber (1979), is that semantic representations should be enriched in such a way that simple pragmatic principles interacting with them will predict what is presupposed. They suggest that all the entailments of a sentence are not on a par; rather an adequate semantic representation would consist of an ordered set of entailments, divided into two sets – **background** and **foreground** entailments. The actual ordering of entailments is logical: if entailment A in turn entails entailment B, then A is ordered before B. However, a sentence may have a number of such chains of entailment, and the importance of one such chain, and the distinction between foreground and background entailments, is determined not by logical considerations, but by grammatical form (including stress). For example, (212) with heavy stress on *Sarah*, will determine the **focal scale** (or chain of entailments) in (213):

(212)   John is married to *Sarah*
(213)   a. John is married to Sarah (*foreground*)
          b. John is married to someone (1st *background* entailment)
          c. John has some property
          d. Something is the case

This scale is obtained by substituting existentially quantified variables (or *someone, something*) for constituents in the sentence, starting with the focus constituent, here *Sarah* (see Chomsky, 1972). Now, the first entailment obtained by substitution of a variable for the focus (here *b*), is the first background entailment; all those entailed by it (here, *c* and *d*) are also part of the background. All entailments ordered above the background, here only *a*, are part of the foreground. Given this much semantic structure, we can then bring a simple pragmatic rule to bear: the background entailments of a sentence are assumed to be not relevant in the context. What is assumed to be relevant, and thus the *point* of saying the sentence, is whatever information has to be added to the background to obtain the foreground – namely the entailments ordered above the background (here *a*). Thus the point of saying (212) would normally be to assert that it is Sarah that is John's spouse, against an assumed background that John is married to someone. Hence, under denial or questioning, the background will continue to be assumed, and only the foreground denied or questioned. In short, so-called 'presuppositions' are just background entailments.

For example, (214) will have the same structure of entailments as (212):

(214)   It is Sarah that John is married to

This semantic structure is again determined by grammatical structure – here by the cleft construction rather than by heavy stress. So the alleged presupposition of clefts is simply the first background entailment, here (213b) above.

The idea of enriching semantic representations so that pragmatic principles can interact with them in complex ways seems the correct theoretical move. However, the use of entailment in this way will again raise all the problems that undermined semantic theories of presupposition, namely the joint difficulties of defeasibility in linguistic and extra-linguistic context, and survival in modal and opaque contexts where entailments cannot survive. We will not willingly re-invoke these difficulties if any alternative can be found. And if Wilson & Sperber wish to retreat to an account in terms of conversational implicatures in complex sentences, then they have not shown us how to do this.

The other approach, advocated by Atlas & Levinson (1981), is to take much more seriously the role of logical form (or the structure of a semantic representation) in the production of pragmatic inferences. We have already argued (in 3.2.2) that conversational implicatures are sensitive to the details of logical form; sentences with the same or similar truth conditions, but different logical forms, can have quite different conversational implicatures. But on what grounds, other than predicting the right entailment relations, should we hypothesize a particular logical form for a sentence? Perhaps these: (a) it should capture the intuitively significant semantic structure of the sentence, (b) it should accurately predict the pragmatic inferences it will generate in context. Amongst the aspects of structure in (a) might be the identification of what a sentence is *about* (Putnam, 1958). (What a sentence is about might then have a close relation to pragmatic notions of what is *given* or assumed in discourse.) For example, there seems to be an intuition that what a sentence is about is indicated by its grammatical structure; and that this has some relation to its logical structure. In simple sentences what a sentence is about seems to coincide with the logical subject: thus *Mary slept* would be about Mary. We might now try and regiment our logical forms for complex sentences so that what such sentences are about coincides with their logical subjects. Such a line leads to quite

complex logical forms, and yet these do seem to capture some
intuitions about the significant semantic structure of sentences. For
example, the logical form hypothesized for the cleft sentence (215)
can be argued on detailed semantic and pragmatic grounds to be
(216):

(215)   It was John that Mary kissed
(216) $\lambda x(x = \text{John})\,(\gamma x \text{Kiss}(\text{Mary}, x))$

We have made use here of two complex logical devices: **lambda-
extraction**, which can be used to construct complex properties
(Allwood, Andersson & Dahl, 1977: 155) and the **group-** or **gamma-
operator**, which constructs collective terms, so that $\gamma x A(x)$ reads 'a
group of individuals x that have the property A'. Thus (216) as a
whole reads 'A group kissed by Mary has the property of being
identical to John'. The logical subject is thus 'A group kissed by
Mary', and this is what the sentence is *about*; this corresponds to the
surface structure clause (*one(s)*) *that Mary kissed*. Such a logical form
will entail that Mary kissed someone, and that Mary kissed John, but
it does not have exactly the same truth conditions as the uncleftled
Mary kissed John (since it entails that Mary kissed just John).

  We now invoke a general pragmatic principle: if a sentence is about
t, then the existence or actuality of t can be assumed to be non-
controversial or given, unless there are specific indications or
assumptions to the contrary. The cleft sentence (215) is about its
logical subject in (216): those kissed by Mary. This logical subject
is responsible for the entailment 'Mary kissed someone'. For
positive cleft sentences we now have the following account: such
sentences entail their alleged presuppositions, but since these propositions are derived from what the sentence is about, and are thus
assumed to be given, they will normally not be the main point
expressed by asserting such sentences.

  For the negative cleft, as in (217):

(217)   It wasn't John that Mary kissed

the account would run as follows. The logical form of (217) is (218),
where negation is (as generally in natural languages) external or
wide-scope.[29] Such logical forms with wide-scope negation are not

---

[29] This is the normal assumption made by *radical pragmatics*, i.e. the attempt
to maximally simplify semantics by developing pragmatics (see Cole, 1981).
However, rather more complex approaches to negation may in fact be
required – see Atlas, 1977, 1979.

very informative: the logical form of (217) merely states that (215) is not the case, without indicating how it fails to be true. However, there is again a general pragmatic principle, the **principle of informativeness** (discussed in Chapter 3), which legitimates the interpretation of wide-scope negation as narrow-scope or predicate negation. The utterance of (217) with the logical form (218) will therefore have the preferred interpretation indicated in (219):

(218) $\sim (\lambda x(x = \text{John})(\gamma x \text{Kiss}(\text{Mary}, x)))$
         i.e. 'It is not the case that a group that Mary kissed has the property of being identical to John'

(219) $\lambda x(x \neq \text{John})(\gamma x \text{Kiss}(\text{Mary}, x))$
         i.e. 'A group that Mary kissed has the property of not being identical to John'

Once again, then, the statement will be about its logical subject, 'one(s) who Mary kissed' (in general, if F(a) is about a, $\sim$ F(a) is about a). Now since saying (217) implicates (219), and (219) has the logical subject outside the scope of negation, the implicature (219) entails that Mary kissed someone. So, in the negative cleft, the proposition that Mary kissed someone will be entailed by an implicature, and thus itself implicated. Moreover, it is the logical subject (what the sentence is about) that is responsible for this implicature, so the proposition 'Mary kissed someone' will once again be assumed to be given.

An approach of this sort is meant to have general application, along the following lines. First we motivate the setting up of complex logical forms by making them responsible for capturing aspects of significant semantic structure. Then we examine how these enriched semantic representations interact with pragmatic principles of interpretation, not only of Grice's sort, but of a sort that actually add information to the semantic content of the sentence (e.g. the principle of informativeness). Here we look for general processes: for example, the relation between logical subjects, 'aboutness', and a preferred interpretation in which what a sentence is about can be presumed. The hope is that by enriching both semantic representations and pragmatic principles in this way, they will interact in a more intimate manner, and that this interaction will be seen to be responsible in a systematic way for the apparently *ad hoc* inferences called presuppositions.

There is one immediate objection to any such reduction of presupposition to entailment and implicature: unlike conversational implicatures, presuppositions appear to be **detachable** in Grice's sense (see 3.1 and 3.2.1). That is, whereas in the case of implicatures it is generally impossible to find another way to say the same thing that lacks the same implicatures, in the case of presuppositions the inferences seem to be attached directly to certain aspects of the surface form of linguistic expressions – e.g. to the cleft construction itself.

In fact, though, the difference is more apparent than real. Consider, for example, the verb *regret* which is claimed to have, as an arbitrary additional aspect of its meaning, the presupposition that its complement is true. If the presupposition was really detachable it ought to be possible to find different ways of making the same statement that lacked the presupposition in question. But this is not easy. Consider for example all the near-paraphrases in (220):

(220)   a. John regrets that he ate all the pudding
        b. John is sorry that he ate all the pudding
        c. John repents of having eaten all the pudding
        d. John is unhappy that he ate all the pudding
        e. John feels contrite about eating all the pudding
        f. John feels penitent about eating all the pudding
        g. John feels remorse about eating all the pudding

All of these, and all of their negative counterparts, continue to presuppose what the sentence with *regret* in it does, namely:

(221)   John ate all the pudding

If readers now return to the list of presuppositional phenomena above, and armed with a thesaurus try to find paraphrases, they will discover that it is in fact very difficult to obtain expressions with similar meanings that lack the presuppositions in question. And where exceptionally they can be found, it may often be because the logical forms in question are in fact quite different enough to trigger distinct implicatures.

The reductionist could therefore claim that presuppositions share two very important features with conversational implicatures – namely defeasibility and non-detachability. The only major distinctive characteristic of presuppositions that remains is the projection problem, the behaviour of presuppositions in complex sentences. But this distinction too can easily be eroded, as some examples will indicate. Firstly, survival under modal operators seems to be a feature shared by both presuppositions and implicatures. Thus (222) and (223), where the latter is (222) embedded under a modal, can share the same implicature (224):

(222)   John has some of the tools
(223)   It's possible that John has some of the tools
(224)   (Speaker knows that) John has not got all of the tools

If we then turn to the most specific property of presupposition projection, namely filtering in conditionals and disjunctions, we find again that implicatures can mimic presuppositions. Consider, for example:

(225)   John has some of the tools, if not all of them

where the consequent (= (222)) implicates (224) but the whole sentence does not have this implicature. But this is precisely the circumstance under which presuppositions are filtered, as indicated in the filtering condition in (137) above. Or consider (226):

(226)   Either John has all of the tools, or he has some of them

where the second disjunct implicates (224) but the sentence as a whole lacks this implicature. But this is precisely the condition under which presuppositions are filtered in disjunctions too (see (138) above). So it really is far from clear that presuppositions are distinguished from conversational implicatures by their behaviour in compound and complex sentences.

The reductionist programme thus remains open. The main difficulties that remain are establishing sufficiently rich logical forms to trigger implicatures that will effectively model presuppositions, and some of the more esoteric parts of the projection problem. Recollect, for example, that Gazdar uses implicatures to cancel presuppositions and in this way obtains remarkably accurate predictions of presuppositional behaviour in complex sentences. How can the reductionist use the same apparatus, given that he would have to use implicatures to cancel implicatures? In fact it is possible in a very large range of cases to adapt Gazdar's mechanisms, allowing entailments to cancel implicatures and allowing implicatures due to higher constructions to cancel inconsistent implicatures that arise from embedded clauses. Thus in (227) the implicature from the embedded sentence (228) is (229):

(227)   Some of the boys went to the party, if not all

(228)   Some of the boys went to the party
(229)   Not all of the boys went to the party

but this is cancelled – on this theory – because there is an inconsistent implicature from the matrix sentence, namely (230) due to the conditional construction:

(230)   It is consistent with all the speaker knows that it is not the case that (229) is true

This principle of 'matrix wins' works extremely well for the majority of cases. It is too early to know whether or not this approach, or something similar, is ultimately viable.

4.5 Conclusions

We began this Chapter by noting that philosophical and linguistic treatments of presupposition deal with a very much narrower range of phenomena than are included within the ordinary language sense of the term. The general pragmatic effects of foregrounding and backgrounding information within a sentence can be achieved in many ways that are not presuppositional in this narrow sense, e.g. by changing word order, utilizing syntactic subordination, prosodic emphasis or the emphatic particles provided by many languages. There is considerable overlap, but no equivalence, between presuppositional accounts and accounts in terms of the **topic /comment** distinction (not reviewed in this book; see e.g. Clark & Haviland, 1977; Gundel, 1977; Foley & Van Valin, in press). Yet even within this narrow scope, we have shown that there are considerable problems to be overcome. Above all, if, as seems likely, presuppositions are not correctly treated as inferences associated with linguistic elements item-by-item in a non-predictable way, then at present we have no adequate theory at all. In that case, what we need is a theory that predicts presuppositions from the semantic specification of linguistic expressions. Such a theory would be an essentially hybrid account: presuppositions would not be *sui generis*, but rather the result of complex interactions between semantics and pragmatics. But to model such interactions we need to know considerably more about both the structure of semantic representations and the pragmatic principles that interact with them. We conclude that presupposition remains, ninety years after Frege's remarks on the subject, still only partially understood, and an important ground for the study of how semantics and pragmatics interact.

5
Speech acts

5.0 Introduction[1]

Of all the issues in the general theory of language usage, **speech act theory** has probably aroused the widest interest. Psychologists, for example, have suggested that the acquisition of the concepts underlying speech acts may be a prerequisite for the acquisition of language in general (see e.g. Bruner, 1975; Bates, 1976), literary critics have looked to speech act theory for an illumination of textual subtleties or for an understanding of the nature of literary genres (see e.g. Ohmann, 1971; Levin, 1976), anthropologists have hoped to find in the theory some account of the nature of magical spells and ritual in general (see e.g. Tambiah, 1968), philosophers have seen potential applications to, amongst other things, the status of ethical statements (see e.g. Searle, 1969: Chapter 8), while linguists have seen the notions of speech act theory as variously applicable to problems in syntax (see e.g. Sadock, 1974), semantics (see e.g. Fillmore, 1971a), second language learning (see e.g. Jakobovitz & Gordon, 1974), and elsewhere. Meanwhile in linguistic pragmatics, speech acts remain, along with presupposition and implicature in particular, one of the central phenomena that any general pragmatic theory must account for.

Given this widespread interest, there is an enormous literature on the subject, and in this Chapter we cannot review all the work within linguistics, let alone the large and technical literature within philosophy, from which (like all the other concepts we have so far reviewed) the basic theories come. Rather, what is attempted here is a brief sketch of the philosophical origins, and a laying out of the different positions that have been taken on the crucial issues, together

[1] Parts of this Chapter are based on an earlier review article (Levinson, 1980).

with indications of some general problems that all theories of speech acts have to face.

5.1 Philosophical background

Issues of truth and falsity have been of central interest throughout much of the discussion of deixis, presupposition and implicature. Indeed those issues derive much of their interest from the way in which they remind us of the strict limitations to what can be captured in a truth-conditional analysis of sentence meaning. Nevertheless in the 1930s there flourished what can now be safely treated as a philosophical excess, namely the doctrine of **logical positivism**, a central tenet of which was that unless a sentence can, at least in principle, be *verified* (i.e. tested for its truth or falsity), it was strictly speaking *meaningless*. Of course it followed that most ethical, aesthetic and literary discourses, not to mention most everyday utterances, were simply meaningless. But rather than being seen as a *reductio ad absurdum*, such a conclusion was viewed by proponents of logical positivism as a positively delightful result (see the marvellously prescriptive work by Ayer (1936)), and the doctrine was pervasive in philosophical circles at the time. It was this movement (which Wittgenstein had partly stimulated in his *Tractatus Logico-Philosophicus* (1921)) that the later Wittgenstein was actively attacking in *Philosophical Investigations* with the well known slogan "meaning is use" (1958: para. 43) and the insistence that utterances are only explicable in relation to the activities, or **language-games**, in which they play a role.

It was in this same period, when concern with verifiability and distrust of the inaccuracies and vacuities of ordinary language were paramount, that Austin launched his theory of speech acts. There are strong parallels between the later Wittgenstein's emphasis on language usage and language-games and Austin's insistence that "the total speech act in the total speech situation is the *only actual* phenomenon which, in the last resort, we are engaged in elucidating" (1962: 147). Nevertheless Austin appears to have been largely unaware of, and probably quite uninfluenced by, Wittgenstein's later work, and we may treat Austin's theory as autonomous.[2]

---

[2] See Furberg, 1971: 50ff and Passmore, 1968: 597, who trace Austin's ideas rather to a long established Aristotelian tradition of concern for ordinary language usage at Oxford, where Austin worked (Wittgenstein was at

In the set of lectures that were posthumously published as *How To Do Things With Words*,[3] Austin set about demolishing, in his mild and urbane way, the view of language that would place truth conditions as central to language understanding. His method was this.

First, he noted that some ordinary language declarative sentences, contrary to logical positivist assumptions, are not apparently used with any intention of making true or false statements. These seem to form a special class, and are illustrated below:

(1)   I bet you six pence it will rain tomorrow
                I hereby christen this ship the H.M.S. Flounder
                I declare war on Zanzibar
                I apologize
                I dub thee Sir Walter
                I object
                I sentence you to ten years of hard labour
                I bequeath you my Sansovino
                I give my word
                I warn you that trespassers will be prosecuted

The peculiar thing about these sentences, according to Austin, is that they are not used just to *say* things, i.e. describe states of affairs, but rather actively to *do* things.[4] After you've declared war on Zanzibar, or dubbed Sir Walter, or raised an objection, the world has changed in substantial ways. Further, you cannot assess such utterances as true or false – as is illustrated by the bizarre nature of the following exchanges:

Cambridge). Both philosophers worked out their later theories at about the same time, the late 1930s (judging from the claim in the introduction to Austin's basic work *How To Do Things With Words*, delivered as lectures for the last time in 1955, and not published till 1962). Wittgenstein's ideas in the late 1930s were only available in manuscript form (see Furberg, 1971: 51).

[3] This is the central source for Austin's theory of speech acts, but see also Austin, 1970b, 1971. His views on word-meaning, truth and propositional content – which do not all mesh closely with his theory of speech acts – can be found in Chapters 3, 5 and 6, respectively, of Austin, 1970a. For commentaries on Austin's work, the reader should see the collection in Fann, 1969, and the monographic treatments in Graham, 1977 and especially Furberg, 1971.

[4] Here, as so often in the literature on speech acts, it is tacitly assumed that we are not considering *metalinguistic* uses of sentences, as in linguistic examples, or other special uses in which sentences do not carry their full pragmatic force or interpretation, as in novels, plays and nursery rhymes.

(2)   A: I second the motion
             B: That's false
(3)   A: I dub thee Sir Walter
             B: Too true

Austin termed these peculiar and special sentences, and the utterances realized by them, **performatives**, and contrasted them to statements, assertions and utterances like them, which he called **constatives**.

Austin then went on to suggest that although, unlike constatives, performatives cannot be true or false (given their special nature, the question of truth and falsity simply does not arise), yet they can go wrong. He then set himself the task of cataloguing all the ways in which they can go wrong, or be 'unhappy', or **infelicitous** as he put it. For instance, suppose I say *I christen this ship the Imperial Flagship Mao*, I may not succeed in so christening the vessel if, for instance, it is already named otherwise, or I am not the appointed namer, or there are no witnesses, slipways, bottles of champagne, etc. Successfully naming a ship requires certain institutional arrangements, without which the action that the utterance attempts to perform is simply null and void. On the basis of such different ways in which a performative can fail to come off, Austin produced a typology of conditions which performatives must meet if they are to succeed or be 'happy'. He called these conditions **felicity conditions**, and he distinguished three main categories:

(4)   A. (i)   There must be a conventional procedure having a
                      conventional effect
                 (ii) The circumstances and persons must be appropriate,
                      as specified in the procedure
             B. The procedure must be executed (i) correctly and (ii)
                completely
             C. Often, (i) the persons must have the requisite thoughts,
                feelings and intentions, as specified in the procedure, and
                (ii) if consequent conduct is specified, then the relevant
                parties must so do

As evidence of the existence of such conditions, consider what happens when some of them are not fulfilled. For example, suppose, as a British citizen, I say to my wife:

(5)   I hereby divorce you

I will not thereby achieve a divorce, because there simply is no such procedure (as in A (i)) whereby merely by uttering (5) divorce can be achieved. In contrast, in Muslim cultures there is such a procedure, whereby the uttering of a sentence with the import of (5) three times consecutively does thereby and *ipso facto* constitute a divorce. As an illustration of a failure of condition A (ii), consider a clergyman baptizing the wrong baby, or the right baby with the wrong name (Albert for Alfred, say), or consider the case of one head of state welcoming another, but addressing the attendant bodyguard in error. As for condition B (i), the words must be the conventionally correct ones – the response in (6) simply will not do in the Church of England marriage ceremony:

(6)   Curate: Wilt thou have this woman to thy wedded wife
                 ... and, forsaking all other, keep thee only unto
                 her, so long as ye both shall live?
        Bridegroom: Yes

The bridgegroom must say *I will*. Further, the procedure must be complete as required by B (ii): if I bet you six pence that it will rain tomorrow, then for the bet to take effect you must ratify the arrangement with *You're on* or something with like effect – or in Austin's terminology, there must be satisfactory **uptake**. Finally, violations of the C conditions are insincerities: to advise someone to do something when you really think it would be advantageous for you but not for him, or for a juror to find a defendant guilty when he knows him to be innocent, would be to violate condition C (i). And to promise to do something which one has no intention whatsoever of doing would be a straightforward violation of C (ii).

Austin notes that these violations are not all of equal stature. Violations of A and B conditions give rise to **misfires** as he puts it – i.e. the intended actions simply fail to come off. Violations of C conditions on the other hand are **abuses**, not so easily detected at the time of the utterance in question, with the consequence that the action is performed, but infelicitously or insincerely.

On the basis of these observations Austin declares that (a) some sentences, performatives, are special: uttering them *does* things, and does not merely say things (report states of affairs); and (b) these performative sentences achieve their corresponding actions because there are specific *conventions* linking the words to institutional procedures. Performatives are, if one likes, just rather special sorts of ceremony. And unlike constatives, which are assessed in terms of truth and falsity, performatives can only be assessed as felicitous or infelicitous, according to whether their felicity conditions are met or not.

But Austin is playing cunning: given this much, he has his wedge into the theory of language and he systematically taps it home. Readers of *How To Do Things With Words* should be warned that there is an internal evolution to the argument, so that what is proposed at the beginning is rejected by the end. Indeed what starts off as a theory about some special and peculiar utterances – performatives – ends up as a general theory that pertains to all kinds of utterances. Consequently there are two crucial sliding definitions or concepts: firstly, there is a shift from the view that performatives are a special class of sentences with peculiar syntactic and pragmatic properties, to the view that there is a general class of performative utterances that includes both **explicit performatives** (the old familiar class) and **implicit performatives**, the latter including lots of other kinds of utterances, if not all.[5] Secondly, there is a shift from the dichotomy performative/constative to a general theory of **illocutionary acts** of which the various performatives and constatives are just special sub-cases. Let us take these two shifts in order, and review Austin's arguments for the theoretical "sea-change", as he puts it.

If the dichotomy between performatives and constatives is to bear the important load that Austin indicates, namely the distinction between truth-conditionally assessed utterances and those assessed in terms of felicity, then it had better be possible to tell the difference – i.e. to characterize performatives in independent terms. Austin therefore teases us with an attempt to characterize performatives in linguistic terms. He notes that the paradigm cases, as in (1) above, seem to have the following properties: they are first person indicative active sentences in the simple present tense. This is hardly surprising, since, if in uttering a performative the speaker is concurrently performing an action, we should expect just those properties. Thus we get the

---

[5] Austin does not oppose the terms *sentence* and *utterance* in the way done in this book – he talks about *performative sentences* and *performative utterances* pretty much interchangeably (although he notes that not all utterances are sentences – Austin, 1962: 6). In our terminology, in so far as it is possible to characterize performative utterances as being performed by specific types of sentence it makes sense to talk about performative sentences too – this being less obviously possible for implicit performatives.

contrast between the following sentences: only the first can be uttered performatively.

(7)   a. I bet you five pounds it'll rain tomorrow
           b. I am betting you five pounds it'll rain tomorrow
           c. I betted you five pounds it'll rain tomorrow[6]
           d. He bets you five pounds it'll rain tomorrow

The progressive aspect in (7b) renders that (most probably) a reminder, as does the third person in (7d), while the past tense in (7c) indicates a report; none of these constatives seems, then, to be capable of doing betting, unlike the performative (7a). However, convincing though this paradigm is at first sight, there are plenty of other uses of first person indicative active sentences in the simple present, for example:

(8)   I now beat the eggs till fluffy

which can be said in demonstration, simply as a report of a concurrent action. So we shall need other criteria as well if we are to isolate performatives alone. Here one might fall back on a vocabulary definition – only some verbs appear to be usable in this performative syntactic frame with the special property of performing an action simply by being uttered. To distinguish the performative simple present from other kinds, one can note that only the performative usage can co-occur with the adverb *hereby*; and thus one can isolate out the **performative verbs** by seeing whether they will take *hereby*:

(9)   a. I hereby declare you Mayor of Casterbridge
           b. ?I hereby now beat the eggs till fluffy
           c. ?I hereby jog ten miles on Sundays

Declare is shown thereby to be a performative verb, while *beat* and *run* are clearly not. So now we can take all these criteria together: performative utterances are identifiable because they have the form of first person indicative active sentences in the simple present with one of a delimited set of performative verbs as the main verb, which will collocate with the adverb *hereby*.

However that won't quite do either. Consider (10) – could this performative not be expressed equally well as (11)? Or (12) as (13), or even (14)?

---

[6] Some varieties of English have past tense *bet*; readers finding (7c) odd may try substituting *did bet* for *betted*.

(10)   I hereby warn you
(11)   You are hereby warned
(12)   I find you guilty of doing it
(13)   You did it
(14)   Guilty!

But if that is so, then the grammatical properties of performatives go by the board. Nor can we just fall back on the vocabulary definition alone, for performative verbs can be used non-performatively as in (7b) above, and (14) contains no verb at all. Moreover even when all the conditions we have collected so far are met, utterances exhibiting these properties are not necessarily performative, as illustrated by (15):

(15)   A: How do you get me to throw all these parties?
         B: I promise to come

So what Austin suggests is that explicit performatives are really just relatively specialized ways of being unambiguous or specific about what act you are performing in speaking. Instead, you can employ cruder devices, less explicit and specific, like mood[7] (as in *Shut it*, instead of *I order you to shut it*), or adverbs (as in *I'll be there without fail* instead of *I promise I'll be there*), or particles (like *Therefore, X* instead of *I conclude that X*). Or you can rely on intonation to distinguish *It's going to charge* as a warning, a question or a protest; or simply allow for contextual disambiguation. Perhaps, he suggests, only "developed" literate cultures will find much use for the explicit performative.

Nevertheless, despite the fact that Austin has now conceded that utterances can be performative without being in the *normal form* of explicit performatives, he suggests that performative verbs are still the best way into a systematic study of all the different kinds of performative utterance. This suggestion seems to rely on the claim that every non-explicit performative could in principle be put into the form of an explicit performative, so that by studying the latter alone we shall not be missing any special varieties of action that can be achieved only by other kinds of utterance. (A principle reified by Searle (1969: 19ff) as a general **principle of expressibility** – "anything that can be meant can be said"; Austin was, as always, more cautious (see Austin, 1962: 91).) The aim is to produce a

---

[7] This is Austin's term: below we shall distinguish *mood* from *sentence-type*.

systematic classification of such acts, and Austin sees this as just a matter of "prolonged fieldwork" (1962: 148), using the *hereby* test to extract performative verbs from a dictionary. He produces a tentative five-fold classification that he implies emerges naturally, as genera might if you were collecting butterflies, into which may be sorted the many thousands of performative verbs that he estimates to be in the language. Since many other classificatory schemes have since been advanced, there appears to be little to justify his own, and we shall not recount the details here, although the taxonomic issue will recur below.

Let us now turn to the other major shift in Austin's work, from the original distinction between constatives and performatives to the view that there is a whole family of speech acts of which constatives and the various performatives are each just particular members. How this substantial change comes about is this. First, the class of performatives has been, as we have seen, slowly extended to include *implicit performatives*,[8] so that the utterance *Go!*, for example, may be variously performing the giving of advice, or an order, or doing entreating, or daring, according to context. So pretty soon the only kinds of utterances that are *not* doing actions as well as, or instead of, simply reporting facts and events, are statements or constatives. But then are statements really such special kinds of utterance? May they too not have a performative aspect?

Once the doubt is voiced, a few observations will confirm the insubstantial nature of the performative/constative dichotomy. For example, there is clearly no real incompatibility between utterances being truth-bearers, and simultaneously performing actions. For example:

(16)   I warn you the bull will charge

seems simultaneously to perform the action of warning, and to issue a prediction which can be assessed as true or false. But, most convincingly, it can be shown that statements (and constatives in general) are liable to just the infelicities that performatives have been shown to be. Indeed for each of the A, B, and C conditions in (4) above, we can find violations of the sort that rendered performatives

---

[8] Austin preferred the term **primary** to **implicit**, in order to emphasize the rather specialized nature of explicit performatives (1962: 69); but the usage is no longer current.

void or insincere. For example, take the condition A (ii), requiring that the circumstances and persons must be appropriate for the relevant action to be performed. Then, just as (17) fails if I do not own a Raphael, so (18) fails if John does not in fact have any children:

(17)   I bequeath you my Raphael
(18)   All of John's children are monks

Presupposition failure is thus, in the domain of constatives, clearly paralleled in the domain of performatives, where it renders the utterance infelicitous or void. Similarly, if one offers advice or delivers a warning, one is obligated to have good grounds for the advice or warning, in just the same way as one should be able to back up an assertion or constative. If the grounds are feeble, all three kinds of utterance share the same kind of infelicity. Or, considering the C condition, requiring the appropriate feelings and intentions, one can see that just as promises require sincere intentions about future action, so statements require sincere beliefs about the factuality of what is asserted. Hence the close parallel between the infelicity of (19) and the infelicity of the statement in (20) ('Moore's paradox'):

(19)   I promise to be there, and I have no intention of being there
(20)   The cat is on the mat, and I don't believe it

The critic might hold that, nevertheless, truth and felicity are quite different kinds of thing – there may be degrees of felicity and infelicity, but there is only either true or false. But Austin points out that statements like those in (21) are not so easily thought of in such black and white terms:

(21)   France is hexagonal
         Oxford is forty miles from London

One wants to say of such statements that they are more or less, or roughly, true. Austin concludes that the dichotomy between statements, as truth-bearers, and performatives, as action-performers, can no longer be maintained. After all, is not (22) a statement in the performative normal form?

(22)   I state that I am alone responsible

The dichotomy between performatives and constatives is thus rejected in favour of a general full-blown theory of speech acts, in which statements (and constatives in general) will merely be a special case.

So it is now claimed that all utterances, in addition to meaning whatever they mean, perform specific actions (or 'do things') through having specific **forces**, as Austin was fond of saying:

> Besides the question that has been very much studied in the past as to what a certain utterance *means*, there is a further question distinct from this as to what was the *force*, as we call it, of the utterance. We may be quite clear what 'Shut the door' means, but not yet at all clear on the further point as to whether as uttered at a certain time it was an order, an entreaty or whatnot. What we need besides the old doctrine about meanings is a new doctrine about all the possible forces of utterances, towards the discovery of which our proposed list of explicit performative verbs would be a very great help. (Austin 1970a: 251)

But if this notion that, in uttering sentences, one is also doing things, is to be clear, we must first clarify in what ways in uttering a sentence one might be said to be performing actions. Austin isolates three basic senses in which in saying something one is doing something, and hence three kinds of acts that are simultaneously performed:

(i)   **locutionary act**: the utterance of a sentence with determinate sense and reference

(ii) **illocutionary act**: the making of a statement, offer, promise, etc. in uttering a sentence, by virtue of the conventional *force* associated with it (or with its explicit performative paraphrase)

(iii) **perlocutionary act**: the bringing about of effects on the audience by means of uttering the sentence, such effects being special to the circumstances of utterance

It is of course the second kind, the illocutionary act, that is the focus of Austin's interest, and indeed the term **speech act** has come to refer exclusively (as in the title of this Chapter) to that kind of act. Austin is careful to argue that (i) and (ii) are detachable, and therefore that the study of meaning may proceed independently, but supplemented by a theory of illocutionary acts. More troublesome, it seemed to him, was the distinction between (ii) and (iii). Some examples of his will indicate how he intended it to apply:

(23)   Shoot her!

One may say of this utterance that, in appropriate circumstances, it had the **illocutionary force** of, variously, ordering, urging, advising the addressee to shoot her; but the **perlocutionary effect** of persuading, forcing, or frightening the addressee into shooting her. (Or, he might have added, it might have the perlocutionary effect of frightening *her*.) Similarly, the utterance of (24) may have the illocutionary force of protesting, but the perlocutionary effects of checking the addressee's action, or bringing him to his senses, or simply annoying him.

(24)   You can't do that

In sum, then, the illocutionary act is what is directly achieved by the conventional force associated with the issuance of a certain kind of utterance in accord with a conventional procedure, and is consequently determinate (in principle at least). In contrast, a perlocutionary act is specific to the circumstances of issuance, and is therefore not conventionally achieved just by uttering that particular utterance, and includes all those effects, intended or unintended, often indeterminate, that some particular utterance in a particular situation may cause. The distinction has loose boundaries, Austin admits, but as an operational test one may see whether one can paraphrase the hypothetical illocutionary force of an utterance as an explicit performative: if one can, the act performed is an illocutionary act; if not, the act performed is a perlocutionary act. One particular problem is that, while one would like to be able to identify the perlocutionary effects with the *consequences* of what has been said, illocutionary acts too have direct and in-built consequences – there is the issue of **uptake** (including the *understanding* of both the force and the content of the utterance by its addressee(s) – see Austin, 1962: 116), and the need for the ratification of, for example, a bet or an offer, while certain illocutions like promising or declaring war have consequent actions specified. This interactional emphasis (on what the recipient(s) of an illocutionary act must think or do) in Austin's work has unfortunately been neglected in later work in speech act theory (see Austin, 1962: Lecture IX).

These seem to be Austin's main contributions to the subject; his work, though, is not easy to summarize as it is rich with suggestions that are not followed up, and avoids dogmatic statements of position. Of the large amount of philosophical work that it has given rise to, two developments in particular are worth singling out. One is the very influential systematization of Austin's work by Searle, through whose writings speech act theory has perhaps had most of its impact on linguistics, and the other is a line of thought that attempts to link up closely Grice's theory of meaning-nn (Grice, 1957; discussed in 1.2 above) with illocutionary force. We may approach the latter through a brief review of Searle's work.

In general, Searle's theory of speech acts is just Austin's systematized, in part rigidified,[9] with sallies into the general theory of meaning, and connections to other philosophical issues (see Searle, 1969, 1979b). If illocutionary force is somehow conventionally linked with explicit performatives and other illocutionary force indicating devices (let us call them IFIDs), then we should like to know exactly how. Searle appeals to a distinction by Rawls (1955) between **regulative rules** and **constitutive rules**. The first are the kind that control antecedently existing activities, e.g. traffic regulations, while the second are the kind that create or constitute the activity itself, e.g. the rules of a game. The latter have the conceptual form: 'doing X counts as Y', e.g. in soccer, kicking or heading the ball through the goal-posts counts as a goal. Essentially, the rules linking IFIDs with their corresponding illocutionary acts are just of this kind: if I warn you not to touch the dog, that counts as an undertaking that it is not in your best interests to touch that animal. Of course, as Austin points out, it will only be a felicitous warning if all the other felicity conditions are also met (Searle assimilates the 'uttering IFID X counts as doing Y' condition to the same schema, calling it the **essential condition**).

This prompts Searle to suggest that felicity conditions are not merely dimensions on which utterances can go wrong, but are actually jointly constitutive of the various illocutionary forces. For example, suppose that, by means of producing the utterance U, I promise sincerely and felicitously to come tomorrow. Then in order to perform that action it must be the case that each of the conditions below has been met:

(25)   1. The speaker said he would perform a future action

---

[9] Especially in the sense that where Austin's characterizations of speech acts are in terms of loose 'family relationships', Searle prefers strict delimitations in terms of necessary and sufficient conditions. There are reasons to think that Searle's treatment here is much too strong and inflexible (see e.g. sections 5.5 and 5.7 below). In general, students are well advised to turn back to Austin's often more subtle treatment of the issues.

2. He intends to do it
3. He believes he can do it
4. He thinks he wouldn't do it anyway, in the normal course of action
5. He thinks the addressee wants him to do it (rather than not to do it)
6. He intends to place himself under an obligation to do it by uttering U
7. Both speaker and addressee comprehend U
8. They are both conscious, normal human beings
9. They are both in normal circumstances – not e.g. acting in a play
10. The utterance U contains some IFID which is only properly uttered if all the appropriate conditions obtain

Now some of these are clearly general to all kinds of illocutionary act, namely 7–10. Factoring these out, we are left with the conditions specific to promising: and these (namely 1–6) are actually constitutive of promising – if one has met these conditions then (if 7–10 also obtain) one has effectively promised, and if one has effectively (and sincerely) promised then the world meets the conditions 1–6 (and also 7–10).

We can now use these felicity conditions as a kind of grid on which to compare different speech acts. To do so it will be useful to have some kind of classification of felicity conditions, like Austin's in (4) above; Searle suggests a classification into four kinds of condition, depending on how they specify **propositional content**, **preparatory** preconditions, conditions on **sincerity**, and the **essential** condition that we have already mentioned. An example of a comparison that can be made on these dimensions, between requests and warnings (see Table 5.1), should make the typology clear (drawn from Searle, 1969: 66–7).

But Searle is unsatisfied with this procedure as a classificatory method. For sub-types of questions, for example, can be proliferated, and there may be an indefinite number of tables like the one above that can be compared. What would be much more interesting would be to derive some overall schema that would delimit the kinds of *possible* illocutionary force on principled grounds. Now Austin thought that one could come to an interesting classification through a taxonomy of performative verbs, but Searle seeks some more abstract scheme based on felicity conditions. In fact he proposes

Table 5.1. *A comparison of felicity conditions on requests and warnings*

Conditions	REQUESTS	WARNINGS
propositional content	Future act A of H	Future event E
preparatory	1. S believes H can do A 2. It is not obvious that H would do A without being asked	1. S thinks E will occur and is not in H's interest 2. S thinks it is not obvious to H that E will occur
sincerity	S wants H to do A	S believes E is not in H's best interest
essential	Counts as an attempt to get H to do A	Counts as an undertaking that E is not in H's best interest

(Searle, 1976) that there are just five basic kinds of action that one can perform in speaking, by means of the following five types of utterance:

(i) **representatives**, which commit the speaker to the truth of the expressed proposition (paradigm cases: asserting, concluding, etc.)

(ii) **directives**, which are attempts by the speaker to get the addressee to do something (paradigm cases: requesting, questioning)

(iii) **commissives**, which commit the speaker to some future course of action (paradigm cases: promising, threatening, offering)

(iv) **expressives**, which express a psychological state (paradigm cases: thanking, apologizing, welcoming, congratulating)

(v) **declarations**, which effect immediate changes in the institutional state of affairs and which tend to rely on elaborate extra-linguistic institutions (paradigm cases: excommunicating, declaring war, christening, firing from employment)

The typology, though perhaps an improvement on Austin's, is a disappointment in that it lacks a principled basis; contrary to Searle's claims, it is not even built in any systematic way on felicity conditions. There is no reason, then, to think that it is definitive or exhaustive. Indeed, there are now available a great many other rival classificatory schemes (see Hancher, 1979 for a review of five of the more interesting, including Searle's; see also Allwood, 1976; Lyons, 1977a: 745ff; Bach & Harnish, 1979). Here the other main strand of post-Austinian thought, which attempts to relate illocutionary force closely to Grice's theory of meaning-nn or communicative intention, may ultimately prove helpful. Strawson (1964) claims that Austin was misled about the nature of illocutionary force by taking as his paradigm cases institutionally-based illocutions like christening, pronouncing man and wife, finding guilty and the like, which require the full panoply of the relevant social arrangements. Rather, the "fundamental part" of human communication is not carried out by such conventional and culture-bound illocutions at all, but rather by specific classes of *communicative intention*, in the special sense sketched by Grice (1957) in his theory of meaning (see 1.2 above). This view suggests that given Searle's essential condition, which generally states the relevant intention, the felicity conditions on each of the major illocutionary acts will be predictable from general considerations of rationality and co-operation of the sort represented by Grice's maxims (a point admitted by Searle (1969: 69); see also Katz, 1977). A principled classification of such possible communicative intentions may then, it is hoped, be based on the nature of such intentions themselves and the kinds of effects they are meant to achieve in recipients. An attempt at such a classification is made by Schiffer (1972: 95ff), and this makes a first cut between classes of intention similar to Searle's *directives*, and a class similar to his *representatives*, and proceeds to finer categories within each of these.[10]

However, it can be argued that the enthusiasm for this kind of classificatory exercise is in general misplaced. The lure appears to be that some general specification of all the possible *functions* of language (and thus perhaps an explication of the "limits of our language" that so intrigued Wittgenstein) may thereby be found. But if illocutions are perhaps finite in kind, perlocutions are clearly not so in principle, and there seems to be no clear reason why what is a perlocution in one culture may not be an illocution in another. Or alternatively, one could say that the exercise made sense if Searle's *principle of*

---

[10] Grice, in an unpublished paper (1973), has himself suggested such a classification under a further restriction: he hopes to achieve a motivated taxonomy by building up complex communicative intentions, or illocutionary forces, from just two primitive propositional attitudes, roughly *wanting* and *believing*.

expressibility, which holds that "anything that can be meant can be said" (Searle, 1969: 18ff), was tenable; but the distinction between illocution and perlocution seems to belie the principle (see also the critique of the principle in Gazdar, 1981). Nevertheless there are certain recurring *linguistic* categories that do need explaining; for example, it appears that the three basic **sentence-types**, *interrogative*, *imperative*, and *declarative* are universals – all languages appear to have at least two and mostly three of these (see Sadock & Zwicky, in press).[11] On the assumption (to be questioned below) that these three sentence-types express the illocutions of questioning, requesting (or ordering) and stating, respectively, then a successful typology of illocutions might be expected to predict the predominance of these three sentence-types across languages. No such theory exists.

Finally we should briefly mention that the distinction between illocutionary force and propositional content can in fact be found in another philosophical tradition stemming from Frege. Frege himself placed considerable emphasis on the distinction between the "thought" or proposition, and its assertion or "judgement" as true. To make the distinction systematically clear, Frege was careful to place a special assertion sign in front of an asserted sentence (see Dummett, 1973; Atlas, 1975a). This distinction was honoured by Russell & Whitehead (1910), and plays an essential role in Strawson's (1950) views on presupposition (see Chapter 4) and truth. Hare (1952) introduced the terms **phrastic** for propositional content (certainly preferable for WH-questions which do not, arguably, express complete propositions), and **neustic** for illocutionary force. He later went on to suggest (Hare, 1970) that illocutionary force was in fact an amalgam of *neustic* (speaker commitment) and a further element, the **tropic** (the factuality of the propositional content), and Lyons (1977a: 749ff) sees some linguistic merit in these distinctions.

Before proceeding, it is important to emphasize some distinctions essential to a clear discussion of speech acts. First, the distinction between linguistic expressions (sentences) and their use in context, on concrete occasions for particular purposes (utterances), must never be lost sight of, even though a number of theories of speech acts

---

[11] These authors also draw attention to the occurrence of language-specific **minor sentence-types** – e.g. English exclamations like *How shoddy that is!*, or *Boy, can he run!* These will not be treated here, though obviously they are of substantial pragmatic interest (see Quirk, Greenbaum, Leech & Svartvik, 1972: 406–14).

attempt to conflate them systematically. Secondly, the term *speech act* is often used ambiguously, or generally, to cover both a type of illocutionary act characterized by a type of illocutionary force (like requesting) and a type of illocutionary act characterized- by an illocutionary force and a particular propositional content (like requesting someone to open the door). Thirdly, and most importantly, we must be careful to distinguish the set of terms *imperative*, *interrogative*, and *declarative* from the set of terms *order* (or *request*), *question* and *assertion* (or *statement*). The first set are *linguistic* categories that pertain to sentences, the second set are categories that pertain only to the *use* of sentences (i.e. to utterances and utterance-types). Now the term **mood** is often used to designate the first set, but this is inaccurate as *mood*, in traditional grammar at any rate, is a category of verbal inflection, and on this dimension *imperative* contrasts with *indicative* and *subjunctive* rather than *declarative* and *interrogative*. Lyons (1977a: 747ff) therefore proposes a change in terminology; nevertheless we shall retain the familiar terms *imperative*, *interrogative* and *declarative*, using however the cover term **sentence-types** instead of the misleading term *mood*. (Here see also the helpful discussion in Sadock & Zwicky, in press.)

5.2 Thesis: speech acts are irreducible to matters of truth and falsity

We shall here summarize, at the risk of repetition, those aspects of the philosophical work on speech acts that have had the most direct impact on linguistic theorizing. From Austin's work, and in large part through Searle's systematization of it, there has emerged a coherent theory of speech acts that demands the linguist's attention. This position, which is a judicious selection and slight abstraction from Austin and Searle's particular views, we may call the *irreducibility thesis*, or *Thesis* for short. In brief, the position can be formulated as follows. First, all utterances not only serve to express propositions, but also perform actions. Secondly, of the many ways in which one could say that in uttering some linguistic expression a speaker was *doing* something, there is one privileged level of action that can be called the illocutionary act – or, more simply, the speech act. This action is associated by convention (*pace* Strawson, 1964 and Schiffer, 1972) with the form of the utterance in question, and this distinguishes it from any perlocutionary actions that may accompany the central illocutionary act, and be done via that central action. Thirdly, although any particular illocutionary force may be effectively conveyed in various ways, there is at least one form of utterance that (in some languages at any rate) directly and conventionally expresses it – namely, the explicit performative, which in English has the normal form of (26):

(26)   I (hereby) V_p you (that) S'

where V_p is a **performative verb** drawn from the limited and determinate set of performative verbs in the language in question, S' is a complement sentence (the content of which is often restricted by the particular performative verb), and V_p is conjugated in the simple present indicative active. There are variations, of no great significance (but see Searle, 1976), about whether a particular performative verb takes a *that* complement (as in *I state that p*) or a *for -ing* complement (as in *I apologize for laughing*) and so on. We may also treat the three basic sentence-types in English (and most languages), namely the imperative, the interrogative and the declarative, as containing grammaticalized conventional indicators of illocutionary force, namely those associated respectively with the explicit **performative prefixes** (or phrases)[12] *I request you to, I ask you whether, I state to you that* (with the single proviso that explicit performatives, although in declarative form, have the force associated with the overt performative verb in each case). We may say that sentences in the imperative, interrogative or declarative, and perhaps other kinds of sentence format, are **implicit performatives**. Fourthly, the proper characterization of illocutionary force is provided by specifying the set of **felicity conditions** (or FCs) for each force. FCs may be classified, following Searle, into **preparatory conditions** that concern real-world prerequisites to each illocutionary act, **propositional content conditions** that specify restrictions on the content of S' in (26), and **sincerity conditions**, that state the requisite beliefs, feelings and intentions of the speaker, as appropriate to each kind of action. (There is also in Searle's schema, as we noted, an **essential**

---

[12] The term *performative prefix* is used here, as in the speech act literature, as a shorthand for 'sentence-initial performative phrase' or the like; from a linguistic point of view, of course, such a phrase is not a prefix, but the performative clause minus one argument, namely the complement of the performative verb, which expresses the propositional content (see immediately below).

condition, which is of a rather different order.) Thus to provide the felicity conditions for some illocutionary act is to specify exactly how the context has to be in order for a particular utterance of a sentence that is conventionally used to perform that type of act to actually perform it on an occasion of utterance. Given that felicity conditions jointly define and constitute the nature of any specific speech act, there is hope that a more abstract and principled classification of speech acts can be provided in terms of FCs than emerges (*pace* Austin) from a study of performative verbs alone.

These claims imply that the illocutionary force and the propositional content of utterances are detachable elements of meaning. Thus the following sentences, when uttered felicitously, would all share the same propositional content, namely the proposition that the addressee will go home:

(27)   a. I predict that you will go home
         b. Go home!
         c. Are you going to go home?
         d. I advise you to go home

but they would normally be used with different illocutionary forces, i.e. perform different speech acts.[13] There is a problem for this view, namely that in the case of the explicit performatives, the propositional content appears to include the force-indicating device. For if, as this version of speech act theory suggests, the propositional aspect of meaning is to be treated one way, and the illocutionary aspect another, then the meaning of *promise* in *I hereby promise to come* is different from the meaning of *promise* in *He promised to come*. In the first, it has a performative usage, in the second, a descriptive usage; in the first it is explicated by reference to FCs, in the second by appeal to the semantic concepts of sense and reference. One solution to this problem, adopted by Searle but not by Austin, is to claim that the propositional aspect of meaning is not after all so distinct in kind: one can provide **usage conditions** for the descriptive usage of *promise* in just the way that one can apply felicity conditions for the performative usage. Searle (1969, 1979b) thereby attempts to extend speech act theory into a general theory of semantics. There are many objections to such a theory (see Kempson, 1977 for discussion), and

---

[13] Gazdar (1981) points to some significant difficulties with the notion of propositional content employed here (as e.g. by Katz (1977)).

we shall continue to be interested here in speech act theory solely as a theory of illocutionary force. This does, however, leave quite unsolved the issue of the way in which performative and descriptive uses of the same words are to be related. (One possible line for Thesis theorists is to claim that explicit performative prefixes are indeed treated semantically just like other non-performative clauses, but that *in addition* performative clauses have a force-indicating function irreducible to ordinary semantics.)

We are now in a position to state the central tenet of Thesis: illocutionary force is an aspect of meaning, broadly construed, that is quite irreducible to matters of truth and falsity. That is, illocutionary force constitutes an aspect of meaning that cannot be captured in a truth-conditional semantics. Rather, illocutionary acts are to be described in terms of felicity conditions, which are specifications for appropriate usage. The reason is that while propositions *describe* (or are in correspondence with) states of affairs, and may thus be plausibly characterized in terms of the conditions under which they would be true, illocutionary forces indicate how those descriptions are to be taken or what the addressee is meant to do with a particular proposition that is expressed, e.g. for an assertion the addressee may be meant to believe the proposition expressed, for an order he will be meant to make the proposition true, and so on (see Stenius, 1967). Illocutionary force belongs firmly in the realm of *action*, and the appropriate techniques for analysis are therefore to be found in the theory of action, and not in the theory of meaning, when that is narrowly construed in terms of truth-conditional semantics. Thesis is thus a theory that proposes to handle illocutionary force in an entirely pragmatic way.

5.3 Antithesis: the reduction of illocutionary force to ordinary syntax and semantics

Directly opposed to Thesis is a position that we may call *Antithesis*: according to Antithesis there is no need for a special theory of illocutionary force because the phenomena that taxed Austin are assimilable to standard theories of syntax and truth-conditional semantics.

The opening move here is to attack Austin's handling of explicit performatives. Basic to Austin's theory is the claim that the utterance of *I bet you six pence* is simply not assessed, or sensibly assessable, in terms of truth and falsity: you either did or did not manage to bet successfully, and that depends on whether the FCs were met or not. Early on there were dissenters to this (see e.g. Lemmon, 1962; Hedenius, 1963): why not claim instead that simply by uttering sentences of that sort the speaker makes them true? In this respect performatives would be similar to other sentences that are verified simply by their use, like:

(28)   I am here
         I can speak this loud
         I can speak some English

There seems to be nothing incoherent with this view held generally for explicit performatives; for example, if you say *I hereby warn you not to get in my way*, then what you have said is true – you have indeed so warned. Whatever Austin thought of as usage conditions for *bet*, *warn* and the like, are simply part of the meaning of those words.[14]

To generalize the attack on Thesis, we may then bring in the **performative analysis** (or **performative hypothesis**) to handle implicit performatives. According to this hypothesis, which we may refer to as the PH, every sentence has as its highest clause in deep or underlying syntactic structure a clause of the form in (26) – i.e. a structure that corresponds to the overt prefix in the explicit performative, whether or not it is an overt or explicit performative in surface structure. Such an analysis can be put forward on what seem to be plausible independent grounds, namely that it captures a number of syntactic generalizations that would otherwise be lost (see Ross, 1970; Sadock, 1974). The syntactic arguments are of two major kinds. The first uses anaphoric processes along the following lines: some constituent X of a subordinate clause is first shown to be acceptable only if there is another constituent Y in the matrix clause; thus

---

[14] This line is more awkward for those performatives involved in illocutionary acts (like christening, declaring war, even ordering) that require specific institutional arrangements; here, perhaps, one must allow for falsification, as well as verification, by use: thus *I declare war on Wales* said by someone not so empowered may fail to be true in a way parallel to the falsity of a (non-recorded, non-relayed) utterance of *I am not here*. There are also difficulties with (metalinguistic) *mention* as opposed to (performative) *use* of such sentences, but these difficulties are shared by most theories of speech acts. Finally, there are problems with the semantic interpretation of the tense and aspect of performative utterances (which Kempson, 1977: 64–8 claims to be illusory).

without Y, X may not appear in the lower clause. We now turn to some *implicit* performatives and find, contrary to our generalization, some X in the matrix clause, unlicensed by an overt Y in a higher clause. Either our generalization about the Y-dependency of X is wrong, or there is in fact a covert Y in an underlying deleted matrix clause. We then show that if the PH is assumed, i.e. there is a higher implicit performative clause, then there would in fact be just the required Y in a higher clause, and our generalization can be preserved. For example, in (29) the reflexive pronoun *himself* seems to be licensed by the higher co-referential noun phrase, *the President*:

(29)   The President said that solar energy was invented by God and himself

But in breach of the generalization, the *myself* in (30) seems to lack any such corresponding antecedent:

(30)   Solar energy was invented by God and myself

Note that such usages are highly restricted; e.g. third person reflexives as in (31) are unacceptable (at least at the beginning of a discourse):

(31)   ?Solar energy was invented by God and herself

Therefore the acceptability of (30) seems puzzling. The puzzle disappears, according to the PH, if we note that (32) is acceptable for just the same reasons that (29) is, and if we claim that in fact (30) is derived from (32) by a regular process of performative clause deletion:

(32)   I say to you that solar energy was invented by God and myself

Using anaphoric arguments of this kind, it is possible to argue that every feature of the covert performative clause is motivated by independent syntactic requirements (see Ross, 1970). For example, on the basis of the parallelism between the following two sentences:

(33)   Herbert told Susan that people like herself are rare
(34)   People like yourself are rare

we may argue that there must in fact be an implicit second person antecedent in the second, which would be conveniently provided by the indirect object of the hypothesized performative clause. And evidence for the presence of a covert performative verb itself seems to be offered by the adverbial data to which we now turn.

Another major kind of argument is based on the fact that there appear to be adverbs that modify performative clauses appearing in sentences without such overt performative clauses, as in (35) and (36):

(35)   Frankly, I prefer the white meat
(36)   What's the time, because I've got to go out at eight?

where a natural interpretation is that in (35) *frankly* is an adverb on an implicit *I tell you* performative prefix, and in (36) the *because*-clause is an adverb on an implicit *I ask you* prefix.

There are in addition a number of minor arguments. Most of these have as a basis the claim that certain syntactic generalizations that would otherwise have exceptions manifested in the matrix clauses of implicit performatives, will be fully general if the PH is in fact assumed. For example, sentences generally require overt subjects in English and many other languages, but the imperative is an exception. If, however, we assume the PH, then (37) will have an underlying performative clause of the sort made overt in (38):

(37)   Wash the dishes!
(38)   I order you to wash the dishes
(39)   *I order you that you wash the dishes

Now (39) is ungrammatical because Equi-NP deletion must apply,[15] given that *order* requires that the subject of the complement clause be co-referential with the indirect object of the matrix clause. Therefore, on performative clause deletion, one will be left with (37), providing that Equi-NP deletion applies first. Thus we have simultaneously an explanation for the subjectless nature of imperatives, and the understanding that there is a covert second person subject in imperatives (see Sadock, 1974: 32–3). Further, if a performative clause was always available, certain morphological problems that arise with honorifics, of the sort we encountered in Chapter 2, might be solved: the subject and object of the performative verb could be assigned a syntactic feature indicating level of politeness, and honorific concord be achieved by requiring the same features on all co-referent noun phrases (see Sadock, 1974: 41ff). Indeed, the description of deixis in general might be facilitated by the presence of the crucial deictic reference points – speaker, addressee and time

---

[15] Equi-NP deletion is a transformational rule that deletes subjects of subordinate clauses under identity with the subject or indirect object of the next-higher clause (see Sadock, 1974: 5, 34–5).

of utterance (encoded by the tense of the performative) – in underlying structure (see G. Lakoff, 1972, 1975).

The adoption of the PH thus seems, at first sight, to offer a significant and general improvement over the earlier suggestions for dealing with the syntax of sentence-types. Chomsky (1957) had originally suggested optional transformations to derive the subject-auxiliary inversion of English interrogatives, and the subject-deletion of English imperatives, from declaratives; while Katz & Postal (1964) had proposed two underlying morphemes, call them Q and I, that would not only trigger the necessary transformations, but also be available in deep structure for semantic interpretation. The PH achieves all that these proposals achieved, providing both triggers for the necessary adjustments in surface structure and structures for semantic interpretation, but in a much less arbitrary way (substituting natural language expressions for Q and I, for example; see Sadock, 1974: 17).

On the basis of arguments like these, we may then formulate (following Gazdar, 1979a: 18) the strongest version of the PH as follows:

(40)   1. Every sentence has a performative clause in deep or under-lying structure
        2. The subject of this clause is first person singular, the indirect object second person singular, and the verb is drawn from a delimited set of performative verbs, and is conjugated in the indicative active simple present tense (or is associated with the underlying representation thereof)
        3. This clause is always the highest clause in underlying structure, or at the very least always occurs in a determinable position in that structure
        4. There is only one such clause per sentence
        5. The performative clause is deletable, such deletion not changing the meaning of the sentence
        6. Illocutionary force is semantic (in the truth-conditional sense) and is fully specified by the meaning of the performative clause itself

In actual fact, the various proponents of the PH have usually adopted only some sub-set of these claims – for example, G. Lakoff (1972) avoids claim 2 in order to allow singular and plural speakers and addressees; Sadock (1974) has abandoned claim 4 and the first part of claim 3 for syntactic reasons; G. Lakoff (1975) abandons claim 1 for sentences not being actively asserted or expressing timeless truths; while Lewis (1972) avoids the same claim just in the case of declarative sentences (for semantic reasons which we will consider in due course). We cannot review all these distinct but closely related positions here (see Gazdar, 1979a: Chapter 2), but the very variety of them, and the general retreat from the strong version of the PH expressed by the claims in (40), reflects the considerable difficulties that each of those claims faces, as we shall see.

Armed with the PH, Antithesis theorists may now claim that they have a complete reduction of speech act theory to matters of syntax and truth-conditional semantics. That every sentence when uttered has what appears to be an 'illocutionary force' is accounted for by the guaranteed presence of an underlying or overt performative clause, which has the peculiar property of being true simply by virtue of being felicitously said – hence the intuition that it makes no sense to consider its falsity. The particular so-called 'felicity conditions' on different speech acts are simply part of the meaning of the implicit or explicit performative verbs, capturable either in terms of entailment or semantic presupposition (see e.g. Lewis, 1972, and especially G. Lakoff, 1975). The basic result is that illocutionary force is reduced to "garden variety semantics" (G. Lakoff, 1972: 655).

5.4 Collapse of Antithesis

Antithesis is clearly an elegant theory, promising to reduce what seems to be an apparently irreducibly pragmatic aspect of meaning to relatively well-understood areas of linguistic theory. However, it is now all but certain that Antithesis, at least in its full form, is untenable. For it runs into insurmountable difficulties on both the semantic and syntactic fronts. Let us take these in turn.

5.4.1 *Semantic problems*

Although a widely held belief is that truth-conditional semantics cannot deal with non-assertoric utterances, using the PH and the notion that performative sentences are verified simply by their use, such a semantics handles non-declaratives without too much difficulty. Paradoxically enough, where the problems arise is with assertions and declaratives. Consider for example:

(41)   I state to you that the world is flat

On the normal Antithesis assumption, such a sentence will have the value *true* simply by virtue of being felicitously uttered. Also by Antithesis, (42) will have as its underlying form something corresponding closely to (41):

(42)   The world is flat

By hypothesis, (41) and (42) should have the same truth conditions, so (42) will be true just in case the speaker so states. But clearly such an argument amounts to a *reductio ad absurdum*. For, whatever our intuitions about (41), (42) is, given the way the world actually is, simply false (see Lewis, 1972 for the full argument).

To this difficulty G. Lakoff (1975) had a response. Let us say that an assertion is true if, and only if, both the performative clause and its complement clause are true. However, the response lands one in further difficulties.[16] Consider:

(43)   I stated to you that the world is flat

Here it is sufficient for the truth of (43) simply that I did so state, the truth or falsity of the complement clause (*the world is flat*) playing no role in the overall truth conditions. Hence the non-performative usages (as in (43)) of performative verbs like *state* seem to have different truth conditions from the performative usages of the same verb. But in that case, we have in fact *failed* to reduce performative usages to straightforward applications of uniform semantical procedures, as Antithesis claims to be able to do.

Various attempts may be made to salvage the PH from this semantic difficulty, and it is worth considering carefully, at the risk of belabouring the point, the different options that are open to its die-hard supporters. Sadock (in preparation), for example, hopes to escape the dilemma by appealing to two distinct kinds of truth (and falsity), namely a semantic truth (call it T1) which holds of propositions, and a pragmatic concept of truth (call it T2) which holds only of statements or assertions. We might then say that the ordinary language use of the English word *true*, namely the pragmatic concept T2, can only sensibly be predicated of the complements of overt or covert performative clauses. Thus we ordinarily say that (41) is true (i.e. T2) only if we agree that (42) is true. However, technically, in the theoretical sense (i.e. T1), the

[16] This was pointed out to me by Gerald Gazdar.

proposition expressed by both sentences (which is identical on the assumption of PH) is T1 only if the performative clause (*I state to you that p*), and on some views the complement *p* too, is true (T1). Thus, one could claim, the view that (41) is true while (42) is false is due to predicating T1 of (41) and T2 (or rather F2) of (42) – i.e. to a conflation of the two kinds of truth (see Sadock, in preparation; also G. Lakoff, 1975). Nevertheless, although such a distinction may indeed be salutary, this will not solve the present problem. For that problem is precisely that it seems to be impossible to maintain a coherent and uniform application of the semantic notion of truth conditions to sentences if one adopts the PH. Let us restate the difficulty.

(44)   Snow is green
(45)   I state that snow is green
(46)   I stated that snow is green

To accommodate the PH we must find some way in which (44) and (45) may reasonably be held to be identical in truth conditions, as they will have identical underlying structures and semantic representations on that hypothesis. Let us adopt the following conventions: let *s* be the performative prefix *I state to you that* (or any of its alternatives), *p* be the complement clause of the overt or covert performative verb, *p'* be the past report of a statement (as in (46)), and *s(p)* be the overt performative sentence (as in (45)); further, let [*p*] mean 'the proposition expressed by *p*', and so on for [*p'*], etc. Then, to make (44) and (45) parallel in truth conditions, we may take one of the following lines. We can, as G. Lakoff (1975) suggested, assign truth conditions on the following basis (where *true* is always T1):

(47)   (i)   '*p*' is true iff [*p*] is true and [*s(p)*] is true
         (ii) '*s(p)*' is true iff [*p*] is true and [*s(p)*] is true
         (iii) '*p'*' is true iff [*p'*] is true and [*s(p')*] is true, regardless of the truth or falsity of the complement *p* of the verb *state* in *p'*

The problems then are (a), (44) can only be true if someone is in fact stating it, which seems a short road to solipsism, and (b) the solution forces us (as we noted above) into two kinds of truth conditions for *state*, those for performative usages, as in (45) (where the truth of the complement is relevant to the truth of the whole), and those for non-performative usages, as in (46) (where the truth of the complement is irrelevant to the truth of the matrix sentence). Alternatively, finding this untenable, we could hold instead:

(48)   (i)   '*p*' is true iff [*p*] is true
         (ii) '*s(p)*' is true iff [*p*] is true
         (iii) '*p*'' is true iff [*p*'] is true

The problem here is that we have in effect made the performative clause, whether covert or overt, 'invisible' to truth conditions. But in that case we have failed to give a semantic characterization of the performative clause at all. Such a solution might well be congenial to Thesis theorists, leaving open a pragmatic interpretation of both explicit performatives and sentence-types, but it is hardly a route open to the proponents of Antithesis. Another alternative would be:

(49)   (i)   '*p*' is true iff [*s(p)*] is true, regardless of the truth of *p*
         (ii) '*s(p)*' is true iff [*s(p)*] is true, regardless of the truth of *p*
         (iii) '*p*'' is true iff [*s(p')*] is true, regardless of the truth of *p'*
               (or *p*)

i.e. the truth of the whole depends solely on the truth of the performative clause, implicit or explicit. But clearly such a view has the consequence that the truth conditions for all declaratives would be effectively the same, which would be absurd: for any declarative clause *p*, both *I state that p* and simply *p*, will be true iff the speaker does so state. But we are now full circle, for that claim, which may be tenable for explicit performatives, seems clearly wrong for sentences without the performative prefix, as we noted initially in connection with example (42).[17] Any semantic theory that for an arbitrary declarative sentence gave as its truth conditions only the conditions under which it would be successfully stated would signally fail to connect language to the world – to utter a declarative would simply be to guarantee that one was issuing correctly a string of morphemes, and not in any way to affirm the way the world is.

We are left with the conclusion that it seems simply impossible to achieve the semantical parallelism between (44) and (45) that the PH

---

[17] Indeed the only thorough attempt to work out the truth conditions for performatives, namely that by Aqvist (1972), would assign to (41) (at least if it incorporated *hereby*) a meaning that we can paraphrase as: 'I communicate this sentence to you in this situation and, by doing so, I make a statement that the world is flat'. Such a paraphrase makes clear the peculiar self-referential or **token-reflexive** (see 2.2.4) nature of performative sentences, which sets them apart from non-performatives (see Lyons, 1977a: 781).

requires. One can retreat and accept the PH for all sentences other than declaratives, as Lewis (1972) does, but that is an asymmetry that few linguists would be attracted to, and indeed one which the syntactic arguments for the PH will simply not allow. One should note too that whatever the *semantic* relation of (44) to (45), there is a significant *pragmatic* difference, which will become immediately clear if the reader prefixes each of the sentences in this paragraph with *I hereby state* (R. Lakoff, 1977: 84–5). But if the PH is part of a general programme to reduce pragmatics to ordinary semantics, then appeal can hardly be made to the semantic/pragmatic distinction in order to explain the different usages of (44) and (45) (Gazdar, 1979a: 25).

Now some of the most persuasive evidence for the PH comes from adverbs like *frankly* that appear to modify performative verbs (let us call these **performative adverbs** without prejudging whether in fact they do actually modify such verbs). However, there are significant semantic difficulties here too. Firstly, it is simply not clear that the meanings of the relevant adverbs are indeed parallel in the explicit performative, the (allegedly) implicit performative and the reported performative usages:

(50)   I tell you frankly you're a swine
(51)   Frankly, you're a swine
(52)   John told Bill frankly that he was a swine

According to the PH, *frankly* should modify the verb *tell* (implicit in (51)) in each of these in just the same way. But what *frankly* seems to do in (51) is warn the addressee that a criticism is forthcoming, whereas in (52) it modifies the manner in which the telling was done (Lyons, 1977a: 783). The explicit performative in (50) perhaps allows both interpretations (though prosody, especially a pause after the adverb, can favour a reading as in (51); cf. Sadock, 1974: 38–9). The alleged symmetry here certainly does not unequivocably exist.

A second fact to note is that there are some adverbs that can *only* modify explicit performatives, notably *hereby*, as the following sentences make clear:

(53)   I hereby order you to polish your boots
(54)   ?Hereby polish your boots

Other adverbs, while they may occur with reported performatives (unlike *hereby*), nevertheless can only modify the illocutionary act concurrent with the utterance. Thus *in brief* in both (55) and (56)

modifies the current speech act, and not the reported one in the second
example:

(55)   In brief, the performative analysis is untenable
(56)   Harvey claimed, in brief, that the performative analysis is
        untenable

Such asymmetries make it plausible that performative adverbs cannot
in general be assimilated to ordinary adverbs on verbs of communication (but see Sadock, 1974: 37ff).

   Thirdly, it is sometimes claimed that complex adverbial expressions
like the following are evidence in favour of the PH (Davison, 1973;
Sadock, 1974: 38):

(57)   John's at Sue's house, because his car's outside

However, it is clear that the *because*-clause here does not in fact
modify any implicit *I state* or *I claim*, but rather an understood *I know*
as made explicit in (59):

(58)   I state John's at Sue's house because his car's outside
(59)   I know John's at Sue's house because his car's outside

For if (57) had an underlying structure similar to (58), then John's
car's location would have to be taken as the reason for *stating*, whereas
in fact it is clearly being offered as grounds for *believing* what is stated.
Now whereas it may be true that believing or knowing that *p* may
be a FC on asserting that *p*, and thus true that such reason adverbials
provide evidence for certain aspects of speech act theory in general,
the fact that they do not always modify the implicit performative verb
shows that they do not provide direct evidence for the PH. Rather,
it seems to be appropriate to provide evidence in such a clause that
certain pragmatic conditions on the speech act hold (see Mittwoch,
1977: 186ff). In a similar way note that *briefly* in (60) does not
paraphrase as (61), but rather as (62):

(60)   Briefly, who do you think will win the gold medal?
(61)   I ask you briefly who you think will win the gold medal
(62)   Tell me briefly who will win the gold medal

but the relevant implicit performative verb must be one of asking not
one of telling (though see here the theory that performatives **lexically
decompose** so that asking is derived from requesting to tell,
expounded in Sadock, 1974: 149ff).

Finally, performative adverbs participate in the general problem associated with the truth-conditional assessment of declaratives. The issue is this. If we argue that the adverb in (63) is evidence for an implicit performative clause, as in (64), then (63) should have the same truth conditions as (64). But as we have seen, (63) seems to be true just in case semantics is a bore, and (64) true just in case I say so.

(63)   Confidentially, semantics is a bore
(64)   I say to you confidentially that semantics is a bore

So to assimilate (63) to (64), however it may help us understand the *syntax* of performative adverbs, ultimately only clouds our understanding of their semantics. Nevertheless to reject the PH lands us equally in a quandary, for then we are left with the 'dangling' adverb in (63) – how is this to be interpreted in the absence of a verb it might modify?

Boër & Lycan (1978) term one version of this dilemma the **performadox**. Assuming for purposes of argument that the PH is syntactically correct, they argue that either (a) one takes the Thesis view, namely that the performative clause itself is not *semantically* interpreted in terms of truth conditions at all, in which case the associated adverbs (as in (63) and (64)) must also be uninterpreted, which seems quite *ad hoc*, or (b) one does interpret the performative clause, in which case one invariably gets the truth conditions wrong. Note that if we reject the PH, and allow (63) and (64) to have different truth conditions, we are still left with the dangling adverb in (63). We could claim that *confidentially* is ambiguous between a sentence-modifying reading appropriate to (63) and a predicate-modifying reading appropriate to (64), but then we would have to claim this for *all* performative adverbs that can show up without explicit performatives, including the productive adverbial modifiers with *because*, *since*, *in case*, etc., as in (65):

(65)   Semantics is a bore, since you ask
         Semantics is a bore, in case you didn't know

(see Rutherford, 1970 for further examples, and the discussion in Cresswell, 1973: 233–4). It must be confessed that the 'performadox' is ultimately a problem for Thesis theorists too. Cresswell's (1973: 234) inelegant solution is to consider (63) strictly speaking ill-formed, and pragmatically elliptical for (64). Boër & Lycan (1978) simply

257

propose a compromise, which is to accept the PH for implicit performatives just where one is forced to by dangling performative adverbs, and reject it elsewhere, reaping the reduced harvest of semantic incoherencies that one has then cultivated.[18]

We may conclude this discussion of performative adverbs by noting that although they seem at first sight the strongest evidence for the PH, they in fact raise a host of problems which the PH in no way solves. As such, they certainly do not constitute evidence in favour of it.

There are further difficulties for attempts to reduce illocutionary force to truth-conditional semantics. Take, for example, the attempted reduction of FCs to aspects of the meaning of the performative verbs that they are associated with. It soon becomes clear that the relevant aspects of meaning cannot be truth-conditional. Consider, for example, (66) and its corresponding implicit performative version (67):

(66)   I request you to please close the door
(67)   Please close the door

Due to the presence of an explicit or implicit verb of requesting, these would have as part of their meaning the FC in (68):

(68)   The door is not closed (or at least will not be at the time the request is to be complied with)

If (68) was an entailment from (66) or (67), simply by virtue of the meaning of *request*, then (69) should entail (70), and (71) be a contradiction.

(69)   John requested Bill to close the door
(70)   At the time the action was to be carried out, the door was not closed
(71)   John requested Bill to close the door, but it was already closed

Again, these are the wrong results, and by *reductio* we must abandon the assumption that FCs can be captured truth-conditionally as part of the semantics of the verbs in question. The properties of most FCs

---

[18] Other theorists hope to escape some of these dilemmas by alternative versions of the PH. Thus Lyons (1977a: 782) and Mittwoch (1977) suggest that the associated implicit performative clause should be *paratactically* juxtaposed with, rather than superordinate to, the content of the utterance. But as Boër & Lycan (1978) show, all such suggestions flounder equally in the 'performadox'.

are in any case far too general to be attributed to the meanings of particular lexical items (Allwood, 1977). For example, the **ability conditions** (i.e. the preparatory conditions requiring that the speaker or addressee can perform the relevant actions required) on promising and offering seem to be based on the simple rational criterion that it makes no sense to commit oneself to attempting actions one knows one cannot achieve; similarly, for the ability conditions on requests, commands and suggestions: it would simply be less than rational to sincerely attempt to get other agents to do what one knows they cannot. Such constraints on rational action in general are quite independent of language, let alone part of the meaning of performative verbs. One might try to assimilate FCs to the category of pragmatic presupposition, but they can be shown to have quite different properties from core examples of presupposition, and would be better assimilated to the category of conversational implicature (see Rogers, 1978).

Finally, even if it turned out that performative sentences, implicit and explicit, could be simply handled within a truth-conditional framework (as Sadock (in preparation) continues to hope), some of the basic intuitions that underlay Austin's work would still not have been accounted for. For the notion of illocutionary force was specifically directed to the action-like properties of utterances, and these would in no way be captured by such a treatment. For, essentially, an utterance like (72) would not be treated as basically different in kind from (73); both would be reports of events, but the event reported in the first would simply be concurrent with the utterance.

(72)   I bet you six pence I'll win the race
(73)   I betted you six pence that I'd win the race

Our sense is that there is something over and above a mere concurrent report in (72), which is curiously lacking in other formats for concurrent reports like that in (74):

(74)   I am betting you six pence I'll win the race

That utterances do have action-like properties is clear from simple observations like the following. Some utterances, e.g. requests and promises, have actions as rule-governed consequences; actions can substitute for many utterances and vice versa (consider, for example,

259

the utterances accompanying a small purchase in a shop); some utterances do rely, as Austin insisted, on elaborate non-linguistic arrangements, and in such arrangements linguistic and non-linguistic actions are systematically inter-leaved (consider christening a ship, performing a marriage service, etc.). Finally, Austin correctly attached some importance to what he called *illocutionary uptake*; thus if I utter (72) in such a way that you fail to hear, it is fairly clear that (73) would be false as a report of what had transpired. It seems therefore that in order for a speech act to 'come off', it is ordinarily required that the addressee(s) may be supposed to have heard, registered and in some cases (like (72)) responded to what has been said (exceptions, perhaps, are things like curses, invocations and blessings).

5.4.2   *Syntactic problems*

In addition to these semantic incoherencies and in-adequacies, the PH required by Antithesis is assailed by syntactic problems. We can do no more here than indicate the scope of these (the reader is referred to Anderson, 1971, Fraser, 1974a, Leech, 1976 and Gazdar, 1979a: Chapter 2, for further details). But the following is a sample of the problems. First, as Austin himself noted, there are many cases where explicit performatives do not refer to the speaker, as in the following examples:

(75)   The company hereby undertakes to replace any can of Doggo-Meat that fails to please, with no questions asked
(76)   It is herewith disclosed that the value of the estate left by Marcus T. Bloomingdale was 4,785,758 dollars

and others where the addressee is not the *target* (see 2.2.1) as in:

(77)   Johnny is to come in now

However such examples were handled, they would considerably complicate the PH. For unless the performative clause has strictly definable properties, it will be impossible to specify it uniquely in syntactic terms; and if that cannot be done then the very special, indeed extra-ordinary, syntactic rules that apply just to performative clauses (notably, wholesale performative clause deletion) cannot be properly restricted. One such crucial defining property might be that the performative clause is always the highest clause in any sentence. However, examples like (78) seem to be clear counter-examples to such a generalization:

(78)   We regret that the company is forced by economic circumstances to hereby request you to tender your resignation at your earliest convenience

Proponents of the PH are forced by such examples either to entertain otherwise unmotivated rules of 'performative clause lowering', or to claim that the illocutionary force of (78) is in fact assertoric, and only by pragmatic implication a request.

Further problems arise from the fact that many sentences seem to involve more than one illocutionary force. For example, (79) has a non-restrictive relative clause that is clearly assertoric in force despite being embedded within a question:

(79)   Does John, who could never learn elementary calculus, really intend to do a PhD in mathematics?

If every sentence has only one performative clause, it would seem to be necessary to derive (79) from an 'amalgamation' of two distinct derivations (see G. Lakoff, 1974). Similar difficulties arise even with tag-questions like:

(80)   Wittgenstein was an Oxford philosopher, wasn't he?

where the tag carries a question force that modifies the assertoric force of the declarative clause (see Hudson, 1975 for discussion). And even where we have one unitary syntactic clause in surface structure, in order to capture the intuitive illocutionary force we may have to hypothesize a conjunction of two underlying performative clauses. Thus (81) has been analysed as having an underlying structure similar to (82) (Sadock, 1970; but see Green, 1975):

(81)   Why don't you become an astronaut?
(82)   I ask you why you don't become an astronaut and I suggest that you do

But clearly a better paraphrase would be:

(83)   I ask you why you don't become an astronaut, and if you can think of no good reasons why not, I suggest that you do

Yet clearly (83) is not *syntactically* related to (81). There therefore seem to be distinct limits to the extent to which one can hope for illocutionary force to be mirrored in syntactic structure.

But perhaps the most important syntactic objections to the PH are the following. Firstly, it would require an otherwise atypical and unmotivated rule of performative deletion in the majority of cases (for all implicit performatives), and much more complex rules, again not independently motivated, to deal with cases like (78)–(81). Secondly, exactly the same reasoning that led to the positing of the performative clause in the first place leads to arguments that undermine it. For example, the same anaphoric arguments that were discussed above as motivations for the performative analysis, lead to the conclusion that there must in fact be a clause still higher than that, and so on ad infinitum (see Gazdar, 1979a: 21). Further, the anaphoric phenomena themselves seem to be pragmatically conditioned rather than syntactically conditioned (as indicated by the qualification we had to make about the unacceptability of (31), discourse-initially). Even the facts about the adverbs that seem to modify implicit performatives, do not in fact support the PH (Boër & Lycan, 1978). For performative adverbs unfortunately turn up in syntactic locations that are not easily reconciled with the claim that they modify the highest (performative) clause (Mittwoch, 1977). Note, for example, the following possible locations for *frankly*:

(84)   It's because, frankly, I don't trust the Conservatives that I voted for Labour

(85)   I voted for Labour because, frankly, I don't trust the Conservatives

There seems to be no independently required syntactic apparatus that can be held responsible for lowering these adverbs from their hypothetical location in the performative clause into the embedded clauses in which they in fact appear. In the case of (85), one might try to rescue the hypothesis by claiming that there are in fact two performative clauses and *frankly* modifies the second, as in (86):

(86)   I tell you that I voted for Labour because I tell you frankly I don't trust the Conservatives

But that of course gets the semantics of the *because*-clause wrong: (86) asserts that I'm telling you something because I'm telling you something else, which is not the meaning of (85) at all (see Mittwoch, 1977: 179 for further syntactic difficulties with performative adverbs). Finally, as we shall see when we come to talk of **indirect speech acts**, the syntactic mechanisms that are required to handle those phenomena are powerful enough to entirely replicate the effects of the PH without actually having performative clauses (see Sadock, 1975).

For all these reasons, and others, Antithesis cannot be considered an adequate theory of illocutionary force. It fails both on internal grounds, because it leads to semantic and syntactic incoherencies, and on external grounds because it fails to capture the basic intuitions that led to the theory of speech acts in the first place. The collapse of Antithesis would appear to leave Thesis unassailed, though not without its own problems. For of course it inherits in part the problems with the evaluation of performative adverbs, and is obliged to offer some pragmatic account of all the distributional phenomena that prompted the PH in the first place. No such account has been worked out in detail, and in general there has been surprisingly little recent thought on how the apparent pragmatic conditioning of syntactic facts should be accommodated within a general linguistic theory (what ideas there have been will be considered in section 5.5; see also the remarks in earlier Chapters in connection with deixis (2.2), conventional implicature (3.2.3) and presupposition (4.2)). However, there are further reasons to doubt the adequacy of Thesis too, and there is at least one alternative and elegant way of thinking about speech acts. Before proceeding to it, let us discuss a pervasive phenomenon that is a serious problem for both Thesis and Antithesis as they are usually advanced.

5.5 Indirect speech acts: a problem for Thesis and Antithesis

A major problem for both Thesis and Antithesis is constituted by the phenomena known as **indirect speech acts** (or ISAs for short). The notion only makes sense if one subscribes to the notion of a **literal force**, i.e. to the view that illocutionary force is built into sentence form. Let us call this the **literal force hypothesis** (or LFH for short). As Gazdar (1981) has pointed out, LFH will amount to subscribing to the following:

(87) (i) Explicit performatives have the force named by the performative verb in the matrix clause

(ii) Otherwise, the three major sentence-types in English, namely the imperative, interrogative and declarative, have the forces traditionally associated with them, namely ordering (or requesting), questioning and stating respectively

(with, of course, the exception of explicit performatives which happen to be in declarative format)

It is clear that Antithesis theorists have to subscribe to LFH by virtue of their commitment to the PH: by that hypothesis explicit performatives directly express their illocutionary forces, and the three basic sentence-types will be reflexes of underlying performative verbs of ordering, questioning and stating. However, Thesis theorists are also committed to LFH in so far as they think that they are engaged in a semantical exercise characterizing the meaning of the various IFIDs (illocutionary force indicating devices), which clearly include explicit performatives and the main sentence-types. Certainly Searle is overtly committed to LFH, and Austin's emphasis on the "conventional" nature of illocutionary force and its indicators would seem also to commit him to LFH.

Given the LFH, any sentence that fails to have the force associated with it by rule (i) or (ii) in (87) above is a problematic exception, and the standard line is to claim that, contrary to first intuitions, the sentence does in fact have the rule-associated force as its *literal* force, but simply has in addition an inferred *indirect* force. Thus any usages other than those in accordance with (i) or (ii) are *indirect speech acts*.

The basic problem that then arises is that *most* usages are indirect. For example, the imperative is very rarely used to issue requests in English; instead we tend to employ sentences that only indirectly do requesting. Moreover the kinds of sentences that are thus employed are very varied (see e.g. Ervin-Tripp, 1976 for some empirical generalizations). For example, we could construct an indefinitely long list of ways of indirectly requesting an addressee to shut the door (see also Searle, 1975):

(88)   a. I want you to close the door
             I'd be much obliged if you'd close the door
       b. Can you close the door?
             Are you able by any chance to close the door?
       c. Would you close the door?
             Won't you close the door?
       d. Would you mind closing the door?
             Would you be willing to close the door?
       e. You ought to close the door
             It might help to close the door
             Hadn't you better close the door?
       f. May I ask you to close the door?

Would you mind awfully if I was to ask you to close the
door?
I am sorry to have to tell you to please close the door
g. Did you forget the door?
Do us a favour with the door, love
How about a bit less breeze?
Now Johnny, what do big people do when they come in?
Okay, Johnny, what am I going to say next?

Given that the primary function of each of these could, in the right
circumstances, amount to a request to close the door, the LFH
theorist has to devise some way of deriving their request force from
sentence forms that, according to rule (ii) in (87) above, are
prototypically assertions and questions rather than requests (since
they are not, with one exception, in imperative form).

The diversity of actual usage thus constitutes a substantial challenge
to LFH, the theory that there is a simple form:force correlation.
On the face of it, what people *do* with sentences seems quite
unrestricted by the surface form (i.e. sentence-type) of the sentences
uttered. However, before we ask how Thesis and Antithesis theorists
might respond to this challenge, we should first consider another but
related problem that is posed by ISAs. This problem is that ISAs
often have syntactic (or at least distributional) reflexes associated not
only with their surface sentence-type (and thus, on LFH, with their
literal force), but also with their indirect or effective illocutionary
force. A few examples of this phenomenon will make the dimensions
of the problem clear.

First, consider the quite restricted distribution of *please* in the
pre-verbal position – it occurs in direct requests as in (89), but not
in non-requests as in (90) (the ? here indicates at least pragmatic
anomaly, and some would claim ungrammaticality):

(89)   Please shut the door
         You please shut the door
         I ask you to please shut the door
(90)   ?The sun please rises in the West
         ?The Battle of Hastings please took place in 1066

However, *please* also occurs pre-verbally in certain indirect requests
(roughly, those that incorporate the propositional content of the
direct request), as in:

(91)   Can you please close the door?
        Will you please close the door?
        Would you please close the door?
        I want you to please close the door

Consequently, in order to describe succinctly the distribution of this English morpheme, we seem to need to refer to a single functional class, namely the set of effective requests, direct or indirect (for further discussion see Gordon & Lakoff, 1971; Sadock, 1974: 88–91, 104–8).

Similarly, consider a performative adverb like *obviously*, or a parenthetical clause like *I believe*, which seem to be restricted to assertions, as (93) makes clear:

(92)   a. The square root of a quarter is, obviously, a half
        b. The square root of a quarter is, I believe, a half
(93)   a. ?Is, obviously, the square root of a quarter a half?
        b. ?Is, I believe, the square root of a quarter a half?

However, such expressions can occur not only with direct assertions as in (92), but with assertions in the guise of interrogatives as in (94) or in the form of imperatives as in (95):

(94)   a. May I tell you that, obviously, the square root of a quarter
           is a half?
        b. May I tell you that, I believe, the square root of a quarter
           is a half?
(95)   a. Let me tell you that, obviously, the square root of a quarter
           is a half
        b. Let me tell you that, I believe, the square root of a quarter
           is a half

Again the generalization is that these modifiers seem restricted to utterances that can have the force of an assertion, whatever the sentence-type of the linguistic expression that performs the assertion (see Davison, 1975). Similar remarks can be made for certain kinds of *if*-clause that seem to mention felicity conditions on the illocutionary act being performed, as in:

(96)   Pass me the wrench, if you can

where the *if*-clause serves to lift the normally assumed ability condition on requests. Now notice that such a clause occurs happily with indirect requests, as in (97), but not with questions, whether direct or indirect, as in (98) (see Heringer, 1972):

(97)   a. I want you to pass me the wrench, if you can
         b. Will you pass the wrench, if you can
         c. Let me have the wrench, if you can
(98)   a. ?Have you got the wrench, if you can
         b. ?I want to know if you have the wrench, if you can
         c. ?Let me ask you if you have the wrench, if you can

Again, we seem to need to refer to the effective force of an utterance, irrespective of its form, if we are to express the restrictions on these clauses.

Another kind of distributional pattern that is associated with ISAs is the sort of contraction or deletion illustrated by the sentences below:

(99)   a. Why don't you read in bed?
         b. Why not read in bed?

Here the first sentence can either be used as a genuine request for reasons, or as a suggestion, but the form with *do*-deletion in the second sentence seems only to allow the suggestion interpretation (Gordon & Lakoff, 1975). Similarly, the contraction from (100a) to (100b) forces an advice interpretation of the latter:

(100)   a. You ought to pay your bills on time
         b. Oughta pay your bills on time

and this explains the oddity of:

(101)   ?Oughta pay your bills on time, and you do

since one cannot felicitously advise a course of action that has already been adopted (Brown & Levinson, 1978: 275). Such examples, of which there are many, appear at least to provide *prima facie* evidence for the systematic pragmatic conditioning of various syntactic, or at least distributional, processes.

There are many other kinds of apparent interaction between syntax and indirect illocutionary force (for further examples see Sadock, 1974: Chapter 4; Mittwoch, 1976; Gazdar, 1980a). Ross (1975) concluded, on the basis of one such putative interaction, that pragmatic constraints must be referred to during the syntactic derivation of sentences and suggested that just as Generative Semanticists have argued for a hybrid 'semantax', so these facts motivate a general 'pragmantax'. An alternative, much more in line with current thinking, is not to restrict the syntax by pragmatic constraints at all (thus generating all the ? sentences above), but to have an additional set of pragmatic filters that screen out pragmatically anomalous collocations. But in any case, a general linguistic theory seems called upon to provide an account of the interaction between illocutionary force, both direct and indirect, and apparently syntactic processes.

The LFH is thus confronted with a two-pronged problem: on the one hand, it seems to make the wrong predictions about the assignment of *force* to sentence *form*, and on the other it needs to provide an account of how and why sentences seem able to bear the syntactic stigmata, or distributional markers, of their indirect forces. Two basic kinds of theory have been proposed to rescue LFH, which we may call **idiom theory** and **inference theory**.

According to idiom theories, the indirectness in many putative cases of ISAs is really only apparent. Forms like those in (88a)–(88d) are in fact all *idioms* for, and semantically equivalent to, 'I hereby request you to close the door'. Forms like *Can you VP?* are idioms for 'I request you to VP' in just the same way that *kick the bucket* is an idiom for 'die', i.e. they are not compositionally analysed, but merely recorded whole in the lexicon with the appropriate semantic equivalence. As a point in their favour, idiom theorists can point to lexical idiosyncrasies of ISA formats – for example *Can you VP?* seems a more standard format for indirect requests than *Are you able to VP?*; there are moreover forms like *Could you VP?* that seem difficult to interpret appropriately in a literal way at all. Further, there appear to be some ways in which the hypothesized idioms behave syntactically like their corresponding non-idiomatic direct counterparts. For example, consider again the distribution of pre-verbal *please* in direct requests and apparently indirect requests. But suppose the latter are really idioms for requests, then they will have the same underlying structure or semantic representation as direct requests (indeed, they are also direct requests, in the relevant sense of *direct*). Therefore, on the idiom theory the distributional constraint can be simply captured: pre-verbal *please* can be conditioned so that it can only occur if there is a verb of requesting in the highest clause of the underlying structure or the semantic representation (the actual mechanisms involved are dependent, of course, on views of the nature of, and the relations between, semantics and syntax).

Idiom theory has been seriously and energetically maintained, especially by Sadock (1974, 1975; see also Green, 1975). However, there are overwhelming problems for it. First, responses to utterances can attend to both the literal force (i.e. that associated by rule (i) or (ii) in (87) above with the syntactic form in question) and the alleged idiomatic force, as in (102):

(102)   A: Can you please lift that suitcase down for me?
          B: Sure I can; here you are

This suggests at least that both readings are simultaneously available and utilized, but not in the way that they might be in a pun. Secondly, the argument that idiom theory is the only way to get the syntactic or distributional facts right for phenomena like pre-verbal *please* has the embarrassment that whenever there's a grammatical reflex of indirect force, idiom theorists must claim an idiom. It follows that every sentence (other than direct requests) with pre-verbal *please* must be an idiom with requesting force, e.g. the sentences in (103):

(103)   I'd like you to please X
          May I remind you to please X
          Would you mind if I was to ask you to please X
          I am sorry that I have to tell you to please X

Unfortunately this list seems to be of indefinite length, so if we are to treat these forms as idioms for 'I request you to X', the lexicon will have to contain an indefinite number of such forms. But lexicons are strictly finite, and this suggests that forms like those in (103) are not really idioms at all.[19]

   Thirdly, idiom theory suggests that there should be a considerable comprehension problem: forms like *Can you VP?*, *Will you VP?* and so on will each be *n*-ways ambiguous. How does a listener know what's meant? Although prosodic, and particularly intonational, factors may clearly help, they do not seem to fully 'disambiguate' the forces with which sentences are being used (Liberman & Sag, 1974). In effect, idiom theory will need to be complemented by a powerful pragmatic theory that will account for which interpretation will be taken in which context, i.e. a theory that will bridge the gap

---

[19] A corollary of this point is that the set of ISAs that allows the syntactic or distributional marking of their indirect force is not coincident with the set of idiomatic ISAs (see Brown & Levinson, 1978: 144ff); in which case the attempt to solve the distributional problems of ISAs by appeal to idiom theory fails in any case.

between what is said and what is meant (intended). But if such a theory is required anyway, then we don't need idiom theory at all, because we will in effect have need of an *inference* theory in any case (see below). Similarly, since idiom theory could at most handle cases like (88a)–(88d) (and not (88e)–(88g)), we would need an independent inference theory to get the rest of the ISAs which are based on the inventive use of hints and the like, in which case again we could use such a theory to do what idiom theory does.

Finally, idioms are by definition non-compositional, and are therefore likely to be as idiosyncratic to speech communities as the arbitrary sound–meaning correspondences of lexical items. However, most of the basic ISA structures translate across languages, and where they don't it is usually for good semantic or cultural reasons (see Brown & Levinson, 1978: 143–7). Such strong parallels across languages and cultures in the details of the construction of ISAs constitute good *prima facie* evidence that ISAs are not, or not primarily, idioms.

We are left with inference theories as the only way of maintaining LFH. The basic move here is to claim that ISAs have the literal force associated with the surface form of the relevant sentence by rules (i) and (ii) in (87) above. So, *Can you VP?* has the literal force of a question; it may also in addition have the conveyed or indirect force of a request, by virtue of an inference that is made taking contextual conditions into account. One can think of the additional indirect force as, variously, a perlocution, a Gricean implicature, or an additional conventionally specified illocution. There are, therefore, a number of distinct inference theories, but they share the following essential properties:

(i)   The literal meaning and the literal force of an utterance is computed by, and available to, participants

(ii) For an utterance to be an *indirect* speech act, there must be an inference-trigger, i.e. some indication that the literal meaning and/or literal force is conversationally inadequate in the context and must be 'repaired' by some inference

(iii) There must be specific principles or rules of inference that will derive, from the literal meaning and force and the context, the relevant indirect force

(iv) There must be pragmatically sensitive linguistic rules or constraints, which will govern the occurrence of, for example, pre-verbal *please* in both direct and indirect requests

The first such inference theory was that proposed by Gordon & Lakoff (1971, 1975). In that theory, property (i) was met by assuming the PH; while the trigger in (ii) was provided whenever the literal force of an utterance was blocked by the context. For property (iii), some specific inference rules were offered, **conversational postulates**, modelled on Carnap's **meaning postulates** (which state analytic equivalences not captured elsewhere in a semantical system – see Allwood, Andersson & Dahl, 1977: 144), but with additional reference to contextual factors. Thus, an inference rule was suggested that stated that if a speaker says *Can you VP?* (or any other expression of the same concepts) in a context in which a question reading could not be intended, then his utterance would be equivalent to his having said *I request you to VP*. Similar rules were proposed for *Will you VP?*, *I want you to VP*, and so on. So far this was merely a descriptive enterprise, but Gordon & Lakoff went on to note a compact generalization behind such inference rules, namely that to state or question a felicity condition on a speech act (with some restrictions), where the literal force of such a statement or question is blocked by context, counts as performing that specific speech act. More specifically, Gordon & Lakoff suggested that one can state a *speaker-based* FC as in (104), and question a *hearer-based* FC as in (105):

(104) I want more ice-cream
(105) Can you pass me the ice-cream please?

although a more accurate description would be that one can only state speaker-based FCs, as in (104) (Forman, 1974), while one can state or question all other FCs, although to state them may be less than polite,[20] as in (106):

(106) You will do the washing up
       You can pass me the salt

Such a general principle elegantly captures the kinds of examples of ISAs illustrated in (88a)–(88d). Thus the examples in (88a) are statements of the sincerity condition on requests, that one sincerely wants what one requests; the (88b) examples are questionings of the ability (preparatory) condition on requests, to the effect that one believes that the addressee has the ability to do the thing requested;

---

[20] For some general predictions of what makes speech acts more, or less, polite see Leech, 1977; Brown & Levinson, 1978: 140–1.

the (88c) examples are questionings of the propositional content condition on requests, namely that the propositional content be a specific future act of the addressee's; and the (88d) examples can be claimed to be questionings of the FC that distinguishes requests from orders or demands, namely that the speaker believes that the addressee might not mind doing the act requested (here see Heringer, 1972; cf. Lyons, 1977a: 748–9).

The account is not limited to requests and extends naturally to offers for example, as readers may verify for themselves. Moreover this general principle, that by questioning or asserting a FC on an act one can indirectly perform that act itself, successfully predicts ISAs across quite unrelated languages and cultures (see Brown & Levinson, 1978: 141ff). In fact, the general principle makes the specific *conversational postulates* redundant, for there will be no need, given the general principle, for a language user to learn such specific rules of inference.

Finally, to handle property (iv), Gordon & Lakoff suggested the use of **context-sensitive transderivational constraints**. Transderivational constraints were rules already proposed within the theory of generative semantics that allowed one derivation to be governed by reference to another, and could thus be used to block, for example, certain structural ambiguities (see G. Lakoff, 1973). These could now be used to govern processes like *please*-insertion in indirect requests by reference to the parallel derivation of the explicit performative or direct request. Such rules allowed one to state that the *please* in (107) is acceptable, just because it can also occur in this pre-verbal position in (108), a sentence related to (107) by a conversational postulate – that is, a context-sensitive rule of interpretation.

(107)   Can you please pass the salt?
(108)   I request you to please pass the salt

However, there appear to be serious problems with such rules thought of as syntactic operations. In the first place they belong to the now defunct framework of Generative Semantics. Secondly, syntactic processes are generally thought of as being strictly intra-derivational. But such rules can be equally well stated as pragmatic filtering conditions on syntactic strings (as shown by Gazdar & Klein, 1977). More problematic, perhaps, is a methodological objection:

transderivational rules are so powerful that they undermine, for example, all the arguments for the PH (as Sadock (1975) points out). For, given such rules, the troublesome reflexive pronoun in (30) above could be governed by reference to the parallel derivation of (32), without hypostatizing a covert performative clause in (30) to govern the pronoun instead. However, it is arguable that the elimination of the PH is in fact a desirable result (as argued in section 5.4 above), in which case such rules (or pragmatic filters) provide an alternative account of whatever genuine observations survive the collapse of Antithesis.

Another version of inference theory is suggested by Searle (1975). Property (i) will be handled by his version of speech act theory; property (ii), the trigger requirement, will be provided by Grice's theory of conversational co-operation (Grice, 1975), although on this account the literal force will not be blocked,[21] but rather judged conversationally inadequate alone; and property (iii), the inference principles, will be provided by Grice's general theory of conversational implicature. Since the latter is a general theory of pragmatic inference, this approach, unlike Gordon & Lakoff's, proposes to assimilate ISAs to a broad range of other phenomena that includes metaphor, irony and all other cases where speaker's intent and sentence-meaning are seriously at variance. Such an approach has the great advantage of promising to explain ISAs that are not directly based on FCs, as in (88e)–(88g) above, and thus seems to offer, at least potentially, more than a mere partial solution to the ISA problem. It then becomes necessary, though, to explain why those ISAs based on FCs are so prevalent and successful, and this Searle fails to do satisfactorily (here see an alternative inference theory sketched in Brown & Levinson, 1978: 143).

Incidentally, both these inference approaches fail to attend to the motivation for ISAs: why, for example, do speakers so often prefer the contortions of (110) to the simplicity and directness of (109)? Clearly, on the assumption of Gricean co-operation there must be reason to depart from the direct expression of the relevant speech act.

---

[21] Searle has a problem here which he does not address: he has to claim that, for example, (107) is *literally* a question, and only by additional inference a request, yet (107) used in this way will fail to meet just about all of his FCs on questions (Gazdar, 1981).

(109)   Please lend me some cash

(110)   I don't suppose that you would by any chance be able to lend me some cash, would you?

Labov & Fanshel (1977) suggest that (110) is simply (109) with a bundle of "mitigators", or arbitrary politeness markers, tacked on in front. But this does nothing to explain why the mitigators do the job they do, and besides will not explain the verbal inflection (here -*ing*) in such examples as (111):

(111)   Would you mind lending me some cash, by any chance?

Attempts to explain the rationale behind the **interactional pessimism** in (110), and elsewhere, appeal to the systematic pressures of strategies of politeness (see Brown & Levinson, 1978; also R. Lakoff, 1973b and Leech, 1977). By deviating from the simple and direct (109), one can then communicate by conversational implicature that these omnipresent considerations of politeness are being taken into account in performing the relevant speech act.

However, there is a third solution, more radical than idiom or inference theory, to the problem of ISAs, and that is to reject the fundamental assumption (LFH) that sentences have literal forces at all (see Gazdar, 1981). It will follow that there are no ISAs, and thus no ISA problem, but merely a general problem of mapping speech act force onto sentences in context. Illocutionary force is then entirely pragmatic and moreover has no direct and simple correlation with sentence-form or -meaning. But what would such a radical theorist say about explicit performatives and the major sentence-types, for these seem to embody the corresponding illocutionary forces? What he must say is something along the following lines. The three major sentence-types in English must be given a distinguishing truth-conditional characterization of a very general (and relatively uninformative) sort. For example, the meaning of the interrogative sentence-type can be thought of as an open proposition, closed by the set of appropriate answers (see Hull, 1975), or a particular interrogative may be held to denote the set of its true answers (see Karttunen, 1977; and see Schmerling, 1978 for a similar approach to imperatives). Such meanings are intendedly general, and are consistent with quite different illocutionary forces. Thus interrogatives can be used with the illocutionary forces of 'real' questions, 'exam' questions, rhetorical questions, requests, offers, suggestions, threats and for many other functions, without over-riding some 'literal force' (which concept has been abandoned). Such an approach will fit well with the demonstration that there are no isolable necessary and sufficient conditions on, for example, questionhood, but rather that the nature of the use to which interrogatives are put can vary subtly with the nature of the *language-games* or contexts in which they are used (see Levinson, 1979a for the arguments here). In a similar way, explicit performatives can be assigned truth conditions that are as general as is consistent with their actual use. Contrast this approach with the long-standing tradition, supported by Hare (1949), Lewis (1969: 186), Hintikka (1974), Gordon & Lakoff (1975), and in part by Sadock (1974: 120ff), to the effect that questions in interrogative form are in fact *requests to tell*. Such a view simply does not fit with all the usages of questions, and predicts wrongly, for example, that *no* as a response to a *yes/no* question might be interpretable as a refusal to comply (see Lyons (1977a: 753–68), who suggests that interrogatives simply "grammaticalize the feature of doubt").

Such a radical solution is obviously more than just a way of handling the problem of ISAs; it is also a general approach to speech acts in which semantics plays only a minimal role, by assigning very broad meanings to sentence-types, and also, where appropriate, to explicit performatives. What evidence can be adduced in favour of it? Firstly, it is consistent with the very general use to which the three basic sentence-types are put in English and other languages. For example, imperatives are rarely used to command or request in conversational English (see Ervin-Tripp, 1976), but occur regularly in recipes and instructions, offers (*Have another drink*), welcomings (*Come in*), wishes (*Have a good time*), curses and swearings (*Shut up*), and so on (see Bolinger, 1967). On the alternative set of theories that subscribe to LFH, just about all the actual usages of imperatives in English will therefore have to be considered ISAs, whose understanding is routed through a determination of a literal order or request, usually quite irrelevantly. Even sentences in explicit performative form can be used with different illocutionary forces from those named in the performative verb, as illustrated by (15) above.

Secondly, theorists who hold LFH will find themselves subscribing to an inference theory of ISAs (since the idiom theory has the difficulties outlined above). They therefore hold that the indirect force of an ISA is calculated on the basis of the literal force. But there are a number of cases where this seems not only implausible (as with the use of imperatives in English), but quite untenable. For example, the following would have to have the literal force of a request for permission to remind:

(112)   May I remind you that jackets and ties are required if you wish to use the bar on the 107th floor, sir

Yet (112) cannot felicitously have that force, because reminding is done simply by uttering (112) without such permission being granted. LFH lands one in an awkward position on a number of such examples (see Gazdar, 1981).

Proponents of LFH may perhaps point to the reliable appearance of the three basic sentence-types in the world's languages (see Sadock & Zwicky, in press) as evidence that some such form:force correlation does exist. But it is important to see that a mere approximate correlation of the three sentence-types with their traditional corresponding forces (questions, orders and statements) is not sufficient evidence for LFH. Such a correlation can be accounted for, in so far as it has a firm basis, by assigning truth-conditional meanings to each sentence-type in such a way that rational language users would find them generally useful for the associated purpose. Nevertheless, one may hope that more cross-linguistic work can be brought to bear on the tenability of LFH.

For these and many other reasons, a very good case can be made for abandoning LFH. We are then thrown back on the need for an adequate pragmatic theory of speech acts, or at least a theory that subsumes whatever is valid in the intuitions that lay behind speech act theory in the first place.

5.6   The context-change theory of speech acts

One candidate for such a pragmatic theory of speech acts is a view that treats speech acts as operations (in the set-theoretic sense) on context, i.e. as functions from contexts into contexts. A context must be understood here to be a set of propositions, describing the beliefs, knowledge, commitments and so on of the participants in a discourse. The basic intuition is very simple: when a sentence is uttered more has taken place than merely the expression of its meaning; in addition, the set of background assumptions has been altered. The contribution that an utterance makes to this change in the context is its speech act force or potential. Thus if I assert that p, I add to the context that I am committed to p.

On this view, most speech acts add some propositions to the context, e.g. assertions, promises and orders work in this way. We may express each of these as functions from contexts into contexts very roughly along the following lines:

(i)   An *assertion* that p is a function from a context where the speaker S is not committed to p (and perhaps, on a strong theory of assertion, where H the addressee does not know that p), into a context in which S is committed to the justified true belief that p (and, on the strong version, into one in which H does know that p)

(ii) A *promise* that p is a function from a context where S is not committed to bringing about the state of affairs described in p, into one in which S is so committed

(iii) An *order* that p is a function from a context in which H is not required by S to bring about the state of affairs described by p, into one in which H is so required

Such analyses are capable of considerable refinement, and the reader is directed to work by Hamblin (1971), Ballmer (1978), Stalnaker (1978) and Gazdar (1981) for sophisticated treatments.

One should note that not all speech acts add propositions to the context; some remove them – e.g. permissions, recantations, abolitions, disavowals. Thus, for example, we could characterize the giving of permission as follows:

(iv) A *permission* that (or for) p is a function from a context in which the state of affairs described by p is prohibited, into one in which that state of affairs is not prohibited

thus capturing the intuition that it makes no sense (at least in some systems of deontic logic – see Hilpinen, 1971) to permit what is not prohibited.

One of the main attractions of the context-change theory is that it can be rigorously expressed using set-theoretic concepts. There is no appeal, as there is in most versions of Thesis, to matters of intention and other concepts that resist formalization. The theory is only now becoming generally considered, and it is too early to assess its prospects with any confidence.[22] Important questions that arise, though, are the following:

[22] One may, though, have initial reservations – there are doubts about defining contexts wholly as sets of propositions, and there is also a real possibility that

(i)   How general a theory is it? Can exhortations, curses, expletives, remindings and the like all be adequately expressed in such a framework?

(ii)   Can the full range of speech acts be accommodated with reasonable economy, i.e. how large is the set of primitive concepts, like *commitment*, *obligation* and so on, that have to be marshalled in definitions like those above? The real interest of the theory depends on just how few of these are actually required

(iii) Can such a theory capture the intuitive relations that we feel to exist between some pairs of closely related speech acts, like requests and orders, suggestions and advice, questions and requests, promises and threats?

We await the full-scale theories that would provide answers to these questions. Meanwhile the approach offers hope of systematic formalization in an area of pragmatics that has long resisted it. There are, however, a number of reasons, to which we now turn, why one might be sceptical that any such theory of speech acts will be viable in the long run.

5.7 Beyond theories of speech acts

There are some compelling reasons to think that speech act theory may slowly be superseded by much more complex multi-faceted pragmatic approaches to the functions that utterances perform. The first set of these have to do with the internal difficulties that any speech act theory faces, of which the most intractable is probably the set of problems posed by ISAs. Note that any theory of speech acts is basically concerned with mapping utterances into speech act categories, however those are conceived. The problem then is that either this is a trivial enterprise done by *fiat* (as by LFH), or an attempt is made to predict accurately the functions of sentences in context. But if the latter is attempted, it soon becomes clear that the contextual sources that give rise to the assignment of function or purpose are of such complexity and of such interest in their own right, that little will be left to the theory of speech acts. In the next Chapter we shall review extensive work in conversation analysis that shows

full characterizations of speech acts in terms of deontic, epistemic and other complex propositions will only shift the problems of analysis to another level. Finally, the difficulties associated with the attempt to provide necessary and sufficient conditions for particular illocutionary acts will recur here, albeit in a different form.

278

how the functions that utterances perform are in large part due to the place they occupy within specific conversational (or interactional) sequences.

In this way, speech act theory is being currently undermined from the outside by the growth of disciplines concerned with the empirical study of natural language use (as Austin indeed foresaw). Apart from the important work in conversation analysis dealt with in Chapter 6, there are two major traditions that concern themselves with the details of actual language use in a way pertinent to theories of speech acts. One is the **ethnography of speaking**, which has been concerned with the cross-cultural study of language usage (see the representative collection in Bauman & Sherzer, 1974). A central concept in this work is the notion of a **speech event**, or culturally recognized social activity in which language plays a specific, and often rather specialized, role (like teaching in the classroom, participating in a church service, etc.; see Hymes, 1972). Now given that such cultural events constrain the use of language, there seem to be (as corollaries of such constraints) corresponding inference rules that operate to assign functions to utterances partly on the basis of the social situation that the talk is conducted within (Levinson, 1979a). Thus, in a classroom, the following exchange may have a natural interpretation significantly divergent from the content of what is said:

(113)   Teacher: What are you laughing at?
          Child: Nothing

- roughly, as a command to stop laughing issued by the teacher, and an acceptance of that command, this by virtue of the assumption that laughing (unless invoked by the teacher) is a restricted activity in the classroom (Sinclair & Coulthard, 1975: 30ff). Or consider the following said towards the end of a job interview:

(114)   Interviewer: Would you like to tell us, Mr Khan, why you have
          applied to Middleton College in particular?

where such a leading question does not anticipate replies like "There weren't any other jobs going", but rather, by reference to interview conventions, fishes for compliments on the institution's behalf (see Gumperz, Jupp & Roberts, 1979 for the cross-cultural misunderstandings that can result from not knowing such conventions). Some further examples should serve to indicate just how general such activity-specific inferences seem to be. Thus, the following sentence, delivered in a grocer's shop, and accompanied by a gesture at a lettuce,

(115)   That's a nice one

may count as a request to supply the selected vegetable, and an undertaking to purchase it in due course (Levinson, 1979a). Similarly, utterances that initiate certain kinds of proceedings achieve their effectiveness through assumptions about the nature of those proceedings: hence (116) may serve to constitute the beginning of a committee meeting, of the sort that awaits the arrival of a full complement of personnel:

(116)   Well, we seem to all be here

while some scheduled activity, like a lecture, may be begun by reference to the appropriate schedule:

(117)   It's five past twelve

(see Turner, 1972). All these utterances seem to owe their decisive function in large part to the framework of expectations about the nature of the speech event to which they are contributions. Not only are expectations about the purpose and conduct of the proceedings relevant to this attribution of function, but also, it can be argued, knowledge of social roles. Thus, the following utterance said by one of a pair of students to their landlady may serve as a request for permission, but said by the landlady to the students may be a request for action (Ervin-Tripp, 1981; see also Goody, 1978):[23]

(118)   Can we move the fridge?

Such examples point to the efficacy of Wittgenstein's notion of *language-game*.[24] He denied that there is any small set of functions or speech acts that language may perform; rather, there are as many such acts as there are roles in the indefinite variety of language-games (or speech events) that humans can invent (Wittgenstein, 1958: 10–11). Some support for such a view is offered by the failure of attempts to match up the actual usage of utterances with the felicity conditions proposed by Searle, i.e. with the sets of necessary and sufficient conditions constitutive of specific speech acts. For example,

---

[23] This particular example relies, of course, on the absence of an inclusive/ exclusive distinction in the English first person plural pronoun.

[24] Or the Firthian notion of restricted languages: see e.g. Mitchell, 1975.

questions in actual usage are just too variable and situation-dependent in nature to be captured by any set (or indeed many different sets) of felicity conditions (see Levinson, 1979a), and the same can be shown even for such apparently 'ritualized' speech acts as apologies (see Owen, 1980).

The interpretive corollary of the notion of language-game is the notion of inferential schema, or **frame**, now widely current in artificial intelligence and cognitive psychology (Minsky, 1977; Tannen, 1979). A frame, in this sense, is a body of knowledge that is evoked in order to provide an inferential base for the understanding of an utterance (see e.g. Charniak, 1972), and we may suggest that in the comprehension and the attribution of force or function to utterances like (113)–(118) above, reference is made, as relevant, to the frames for teaching, shopping, participating in committee meetings, lecturing, and other speech events (see e.g. Gumperz, 1977).[25]

The second major empirical tradition that takes us well beyond speech acts narrowly conceived, is the study of language acquisition. Significant advances were achieved here recently when, instead of the emphasis on the grammatical systems lying behind the child's early utterances, attention was shifted to the functions that those utterances perform, and the interactional context they contribute to. It was then seen that, in a sense, the acquisition of speech acts precedes, and systematically pre-figures, the acquisition of speech (Bruner, 1975; Bates, 1976); that is to say that children's gestures and pre-verbal vocalizations play a role in interaction with their caretakers closely similar to the requests and calls for attention that manifest themselves verbally later in development. Thus, with the onset of the child's first use of pre-syntactic utterances (traditionally called *holophrases*), these initial speech functions are already well developed – it seems indeed as if holophrases simply replace gestural indicators of force (Dore, 1975; Griffiths, 1979: 110).[26] An important suggestion that emerges

---

[25] However, there is a significant danger in this line of theorizing, namely that appeal will be made to implicit aspects of context before the full significance of explicit aspects of context – notably prosody and discourse location – have been taken properly into account.

[26] It is interesting that in the holophrase period – from 9–18 months or so – such forces seem very restricted, namely to requests, summonses, greetings and acts of reference. Utterances analysable as unequivocal statements and questions do not seem to appear until the child is nearer 2 (Griffiths, 1979).

is that the acquisition of illocutionary concepts is a precondition for the acquisition of language itself.

However, despite much use of the terms *speech act* and *performative*, this recent work on language acquisition does not really support the importance of the concept of speech act at all; rather it emphasizes the essential roles that communicative intention, utterance function and the interactive context play in the acquisition of language. Indeed the Gricean intentional view of speech acts (as in Strawson, 1964; Schiffer, 1972) seems much more relevant to the description of language acquisition than the convention-based accounts that we have reviewed in such detail in this Chapter. Further, recent work (in part reviewed in Snow, 1979) has stressed the interaction between mother and child that jointly produces discourse. The role of adult interpretations of child utterances, whether those adults are participants or analysts, is thus acknowledged: it is through the responses that adults make on the basis of such interpretations that children "learn how to mean" (Halliday, 1975). Here the other two traditions we have mentioned seem to have promising application. First, conversation analysis is likely to tell us a great deal more than theories of speech acts about the ways in which language is acquired and used by children (see Drew, 1981; Wootton, in press). Secondly, the idea of the speech event and its associated interpretive frame seems very relevant: child-minding is seen as a specific kind of activity in most cultures, associated with a special style of talk by adults ('baby talk' or 'motherese'; see Snow, 1979 for a review of recent work). In such a language-game, expressions of want by the child are not interpreted as requests by virtue of any conversational postulates or the like, but simply because minders tend to see themselves as general want satisfiers (Griffiths, 1979: 109). Further, progress in acquisition can be seen as the acquisition of additional language-games and interpretive frames, extending in a sequence well into adulthood (Keenan, 1976a). Again, then, the study of language acquisition, where the attribution of intent and purpose is often so problematic for both adult participants and analysts, while addressing the issues that lie at the heart of speech act theory, takes us well beyond it.

In conclusion, the future of speech act theory probably rests on the tenability of the LFH. If some version of a strict form:force correlation can be maintained in such a way that the predicted forces match actual usages, then a theory of speech acts is likely to continue to play a role (though not necessarily a central one) in general theories of language usage. If, on the other hand, no such version of LFH can be found (and certainly none now exists), then there is little reason to isolate out a level of illocutionary force that is distinct from all the other facets of an utterance's function, purpose or intent. In that case, we can expect speech act theory to give way to more empirical lines of investigation of the sort briefly reviewed here, and dealt with more extensively in the next Chapter.

6

Conversational structure[1]

6.0 Introduction

In this Chapter we shall be centrally concerned with the organization of conversation. Definitions will emerge below, but for the present **conversation** may be taken to be that familiar predominant kind of talk in which two or more participants freely alternate in speaking, which generally occurs outside specific institutional settings like religious services, law courts, classrooms and the like.

It is not hard to see why one should look to conversation for insight into pragmatic phenomena, for conversation is clearly the prototypical kind of language usage, the form in which we are all first exposed to language – the matrix for language acquisition. Various aspects of pragmatic organization can be shown to be centrally organized around usage in conversation, including the aspects of deixis explored in Chapter 2 where it was shown that unmarked usages of grammatical encodings of temporal, spatial, social and discourse parameters are organized around an assumption of co-present conversational participants. Presupposition may also be seen as in some basic ways

---

[1] Illustrative data in this Chapter are drawn where possible from published sources so that readers can refer to them for additional context or further discussion; in those cases the source heads each extract. Where this has not been possible data have been drawn from transcripts circulated by workers in conversation analysis, such sources being indicated by customary identifying initials (e.g. US, DCD), a large proportion of which have been transcribed by Gail Jefferson; otherwise, data headed by a number (e.g. 176B) are drawn from the author's collection, some of which were transcribed by Marion Owen. Data without a heading are constructed for illustrative purposes unless otherwise indicated in the text. It has not been possible to check transcripts against the original recordings, so there may only be a modicum of consistency in the use of transcription conventions (see Appendix to this Chapter).

organized around a conversational setting: the phenomena involve constraints on the way in which information has to be presented if it is to be introduced to particular participants with specific shared assumptions and knowledge about the world. The issues touch closely on the distinction between **given** and **new** (see e.g. Clark & Haviland, 1977), and concern constraints on the **formulation** of information (that is, the choice of just one out of the indefinitely many possible descriptions of some entity – see Schegloff, 1972b), both of which are important issues in conversational organization. Similarly, implicatures derive from specific assumptions about conversational context: they do not always arise in the same way in all kinds of discourse – rather they are typical of conversation (yet, as we have seen, they have general grammatical reflexes, as in the constraints they impose on lexicalization). In the same way it may be argued that many kinds of speech act are built on the assumption of a conversational matrix – betting, for example, requires *uptake* to be effective, so that the utterance of *I bet you six pence* does not succeed without the interactional ratification typical of conversation. Indeed the conversational dependence of illocutionary force is such that the concept itself can be claimed to be substantially replaced by concepts of conversational function, as we shall see.

Nearly all the pragmatic concepts we have reviewed so far can thus be claimed to tie in closely with conversation as the central or most basic kind of language usage. Now if, as we shall argue, the proper way to study conversational organization is through empirical techniques, this suggests that the largely philosophical traditions that have given rise to pragmatics may have to yield in the future to more empirical kinds of investigation of language usage. Conceptual analysis using introspective data would then be replaced by careful inductive work based on observation. The issue raised here is whether pragmatics is in the long term an essentially empirical discipline or an essentially philosophical one, and whether the present lack of integration in the subject is due primarily to the absence of adequate theory and conceptual analysis or to the lack of adequate observational data, and indeed an empirical tradition. So far, in this book, we have reviewed the philosophically rooted traditions, but in this Chapter we turn to the outstanding empirical tradition in pragmatics. First, however, we should make clear the reasons for preferring this tradition to other approaches to the study of conversation.

285

6.1 **Discourse analysis versus conversation analysis**

In this section some different approaches to the study of conversation are assessed. At the risk of oversimplification, there can be considered to be two major approaches to the analysis of conversation, which we shall designate **discourse analysis** and **conversation analysis** (other distinctive approaches exist, of which the most important is probably the modelling of conversation using computer programs instead of human participants, as yet in its infancy – but see e.g. Power, 1979). Both approaches are centrally concerned with giving an account of how coherence and sequential organization in discourse is produced and understood. But the two approaches have distinctive and largely incompatible styles of analysis, which we may characterize as follows.

Discourse analysis (or DA) employs both the methodology and the kinds of theoretical principles and primitive concepts (e.g. *rule*, *well-formed formula*) typical of linguistics. It is essentially a series of attempts to extend the techniques so successful in linguistics, beyond the unit of the sentence. The procedures employed (often implicitly) are essentially the following: (a) the isolation of a set of basic categories or units of discourse, (b) the formulation of a set of concatenation rules stated over those categories, delimiting well-formed sequences of categories (coherent discourses) from ill-formed sequences (incoherent discourses). There are a number of other features that tend to go with these. There is typically an appeal to intuitions, about, for example, what is and what is not a coherent or well-formed discourse (see e.g. Van Dijk, 1972; Labov & Fanshel, 1977: 72). There is also a tendency to take one (or a few) texts (often constructed by the analyst) and to attempt to give an analysis in depth of all the interesting features of this limited domain (to find out, as some have put it, "what is really going on" – Labov & Fanshel, 1977: 59, 117). Into this broad avenue of work fall not only (and most obviously) the **text grammarians** (like Petöfi and Van Dijk – see de Beaugrande & Dressler, 1981: 24ff for review), but also the rather different work based on speech acts (or related notions) of researchers such as Sinclair & Coulthard (1975), Longacre (1976b), Labov & Fanshel (1977) and Coulthard & Brazil (1979).

In contrast, *conversation analysis* (or CA), as practised by Sacks, Schegloff, Jefferson, Pomerantz and others, is a rigorously empirical approach which avoids premature theory construction (see the collections in Schenkein, 1978; Psathas, 1979; Atkinson & Heritage, in press). The methods are essentially *inductive*; search is made for recurring patterns across many records of naturally occurring conversations, in contrast to the immediate categorization of (usually) restricted data which is the typical first step in DA work. Secondly, in place of a theoretical ontology of *rules* as used in syntactic description, we have an emphasis on the interactional and inferential consequences of the choice between alternative utterances. Again in contrast to DA, there is as little appeal as possible to intuitive judgements – they may, willy-nilly, guide research, but they are not explanations and they certainly do not circumscribe the data; the emphasis is on what can actually be found to occur, not on what one would guess would be odd (or acceptable) if it were to do so. Intuition, it is claimed, is simply an unreliable guide in this area, as indeed it may be in other areas of linguistics (see e.g. Labov, 1972a). There is also a tendency to avoid analyses based on single texts. Instead, as many instances as possible of some particular phenomena are examined across texts, not primarily to illuminate "what is really going on" in some interaction (a goal judged impossible, such illuminations evading participants as well as analysts on many occasions), but rather to discover the systematic properties of the sequential organization of talk, and the ways in which utterances are designed to manage such sequences.

Which is the correct manner in which to proceed? The issue is a live one: DA theorists can accuse CA practitioners of being inexplicit, or worse, plain muddled, about the theories and conceptual categories they are actually employing in analysis (see e.g. Labov & Fanshel, 1977: 25; Coulthard & Brazil, 1979); CA practitioners can retort that DA theorists are so busy with premature formalization that they pay scant attention to the nature of the data. The main strength of the DA approach is that it promises to integrate linguistic findings about intra-sentential organization with discourse structure; while the strength of the CA position is that the procedures employed have already proved themselves capable of yielding by far the most substantial insights that have yet been gained into the organization of conversation.

There may well seem to be room for some kind of accommodation or even synthesis between the two positions; however there are some reasons to think that the DA approach as outlined is fundamentally misconceived. We may start by noting that DA analysts can be divided into two basic categories – the text grammarians and the speech act (or interactional) theorists. The text grammarians believe, at least in the simplest formulations, that discourses can be viewed simply as sentences strung together in much the same way that clauses within sentences can be conjoined with connectives of various kinds. It follows that there are no problems for discourse analysis that are not problems for sentential analysis – "discourse can be treated as a single sentence in isolation by regarding sentence boundaries as sentential connectives" (Katz & Fodor, 1964: 490; see critique in Edmondson, 1978, 1979). However adequate such a view may be for written non-dialogic text, it is simply not feasible as a model for conversation where the links between speakers cannot be paraphrased as sentential connectives – for example (1) does not paraphrase as (2):

(1)   A: How are you?
         B: To hell with you
(2)   How are you and to hell with you
(3)   Anne said "How are you?" and Barry replied "To hell with you"

Even if (1) can be reported as (3), this shows nothing about the reducibility of (1) to (3), but merely that like all other kinds of events conversations are reportable (*contra* Katz & Fodor, 1964: 491).

The DA theorists that are therefore of interest to us are those who have been specifically concerned with conversation as a particular type of discourse, and we shall devote the rest of this section to a critique of their basic methods and assumptions. Here there is a remarkable underlying uniformity of views, a basic assumption (probably right as far as it goes) that the level at which coherence or order in conversation is to be found is not at the level of linguistic expressions, but at the level of the speech acts or the interactional moves that are made by the utterance of those expressions. Or, as Labov & Fanshel (1977: 70) put it: "obligatory sequencing is not to be found between utterances but between the actions that are being performed". It is thus possible to formulate the general properties of the whole class of models to which, in one guise or another, most DA theorists of conversation would subscribe (see e.g. Labov, 1972b; Sinclair & Coulthard, 1975; Longacre, 1976b; Labov & Fanshel, 1977; Coulthard & Brazil, 1979; Edmondson, 1981):

(4)   (i)   There are unit acts – *speech acts* or *moves* – that are
               performed in speaking, which belong to a specifiable,
               delimited set

        (ii)   Utterances[2] are segmentable into unit parts – *utterance-
               units* – each of which corresponds to (at least) one unit act

        (iii) There is a *specifiable function*, and hopefully a *procedure*,
               that will map utterance units into speech acts and vice
               versa

        (iv)   Conversational sequences are primarily regulated by a set
               of *sequencing rules* stated over speech act (or move) types

The kernel idea here is both simple and highly plausible: since
sequential constraints are clearly not easily stated on the form or
meaning of what is said, utterances have to be 'translated' into the
underlying actions they perform, because on this deeper (or more
abstract) level rules of sequencing will be straightforwardly
describable. Such a model seems to capture the obvious regularities
of the sort that answers generally follow questions, actions or excuses
follow requests, acceptances or rejections follow offers, greetings
follow greetings, and so on. The difficulties are thus generally
considered to lie at the level of (iii) above, the translation from
utterances into acts – "the rules of production and interpretation ...
are quite complex; the sequencing rules are relatively simple"
(Labov & Fanshel, 1977: 110) – and the various theories of indirect
speech acts are therefore a focus of interest.

   If the view is right then we can build up a model of conversation
from a linguistic base by utilizing (while improving) the basic notions
of speech act theory, merely adding a *syntax* for the concatenation of
speech act categories that will capture the simple regularities noted
above.

   However there are some strong reasons to believe that such models
are fundamentally inappropriate to the subject matter, and thus
irremediably inadequate. Some of these have to do with the general
problems that beset speech act theory, which we have already
reviewed in Chapter 5. But in fact there are severe problems for each

---

[2] As noted in Chapter 1, considerable ambiguities attend the use of this term.
We have generally used the term in prior Chapters to denote a sentence-context
pair; however here, and generally elsewhere in this Chapter, it is being used
in the sense of a product of an act of utterance, occurring within a *turn* (see
below) at talk. On the notion *utterance-unit* see Lyons, 1977a: 633ff;
Goodwin, 1981: 25ff.

of the basic assumptions in (4), which should be briefly indicated (see also Levinson, 1981a, 1981b).

First, there are a number of problems with assumption (4)(i). One of these is that some single-sentence utterances clearly perform more than one speech act at a time (if the notion of a speech act is to capture at least what utterances conventionally achieve) – consider, for example, the first utterance in the following exchange:

(5)   A: Would you like another drink?
       B: Yes I would, thank you, but make it a small one

The first utterance seems to be both a question and an offer, as indicated by the response. Now such multiple functions are not in principle problematic for assumptions (4)(i) and (4)(iii), but as they accumulate they do render the whole model considerably less attractive. How, for example, are the sequencing rules in (iv) to operate if more acts are being done than can feasibly be responded to directly? Moreover, as we shall see, the sources for multiple functions often lie outside the utterance in question, in the sequential environment in which it occurs; but such environments are not obviously restricted in kind, so that the existence of a well-defined and delimited set of speech act types, as required by the model, is quite dubious.

However, more problematic for the assumption in (4)(i) is the fact that conversational responses can be directed not just to the *illocutions* performed by utterances, but to their *perlocutions* too. Suppose, for example, that A and his companion B are at a party, and A being bored says to B:

(6)   A: It's getting late, Mildred
       B: a. But I'm having such a good time
          b. Do you want to go?
          c. Aren't you enjoying yourself, dear?

Then B might reply in any of the ways indicated, but none of these addresses the illocutionary force of A's utterance; rather they respond to a number of possible perlocutionary intents that A might have had. But this is highly problematic for the species of model in question: for perlocutions are unlimited in kind and number and any responses based on them will necessarily fall outside the scope of such a model.

There are serious problems too with (4)(ii), the requirement that there be identifiable utterance-units upon which speech acts or moves can be mapped. Single sentences can be used to perform two or more speech acts in different clauses, and each clause (as we have seen) may perform more than one speech act. Further, there are many sub-sentential units that occur as utterances, and it is possible for non-linguistic vocalizations (e.g. laughter), non-vocal actions (like handing someone something requested), and sheer silence (e.g. after a loaded question) to perform appropriate responses to utterances. The problem is that in order for the function in property (4)(iii) to be well-formed, there must be an independently specifiable set of utterance-units onto which actions can be mapped. But in fact it is impossible to specify in advance what kinds of behavioural units will carry major interactional acts; rather the units in question seem to be functionally defined by the actions they can be seen to perform in context.

The requirement (4)(iii), therefore, inherits two problems: for a function to map actions onto utterance-units, there must be well-defined sets of (a) relevant actions and (b) relevant utterance-units. But we have seen that there are not. In addition, for this kind of model to have any real interest, we require not merely an abstract function, but an actual procedure or algorithm that will implement the function. But here we shall be even more disappointed, for as our discussion of speech act theory in Chapter 5 showed, there simply is no simple form-to-force correlation, and the attempts to bridge the gap (between what utterances 'literally' mean and 'actually' do in the way of actions) with theories of indirect speech acts have provided at best only partial solutions. For questions of context, both sequential (or discourse) context and extra-linguistic context, can play a crucial role in the assignment of utterance function. We can expect, therefore, no simple 'force conversion' rules to supply a general solution here, but rather some immensely complex inferential process that utilizes information of many different kinds. In the present state of knowledge, proponents of the kind of model outlined in (4) cannot expect to have even the general outlines of such an algorithm.

But this has an unfortunate consequence for such models, namely that they are unfalsifiable, and therefore essentially vacuous. The reasoning is this: suppose I claim (in accordance with the final assumption in (4)) that, given some set of speech act types or moves (let us call them X, Y and Z), only some sequences of these are *well-formed* or coherent sequences (say, XYZ, XZ, YXX) while all others (like *ZXY, *XYX, *ZX, etc.) are *ill-formed* sequences. Then in order to be able to disprove this hypothesis it must be possible to test independently whether some sequence of utterances in fact corresponds to, say, the string XYZ. But such a test is only possible if there is an explicit procedure for assigning utterances to categories like X, Y and Z. And as there is no such procedure, there is no empirical content to the claim that strings of the form XYX do not or should not occur in discourse.

Finally we come to (4)(iv), the assumption that there is a set of sequencing rules, stated over speech act (or related) categories, which govern the sequential organization of conversation. This assumption is the motivating property of all such models, for the point of 'translating' utterances into the actions they perform is to reduce the problems of sequencing in conversation to a set of rules governing well-formed action sequences. The assumption embodies a strong claim about the 'syntactic' nature of sequential constraints in conversation, and essential to such a claim is that there should be clear cases of ill-formed sequences (like *XYX above) just as there are in sentence grammars (like *on cat the sat mat the). Yet cases of such *impossible* discourses are hard if not impossible to find (see e.g. the successful contextualization by Edmondson, 1981:12ff of the allegedly ill-formed discourses in Van Dijk, 1972). One reason for this is predicted by Grice's theory of implicature: any apparent conversational violation (e.g. a flouting of Relevance) is likely to be treated on the assumption that the utterances involved are in fact interpretable, if additional inferences are made (see Chapter 3 above). Another is that, as mentioned above, responses can be made to perlocutions, and perlocutions are not limited in kind and number and are not solely predictable from the utterances involved. A third is that our intuitions do not seem to be reliable guides in this area – sequences that we might judge 'ill-formed' in isolation do in fact frequently occur. Consider the following example (from Sacks, 1968, April 17):

(7)   A: I have a fourteen year old son
        B: Well that's all right
        A: I also have a dog
        B: Oh I'm sorry

which can seem in isolation quite bizarre, but when re-embedded in the actual conversation from which it is taken – in which A is raising a series of possible disqualifications for apartment rental with the landlord B – it will seem natural and indeed quite unremarkable. So the fundamental basis for the postulation of general sequencing rules, namely the existence and predictability of ill-formed sequences, is seriously called into question.

It is an initial consideration of paired utterances like questions and answers, offers and acceptances (or rejections), greetings and greetings in response, and so on, that motivates the sequencing rules approach. But not only is conversation not basically constituted by such pairs (cf. Coulthard, 1977: 70) but the rules that bind them are not of a quasi-syntactic nature. For example, questions can be happily followed by partial answers, rejections of the presuppositions of the question, statements of ignorance, denials of the relevance of the question, and so on, as illustrated below:

(8)   A: What does John do for a living?
           B: a. Oh this and that
              b. He doesn't
              c. I've no idea
              d. What's that got to do with it?

Rather we want to say that given a question an answer is relevant, and responses can be expected to deal with this relevance (see the explication of the notion of **conditional relevance** in 6.2.1.2 below). Such expectations are more like the maxims proposed by Grice, with their associated defeasible inferences, than like the rule-bound expectancy of an object after a transitive verb in English. This is made clear by, for example, the fact that in conversation inventive co-operative responses following questions may be preferable to answers:

(9)   A: Is John there?
           B: You can reach him at extension thirty-four sixty-two

Finally we should note that sequencing constraints in conversation could in any case never be captured fully in speech act terms. What makes some utterance after a question constitute an answer is not only the nature of the utterance itself but also the fact that it occurs after a question with a particular content – 'answerhood' is a complex property composed of sequential location and topical coherence across two utterances, amongst other things; significantly, there is no proposed illocutionary force of answering. But the model in question skirts the puzzling issue of constraints on topical coherence, despite the fact that their relevance to issues of conversational sequencing is made clear by examples like (7). It seems, then, that it is doubtful that there are rules of a syntactic sort governing conversational sequencing, and that even if such rules could be found they would not give anything but a partial account of constraints on conversational sequences.

The conclusion that can be drawn is that all of the models that fall within the class having the general properties outlined in (4) are beset with fundamental difficulties. In addition, the actual analyses offered within theories of this kind are often quite superficial and disappointing, involving an intuitive mapping of unmotivated categories onto a restricted range of data. Even where this is not so (as in the major work by Labov & Fanshel, 1977), the analyses can often be shown to have obscured basic features of conversational organization (see e.g. the re-analysis of their data in (104) below).

It seems reasonable, then, to turn to CA as the approach that, at least at present, has most to offer in the way of substantial insight into the nature of conversation. It is important to see, though, that the basis for the rejection of DA is that the methods and theoretical tools advocated, namely those imported from mainstream theoretical linguistics, seem quite inappropriate to the domain of conversation. Conversation is not a structural product in the same way that a sentence is – it is rather the outcome of the interaction of two or more independent, goal-directed individuals, with often divergent interests. Moving from the study of sentences to the study of conversations is like moving from physics to biology: quite different analytical procedures and methods are appropriate even though conversations are (in part) composed of units that have some direct correspondence to sentences.

6.2 **Conversation analysis**[3]

Conversation analysis of the sort that will be described in the rest of this Chapter has been pioneered by a break-away group

[3] This Chapter, though relatively long because of the need to cite a considerable amount of data, is only a preliminary introduction. It may be supplemented with the introductory Chapters of Atkinson & Drew, 1979; the exemplary papers by Schegloff & Sacks (1973), Schegloff (1976); and the collections in Schenkein, 1978; Psathas, 1979; Atkinson & Heritage, in press. See also the introduction by Coulthard (1977). It should also be noted that for expositional purposes I have presented in a bold and simplified way a number of findings that are still treated as working hypotheses in conversation analysis.

of sociologists, often known as **ethnomethodologists**. The relevance
of the sociological background to the pragmaticist is the methodological preferences that derive from it. The movement arose in
reaction to the quantitative techniques, and the arbitrary imposition
on the data of supposedly objective categories (upon which such
techniques generally rely), that were typical of mainstream American
sociology. In contrast, it was argued cogently, the proper object of
sociological study is the set of techniques that the members of a
society themselves utilize to interpret and act within their own social
worlds – the sociologist's 'objective' methods perhaps not really
being different in kind at all. Hence the use of the term **ethnomethodology**, the study of 'ethnic' (i.e. participants' own) methods
of production and interpretation of social interaction (see Garfinkel,
1972; Turner, 1974a). Out of this background comes a healthy
suspicion of premature theorizing and *ad hoc* analytical categories:
as far as possible the categories of analysis should be those that
participants themselves can be shown to utilize in making sense of
interaction; unmotivated theoretical constructs and unsubstantiated
intuitions are all to be avoided. In practice this results in a strict and
parsimonious structuralism and a theoretical asceticism – the
emphasis is on the data and the patterns recurrently displayed
therein.

The data consist of tape-recordings and transcripts of naturally
occurring conversation, with little attention paid to the nature of the
context as that might be theoretically conceived within sociolinguistics
or social psychology (e.g. whether the participants are friends or
distant acquaintances, or belong to a certain social group, or whether
the context is formal or informal, etc.).[4] As anyone who works on
conversational data knows, heavy reliance inevitably comes to be
placed on transcriptions and, as in phonetics, issues immediately arise
here as to how **broad** or **narrow** such transcriptions should be, what
notational systems should be used, and to what extent the exercise
of transcription itself embodies theoretical decisions (see Ochs,
1979d). Excerpts from transcripts will here be given in the notation
generally utilized in conversation analysis and listed in the Appendix

[4] It is not that the relevance of these factors is denied *a priori*, but simply that
it is not assumed – if participants themselves can be rigorously shown to
employ such categories in the production of conversation, then they would
be of interest to CA. See e.g. Jefferson, 1974: 198.

to this Chapter: standard orthography will be used in some places where linguists might prefer phonetic transcription, and there is not, unfortunately, an adequate treatment of prosodic, and especially intonational, cues.[5]

In section 6.2.1 we shall present some of the most basic findings that have resulted from this kind of work. These findings are not in themselves, perhaps, of a very surprising sort, but we will then go on to show in later sections (especially, 6.2.2 and 6.2.3) that these apparently disparate little facts about conversation all fit together in a systematic way, and it is only then that one can begin to see that conversation has in fact an elaborate and detailed architecture.

One important *caveat* should be made immediately. The work here reviewed is based almost entirely on English data, especially telephone conversations and group talk, and we simply do not know at the present to what extent these findings extend to other languages and cultures. But although the findings here may be in part culturally specific, the methods employed should be of quite general application.

6.2.1   *Some basic findings*
6.2.1.1   Turn-taking

We may start with the obvious observation that conversation is characterized by **turn-taking**: one participant, A, talks, stops; another, B, starts, talks, stops; and so we obtain an A–B–A–B–A–B distribution of talk across two participants. But as soon as close attention is paid to this phenomenon, how such a distribution is actually achieved becomes anything but obvious. First there are the surprising facts that less (and often considerably less) than 5 per cent of the speech stream is delivered in **overlap** (two speakers speaking simultaneously), yet gaps between one person speaking and another

---

[5] Workers in CA have sometimes used *ad hoc* orthography to represent segmental features, to the irritation of linguists, although no serious theoretical issues seem to be involved (see Goodwin, 1977: 120, 1981: 47). I have taken the considerable liberty of standardizing the orthography of transcripts, but only where non-native speakers might otherwise have difficulty interpreting the text. Punctuation marks are also used by workers in CA to give some indication of intonation (see Appendix) and the original punctuation has therefore been reproduced in examples taken from these printed sources. One hopes that in future work a better system of prosodic transcription will be adopted (as used in e.g. the British tradition by Crystal (1969); O'Connor & Arnold (1973); Brazil, Coulthard & Johns (1980)).

starting are frequently measurable in just a few micro-seconds and they average amounts measured in a few tenths of a second (see Ervin-Tripp, 1979: 392 and references therein). How is this orderly transition from one speaker to another achieved with such precise timing and so little overlap? A second puzzle is that, whatever the mechanism responsible, it must be capable of operating in quite different circumstances: the number of parties may vary from two to twenty or more; persons may enter and exit the pool of participants; turns at speaking can vary from minimal utterances to many minutes of continous talk; and if there are more than two parties then provision is made for all parties to speak without there being any specified order or 'queue' of speakers. In addition the same system seems to operate equally well both in face-to-face interaction and in the absence of visual monitoring, as on the telephone.

Sacks, Schegloff & Jefferson (1974, 1978) suggest that the mechanism that governs turn-taking, and accounts for the properties noted, is a set of rules with ordered options which operates on a turn-by-turn basis, and can thus be termed a **local management system**. One way of looking at the rules is as a sharing device, an 'economy' operating over a scarce resource, namely control of the 'floor'. Such an allocational system will require minimal units (or 'shares') over which it will operate, such units being the units from which **turns** at talk are constructed. These units are, in this model, determined by various features of linguistic surface structure: they are syntactic units (sentences, clauses, noun phrases, and so on) identified as turn-units in part by prosodic, and especially intonational, means. A speaker will be assigned initially just one of these **turn-constructional units** (although the extent of the unit is largely within the speaker's control due to the flexibility of natural language syntax). The end of such a unit constitutes a point at which speakers may change – it is a **transition relevance place**, or TRP. At a TRP the rules that govern the transition of speakers then come into play, which does not mean that speakers will change at that point but simply that they may do so, as we shall see. The exact characterization of such units still requires a considerable amount of linguistic work (see Goodwin, 1981: 15ff), but whatever its final shape the characterization must allow for the **projectability** or predictability of each unit's end – for it is this alone that can account for the recurrent marvels of split-second speaker transition.

There is one other feature of turn-units that has to be mentioned before the rules can be presented, namely the possibility of specifically indicating within such a unit that at its end some particular other party is invited to speak next. Techniques for selecting next speakers in this way can be quite elaborate, but include such straightforward devices as the following: a question (offer, or request, etc.) plus an address term; a tagged assertion plus an address feature; and the various hearing and understanding checks (*Who?*, *You did what?*, *Pardon?*, *You mean tomorrow?*, etc.) which select prior speaker as next.

Operating on the turn-units are the following rules (slightly simplified from Sacks, Schegloff & Jefferson, 1978), where C is current speaker, N is next speaker, and TRP is the recognizable end of a turn-constructional unit:

(10)   Rule 1 – applies initially at the first TRP of any turn
   (a) If C selects N in current turn, then C must stop speaking, and N must speak next, transition occurring at the first TRP after N-selection
   (b) If C does not select N, then any (other) party may self-select, first speaker gaining rights to the next turn
   (c) If C has not selected N, and no other party self-selects under option (b), then C may (but need not) continue (i.e. claim rights to a further turn-constructional unit)
   Rule 2 – applies at all subsequent TRPs
   When Rule 1(c) has been applied by C, then at the next TRP Rules 1 (a)–(c) apply, and recursively at the next TRP, until speaker change is effected

It may be asked whether Rule 1(c) is not just a special case of Rule 1(b), and therefore redundant. However there is some evidence that the self-selecting parties in Rule 1(b) should not properly include current speaker (C): for example, the delays between two turns by different speakers are statistically shorter than between two turn-constructional units produced by a single speaker, suggesting that opportunity for others to speak is specifically provided by Rule 1(b) (see Sacks, Schegloff & Jefferson, 1978: 54 n.30).

Careful consideration will show that the rules provide for the basic observations already noted. On the one hand they predict the following specific details. First, only one speaker will generally be speaking at any one time in a single conversation (although four or more speakers may often conduct more than one conversation simultaneously). However where overlaps do occur, they can be predicted to be, at least in the great majority of cases, precisely placed: overlaps will either occur as competing first starts, as allowed by Rule 1(b) and illustrated in (11), or they will occur where TRPs have been misprojected for systematic reasons, e.g. where a tag or address term has been appended as illustrated in (12), in which case overlap will be predictably brief. The rules thus provide a basis for the discrimination (which we all employ) between inadvertent overlap as in (11) and (12) and violative interruption as in (13):

(11)   *Sacks, Schegloff & Jefferson, 1978 : 16*
    J: Twelve pounds I think wasn't it. =
    D: =//Can you bel*ie*ve it?
    L: Twelve pounds on the Weight Watchers' scale.
(12)   *Sacks, Schegloff & Jefferson, 1978 : 17*
    A: Uh *you* been down here before // havenche.
    B: Yeah.
(13)   *DCD :22*
    C: We:ll I wrote what I thought was a a-a
       rea:s'n//ble explan*a*tio:n
→   F: I: think it was a *very* rude le :tter

It is also predicted that when silence – the absence of vocalization – occurs, it will be differentially assigned, on the basis of the rules, as either (i) a **gap** before a subsequent application of Rules 1(b) or 1(c), or (ii) a **lapse** on the non-application of Rules 1(a), (b) and (c), or (iii) a selected next speaker's **significant** (or **attributable**) **silence**[6] after the application of Rule 1(a). Thus in (14) we have first a *gap* by delay of the Rule 1(b) option for just one second, then a lapse of sixteen seconds:

(14)   *Sacks, Schegloff & Jefferson, 1978 : 25*
    C: Well no I'll drive (I don't mi//nd)
    J: hhh
→   (1.0)
    J: I meant to *offer*.
→   (16.0)
    J: Those shoes look nice ...

While in (15) we have two clear cases of *attributable silence*, by virtue

---

[6] Henceforth the term *silence* is sometimes used in this technical sense, while the term *pause* is used as a general cover term for these various kinds of periods of non-speech. Other usages will be clear from the context.

of the fact that A's utterances select B as next speaker, and by Rule
1(a) B should then speak:

(15)   *Atkinson & Drew, 1979 : 52*
         A: Is there something bothering you or not?
→   (1.0)
         A: Yes or no
→   (1.5)
         A: Eh?
         B: No.

While making such specific predictions, the rules also allow for the
observable variations in conversation: lapses may or may not occur;
there is no strict limit to turn size given the extendable nature of
syntactic turn-constructional units and the continuations allowed for
by Rule 1(c); there is no exclusion of parties; the number of parties
to a conversation can change. These diverse variations are allowed for
basically because the system is **locally managed**, i.e. it operates on
a turn-by-turn basis, organizing just the transition from current
speaker to next, and is therefore indifferent to, for example, the pool
of potential next speakers.[7]

An important consequence of the system is that it provides,
independently of content or politeness considerations, an intrinsic
motivation for participants to both listen and process what is said – for
the transition rules require prior location of next speaker selection
should it occur, and the projection of upcoming TRPs.

Where, despite the rules, overlapping talk occurs, detailed study
has revealed the operation of a resolution system that is integrated
into the main turn-taking system. First, if overlap occurs, one speaker
generally drops out rapidly, as in (16):

(16)   *Atkinson & Drew, 1979 : 44 (simplified)*
         D: ... he's got to *talk* to someone (very sor) supp*o*rtive way
            towards you (.)
→   A: //Greg's (got wha-)*
         G: Think you sh* – think you should have *one* to: hold him

Secondly, as soon as one speaker thus emerges into 'the clear', he
typically recycles precisely the part of the turn obscured by the
overlap, as in G's turn in (16). Finally, if one speaker does not
immediately drop out, there is available a competitive allocation

---

[7] Although such factors do influence, for example, the details of techniques
for next-speaker selection.

system which works roughly on a syllable-by-syllable basis, whereby the speaker who 'upgrades' most wins the floor, upgrading consisting of increased amplitude, slowing tempo, lengthened vowels and other features, as illustrated in (17):

(17)   *US: 43*
→   J: But dis // person thet *DID* IT* IS GOT TO BE::
       V: If I see the person
       J: .hh taken care of

There is, then, quite an elaborate back-up machinery for resolving overlap if, despite the rules, it should occur (see Jefferson & Schegloff, 1975).

It is important to see that, although the phenomenon of turn-taking is obvious, the suggested mechanism organizing it is not.[8] For a start, things could be quite otherwise: for example, it is reported of the African people, the Burundi (see Albert, 1972: 81ff), that turn-taking (presumably in rather special settings) is pre-allocated by the rank of the participants, so that if A is of higher social status than B, and B than C, then the order in which the parties will talk is A–B–C. Of course in English-speaking cultures too there are special non-conversational turn-taking systems operative in, for example, classrooms, courtrooms, chaired meetings and other 'institutional' settings, where turns are (at least in part) pre-allocated rather than determined on a turn-by-turn basis, and these too emphasize that the rules in (10) are not the only possible or rational solution to the organization of the 'economy' of turns at talk. Nevertheless, there is good reason to think that like many aspects of conversational organization, the rules are valid for the most informal, ordinary kinds of talk across all the cultures of the world. There is even evidence of ethological roots for turn-taking and other related mechanisms, both from work on human neonates (see e.g. Trevarthen, 1974, 1979) and primate research (see e.g. Haimoff, in press).

Another indication that the suggested mechanism is far from obvious is that psychologists working on conversation have suggested a quite different solution to how turn-taking works. According to this

---

[8] It is also worth pointing out that the motivation for turn-taking is not as obvious as it may seem: as Miller has noted (1963: 418) turn-taking "is not a necessary consequence of any auditory or physiological inability to speak and hear simultaneously; one voice is poor masking for another" (cited in Goodwin, 1977: 5). The possibility of simultaneous translation bears witness to this (see Goldman-Eisler, 1980).

other view, turn-taking is regulated primarily by *signals*, and not by opportunity assignment rules at all (see e.g. Kendon, 1967; Jaffé & Feldstein, 1970; Duncan, 1974; Duncan & Fiske, 1977). On such a view a current speaker will signal w̄hen he intends to hand over the floor, and other participants may bid by recognized signals for rights to speak – a practice similar to the 'over' announcement on a field radio transmitter. One of the most plausible candidates for such signals is **gaze** : it seems roughly true, for example, that a speaker will break mutual gaze while speaking, returning gaze to the addressee upon turn completion (Kendon, 1967; Argyle, 1973: 109, 202; but see contrary findings in Beattie, 1978a; and see Goodwin, 1977, 1981 for a CA approach to gaze). The problem here is that if such signals formed the basis of our turn-taking ability, there would be a clear prediction that in the absence of visual cues there should either be much more gap and overlap or that the absence would require compensation by special audible cues. But work on telephone conversation shows that neither seems to be true – for example, there is actually less gap and shorter overlap on the telephone (see Butterworth, Hine & Brady, 1977; Ervin-Tripp, 1979: 392), and there is no evidence of special prosodic or intonational patterns at turn-boundaries on the telephone (although there is evidence that such cues are utilized both in the absence and presence of visual contact to indicate the boundaries of turn-constructional units – see e.g. Duncan & Fiske, 1977). In any case it is not clear how a signal-based system could provide for the observed properties of turn-taking anyway: for example, a system of intonational cues would not easily accomplish the observable *lapses* in conversation, or correctly predict the principled basis of overlaps where they occur, or account for how particular next speakers are selected (see Goodwin, 1979b, 1981: 23ff). Therefore the signalling view, plausible as it is, viewed as a complete account of turn-taking seems to be wrong: signals indicating the completion of turn-constructional units do indeed occur, but they are not the essential organizational basis for turn-taking in conversation. That organization seems rather to be based on an opportunity assignment of the sort specified by the rules in (10).

Another possible view that also seems to be incorrect is that, while turn-taking is indeed an option-based system, the options are organized not around surface-structural units, as suggested by Sacks,

Schegloff & Jefferson (1978), but rather around functional units – speech acts, moves, or perhaps ideational units (as in Butterworth, 1975). Such a view has an initial plausibility: as a participant one should wait until one sees what interactional contribution the other party is making, and then perform one's own. Again, however, such a view makes the wrong predictions – for example, since greetings, expressions like *How are you?*, etc., are generally precisely predictable, they ought to get regularly overlapped, but this is not the case. Similarly, where a speaker fails to make himself audible or comprehensible to a recipient, requests for **repair** ought to occur immediately after the 'repairable', whereas in fact the initiation of repair generally awaits the next TRP (see Sacks, Schegloff & Jefferson, 1978: 39, and section 6.3.2 below). And in general, given the apparent projectability of other persons' utterances, we should expect the majority of turns to be completed in overlap – and of course such is not the case. So despite its plausibility, this view too seems to be wrong: turn-taking is firmly anchored around the surface-structural definition of turn-units, over which rules of the sort in (10) operate to organize a systematic distribution of turns to participants.

6.2.1.2 Adjacency pairs

We now turn to another local management organization in conversation, namely **adjacency pairs** – the kind of paired utterances of which question–answer, greeting–greeting, offer–acceptance, apology–minimization, etc., are prototypical. We have already noted that these are deeply inter-related with the turn-taking system as techniques for selecting a next speaker (especially where an address term is included or the content of the first utterance of the pair clearly isolates a relevant next speaker). Once again, the existence of such paired utterances is obvious, but a precise specification of the underlying expectations upon which the regularities are based is not so easy. Schegloff & Sacks (1973) offer us a characterization along the following lines:

(18)   *adjacency pairs* are sequences of two utterances that are:
         (i)   adjacent
         (ii) produced by different speakers
         (iii) ordered as a **first part** and a **second part**
         (iv) typed, so that a particular first part requires a particular
               second (or range of second parts) – e.g. offers require

> acceptances or rejections, greetings require greetings, and
> so on

and there is a rule governing the use of adjacency pairs, namely:

(19)   Having produced a first part of some pair, current speaker must
         stop speaking, and next speaker must produce at that point a
         second part to the same pair

Adjacency pairs seem to be a fundamental unit of conversational organization – indeed it has been suggested that they are *the* fundamental unit (see e.g. Goffman, 1976; Coulthard, 1977: 70). Such a view seems to underlie the speech act models of conversation reviewed in section 6.1 above. However there are many other kinds of more complex sequential organizations operating in conversation, as we shall see, nor indeed can the constraints across such pairs be properly modelled by formation rules analogous to syntactic rules. It is therefore important to see that the characterization of adjacency pairs in (18) and (19) is only a first approximation, and is in fact inadequate in a number of important respects.

There are problems with each of the conditions in (18), but we shall focus on (i), adjacency, and (iv), the kinds of expectable second parts. First, strict adjacency is actually too strong a requirement: there frequently occur **insertion sequences** (Schegloff, 1972a) like the following in which one question–answer pair is embedded within another (where Q1 labels the first question, A1 its answer, and so on):

(20)   *Merritt, 1976: 333*
         A: May I have a bottle of Mich?   ((Q1))
         B: Are you twenty one ?   ((Q2))
         A: No   ((A2))
         B: No   ((A1))

or like the following where a notification of temporary interactional exit and its acceptance are embedded within a question–answer pair:[9]

(21)   *144/6*
         B: U:hm (.) what's the price now eh with V.A.T.
            do you know eh   ((Q1))
         A: Er I'll just work that out for you=   ((HOLD))

---

[9] *Hold* and *accept(ance)* are *ad hoc* terms for the parts of the adjacency pair that are used to initiate an interactional interlude or 'time out'. Interaction may then, but need not, be re-initiated by another adjacency pair (*Hello?*; *Hello*).

B: =thanks   ((ACCEPT))
    (10.0)
A: Three pounds nineteen a tube sir   ((A1))

Indeed numerous levels of embedding are not at all infrequent, with
the consequence that, say, a question and its answer may be many
utterances apart; nevertheless the relevance of the answer is merely
held in abeyance while preliminaries are sorted out, and insertion
sequences are thus restricted in content to the sorting out of such
preliminaries. In fact (21) is extracted from the larger sequence of
nested adjacency pairs in (22) (here R labels a request first part, Q
and A question and answer, respectively, and turns are numbered T1,
T2, etc., for reference):

(22)   *144/6*
T1   B: ... I ordered some paint from you uh a couple
                of weeks ago some vermilion
T2   A: Yuh
T3   B: And I wanted to order some more the name's
                Boyd   ((R1))
T4   A: Yes // how many tubes would you like sir   ((Q1))
T5   B: An-
T6   B: U:hm (.) what's the price now eh with V.A.T.
                do you know eh   ((Q2))
T7   A: Er I'll just work that out for you=   ((HOLD))
T8   B: =Thanks   ((ACCEPT))
                (10.0)
T9   A: Three pounds nineteen a tube sir   ((A2))
T10   B: Three nineteen is it =   ((Q3))
T11   A: =Yeah   ((A3))
T12   B: E::h (1.0) yes u:hm ((dental click)) ((in paren-
                thetical tone)) e:h jus-justa think, that's what
                three nineteen
                That's for the large tube isn't it   ((Q4))
T13   A: Well yeah it's the thirty seven c.c.s   ((A4))
T14   B: Er, hh I'll tell you what I'll just eh eh ring you
                back I have to work out how many I'll need.
                Sorry I did- wasn't sure of the price you see   ((ACCOUNT
                                                                FOR
                                                                NO A1))
T15   A: Okay

A number of points may be parenthetically made here. First,
insertion sequences, which are of great interest in their own right, can

effectively structure considerable stretches of conversation. So what is strictly a local system, operating over just two turns – namely adjacency pair organization – can by means of the accumulation of first pair parts project a large sequence of expectable seconds, as in the structure schematized in (23):

(23) $(Q_1(Q_2(Q_3(Q_4-A_4)A_3)A_2)A_1)$

Secondly, we should note that in (22) neither the initial request (R1) nor the first question (Q1) ever receives its second part (an acceptance or rejection, and an answer, respectively). Nevertheless what takes place after these two turns, T3 and T4, takes place under the umbrella of the expectation that the relevant second parts will be forthcoming. Finally in T14 an explanation or **account** is provided for the failure to provide an A1 for Q1, showing that there is an orientation to the expected appropriate second part even though it never occurs.˙ Further, note that the acknowledged failure to produce an A1 is sufficient to explain the absence of any response to R1: failure to resolve an insertion sequence regularly aborts the entire umbrella sequence too.

But the main point is that we need to replace the strict criterion of adjacency with the notion of **conditional relevance**, namely the criterion for adjacency pairs that, given a first part of a pair, a second part is immediately relevant and expectable (Schegloff, 1972a: 363ff). If such a second fails to occur, it is noticeably absent; and if some other first part occurs in its place then that will be heard where possible as some preliminary to the doing of the second part, the relevance of which is not lifted until it is either directly attended to or aborted by the announced failure to provide some preliminary action. What the notion of conditional relevance makes clear is that what binds the parts of adjacency pairs together is not a formation rule of the sort that would specify that a question must receive an answer if it is to count as a well-formed discourse, but the setting up of specific expectations which have to be attended to. Hence the non-occurrences of an R1 and an A1 in (22) do not result in an incoherent discourse because their absences are systematically provided for.

A second kind of problem that arises with the notion of an adjacency pair concerns the range of potential seconds to a first part. Unless for any given first part there is a small or at least delimited set of seconds, the concept will cease, it seems, to describe the tight organization in conversation that is its principal attraction. But in fact there are, for example, a great many responses to questions other than answers which nevertheless count as acceptable seconds (rather than, say, beginnings of insertion sequences prior to answers) – including protestations of ignorance, 're-routes' (like *Better ask John*), refusals to provide an answer, and challenges to the presuppositions or sincerity of the question (and see (8) above). For example, we noted in (22) that in T14, the slot for an answer to Q1, we have not an answer but a promise to provide an answer at a later date, together with an account explaining the deferral. So while responses to, for example, questions may be restricted, they certainly do not constitute a small set, and this does seem to undermine the structural significance of the concept of an adjacency pair.

However the importance of the notion is revived by the concept of **preference organization**. The central insight here is that not all the potential second parts to a first part of an adjacency pair are of equal standing: there is a ranking operating over the alternatives such that there is at least one **preferred** and one **dispreferred** category of response. It must be pointed out immediately that the notion of *preference* here introduced is not a psychological one, in the sense that it does not refer to speakers' or hearers' individual preferences. Rather it is a structural notion that corresponds closely to the linguistic concept of **markedness**. In essence, preferred seconds are **unmarked** – they occur as structurally simpler turns; in contrast dispreferred seconds are **marked** by various kinds of structural complexity. Thus dispreferred seconds are typically delivered: (a) after some significant delay; (b) with some preface marking their dispreferred status, often the particle *well*; (c) with some account of why the preferred second cannot be performed. For the present (but see 6.3) a contrastive pair of examples will suffice to illustrate the notion:

(24)   *Wootton, in press*
         Child: Could you .hh could you put on the light for my
                     .hh room
         Father: Yep

---

[10] In examples from telephone calls, where the roles of caller and receiver may be relevant to the interpretation, caller is labelled C, receiver R.

(25) $176B^{10}$

C: Um I wondered if there's any chance of seeing you tomorrow
   sometime (0.5) morning or before the seminar

→   (1.0)

R: Ah um (.) I doubt it

C: Uhm huh

R: The reason is I'm seeing Elizabeth

In (24) a granting of a request is done without significant delay and with a minimal granting component *Yep*. In contrast in (25), a rejection of a request for an appointment is done after a one second delay, and then, after further delay components (*ah um*, the micro-pause (.)), by a non-minimal turn (compare *I doubt it* with *No*), followed by an account or reason for the difficulty. In fact, rejections of requests are normally done in this marked way. Thus we can say grantings are preferred seconds (or **preferreds** for short) to requests, rejections are dispreferred seconds (or **dispreferreds**). This is a general pattern: in contrast to the simple and immediate nature of preferreds, dispreferreds are delayed and contain additional complex components; and certain kinds of seconds like request rejections, refusals of offers, disagreements after evaluative assessments, etc., are systematically marked as dispreferreds.

Preference organization is described in detail in section 6.3 below, but the relevance here is that by ordering seconds as preferreds and dispreferreds, the organization allows the notion of an adjacency pair to continue to describe a set of strict expectations despite the existence of many alternative seconds to most kinds of first parts.[11]

6.2.1.3   Overall organization

We have now described two kinds of local organization operating in conversation – local in the sense that turn-taking and adjacency pair organization operate in the first instance across just two turns, current and next. But there are quite different orders of organization in conversation: for example, there are certain recurrent kinds of sequence definable only over three or four or more turns, like those treated in following sections that deal with **repair** (6.3) or begin with **pre-sequences** (6.4). Further, there are some that can be called **overall organizations** in that they organize the totality

----

[11] The exceptions here include greetings, where return greetings are more or less the only kind of second.

of the exchanges within some specific kind of conversation, and it is these that we shall illustrate here.

One kind of conversation with a recognizable overall organization that has been much studied is the telephone call. But it is not by virtue of 'being on the telephone' that such conversations have most of the features of overall organization that they display: rather they belong fairly clearly to a class of verbal interchanges that share many features, namely those that are social activities effectively constituted by talk itself, like a chat on a chance meeting in the street, or a talk over the garden fence. These tend to have clear beginnings and carefully organized closings. Thus in telephone calls we can recognize the following typical components of an **opening section**: the telephone rings and, upon picking up the receiver, the person at the receiving end almost invariably speaks first, either with a *station identification* (name of a firm, a telephone number, etc.) or a plain *Hello*, whereupon the caller produces a *Hello*, often with a self-identification. If the call is between two friends or acquaintances we may expect an exchange of *How are you*s. Then at that point we expect some announcement from the caller of the reason for the call, and we thereby find ourselves projected into the substance of the call, and thus (as we shall see) into matters of topical organization.

To say this is to say little more than that telephone conversations have recognizable openings. But there is much elaborate structure here. For a start we may note that such openings are constructed largely from adjacency pairs: thus we typically get paired *Hello*s as an exchange of greetings, we may get self-identifications with paired recognitions, and an exchange of *How are you*s each with their paired responses (see Schegloff, 1972a, 1979a; Sacks, 1975, respectively, for each of these). There is, moreover, a puzzle about why the receiver, the person with the least information about the identity and purposes of the other, almost invariably talks first. The puzzle dissolves when we assimilate the openings of telephone conversations to **summons–answer** sequences. Such sequences in face-to-face interaction run typically in any of the following ways:

(26)   *Terasaki, 1976 : 12,13*
     (a) A: Jim? (b) A: Mo:m (c) A: ((knock knock knock))
         B: Yeah?   B: What?   B: Come in::
(27)   *Atkinson & Drew, 1979 : 46*
     Ch: Mummy

> M: Yes dear
> (2.1)
> Ch: I want a cloth to clean (the) windows

where the first utterance (or action) is a **summons**, the second an **answer** to the summons, the exchange establishing an open channel for talk. Schegloff (1972a) suggests that the ringing of the telephone is the summons component in such an adjacency pair, so that the first turn at talk (the receiver's *Hello*) is actually the second interactional move. This explains a number of features of telephone openings, including the strong compulsion to respond, and the reportable inference which motivates it – namely that (by conditional relevance) no response 'means' that 'no one is at home'. It even explains the mechanical ring–pause–ring, which imitates the recursive repetition of a verbal summons that is not attended to. That repetition is in turn the basis of the rare exceptions to the generalization that the receiver speaks first, for these occur where the receiver upon picking up the telephone after the first (mechanical) summons, fails to respond – we then get a repeated summons (now verbal) from the caller.

A moment's consideration will show too that summons–answer sequences are a little different from other adjacency pairs (like greetings–greetings, offers–acceptances/refusals) in that they are always a prelude to something. Moreover the something in question can be expected to be produced by the summoner as the reason for the summons. So summons–answer sequences are actually elements of (minimally) three-turn sequences, as illustrated below (and in (27) above):

(28)

T1	A: John?	((SUMMONS))
T2	B: Yeah?	((ANSWER))
T3	A: Pass the water wouldja?	((REASON FOR SUMMONS))

The three-part structure is evidenced by the common use of question components in T2 (like *What?*, *What is it?*, *Yeah?*), which, by simultaneously being the second part to the summons and a first part requesting reasons for the summons, provide for a three-turn structure constructed out of two adjacency pairs. One may also note the obligation that the summoner often feels, for example, in calling a store to find if it is open, to produce a T3 (e.g. *Oh I was just calling to see if you were open*) even though the presence of a T2 was sufficient to make the third turn redundant. It is the three-turn structure of such sequences that establishes not only the obligation for the summoner to produce a T3, but an obligation for a recipient who has produced a T2 to attend to a T3. The sequence thereby serves to establish the co-participation necessary to conversation.

One important feature of opening sections in telephone conversations is the immediate relevance, and the potential problems, of *identification* and *recognition* (Schegloff, 1979a). Many telephone conversations have as their first three turns the following, or something closely similar:

(29)   C: ((causes telephone to ring at R's location))
T1   R: Hello
T2   C: Hi
T3   R: Oh hi::

Such openings illustrate a basic finding of CA, namely that a single minimal utterance or turn can be the locus of a number of quite different overlapping constraints – it can thus perform, and can be carefully designed to perform, a number of quite different functions at once. Here for example, T1, despite being the first turn in the conversation, is not (as we have seen) the first move in the interaction: the ring is the summons, and T1 its answer. But T1 is also simultaneously a display for recognitional purposes of recipient's identity (in cases where recognition is relevant, as not always, e.g. in business calls), and it is notable that speakers tend to use a 'signatured' prosody or voice-quality in this turn (Schegloff, 1979a: 67). Despite the apparent greeting token in T1, greeting is not what the turn appears to do, as the discussion of T3 will make clear. T2 on the other hand is indeed a greeting token that does greetings, and greetings being adjacency-paired, T2 gets a return greeting in T3 (this showing that T1 is hardly a greeting after all, greetings being in general not reiterable kinds of things). But that is not all, indeed the least, of what is going on in T2 and T3.[12] T2, by virtue of its minimal greeting form, actually claims recognition of the recipient on the sole basis of the voice-quality sample offered in T1; and moreover T2 claims that the recipient should likewise be able to recognize the caller on the basis of the minimal voice-quality sample it provides. T3 then, in

---

[12] Note that the *Oh* in T3, normally a marker of receipt of new information, only makes sense if more than greetings are going on in T2 and T3 (see Heritage, in press).

performing return greetings, also claims to have recognized the caller. The overlapping organizations here are thus: (a) telephone (and other related) conversations begin with summons–answer pairs; (b) reciprocal greetings are relevant at the very beginning of calls; (c) also at the very beginning of calls, recognition (or identification) is a prime concern. Note that T2 is the slot for recognitions to be begun, recipient clearly not being able to do this in T1 in the absence of any evidence of who the caller might be. And despite the total absence in (29) of any *overt* recognitional devices (e.g. *Hi, Sam*), the expectation, based on overall organization, of the recognitional relevance of T2 is strong enough invariably to impose on *Hi, Hello,* and other minimal greeting components in T2, a claim that recognition of the recipient by the caller has been achieved (see discussion of (45), (46), and (81)–(85) below, and Schegloff, 1979a). We may summarize this as follows:

(30)   C: ((rings))   ((SUMMONS))
T1   R: Hello   ((ANSWER)) + ((DISPLAY   FOR   RECOGNITION))
T2   C: Hi   ((GREETINGS 1ST PART))
                        ((CLAIM THAT C HAS RECOGNIZED R))
                        ((CLAIM THAT R CAN RECOGNIZE C))
T3   R: Oh hi::   ((GREETINGS 2ND PART))
                        ((CLAIM THAT R HAS RECOGNIZED C))

We are introduced here to the richness of the communicational content that is mapped onto minimal utterances by virtue of **sequential location** – here a location whose specificity is due to the structure of opening sections of the overall organization of telephone calls.

The opening section of a telephone call is usually followed in what may be called **first topic slot** by an announcement by the caller of the reason for the call:

(31)   *Schegloff, 1979a: 47*
         R: Hello.
         C: Hello Rob. This is Laurie. How's everything.
         R: ((sniff)) Pretty good. How 'bout you.
→   C: Jus' fine. The reason I called was ta ask ...

The first topic slot immediately after the opening section is a privileged one: it is the only one that is likely to be almost entirely free from topical constraints arising from prior turns. The main body of a call is thus structured by topical constraints: the content of the first slot is likely to be understood as the main reason for the call (whether or not, of course, from the point of view of the caller, it 'really' is),[13] and after that topics should by preference be 'fitted' to prior ones – topics therefore often being withheld until such a 'natural' location for their mention turns up (Schegloff & Sacks, 1973: 300ff). Evidence for this preference for linked transitions from topic to topic can be found in the common experience of having things to say that one never manages to get in, and more demonstrably in the *marked* nature of the other main kind of transition, unlinked topic 'jumps'. Thus, for example, in the arrowed utterance in (32), a topic jump is signalled in a typical way by the features of increased amplitude, raised pitch, markers of self-editing and hesitancy (see Schegloff, 1979b) and a marker of discontinuity, *Hey*.

(32)   *163*
         R: It's o – it's okay we'll pop down tomorrow Gertrude
         C: You sure you don't, it is an awful lot of it, you want to quickly nip down now for it
→   R: Okay I will. Er *HEY* you hmm that is have you been lighting a fire down there?

Sacks remarks (1971, April 5) that the relative frequency of marked topic shifts of this sort is a measure of a 'lousy' conversation. Instead, what seems to be preferred is that, if A has been talking about X, B should find a way to talk about Z (if Z is the subject he wants to introduce) such that X and Z can be found to be 'natural' fellow members of some category Y. However it should not be thought from this that such co-class membership is somehow antecedently given; rather it is something that is actually achieved in conversation.

This last point needs a little elaboration. It has been suggested, very plausibly, that topic can be characterized in terms of **reference**: A and B are talking about the same topic if they are talking about the same things or sets of referents (see Putnam, 1958; but see Keenan

[13] In some cultures there seems to be a preference for displacing the business of a conversation to later on – however, one needs to distinguish here an elaboration of openings to include conventional inquiries about health, family and so on, from a true difference in the use of the first free topic slot.

& Schieffelin, 1976). Alternatively, we can say that A and B are talking about the same topic if they are talking about the same or linked **concepts** (de Beaugrande & Dressler, 1981: 104). However it is easy to show that co-referentiality, or a set of shared concepts, is neither sufficient nor necessary to establish topical coherence. Consider, for example:

(33) *Sacks, 1968, April 17: 16*
A: God any more hair on muh chest an' I'd be a fuzz boy.
B: 'd be a *what*.
C: A // fuzz boy.
A: Fuzz boy.
B: What's that.
A: Fuzz mop.
C: Then you'd have t'start shaving.
(1.0)
→   B: Hey I shaved this morni- I mean last night for you.

Here the last two utterances both mention shaving, and share that concept, and also on the logical analysis of predicates (see Allwood, Andersson & Dahl, 1977: 72ff) would share some of their referents.[14] But, as Sacks (1968, April 17) points out, B's utterance is produced in such a way as to indicate that it is *not* topically tied to what has gone before. Rather the *Hey* marks (as it can be shown to do generally) the introduction of a new topic 'touched off' by the prior utterance, which is just evoked from memory by some chance association to the content of the prior turn.

But if shared reference, or a set of shared concepts, across turns is not sufficient to ensure shared topic, neither is it necessary for two turns to share some referents, or concepts, in order for topic to be

---

[14] It may be objected that the example indicates only that use of the same words, e.g. *shaving*, does not entail identity of reference. However, it is easy to show that identical referents may be picked out by terms either side of a topic break, here marked by *By the way* and increased amplitude following a pause:

Owen 8b
B: Probably *is* because of that I should think, yes, mm
A: Mm
(1.2)
A: ((louder)) By the way, do you want any lettuces

Here of course *I* and *you* both refer to the same entity, namely B, but neither topic is in any ordinary sense 'about B'. So the argument can be generalized: neither identical reference, nor the use of identical terms or concepts (with same or different reference) is sufficient to engender topical continuity.

preserved. For example, C's utterance below is topically tied to prior utterances:

(34)   *Sacks, 1968, April 17*
         A: If yer gonna be a politician, you better learn how to smoke cigars
         B: Yeah that's an idea Rog
         C: I heard a very astounding thing about pipes last night

but *pipes* and *cigars* are distinct concepts, and are terms with no overlapping sets of referents. Of course we can retreat and say: two utterances share the same topic or are at least topically tied only if there is some superordinate set which includes referents or concepts from both utterances (here, say, the set of 'smokables'). But then any two utterances share a topic (or at least are topically tied) because for *any* two sets of referents or concepts one can invent a superordinate set that includes them both – nor is this conversationally absurd (see e.g. (7) above where the shared class was 'apartment rental disqualifiers', hardly some 'natural' class).

The point is simply that topical coherence cannot be thought of as residing in some independently calculable procedure for ascertaining (for example) shared reference across utterances. Rather, topical coherence is something *constructed* across turns by the collaboration of participants. What needs then to be studied is how potential topics are introduced and collaboratively ratified, how they are marked as 'new', 'touched off', 'misplaced' and so on, how they are avoided or competed over and how they are collaboratively closed down.[15]

Now such collaborative procedures for opening, changing and closing down topics are not strictly part of the overall organization of telephone calls: they are local procedures that can operate throughout a call. But they interact in complex ways with matters of overall organization, hence their treatment here. For example, as we noted, later topical constraints give the first topic slot after the opening section a special importance, reinforced by the expectation that, after a summons and its answer, a reason for the summons will be presented. Further, the elaboration of *How are you*s provides a route into topical talk that can displace the reason for the call and its

---

[15] Relatively little work has been done here, but see Sacks, 1967–72 passim and summary in Coulthard, 1977: 78ff; Button & Casey, in press; Jefferson, in press; Owen, 1982.

first topic slot to later in the call, thereby providing a powerful motive for escaping from such elaborations (see Sacks, 1975). And techniques for topic closing are intimately connected to the introduction of the **closing section** shutting down the conversation: the closure of any topic after the privileged first one makes the introduction of the closing section potentially imminent, matters dealt with below. Finally, some kinds of telephone calls have an expectable overall organization that admits just one topic – such **monotopical** calls being typical of routine business calls or service inquiries. Interestingly, such calls are monotopical not in the sense that no more than one topic is ever addressed within them, but in the sense that the caller orients to the expectation of a single topic in the very introduction of further topics. Thus one finds, not only initial announcements in first topic slot that the caller has in fact more than one thing to say, but also careful tracking of the progress through the list of topics:

(35) *Birmingham Discourse Project TD.C1.2 (After initial inquiry)*
B: Yeah er two other things firstly do you know the eventual street number of plot 36
((several turns later))
Erm the other thing is erm ((ahem)) presumably be okay for somebody to have access to it before we move in to put carpets down and that

So matters of overall organization and of topical organization can be closely interlinked.

We come finally to the **closing sections** of the overall organization of telephone calls or similar kinds of conversation. Closings are a delicate matter both technically, in the sense that they must be so placed that no party is forced to exit while still having compelling things to say, and socially in the sense that both over-hasty and over-slow terminations can carry unwelcome inferences about the social relationships between the participants. The devices that organize closings are closely attuned to these problems. We find typically that conversations close in the following sort of manner:

(36) *172B(7)*
R: Why don't we all have lunch
C: Okay so that would be in St Jude's would it?
R: Yes
(0.7)
C: Okay so:::

```
R: One o'clock in the bar
C: Okay
R: Okay?
C: Okay then thanks very much indeed George=
R: =All right
C: //See you there
R:     See you there
C: Okay
R: Okay // bye
R:          Bye
```

The typical features here are the arrangements for a next meeting, a sequence of *Okays* closing down the arrangements (or other topic), a *Thank you* produced by the caller, and a further sequence of *Okays* just prior to a final exchange of *Good-byes*. One very general schema for closing sections, of which (36) is merely one instantiation, might be represented thus:

(37)   (a) a closing down of some topic, typically a **closing implicative** topic; where closing implicative topics include the making of arrangements, the first topic in monotopical calls, the giving of regards to the other's family members, etc.

(b) one or more pairs of **passing turns** with **pre-closing items**, like *Okay*, *All right*, *So* : :, etc.

(c) if appropriate, a **typing** of the call as e.g. a favour requested and done (hence *Thank you*), or as a checking up on recipient's state of health (*Well I just wanted to know how you were*), etc., followed by a further exchange of pre-closing items

(d) a final exchange of terminal elements: *Bye, Righteo, Cheers*, etc.

The crucial elements here (after (a) has been achieved) are (b) and (d). Essentially what the two components jointly achieve is a co-ordinated exit from the conversation: they do this by providing, in the form of the topic-less passing turns in (b), a mutual agreement to talk no more, this being a prelude to the exchange of the terminal adjacency pair in (d) that closes down the conversation. The mutual agreement is secured by one party producing a topic-less passing turn, indicating that he has no more to say, whereupon the other party – if he too has no more to say – may produce another such turn. The technical and social problems that closings raise are thus initially dealt with by providing that the closing section as a whole is placed in a location that is interactively achieved: a pre-closing offer to close is issued in the form of *Okay*, *Right*, etc., and only if taken up do closings proceed. Further motivation for this pattern in closing sections will be provided below (but see Schegloff & Sacks, 1973).

A final point about closing sections that is of interest here is that components of the sort in (37)(c) indicate that the placement and content of closing sections is attuned to other aspects of overall organization. Thus, for example, the *Thanks* in (36) is oriented to the specific content of the first topic slot of that call, namely a request for a favour. Similarly one finds in closings reference to aspects of opening sections, as in *Sorry to have woken you up* referring back to *I hope I'm not calling too early*, or *Well I hope you feel better soon* referring back to responses to *How are you*s, and so on. Each aspect of overall organization, then, can be oriented to other aspects, as is exemplified in the attention paid in the opening sections of expectably monotopical calls to the imminence of closing immediately after the first topic is closed down (the attention revealed in the *Just two things* kind of bid for more than one topic).

We are now in a position to give a more technical characterization of what a conversation is. We must first distinguish the unit **a conversation** from **conversational activity**. The latter is something characterizable in terms of local organizations, and especially the operation of the turn-taking system in (10); there are many kinds of talk – e.g. sermons, lectures, etc. – that do not have these properties and which we would not want to consider conversational. Yet there are also many kinds of talk – e.g. courtroom or classroom interrogation – which exhibit features of conversational activity like turn-taking, but which are clearly not conversations. Conversation as a unit, on the other hand, is characterizable in terms of overall organizations of the sort sketched here in addition to the use of conversational activities like turn-taking (Schegloff & Sacks, 1973: 325; Sacks, Schegloff & Jefferson, 1974: 730–7).

6.2.2   *Some remarks on methodology*

The basic findings in the prior section have been presented (for the sake of brevity) in a way that CA workers would in fact be careful to avoid. The reason is that, for each substantial claim, the methodology employed in CA requires evidence not only that some aspect of conversation *can* be viewed in the way suggested, but that it actually is so conceived by the participants producing it. That is, what conversation analysts are trying to model are the procedures and expectations actually employed by participants in producing and understanding conversation. In addition, for each conversational device we should like, by way of explanation, to elucidate the interactional problems that it is specifically designed to resolve – that is, to provide *functional* explanations, or expositions of rational design, for the existence of the device in question. There are, then, two basic methods to be employed in CA-style investigation:

(a) We should attempt to locate some particular conversational organization, and isolate its systematic features, by demonstrating participants' orientation to it

(b) We should ask, (i) what problems does this organization solve, and (ii) what problems does this organization raise – and therefore what implications does it have for the existence of further solutions to further problems?

These methods are important because they offer us a way of avoiding the indefinitely extendable and unverifiable categorization and speculation about actors' intents so typical of DA-style analysis. Let us therefore look at some illustrations of how the methods may be applied to yield and then confirm results of the kind we have reviewed.

We may start with the problem of demonstrating that some conversational organization is actually oriented to (i.e. implicitly recognized) by participants, rather than being an artefact of analysis. One key source of verification here is what happens when some 'hitch' occurs – i.e. when the hypothesized organization does not operate in the predicted way – since then participants (like the analyst) should address themselves to the problem thus produced. Specifically, we may expect them either to try to repair the hitch, or alternatively, to draw strong inferences of a quite specific kind from the absence of the expected behaviour, and to act accordingly.

Where hitches of these sorts are a recurrent possibility, there is likely to be a regularized repair procedure. Such occurs, we noted, in association with the turn-taking system, where a special set of procedures operates to reduce and resolve overlap, should this arise despite the rules assigning turns. But there are overlaps allowed (and thus their location and nature predicted) by the rules, and overlaps that contravene the rules (*interruptions*). When the latter occur, they are subject not only to the standard resolution procedures, but also to overt reprimands and sanctions – and such overt attention to interruptions again indicates participants' orientation to the basic expectations provided by the rules:

(38)   *DCD : 28*
        Collins: Now // the be:lt is meh*
        Fagan: is the sa:me mater*ial as // thi:s
→   Smythe: Wait a moment
           Miss Fagan

Similarly, the conditional relevance of a second part of an adjacency pair given a first part is easily shown to be more than just an analyst's fancy. Consider for example what happens when, employing Rule 1(a) of the turn-taking system, a speaker addresses a recipient with the first part of a pair and receives no immediate response. Strong inferences are immediately drawn, either of the sort 'no response means no channel contact', or, if that is clearly not the case, then 'no response means there's a problem'. So, in the case of a failure to respond to a summons, the absence of a second part can, in the case of the telephone, be understood as 'recipient is not at home', or in face-to-face interaction as 'recipient is sulking or giving the cold shoulder' (Schegloff, 1972a: 368ff). Or, consider:

(39)   *172B(7)*
T1   C: So I was wondering would you be in your office on Monday
           (.) by any chance?
T2   (2.0)
T3   C: Probably not
T4   R: Hmm yes =
T5   C: = You would?
T6   R: Ya
T7   C: So if we came by could you give us ten minutes of your time?

Here a two-second pause after the question in T1 is actually taken by C to indicate a (negative) answer to the question. How can this come about? Note first that (by Rule 1(a) of the turn-taking system) C has selected R to speak (a feature of address not being necessary as there are only two participants here). Therefore the two-second pause is not just anyone's pause or nobody's pause (i.e. a lapse): rather it is assigned by the system to R as R's silence. Then recollect that adjacency pairs can have dispreferred seconds, these in general being marked by delay (amongst other features). Therefore the pause can be heard as a preface to a dispreferred response. Now in full sequential context it is clear that C's question is a prelude to a request for an appointment, and for such questions it turns out that negative answers (answers that block the request) are dispreferred (see 6.3 and 6.4 below). Hence C draws the inference from R's silence that he makes explicit in T3. (That he got it wrong, as indicated by R in T4, does not affect the point – such inferences are made, often correctly, though sometimes not.) Note here the remarkable power of the turn-taking system to assign the absence of any verbal activity to some particular participant as his turn: such a mechanism can then quite literally make something out of nothing, assigning to a silence or pause, itself devoid of interesting properties, the property of being A's, or B's, or neither A's nor B's, and further, through additional mechanisms, the kind of specific significance illustrated in (39) (a point taken up below).[16]

A fundamental methodological point can be made with respect to (39), and indeed most examples of conversation. Conversation, as opposed to monologue, offers the analyst an invaluable analytical resource: as each turn is responded to by a second, we find displayed in that second an *analysis* of the first by its recipient. Such an analysis is thus provided by participants not only for each other but for analysts too. Thus in (39) the turn in T3 displays how the pause in T2 was interpreted. Hence "the turn-taking system has, as a by-product of its design, a proof procedure for the analysis of turns" (Sacks, Schegloff & Jefferson, 1978: 44). A good case can therefore be made for the methodological priority of the study of conversation over the study of other kinds of talk or other kinds of text.

Having shown that participants themselves orient to the conditional relevance of, for example, an answer after a question, let us now briefly consider the kind of evidence that could be used to show that

[16] Examples of this sort provide a clue to the nature of conversational constraints. Participants are constrained to utilize the expected procedures not (or not only) because failure to do so would yield 'incoherent discourses', but because if they don't, they find themselves accountable for specific inferences that their behaviour will have generated. Thus defendants in political trials may hope that silence will count as rejection of the proceedings, only to find it read as admission of guilt. Or, in (39), R's disregard of the expectation that preferred responses will be immediate not only produces an unintended inference that has to be corrected, but, if sustained, may produce an inference of general reluctance to co-operate. Conversationalists are thus not so much constrained by rules or sanctions, as caught in a web of inferences.

the overall organizations we have claimed to be operative in conversation are actually oriented to by participants. As already noted, closing sections may refer back to opening sections and vice versa, indicating that "the unit 'a single conversation' is one to which participants orient throughout its course" (Schegloff & Sacks, 1973: 310). Further, if closing sections have the character suggested above, then a co-ordinated determination to close is mutually accepted by an exchange of pre-closings like *Okay*, and we expect thereupon the immediate exchange of terminal elements like *Bye*. But every now and then closings are in fact re-opened, and if these re-openings occur after the exchange of pre-closings, then they are typically *marked* as grossly misplaced, as in the extract below:

(40)   *Schegloff & Sacks, 1973: 320*
          C: Okay, thank you.
          R: Okay dear.
→   C: OH BY THE WAY. I'd just like to say ...

Such misplacement markers demonstrate an orientation to the closing section as a unit not properly taking such interpolations, and thus once embarked on, properly final.

Let now consider the other basic methodological procedure, namely the search for the *raison d'être* of particular conversational organizations, and then the implications that the existence of one device has for the necessity for others. We may show in this way how all the structural facts we have reviewed (and indeed others too) are in fact closely integrated; and in doing so we may illustrate how in discovering one such organization the analyst is provided with a lever for prying up further levels of organization. So the assumption of functional inter-connection actually yields a powerful discovery technique.

Suppose we take the turn-taking system as the fundamental device, our initial discovery. What we then have is a system primarily designed to (a) organize the change of speakers and (b) keep only one speaker speaking at a time. But then we may ask: how is such a device 'cranked up', how is the machinery to be got rolling? Clearly we need some device that will establish (for the case of two parties) the A–B–A–B pattern of turns, while launching us into the business of the interaction. An adjacency pair, it would seem, would nicely do the job, setting up an initial A–B sequence. However, as the turn-taking rules permit a conversation to lapse, that is all such a pair might achieve: A–B, finish. So we need an opening section that has at least a three-turn structure, wherein the first requests attendance from the other party, the second provides a slot for that other party to commit himself to an initiation of interaction, and the third turn is the slot for the initiating party to provide some initial business for the interaction. We then have the familiar structure, summons–answer–first topic, which establishes a co-ordinated co-participation, assigns speaking and receiving roles to the two parties for the first three turns, and thus cranks up the turn-taking machinery as minimally required. Small details of the design of such sequences reflect their adaptation to this task – e.g. the tendency (in face-to-face interaction) for the second turn to be an open question requiring by adjacency pair format the third turn necessary for the proper initiation of talk (as already noted). There is thus nothing *ad hoc* or arbitrary about the design of conversational sequences like summons sequences: they are rational solutions to particular organizational problems.

We now have the turn-taking machinery started up. But then the question arises: how do we suspend it? Consider: A and B are talking and A now wants, in response to B's remark, to tell an apposite story. But how is A to get such a substantial section of talk, when by the rules of the turn-taking system B is allowed at the very first TRP to compete by first start for the floor? Clearly obtaining such an extended turn at talk (by other than sheer listener apathy) requires special techniques. One such special device is a story announcement sequence of the stereotypical sort illustrated below:

(41)   A: Have you heard the one about the pink Martian?
        B: No
        A: ((Story))

where a bid is specifically made for an extended space for the telling of a story, the telling being conditional on the acceptance of the bid. Or, from a recording:

(42)   *Sacks, 1974: 338*

T1   K: You wanna hear muh- eh my sister told me a story last night.
T2   R: I don't wanna hear it. But if you must,
           (1.0)
T3   A: What's purple an' an island. Grape-Britain. That's what
           iz sis//ter -
T4   K: No. To stun me she says uh there was these three
           girls ...((Story follows))

Here, in T2, R gives a reluctant go-ahead, while in T3 the other intended recipient produces a 'guess' at what kind of a story it is as a potential dismissal (T3), itself dismissed by the story teller in T4. Such sequences contain (minimally) in T1 an offer to tell, in T2 a 'go-ahead' or rejection, and then contingent on the 'go-ahead' the telling of the story in T3 (see 6.4 below). What such a structure achieves is the collaborative suspension of the turn-taking machinery, by joint agreement, for the duration of the story (there are of course other techniques for doing this – see Terasaki, 1976; Jefferson, 1978; Ryave, 1978).

But if we have achieved a suspension of speaker transition relevance over an extended period of talk, we now have yet another problem, namely how to start up the turn-taking machinery once again (or more strictly, since co-participation is still assured, re-invoke the relevance of TRPs). A solution here had better provide for the recognizability of *story endings* – for if they are recognizable then on such a completion the normal turn-taking machinery can once again automatically resume. So stories must be recognizable units if turn-taking is to be adjusted around them; and of course they are: stories, if of the 'funny' variety, typically have punchlines, whereupon laughter by listeners is immediately relevant (Sacks, 1974: 347ff); or if they are topically tied to the sequential locus in which they occur then endings are recognizable in part because they return participants to that particular topic (Jefferson, 1978); or other recognizable ending formats are used (Labov & Waletsky, 1966; Sacks, 1972).

Once again, then, we have the turn-taking machinery operating normally. But now let us suppose we want not merely to suspend it, but to close it down, i.e. to finish the conversation. Again some special device is needed which will provide a solution to the following problem: "how to organize the simultaneous arrival of co-conversationalists at a point where one speaker's completion will not occasion another speaker's talk and that will not be heard as some speaker's silence" (Schegloff & Sacks, 1973: 294–5). Again one basic ingredient suggests itself: an adjacency pair such that the first part announces imminent closure and the second part secures it. And we do indeed have the terminal exchange generally realized as A: *Bye*; B: *Bye*.

However there would be substantial problems for the use of the terminal exchange alone as a solution to the closing problem. For A might have said all he wants to say, and therefore have issued a *Bye*, whereupon B, despite perhaps having important things to say (things perhaps that *must* be said in this conversation – see Sacks, 1975), would be constrained by the adjacency pair format to produce a second *Bye* that terminated the interaction. Therefore there needs to be some pre-terminal section where undelivered news and the like can be fitted in. This need is strongly reinforced by the topical organization we reviewed, since (a) one is constrained not to mention in first topic slot anything that one doesn't want to be taken as the main reason for engaging in interaction, and is therefore forced to hang on to these other 'mentionables', and (b) after first topic slot, mentionables should by preference be fitted to prior topics, requiring that one waits for a suitable slot for such deferred mentionables. However, such a slot may never come up, and there is therefore a need for some slot towards the end of a conversation specifically set aside as the place where such deferred mentionables can be unburdened.

What is needed for effective closings is therefore a device which (a) offers each party a turn for such deferred mentionables, (b) if such a turn is taken up, recycles the opportunity in (a), and (c), consequent upon no party taking up the opportunity in (a), makes the terminal exchange immediately relevant. And it is this that motivates the familiar four-turn closing section:

(43)   A: Okay
         B: Okay
         A: Bye
         B: Bye

where the first *Okay* yields the floor to the other party for any deferred mentionables that he may have, the second indicates that no such items have been withheld, and thus the exchange of topic-less passing turns may be taken as a mutual agreement that termination should now commence. The exchange of *Okay*s can thus be called *pre-closings* – producing the forewarning and collaborative co-ordination of closure, which the turn-taking system and topical organization independently but jointly require.

So in the way thus informally sketched, from one kind of conversational organization one can foresee the need for other kinds of organizations with specific properties, providing simultaneously both a search procedure for conversational organizations and explanations for their existence and design.

One further methodological preference is a growing tendency in CA to work with increasing numbers of instances of some phenomenon. Until one knows how, for example, certain kinds of sequence normally unfold, the analysis of individual complex cases will not yield up the rich texture they almost invariably conceal (see e.g. the analysis of (49) and (104) below).

In summary, then, CA methodology is based on three basic procedures: (a) collecting recurrent patterns in the data, and hypothesizing sequential expectations based on these; (b) showing that such sequential expectations actually are oriented to by participants; and (c) showing that, as a consequence of such expectations, while some organizational problems are resolved, others are actually created, for which further organizations will be required.

6.2.3   *Some applications*
          In this section we illustrate how the observations above may be applied to yield insight into particular instances of talk. We will start by considering what is apparently just one phenomenon – silence, or a period of non-speech – and show how such pauses can be discriminated into many different kinds with quite different significances on the basis of their structural locations. Then we will summarize an analysis by Schegloff of an opaque little sequence rich in structural detail, showing that detailed analysis of individual segments of talk is made possible by the use of the general findings and techniques already reviewed. These examples should suffice to indicate how much organization there is to be discovered in the smallest extract of talk, and how powerful *sequential location* can be in the assignment of multiple functions to individual utterances.

There have been many theories about the significance of pauses and hesitations in conversation: some analysts, for example, have seen pauses as evidence of verbal planning, i.e. 'time out' for psychological processing either in the routine preparation of the fluent phases that often follow (Butterworth, 1975) or in the production of complex syntax (Goldman-Eisler, 1968; Bernstein, 1973). But the following observations show that any unitary account of pauses, and any account that does not take into consideration their role as potentially symbolic devices, will be fundamentally misguided.

The turn-taking system itself assigns different values to pauses within conversation. We have already described how the rules in (10) discriminate between *gaps* (delays in the application of Rules 1(b) or 1(c)), *lapses* (non-application of the rules) and next speaker *silence* (after application of Rule 1(a)), as illustrated in (14) and (15) above. Where these rules assign a pause to some speaker as a silence, additional factors systematically play a role in its interpretation. For example, we have seen in (39) how a silence after a question of a special sort (a prelude to a request – a **pre-request** – see section 6.4 below) can be read, by virtue of preference organization, as indicating a negative answer. Or, consider the three-second silence in (44):

(44)   *Drew, 1981 : 249*
          M: What's the time- by the clock?
          R: Uh
          M: What's the time?
→   (3.0)
          M: (Now) what number's that?
          R: Number two
          M: No it's not
             What is it?
          R: It's a one and a nought

Here, in the turn prior to the pause, a mother asks her child to try and tell the time. So, by Rule 1(a) in (10), the pause is a silence, attributable to the child R. But just because the question is an 'exam question' (and not, say, a pre-request), the silence here can be understood as 'answer unknown'. Such an analysis is made clear by the mother's next turn, where an easier question is asked that, if answered, might provide a partial solution to the first question.

Now in (45) we have a small pause after the second turn in the opening of a telephone call:

(45)   *Schegloff, 1979a : 37*
          C: ((rings))
T1   R: Hello?
T2   C: Hello Charles.
    →   (0.2)
T3   C: This is Yolk.

As noted earlier, for a caller to provide a greeting in T2 (his first verbal turn) is to claim that the recipient should be able to recognize the caller on the basis of this sample of voice-quality alone. The second turn, we noted, is in fact the first part of an adjacency greeting pair; a second is therefore due. Once again, then, the delay (short though it is) is R's delay and can be taken by C to indicate a problem for R. That the problem is here a problem in identification is shown by the repair C offers, after a significant pause has developed, namely an overt self-identification (*This is Yolk*). That the problem indicated to C by this small delay is not imaginary is shown by examples like the following, where in T3 R has to invite C to repair what C had taken to be an adequate self-identification (the *Hello* in T2):

(46)	*Schegloff, 1979a: 39*
	C: ((rings))
T1	R: Hello?
T2	C: Hello.
→	(1.5)
T3	R: Who's this.

Here a momentary pause is heard immediately as a problem with what is always underway in the first few turns of telephone conversations, namely the business of mutual identification. Therefore the significance of a pause here is determined by that set of overlapping organizations that converge on the first few turns of telephone calls, as indicated in (30) above; that set determines, via adjacency pair organization and the structure of opening sections, just how a pause in this location will be interpreted.

In (47) a pause, which can be analysed as somewhat similar to that in (45), occurs after an invitation. Once again, an invitation is a first part of an adjacency pair, and this assigns next turn to the other party:

(47)	*Davidson, in press*
	A: C'mon down *he*:re, =it's oka:y,
→	(0.2)
	A: I got lotta stuff, =I got *be*:er en stuff

And, as in (45), a short pause occurs, hearable as the other party's silence, and clearly analysed in this (and many related examples) as some problem with A's invitation, which A consequently upgrades – i.e. an attempt is made to make the invitation more attractive (see Davidson, in press on the systematicity of this pattern).

Finally, the following example features the punchline of a dirty joke and the ensuing laughter. As we pointed out, after a story an appreciation is immediately relevant, and the temporary suspension of the turn-transition relevance is lifted. But here we have a two-second delay, and then instead of recipient laughter we have teller's laughter (with a further four-second delay interspersed). Only then does one of the recipients (A) laugh, and then it has the careful syllabicity of mock laughter. The pauses here are assignable to story recipients as *their* silences, and the withholding of appreciation signals 'failed joke' (see Sacks, 1974).

(48)   *Sacks, 1974: 339*
        K: ((tells dirty joke, ending thus:)) Third girl, walks up
        t'her – Why didn' ya *say* anything last night; W' *you* told
        me it was always impolite t'talk with my mouth full,
→   (2.0)
        K: hh hyok hyok,
→   (1.0)
        K: hyok,
→   (3.0)
        A: HA-HA-HA-HA

Many further kinds of significant absences of speech can be found – see e.g. (66), (67), (76) and (77) below – and each kind draws the analyst's attention to the strong kinds of expectations that different conversational organizations, whether local, overall or intermediate in scope, impose on particular sequential slots. The demonstration is the more remarkable in that silence has no features of its own: all the different significances attributed to it must have their sources in the structural expectations engendered by the surrounding talk. So sequential expectations are not only capable of making something out of nothing, but also of constructing many different kinds of significance out of the sheer absence of talk. If conversational organization can map 'meaning' onto silence, it can also map situated significance onto utterances – and in fact can be shown to regularly do so.

Let us now turn to one short extract of conversation and show how the various findings and techniques we have reviewed can be applied to good effect. The argument is a brief résumé of Schegloff, 1976. The extract comes from a radio call-in programme broadcast in the United States, and in it B, who is a High School pupil, is reporting to the compère of the show, A, an argument that he has been having with his history teacher about American foreign policy. The teacher (T) holds that foreign policy should be based on morality, but B thinks it should be based on expediency – 'what is good for America'. It runs as follows:

(49)   *Schegloff, 1976: D9*
T1   B: An' s- an' ( ) we were discussing, it tur- , it comes down,
        he ((T)) s- he says, I-I-you've talked with thi- si- i- about

this many times. *I* ((B)) said, it came down t' this: =
= our main difference: *I* feel that a government, i- the main
thing, is- th-the purpose of the goverment is, what is best
for the country.

T2   A: *Mm*hmm

T3   B: *He* ((T)) says, governments, an' you know he keeps- he
talks about governments, they sh- the thing that they sh'd
do is what's right or wrong.

T4 → A: For *whom.*

T5   B: Well he says-//he-

T6   A: By what *stan*dard.

T7   B: That's what- that's exactly what I mean. He s- but he says
...

The particular interest of this extract is a crucial ambiguity associated
with the utterance *For whom.* It is not, however, an ambiguity that
lies in the linguistic structure of the utterance, nor has it to do with
any lexical ambiguities of the words *for* and *whom*; and unlike
linguistic ambiguities, which scarcely ever cause difficulties in context,
this one demonstrably is (or becomes) ambiguous for the participants.
The ambiguity is this: on one reading (R1) A, in uttering *For whom,*
asks a question that we might paraphrase as 'What exactly did your
teacher say – governments should do what's right *for whom*? Whom
did he have in mind?' On the other reading (R2), A, in asking *For
whom,* is actually trying to show that he agrees with B against B's
teacher (T), and he is trying to show this by offering a potential piece
of B's argument against T. To see this consider that B is reporting
T as saying that foreign policy should be based on what is morally
right – to which B might have retorted by saying *Yes, but right for
whom?*, pointing out that ethical judgements of good or bad depend
upon different parties' points of view. So on this reading, or
interpretation, A in saying *For whom* is providing an utterance that
B might have used against his teacher, thus showing agreement with
B.

That both readings of the utterance become available to B is clear.
First, in T5, he starts off responding to R1, the straightforward
question interpretation, by beginning on a further specification of
what the teacher says. But then A interrupts with a correction; we
know this in part because only corrections of such sorts are priority
items licensing violations of the turn-taking rules. But we also know
that T6 is a correction because it utilizes a standard device for

correcting misunderstandings, namely **reformulation** that makes the same point in different words. In the following turn, B then displays understanding of the alternative reading, by acknowledging A's agreement with him, *that's exactly what I mean*. We can thus show that the ambiguity is a participant's (and not merely an analyst's) ambiguity: each party deals with each reading once – A by correcting B's interpretation, and then reformulating his own intended reading, and B by first beginning to respond to the non-intended reading, and then showing understanding of the second reading as an agreement with him against his teacher, by acknowledging A's agreement.

But how does the ambiguity arise? Since it is clearly not a matter of the grammatical or lexical ambiguity of *For whom*, the source of the ambiguity must lie outside the utterance itself in its sequential location in the conversation. We need now to show that the structural location itself predisposes us to both of the relevant interpretations.

Stories, we noted, require the suspension of the normal turn-taking system, which then requires resumption. This could be provided for, it was argued, if story endings are easily recognizable. One recognizable and recurrent story ending format is a summing up of the story, and that is what we find occurring in our extract – B says *It came down to this: our main difference is* ... and the summary follows. So the slot in which A says *For whom* is the first slot after a story ending. Such a slot is one where story recipients can be expected to do one of two things: they may ask for further details or clarifications of the story – and this is the sequential basis for the simple question interpretation, R1; or they may show understanding and appreciation of the story (as e.g. in the expectable laughter after a joke: see discussion of (48) above), and it is this possibility that forms the basis of the second, more complex, interpretation, R2. For one way of showing understanding is to express agreement in such a way that prior understanding must have taken place, and *For whom* does just this, by showing agreement through displaying understanding of the argument that B was having with his teacher.

But there's another element here: this agreement reading is reinforced by consideration of the kind of story that B's story is, namely an 'opposition story' or a reported argument. Such stories have as features not only an alternation of reported speakers, or an A–B–A–B structure of reported turns, but also, mapped onto the alternation of turns, the alternation of positions, or sides in the argument. So when reported speakers change, the positions being argued for change. Such structural expectations lie behind our ability to understand some minimal story like *Pay the rent. I can't pay the rent* as being a reported argument where one party said *Pay the rent* and the other *I can't pay the rent*. Now it is just because B's story here is an opposition story that we can hear A's *For whom* as taking up B's position against the teacher. For B is reporting an argument in which the teacher (T) and he alternated in turns and positions in a T–B–T–B ... sequence. Further, we can see that it is just because in addition to being an opposition story, it is one which ends with a turn by T, that A can jump in and show story understanding by taking B's turn after T's. And for A to do this is an optimal way of displaying understanding, one of the expectable things to be going on in the first slot after a story.

Analyses of this sort, which show how surrounding conversational structure can impose rich interpretations on utterances, provide important lessons for linguistic and psychological theories of language understanding. First, they indicate that semantic interpretation is only a small and not perhaps the most complex aspect of the communicational significance of an utterance. Secondly, they show that speech act theory and allied theories of utterance function can only be considered crude and (at best) partial accounts of such situated significance (consider, for example, what little of interest speech act theory could say about *For whom*). Thirdly, such analyses suggest that while it is correct to look for the sources of such significance outside the utterance itself, it may be a mistake to look too far afield, and specifically that it can be premature to invoke the application of large quantities of background knowledge, as in the **frames** approach now popular in cognitive psychology and artificial intelligence approaches to language understanding (see e.g. Charniak, 1972).

6.3 Preference organization

6.3.1 *Preferred second turns*

As we have seen (6.2.1.2), alternative second parts to first parts of adjacency pairs are not generally of equal status; rather some second turns are **preferred** and others **dispreferred**. The notion of **preference**, it was noted, is not intended as a psychological claim about speaker's or hearer's desires, but as a label for a structural phenomenon very close to the linguistic concept of **markedness**, especially as used in morphology:[17]

> The intuition behind the notion of markedness in linguistics is that, where we have an opposition between two or more members ..., it is often the case that one member is felt to be more usual, more normal, less specific than the other (in markedness terminology it is unmarked, the others marked). (Comrie, 1976a: 111)

Further, in morphology, "unmarked categories tend to have less morphological material than marked categories" and there is a "greater likelihood of morphological irregularity in unmarked forms" (Comrie, 1976a: 114). The parallel is therefore quite apt, because in a similar way **preferred** (and thus **unmarked**) seconds to different and unrelated adjacency pair first parts have less material than **dispreferreds** (**marked** seconds), but beyond that have little in common (cf. "irregular"). In contrast, dispreferred seconds of quite different and unrelated first parts (e.g. questions, offers, requests, summonses, etc.) have much in common, notably components of delay and parallel kinds of complexity. Some further examples will make this clear, but before proceeding we should point out that, in addition to the structural aspect of preference organization, we will need a rule for speech production, which can be stated roughly as follows: 'try to avoid the dispreferred action – the action that generally occurs in dispreferred or marked format'. (The two essential features of dispreferred actions are thus (a) they tend to occur in a marked format, and (b) they tend to be avoided.) Such a rule is non-circular if we already have an independent characterization of preferred or dispreferred alternatives on structural grounds.

So let us return to a characterization of dispreferred seconds – consider the following pair of invitations and their responses:

(50)   *Atkinson & Drew, 1979: 58*
         A: Why don't you come up and *see* me some//times
         B: I would like to

(51)   *Atkinson & Drew, 1979: 58*
         A: Uh if you'd care to come and visit a little while this morning
            I'll give you a cup of *co*ffee

---

[17] The concept of *markedness* was originally developed by linguists of the Prague School; the classic references are Jakobson, 1932; Trubetzkoy, 1939: Chapter 3; see also Lyons, 1968: 79ff.

$\rightarrow$ B: hehh Well that's awfully sweet of you,
         ((DELAY))((MARKER))((APPRECIATION))
         I don't think I can make it this morning.
         ((REFUSAL or DECLINATION))
         .hh uhm I'm running an ad in the paper and-and uh I have
         to stay near the phone.
         ((ACCOUNT))

Here (as Atkinson & Drew (1979: 58ff) point out) the invitation in the first example has an acceptance as a second part: the acceptance is of simple design and is delivered not only without delay but actually in partial overlap. In contrast, the invitation in the second example receives a refusal or declination as a second, and here we have all the typical features of dispreferreds, namely (as indicated by the glosses in capitals) delay, the particle *Well* which standardly prefaces and marks dispreferreds (and here we have a rival analysis to that offered in Chapter 3 in terms of implicature – see Owen, 1980: 68ff, 1981), an appreciation (notably absent from the acceptance in the prior example),[18] a qualified or mitigated refusal (*I don't think I can*), and an account or explanation for the dispreferred second. (Compare also the request examples in (24) and (25) above.)

The characteristics of dispreferred seconds can be further generalized (see Pomerantz, 1975: 42ff, 1978, in press; Atkinson & Drew, 1979: Chapter 2; Wootton, in press) – such turns typically exhibit at least a substantial number of the following features:

(a) *delays*: (i) by pause before delivery, (ii) by the use of a preface (see (b)), (iii) by displacement over a number of turns via use of *repair initiators*[19] or insertion sequences

(b) *prefaces*: (i) the use of markers or announcers of dispreferreds like *Uh* and *Well*, (ii) the production of token agreements before disagreements, (iii) the use of appreciations if relevant (for offers, invitations, suggestions, advice), (iv) the use of apologies if relevant (for requests, invitations, etc), (v) the use of qualifiers (e.g. *I don't know for sure, but ...*), (vi) hesitation in various forms, including self-editing

(c) *accounts*: carefully formulated explanations for why the (dispreferred) act is being done

(d) *declination component*: of a form suited to the nature of the

---

[18] Of course, appreciations can occur with invitation acceptances, but they typically occur *after* acceptances while they occur *before* rejections.

[19] This term is explained below.

first part of the pair, but characteristically indirect or
mitigated

There follow some examples of each of these (the headings indicate
which features are especially notable in each extract):

(52)   *Wootton, in press (Illustrating (a)(i))*
         Ch: Can I go down an see 'im
             (2.0)
             ( )
             (1.8)
             C'mo::n
             (1.5)
             Come'n te see 'im
             (1.6)
             C'mo::n
         M: No:::

(53)   *33A (Illustrating (a)(ii), (b)(iii), (c), (d))*
         B: She says you might want that dress I bought, I don't know
            whether you do
→   A: Oh thanks (well), let me see I really have lots of dresses

(54)   *Wootton, in press (Illustrating (a)(iii))*
         Ch: I wan my ow:n tea .hh my*self*
→   M: (You) want what?=
         Ch: =My tea my*se :lf*
         M: No:w? We are all having tea together

(55)   *176B (Illustrating (b)(i), (c))*
         R: What about coming here on the way (.) or doesn't that give
            you enough time?
→   C: Well no I'm supervising here

(56)   *176B (Illustrating (b)(v), (d))*
         C: Um I wondered if there's any chance of seeing you
            tomorrow sometime (0.5) morning or before the seminar
            (1.0)
→   R: Ahum (.) I doubt it

(57)   *163 (Illustrating (b)(vi)) (R has been complaining that C's fire in*
      the apartment below has filled R's apartment with smoke)
         C: ...is it-it's all right now- you don't want me to put it out?
→   R: E::r (1.5) well on the whole I wouldn't bother because er
            huhuh (2.0) well I mean what- what (0.5) would it involve
            putting it out
            (0.5)
         C: Hahaha ( ) hahah

(58)   *163 (Illustrating (b)(iv))*
         A: ((to operator)) Could I have Andrew Roper's extension
            please?
             (9.0)

B: Robin Hardwick's telephone (1.0) hello
A: Andrew?
→ B: No I'm awfully sorry Andrew's away all week

Given a structural characterization of preferred and dispreferred turns we can then correlate the content and the sequential position of such turns with the tendency to produce them in a preferred or dispreferred format. And here we find recurrent and reliable patterns, e.g. refusals of requests or invitations are nearly always in dispreferred format, acceptances in preferred format. Table 6.1 indicates the sort of consistent match between format and content found across a number of adjacency pair seconds.

Table 6.1 *Correlations of content and format in adjacency pair seconds*

FIRST PARTS:					
	Request	Offer/Invite	Assessment	Question	Blame
SECOND PARTS:					
Preferred:	acceptance	acceptance	agreement	expected answer	denial[20]
Dispreferred:	refusal	refusal	disagreement	unexpected answer or non-answer	admission

Given such a correlation between the kind of action performed and the way in which it is done, we can then talk not only of preferred turns but also of preferred actions (namely, those normally performed in the preferred format).

Now given these patterns we can see that the analysis can in fact be pushed much further back into the structure, not only of the second part of a pair, but of the first part as well. Take again example (47), in which we noted that the delay of two-tenths of a second seems to be taken as evidence of a dispreferred action – namely an invitation rejection – coming up, so that A then adds further inducements (*lotta stuff* being intended to indicate that plenty of food and drink is available, including the specified beer). Similarly, reconsider (55), where again a small delay (marked (.)) is sufficient to indicate to R

[20] Note that blamings receive denials in simple preferred format, thus indicating again that preference cannot be identified with, for example, blamer's desire; see Atkinson & Drew, 1979: 80.

that there may be a problem with R's suggestion, namely the one R suggests. Or again:

(59)   *144*
         C: ...I wondered if you could phone the vicar so that we could
            ((in-breath)) do the final on Saturday (0.8) morning o:r (.)
            afternoon or
            (3.0)
         R: Yeah you see I'll I'll phone him up and see if there's any
            time free
            (2.0)
         C: Yeah
         R: Uh they're normally booked Saturdays but I don't- it
            might not be

Here over the course of C's first turn there are a number of slots provided where R could have performed the preferred compliance with C's request (these include the prolonged in-breath, the eight-tenths of a second pause, the lengthened *o :r* and its following short pause, and of course the long three-second silence after the turn). Given that preferred actions are properly done without delay, the fact that R's compliance is systematically delayed indicates that significant problems are coming up.

What such examples illustrate is that over the course of a single turn's construction, interactional feedback is being systematically taken into consideration (see Davidson, in press). In this sense a single turn at talk by one speaker can itself be seen to be a joint production, here by virtue of the strong expectations for no gap between the transition of speakers provided by preference organization. There is also further evidence of quite different kinds which shows that a single speaker's turn is often a joint production, in that recipients' non-verbal responses are utilized to guide the turn's construction throughout the course of its production (see Goodwin, 1979a, 1981). Here, though, preference organization, in constraining the construction of second parts of adjacency pairs, can systematically affect the design of first parts – and as we shall see this can happen in more ways than one.

Preference organization, however, extends far beyond the confines of adjacency pairs. There are, for a start, kinds of turns paired less tightly than adjacency pairs, where a first part does not seem to require but rather makes apt some response or second – **action-chains** in Pomerantz's (1978) terminology. For example, after an

assessment (or assertion expressing a judgement) a second assessment is often due, as in:

(60)   *Pomerantz, 1975 : 1*
          J: T's – it's a beautiful day out isn't it?
          L: Yeah it's jus' gorgeous ...
(61)   *Pomerantz, 1975 : 1*
          A: (It) was too depre//ssing
          B: O::::h it is te::rrible

Given a first assessment there is a clear preference for agreement over disagreement. Disagreements here, and after assertions in general, typically have a *yes, but* kind of format (i.e. disagreement, prefaced with token agreement), or they are delayed, or prefaced with *well* like other dispreferreds:

(62)   *Pomerantz, 1975 : 66*
          R: ... Well never mind. It's not important.
→   D: *Well*, it is important.
(63)   *Pomerantz, 1975 : 68*
          R: ... You've really both basically honestly gone your own ways.
→   D: *Essentially*, except we've hadda good relationship at
          //home
→   R: .hhh *Ye:s*, but I mean it's a relationship where ...

We are now in a position to appreciate one kind of complexity that arises, where two different kinds of conversational expectations work in opposing directions. One such area is self-denigration: by the preference for agreement after assessments, if A self-denigrates, an agreement from B is preferred. But by an independent principle of a different order, namely a norm enjoining the avoidance of criticism, B should avoid such an agreement. The latter principle in fact generally takes precedence (if agreements occur at all after self-deprecations they are preceded by disagreements – see Pomerantz, 1975: 101):

(64)   *Pomerantz, 1975 : 93*
          L: ... I'm so dumb I don't even know it. hhh! heh
→   W: Y-no, *y-you're not du :mb*...
(65)   *Pomerantz, 1975 : 94*
          L: You're not bored (huh)?
→   S: Bored? No. We're fascinated.

It follows from this, and the nature of pauses as markers of dispreferred responses, that there is an asymmetry in the significance of a pause after an ordinary assessment like (66) and after a self-deprecating assessment like (67):

(66)   A: God isn't it dreary!
        B: ((SILENCE = DISAGREEMENT))
(67)   A: I'm gettin fat hh
        B: ((SILENCE = AGREEMENT))

Further complexities arise in another special kind of assessment, namely compliments. Once again there are cross-cutting principles at work: a preference for agreement with the compliment, and a norm specifying the avoidance of self-praise. Compromise solutions employed here include down-graded agreements, shifts of praise to third parties, and plain disagreements (Pomerantz, 1978).

6.3.2   *Preferred sequences*

So far we have been concerned with how preference operates over a range of alternative seconds to some prior turn. We have, though, indicated that it can operate to structure that prior turn during the course of its production; we have also briefly indicated that the delay component of a dispreferred second can be realized by what may be called a **next turn repair initiator**, or NTRI, which invites repair of the prior turn in the next turn, as in (54) above, where M asks *You want what?*, or as in the arrowed turn below:

(68)   *Pomerantz, 1975 : 74*
            A: Why *what'sa matter* with y-you sou//nd *HA*:PPY, hh
            B: Nothing
→   B: I sound ha:p//py?
            A: *Ye*:uh
            (0.3)
            B: No:,

A dispreferred 'second' turn can thereby become displaced into fourth turn, by the sequence: A:((ASSESSMENT)), B: ((NTRI)), A: ((RE-ASSESSMENT)), B: ((DISPREFERRED SECOND)). One motive here is that B thereby provides A with an opportunity to re-formulate the first turn in a more acceptable way. So preference organization can and often does spill over into a number of turns subsequent to a first turn.

One area where preference organization routinely operates within and across turns is a central conversational device, the organization of **repair** (Schegloff, Jefferson & Sacks, 1977). As was pointed out above, the tendency for an utterance to attend to those immediately prior to it provides, for both analysts and participants, a 'proof procedure' for checking how those turns were understood. This would be of little use if there was no device for the correction of misunderstandings, mishearings or indeed non-hearings. There is of course such a device and it has the following properties. First, it provides a number of systematic slots across (at least) a three-turn sequence in which repair, or at least its prompting, can be done, as follows:

(69)   T1 (includes repairable item) = first opportunity: here for self-initiated self-repair

          Transition space[21] between T1 and T2 = second opportunity: here again for self-initiated self-repair

          T2 = third opportunity: either for other-repair or for other-initiation of self-repair in T3

          T3 = fourth opportunity: given other-initiation in T2, for other-initiated self-repair

There are two important distinctions here: first, **self-initiated** contrasted to **other-initiated** repair – i.e. repair by a speaker without prompting vs. repair after prompting; secondly, **self-repair**, repair done by the speaker of the problem or repairable item, contrasted to **other-repair**, done by another party. An example of repair in each opportunity should help to make the distinctions clear:

(70)   *Schegloff, Jefferson & Sacks, 1977 : 364*
         (Illustrating self-initiated self-repair in opportunity 1)
         N: She was givin' me a:ll the people that were go:ne
→   this yea:r I mean this quarter y'//know
         J: Yeah

(71)   *Schegloff, Jefferson & Sacks, 1977 : 366*
         (Illustrating repair in opportunity 2, again self-initiated self-repair)
         L: An' 'en but all of the doors 'n things were taped up =
→   = I mean y'know they put up y'know that kinda paper 'r stuff, the brown paper.

(72)   *Schegloff, Jefferson & Sacks, 1977 : 378* *(Illustrating other-initiated other-repair in opportunity 3)*
         A: Lissena *pi*geons.
         (0.7)

[21] *Transition space* labels "the beat that potentially follows the possible completion point of a turn" (Schegloff, Jefferson & Sacks, 1977: 366). A more detailed analysis here might be: first opportunity is immediately after the error, second is at end of turn, third is after recipient delay at end of turn, fourth at T2, fifth at T3, and sixth at still further remove (Schegloff, in prep. a).

→   B: Quail, I think.

(73)   *Schegloff, Jefferson & Sacks, 1977: 367 (Illustrating other-initiation of self-repair in opportunity 3)*
             A: Have you ever tried a clinic?

→   B: *What?*
             A: Have you ever tried a clinic?

(74)   *Schegloff, Jefferson & Sacks, 1977: 368 (Illustrating self-repair in opportunity 4, following other-initiation by NTRI)*
             B: .hhh Well I'm working through the Amfat Corporation.

→   A: The *who?*

→   B: Amfah Corporation. T's a holding company.

The range of phenomena collected here under the concept of *repair* is wide, including word recovery problems, self-editings where no discernible 'error' occurred, corrections proper (i.e. error replacements) and much else besides. The claim (Schegloff, Jefferson & Sacks, 1977) is that the same system handles the repair of all these problems. The examples above are only illustrative: there are many ways, for example, in which self-repair within the turn is signalled (e.g. by glottal stops, lengthened vowels, long schwa, etc.), or other-initiation of self-repair is achieved (e.g. by *What?*, *'Scuse me?*, etc., or by echo-questions, or repetitions of problematic items with stress on problem syllables as in (74), (77) and (78)).

Now the second major component of the repair apparatus is a set of preferences setting up a rank ordering across the opportunity set above. Briefly, the preference ranking is as follows:

(75)   *Preference 1* is for self-initiated self-repair in opportunity 1 (own turn)
             Preference 2 is for self-initiated self-repair in opportunity 2 (transition space)
             Preference 3 is for other-initiation, by NTRI in opportunity 3 (next turn), of self-repair (in the turn after that)
             Preference 4 is for other-initiated other-repair in opportunity 3 (next turn)

The evidence for such a ranking is, first, that this corresponds to the ranking from the most frequently used to the least used resource, (other-repair, for example, being really quite rare in conversation). Secondly, the system is actually set up so that there will be a tendency for self-initiated self-repair, this being the type of repair relevant in the first two opportunities traversed. Thirdly, we have the typical delay by recipient following these two opportunities if they're not immediately utilized, indicating a 'problem' and inviting self-initiated self-repair. Sometimes the invitation by the non-responder is successful as in (76), sometimes not, as in (77):

(76)   *Schegloff, Jefferson & Sacks, 1977: 364*
         K: Did*ju* know the guy up there at-oh. What the hell is'z name use to work up't (Steeldinner) garage did their body work for 'em.
→   (1.5)
         K: Uh::ah, (0.5) Oh:: he meh- uh, (0.5) His wife ran off with Jim McCa:nn.
(77)   *Schegloff, Jefferson & Sacks, 1977: 370*
         A: Hey the first time they stopped me from sellin' cigarettes was this morning.
→   (1.0)
         B: From *sell*ing cigarettes?
         A: From buying cigarettes.

Fourthly, there is clear evidence that even where other parties can do the required repair, they produce an NTRI (i.e. other-initiation of a self-repair) instead of doing other-repair on many and probably most occasions. B's turn in (77) is a case in point, and the fourth turn in the following makes this explicit:

(78)   *Schegloff, Jefferson & Sacks, 1977: 377*
         K: 'E likes that waiter over there,
         A: Wait-*er*?
         K: Waitress, sorry,
→   A: 'Ats better,

Finally in the rare event of other-repair occurring, it is followed by 'modulators' like the *I think* in (72) above, or prefaced by *y'mean*, or otherwise marked:

(79)   *Schegloff, Jefferson & Sacks, 1977: 378*
         L: But y'know *single beds*'r *awfully thin* to *sleep* on.
         S: What?
         L: Single beds. // They're-
→   E: Y'mean narrow?
         L: They're awfully *narrow* yeah.

So the repair apparatus as a whole is strongly biased both by a preference for self-initiation of repair and by a preference for self-repair over repair by others. As a consequence preference organization governs the unfolding of sequences concerned with repair.

We have now widened the scope of preference organization to cover not only rankings of alternative turns, but alternative solutions to problems (like the handling of repair), the solutions being either handled within a single turn or across a sequence of turns. However, preference also seems to operate across *sequence types* – for example, it seems that, if possible, prompting an offer is an action preferable to performing a request (Schegloff, 1979a: 49). Hence, as we shall see in 6.4.3, there is a special utility in a turn designed to prefigure or preface a request (a **pre-request**), for it provides for the possibility of recipient performing an offer instead, as below:

(80)   *176*
→   C: Hullo I was just ringing up to ask if you were going to
             Bertrand's party
          R: Yes I thought you might be
          C: Heh heh
→   R: Yes would you like a lift?
          C: Oh I'd love one

In a similar way, in the initial three turns of telephone calls recognition is done by, and totally submerged within, greetings (where this is possible) in preference to being achieved by a sequence involving overt self-identifications. Thus (81) is the preferred sequence, (82) the dispreferred:[22]

(81)   *Schegloff, 1979a: 35*
          C: ((rings))
T1   R: Hello
T2   C: Hello
T3   R: Hi

(82)   *Schegloff, 1979a: 59*
          C: ((rings))
T1   R: Hello,
T2   C: Hi. Susan?
T3   R: Ye:s,
T4   C: This's Judith (.) Rossman
T5   R: *Ju*dith!

The evidence that self-identification is in general dispreferred is this. Despite the fact that R can be assumed to have a strong interest in learning who is calling, in the first turn by callers (T2) self-identification is often absent; if, given this turn, identification is not

---

[22] This sort of preference may be quite culture-specific; see Godard, 1977 on French conventions.

immediately achieved by R, then C generally leaves a gap or pause for recognition to occur – hence, as we saw in 6.2.3, delay after a minimal T2 is understood as evidence of a problem in R's recognition of C. Only after such a delay does C offer an identification (as in (45) above) or does R request one (as in (46)).

Now given this dispreference for self-identifications, if a caller wishes to avoid overt self-identification but is uncertain that recipient can do identification on a minimal T2 (e.g. *Hello*), then he can produce a T2 that prefigures or prefaces a self-identification while withholding it, thus giving the recipient an opportunity to recognize the caller without actually claiming (as a plain *Hello* would) that recipient can do so. The caller can achieve this by the use of *Hello* plus the name of the recipient, with the characteristic low-rise intonation contour of a 'try' on the name, as in :

(83)   *Schegloff, 1979a : 52*
          R: Hello:,
→   C: Hello *Il*se?
          R: Yes. *Be* :tty.

(Note that a high-rise contour would seem to signal genuine uncertainty about the recipient's identity, whereas a low-rise primarily conveys uncertainty about whether the recipient can recognize the caller – see Schegloff, 1979a: 50.) Now just as a pre-request invites the recipient to provide an offer, thus avoiding the dispreferred request sequence, so *Hello* plus name (with low-rise contour) invites recognition (as in (83)) in preference to the self-identification it prefigures, namely the dispreferred sequence instanced by (82). Hence such a dispreferred sequence, with overt self-identification, will generally only occur if in T3 recipient shows no evidence of recognition, like an address term or enthusiastic response (e.g. *Oh hi! How are you?*). And that it is dispreferred is further shown by the fact that, on the absence of recognition in T3, the caller sometimes provides no more identificatory material in T4 than a further sample of voice-quality:

(84)   *Schegloff, 1979a : 55*
          R: H'llo:?
          C: Harriet?
          R: Yeah?
→   C: Hi!
          R: *Hi* :.

Finally, the dispreferred nature of self-identification is confirmed by the fact that, if it is after all required, it is often received with 'the big hello' – the upgraded recognition component in e.g. T5 in (82), regularly with an account of why recognition was not achieved earlier (e.g. *You sound different* – see Schegloff, 1979a: 48).

So for telephone recognitions between known parties the preference is for caller to provide the minimal cues he judges sufficient for recipient to recognize caller (note here the pause before the provision of the surname in (82)). And such a preference not only ranks T2 cues as in (85):

(85)　　(i)　Hi
　　　　(ii)　Hello
　　　　(iii) Hello. It's me
　　　　(iv) Hello. It's Penny
　　　　(v)　Hello. It's Penny Rankin

but it also ranks the two sequence types, (i) greetings alone, (ii) greetings followed by overt self-identifications and recognitions.

Preference organization thus extends not only across alternative seconds to first parts of adjacency pairs, but backwards into the construction of first parts, forwards into the organization of subsequent turns, and also across entire alternative sequences, ranking sets of sequence types.

6.4　Pre-sequences
6.4.1　*General remarks*

The term **pre-sequence** is used, with a systematic ambiguity, to refer both to a certain kind of turn and a certain kind of sequence containing that type of turn. We will, however, use the abbreviation **pre-s** for the turn-type, reserving *pre-sequence* for the sequence type. Some examples of pre-sequences and pre-s have already been introduced in passing. We have noted for example that a summons prefigures a turn which contains a reason for the summons, as in:

(86)　　*Atkinson & Drew, 1979: 46*
　　　　Ch: Mummy
　　　　M:　Yes dear
　　　　　　(2.1)
　　　　Ch: I want a cloth to clean (the) windows

Since such reasons can be various, summonses are 'generalized pre-s'; most pre-s, however, are built to prefigure the specific kind of action that they potentially precede. For example, pre-closings, often realized as tokens of *Okay*, are recognizable as potential initiations of closings, otherwise closings could not be co-ordinated. Pre-closings illustrate one major motivation for pre-s in general, namely that by prefiguring an upcoming action they invite collaboration in that action (as in pre-closings) or collaboration in avoiding that action (as in pre-self-identifications).

Some of the clearest kinds of pre-s are **pre-invitations**, like the following:

(87)   *Atkinson & Drew, 1979 : 253*
→   A: Whatcha doin'?
           B: Nothin'
           A: Wanna drink?
(88)   *Atkinson & Drew, 1979 : 143*
           R: Hi John
           C: How ya doin =
→   = say wh*at*'r you doing?
           R: Well we're going out. Why?
           C: Oh, I was just gonna say come out and come over here an' talk this evening, but if you're going out you can't very well do that

Notice that in both cases the pre-invitations are treated as transparent by the recipients – so that their responses are clearly attuned to the fact that an invitation (or related act) is potentially forthcoming in the next turn. Thus *Nothing* in (87) can be read as 'nothing that would make the offer of an evening's entertainment irrelevant' or the like, while the formulation of what R is doing in (88) is clearly attuned to the possibility of an upcoming invitation, which the *Why?* requests details of.

A pre-s is not just some turn that comes before some other kind of turn – most turns have that property; it is a turn that occupies a specific slot in a specific kind of sequence with distinctive properties. On the basis of examples like the pre-invitation ones above, we might attempt the following characterization of the structure of such sequences (although such a characterization requires generalization to other kinds of pre-sequence):

(89)   (a) T_1 (Position 1): a question checking whether some precondition obtains for the action to be performed in T_3

T2 (Position 2): an answer indicating that the precondition obtains, often with a question or request to proceed to T3

T3 (Position 3): the prefigured action, conditional on the 'go ahead' in T2

T4 (Position 4): response to the action in T3

(b) *distribution rule*: one party, A, addresses T1 and T3 to another party, B, and B addresses T2 and T4 to A

Of course, a crucial part of the motivation for such a sequence is the conditional or contingent nature of T3 on the nature of T2; so, in the absence of an encouragement in T2, the sequence can be expected to abort along the following lines:

(90)   T1: as in (89)

T2: answer indicates that precondition on action does not obtain – often so formulated as to specifically discourage the foreseeable action

T3: withholding of the prefigured action, usually with a report of what would have been done in T3, by way of explanation for T1

Such a sequence occurs in (88).

Given such a characterization, we then have no difficulty finding further kinds of pre-sequence, e.g. **pre-requests** like the following:

(91)   *Merritt, 1976 : 337*
→   C: Do you have hot chocolate?
            S: mmhmm
→   C: Can I have hot chocolate with whipped cream?
            S: Sure ((leaves to get))
(92)   *Merritt, 1976 : 324*
→   C: Do you have the blackberry jam?
            S: Yes
→   C: Okay. Can I have half a pint then?
            S: Sure ((turns to get))
(93)   *172B(7)*
→   C: So um I was wondering would you be in your office on Monday (.) by any chance (2.0) probably not
            R: Hmm yes =
            C: = You would
            R: Yes yes
               (1.0)
→   C: So if we came by could you give us ten minutes or so?

Similarly one can recognize **pre-arrangements** for future contact, as in:

347

(94)   *176B*
→   R: Erm (2.8) what what are you doing today?
            C: Er well I'm supervising at quarter past
               (1.6)
→   R: Er yuh why (don't) er (1.5) would you like to come by after
               that?
            C: I can't I'm afraid no

Now there is a problem raised for our characterization of such sequences by examples like (93),[23] where the distribution of the characteristic actions is not exactly over the paradigmatic four-turn sequence proposed in (89). Such problems are more acute in examples like the following, where we have two **insertion sequences**, one in T2 and T3 concerned with repair, one in T4 and T5 concerned with establishing a temporary 'hold' in the turn-taking system, both these sequences being inserted between a pre-request on the one hand (in T1), and its response (in T6) with the follow-up request (in T7) on the other.

(95)   *144(3)*
T1   →   C: ... Do you have in stock please any L.T. one eight eight?
               ((POSITION 1))
T2   R: One eight eight ((HEARING CHECK))
T3   C: Yeah= ((CHECK OKAYED))
T4   R: =Can you hold on please ((HOLD))
T5   C: Thank you ((ACCEPT))
               (1.5)
T6   R: Yes I have got the one ((POSITION 2))
T7   →   C: Yes. Could I- you hold that for H.H.Q.G please
               ((POSITION 3))

Intuitively, then, we have two insertion sequences between what would be the paradigmatic turns T1 and T2 in (89). But if we have defined the notion of a pre-sequence in terms of just the sequence of turns in (89), how is this case to be assimilated? What we need here is the distinction introduced recently by Schegloff in the discussion of repair, between **turn location** – i.e. sheer sequential locus of a turn in a sequence by a count after some initial turn – and **position**, the response to some prior but not necessarily adjacent turn. Thus a second part of an adjacency pair separated from its first part by a two-turn insertion sequence will be in *fourth turn* but *second position*. What we want to claim, therefore, is that the structure in (89) actually

---

[23] And compare the different transcription of the same data in (39).

holds across a sequence of *positions* rather than *turns*, and that the utterance T6 in (95) is in *second position* despite being sixth in turn, and likewise T7 is in *third position* though seventh in turn.

But if this distinction between *turn* and *position* is not to render vacuous the claim that pre-sequences ordinarily have the structure in (89), then we must have an independent characterization of each *position*, so that it can be recognized wherever in a sequence of turns it actually shows up. This is not easy to do in a general way for all pre-sequences, but it can certainly be done for sub-classes of pre-sequences, like that including pre-requests, pre-invitations, pre-offers and the like. Indeed the glosses on the content of each turn (or, preferably now, position) in (89) indicate some typical recognizable features of each. Let us take up this problem of characterizing turns in particular positions with respect to one particular type of pre-sequence.

6.4.2 Pre-announcements

One class of pre-s of special interest are **pre-announcements** (see Terasaki, 1976, on whose work the following is based). We have already met the sub-class of these which are bids for story space (see examples (41) and (42) above), noting that they operate to gain ratified access to an extended turn at talk. But there are many other kinds of pre-announcements, like the following:

(96) *Terasaki, 1976: 36*
      D: .hh Oh guess what.
      R: What.
      D: Professor Deelies came in, 'n he- put another book on 'is order.
(97) *Terasaki, 1976: 53*
      D: I forgot to tell you the two best things that happen' to me today.
      R: Oh super = what were they.
      D: I got a B+ on my math test ... and I got an athletic award.
(98) *Terasaki, 1976: 53*
      D: Hey you'll never guess what your dad is lookih-is lookin' at.
      R: What're you looking at.
      D: A radar range.

Let us now attempt to characterize such sequences. One way of thinking about them (and perhaps pre-sequences in general) is that they are made up of two superimposed adjacency pairs: a pre-pair (e.g. A: *Have you heard the news?*, B: *No*) and a second pair (e.g. B: *Tell me*, A: *John won the lottery*) – superimposed in that the second of the first pair and the first of the second pair occur in the same turn or position – namely position 2. Hence we often find in the turn occupying position 2 dual components of the kind in the second turn in (97), where *Oh super* looks backward to the prior turn, and *what were they* is a first part requiring the announcement as a second. We thus have the following structure for pre-announcements:

(99)   *Position 1*: pre-sequence first part, generally checking on newsworthiness of potential announcement in position 3

Position 2: pre-sequence second, generally validating newsworthiness, *and* first part of second pair, namely a request to tell

Position 3: second part to second pair – the announcement delivered

Position 4: news receipt

As required by the distinction between *turn* and *position*, we should attempt to characterize the format of each position independently of its sheer sequential location (though the order of the positions must of course be maintained, so sequential considerations can still play an important part in the recognition of specific positions). Thus we can say of position 1 turns that, although they may be in any of the three main sentence-types (e.g. interrogative in (41) above, imperative in (96), declarative in (97) and (98)), they typically have at least one of the following elements: they *name* the kind of announcement (e.g. *what your dad is looking at* in (98), *the news* in the examples immediately below); and/or they evaluate it e.g. as *good news* in (100), and *terrible news* in (101):

(100)   *Terasaki, 1976 : 33*
        D: Hey we got good news.
        R: What's the good news.
(101)   *Terasaki, 1976 : 28*[24]
        D: Didju hear the terrible news?
        R: No. What.
        D: Y'know your Grandpa Bill's brother Dan?
        R: He died.
        D: Yeah.

[24] This example is a principled exception to the schema in (99), as explained below in terms of a preference for *guessing* over *telling* in the case of bad news.

Further they often date the news (e.g. the specification *today* in (97));
and finally, and most importantly, such position 1 turns generally
have some *variable*, a WH-word (as in *What?* in (96) and (98)) or an
indefinite phrase (*a good thing happened*) or a definite but non-specific
phrase (*the news*). It is of course this variable that these first turns in
the sequence offer to instantiate in position 3.

Position 2 turns are generally characterized by (a), optionally, a
response to position 1 taken as a question (e.g. *No* in (101)), and (b)
almost invariably a question-like component. These question
components are one-word questions like *What* (as in (96)) or echo-
questions or questions like *What were they?* in (97), which copy parts
of position 1's material. That is, they are built like NTRIs (next turn
repair initiators), which include of course echo-questions. What they
share with NTRIs is that they have the same double-directedness –
they look back to prior turn (making possible the truncated format)
and they look forward to next turn (hence the question format). In
this way the format of position 2 turns is designed both as a second
to position 1 turns and as first parts taking position 3 turns as seconds.

Turning to position 3 turns, the announcements themselves, we
find a series of tight constraints on their format. For example, they
sometimes retain the syntactic or case frame of their corresponding
pre-announcements in position 1 (Terasaki, 1976):

(102)   *Terasaki, 1976: 26*
→   D: Oh. You know, Yuri   did   a terrible thing
                       ((SUBJ)) ((VERB)) ((DIRECT OBJECT))
        R: hhh! I kno*w*.
        D: You know?
→   She   committed *suicide*
           ((SUBJ))   ((VERB))   ((DIRECT OBJECT))

Alternatively, position 3 turns provide just the items that would fill
the variable slot (here in bold face for recognitional purposes) typical
in position 1 turns:

(103)   *Terasaki, 1976: 53*
→   D: Y'wanna know **who** I got stoned with a few w(hh)eeks ago?
           hh!
        R: Who.
→   D: Mary Carter 'n her boy(hh) frie(hhh)nd. hh.

Note here too the tie back of position 3 to position 2, since position
3 provides just the information solicited in position 2 (and offered in

position 1). There are other variations, but the point here is that each position is indeed characterizable, independently of absolute location in a sequence of turns, as having certain kinds of (alternative) format.

Clearly, the design of the turn in position 1 is crucial: for it is on the basis of this that the recipient must decide whether or not he already knows the content of the announcement, and thus should abort the sequence. Hence the prefiguring of the syntactic frame of the announcement, as in (102), is a very useful clue to the recipient, as is the characterization of the announcement as 'news' or as a 'joke' or 'story', the dating of reportable events, and the evaluation of 'news' as 'good', 'terrible', etc. So we can appreciate that some phrase like *the two best things that happened to me today* (in (97)) is carefully formulated to prefigure what is coming up – namely two items, good things, and things that happened today.

It is instructive in this regard to reconsider an analysis by Labov & Fanshel (1977) of the very beginning of a psychiatric interview:

(104)   *Labov & Fanshel, 1977 : 363 (transcription conventions converted to CA style)*
          R: I don't (1.0) know, whether (1.5) I- I think I did- the right thing, jistalittle situation came up (4.5) an' I tried to uhm (3.0) well, try to (4.0) use what I- what I've learned here, see if it worked
          (0.3)
          T: Mhm
          R: Now, I don't know if I did the right thing. Sunday (1.0) um- my mother went to my sister's again ... ((story continues))

In seventeen pages of painstaking analysis in DA style, Labov & Fanshel (1977: 113ff) analyse the patient's (R's) first turn here as containing various speech acts including questions, assertions and challenges. To achieve an understanding in such depth they look forward in the interaction to see what *the right thing* and *jistalittle situation* refer to; they then pack back into the gloss or "expansion" of the first turn these details gleaned from later on. Despite the obvious discrepancy between the information thus available to participants (who cannot look ahead in a transcript) and analysts (who can), the authors feel this procedure is justified by the analysts' relative lack of the knowledge available to participants about each other (ibid.: 120). They further argue that the various features here, including the glottalizations and hesitancy, and crucially the "vague reference" in *thing* and *situation*, can be attributed to aspects of "interview style" (ibid.: 129).

Now contrast an analysis in CA style. R's first turn is a pre-announcement, formulated to prefigure (a) the telling of something she did (*I think I did the right thing*), and (b) the describing of the situation that led to the action (*jistalittle situation came up*). We are therefore warned to expect a story with two such components; moreover the point of the story and its relevance to the here and now is also prefigured (*use what I've learned here, see if it worked*). The alleged vagueness of *the right thing* and *jistalittle situation* is in fact the provision of just those variables typical of position 1 turns in pre-announcement sequences. That a pre-sequence analysis seems correct is reinforced by the fact that the recipient, the therapist, does indeed wait for each prefigured segment of the story, receiving the first with *Oh* (a typical news receipt item – see Heritage, in press), and the second with an agreement (*Yes I think you did (the right thing) too*), abstaining from any other substantial turns throughout the story. The point to be made here is that the original DA-style analysis, proceeding in an act-by-act fashion, is not attuned to the larger sequential structures that organize conversation; nor are such structures easily recognizable without a lot of comparative material.[25]

The recognition of pre-announcements can be problematic not only for analysts, but for participants too. Consider, for example, (105):

(105)   *Terasaki, 1976: 45*
T1   Kid: I know where you're going.
T2   Mom: Where.
T3   Kid: To: that (meeting ...)
T4   Mom: Right. Yah!
    →   Do you know who's going to that meeting?
T5   Kid: Who.
T6 →   Mom: I don't know!
T7   Kid: Ou::h prob'ly: Mr Murphy an' Dad said prob'ly Mrs Timpte an' some o' the teachers.

Here in T4 we have a turn in question format: Kid takes it to be a

[25] Incidentally, CA can also provide rival analyses of other features of this first turn – for example, the hesitation and glottal stops attributed in the original analysis to "style" are also the typical markings of self-initiated self-repair, which is characteristic of the production of first topics (see Schegloff, 1979b), and is also used to request listener attention (Goodwin, 1981: Chapter 2).

353

pre-announcement, and for good reasons – the sequential locus is such that given his own use of a guess in T1, he may expect another 'riddle' in return. So in T5 Kid solicits the prefigured announcement, with *Who*. But it turns out that Mom intended T4 as a question, not a pre-announcement, as her response in T6 makes clear. Notice that Kid can then in fact produce an answer in T7, indicating that the *Who* in T5 was only intended as 'Go ahead and tell', not 'I don't know'. An ambiguity of this sort, which is shown here to be an ambiguity for participants like that in (49) above, is a good example of the kind of phenomenon that analysts using intuitions as data have failed to notice. Instead, such theorists might be concerned about another ambiguity, namely that between the 'direct' speech act interpretation of *Do you know p?* (for which *Yes* or *No* would be a complete and adequate response) and the 'indirect' speech act interpretation as a request to tell, which is not an issue for participants here (Schegloff, in prep. b).

What motivates the use of pre-s like these pre-announcements? There seem to be a number of motivations, sometimes working concurrently. We have already sketched, for pre-story turns like that in (42), a motivation based on the turn-taking system: if a speaker wishes to suspend temporarily the relevance of possible transition at each TRP, he may make a bid for ratification of an extended turn. This motivation, Sacks has pointed out, explains the frequent use of pre-announcements by those with restricted rights to speak – hence children's use of formulae like *Want to know something, Daddy?*

However, perhaps the most prominent motivation for pre-announcements is a keen concern with not telling people things that they already know. The concern ramifies through this and other conversational organizations, motivating a general tendency to "oversuppose and undertell" (Sacks & Schegloff, 1979), which we have already met in the domain of telephone identifications (Schegloff, 1979a: 50). Grice's maxim of Quantity, and its basis in rational co-operative efficiency, seems scant motive for the strong interactional aversion to self-repetition. In any case, the extraordinary fact is that everyone is expected to keep an account book, as it were, of every matter talked about with every other co-participant. If uncertainty does arise, or if there is reason to suppose that some other third party may have already imparted the 'news', then recourse can be had to the pre-announcement, which offers to tell contingently upon the 'news' not already being known. Thus solicitations to tell in position 2 will tend to commit the recipient to claiming that he has not previously heard the news (a commitment escapable – but not without loss of grace – by an *Oh that*, or the like, in position 4). A puzzle that then arises is how, from the sometimes fairly non-specific turns in position 1, participants can effectively judge whether what is prefigured is already known, as they confidently do:

(106)   *Terasaki, 1976 : 26*
         D: ... Hey we got good news.
         R: I know.

Here, besides the format of the pre-announcement itself, participants rely on features like sequential context (stories, for example, are often topic-tied to prior turns, providing a resource for guessing what story may now be told – see Jefferson, 1978) and the dating of news provided by the occasion of last meeting (whatever was 'news' then, should have been delivered then, so 'news' now must be 'news' since then – see Sacks, 1975).

We thus see in pre-announcements a concern, reflected in a sequential organization, with the distinction between given and new information that we have discussed elsewhere under the rubrics of presupposition and the maxim of Quantity. The concern runs deep in the usage of pre-announcements: the structure of position 1 turns is often so designed that it provides a frame that is given information, and a variable whose instantiation is thought to be new (as in (98), where the frame is *You'll never guess what your dad is looking at*, given by the situation, and what is delivered in position 3 is just what is new: *A radar range*). Further, in cases where a pre-announcement is delivered to a set of recipients in potentially different states of knowledge, one finds position 1 turns like *Some of you may not have heard the news*; and if one of these recipients is 'in the know' he may produce a 'collaborative' T2 like *Yeah tell 'em about it*, thus carefully excluding himself from those 'in the dark' (Terasaki, 1976: 20ff).

But there are other motivations for pre-announcements besides these. One important one involves preference organization, which we have noted can rank order not only alternative turns but also the choice between alternative entire sequences. Offer sequences can thus be preferred to request sequences (see example (80) and discussion above); and implicit recognition in greetings preferred to overt

355

self-identification sequences in the openings of telephone calls. So also there seems to be, in the case of the delivery of 'bad news', a preference for B guessing over A telling. Just as a pre-request can, in projecting an upcoming request, secure an offer, so a pre-announcement can obtain, and be specifically designed to obtain, a guess:

(107) *Terasaki, 1976 : 29*
       D: I-I-I had something *terr*ible t'tell you.
          So // uh
       R: How terrible *is* it.
       D: Uh, th- as worse it could *be.*
          (0.8)
       R: W- y'mean Edna?
       D: Uh yah.
       R: Whad she do, die?
       D: Mm:hm,

Note here the delay after the third turn, that seems specifically to invite a guess. And note that in (101) above, the first pre-announcement is followed by a second, until recipient guesses. So another motivation for pre-announcements is that by prefiguring a dispreferred action, the telling of bad news, they can prompt a guess by the other party that obviates the need to do the dispreferred action at all.

In this discussion of pre-announcements we have shown that (a) a specific kind of sequence can be properly characterized as an ordered sequence of not necessarily contiguous turns of distinctive type, (b) on inception, it is recognizable to participants by virtue of characteristic position 1 turns, and (c) the usage of such sequences is strongly motivated by various principles of language usage.

6.4.3 *Pre-requests : a re-analysis of indirect speech acts*
       We now have all the ingredients for a powerful re-analysis of the problem of *indirect speech acts.*[26] Strictly speaking, perhaps, we should say that on the CA view the alleged problem does not even arise; and in any case the terms of the two kinds of analyses are so starkly different that what is a problem for the philosophico-linguistic approaches is not for the CA approach, and perhaps vice versa.

---

[26] A number of authors should be credited here: Schegloff, in unpublished work; Goffman, 1976; Merritt, 1976; Coulthard, 1977: 71; Heringer, 1977. The argument also benefits from unpublished work by Paul Drew and John Heritage.

The problem, recollect, from the point of view of speech act theory, is that indirect speech acts do not have the 'literal force' (allegedly) associated by rule with their sentence-types, but rather some other force which a theory of indirect speech acts is concerned to explain. Thus the question is how, for example, sentences like *Is there any more?*, or *Can you reach that book?* or *Will you come here please?* can be effectively employed to perform requests. Let us restrict ourselves to requests as the variety of indirect speech act which has received the most attention.

A CA analysis might go roughly as follows. Pre-request sequences, we noted, properly have a four-position structure, providing the following kind of analysis:

(108)   *Merritt, 1976 : 324*
          Position 1: A: Hi. Do you have uh size C flashlight batteries?
                                                    ((PRE-REQUEST))
          Position 2: B: Yes sir   ((GO AHEAD))
          Position 3: A: I'll have four please ((REQUEST))
          Position 4: B: ((turns to get))   ((RESPONSE))

Now, as we have argued, it is possible to distinguish sheer sequential location in a sequence of turns, from position or location in a sequence of responses. So we need an independent characterization of, for example, position 1 turns in pre-request sequences, thus giving an account of how they can be recognized prior to position 3 turns being performed. One characteristic, we noted, for a wide range of pre-sequences, is that position 1 turns check that conditions for successful position 3 turns obtain. Why should this be so?

In the case of requests it seems clear that one prime motivation for employing pre-requests is provided by the preference ranking which organizes responses to requests themselves. Request refusals are dispreferred: therefore, by the accompanying rule for production, to be avoided if possible. One major reason for utilizing a pre-request is, then, that it allows the producer to check out whether a request is likely to succeed, and if not to avoid one in order to avoid its subsequent dispreferred response, namely a rejection. Given which, in cases of doubt, pre-requests are to be preferred to requests.

One kind of evidence for this is that not just any precondition on a request is generally usable in a pre-request: rather just those that are, in the particular circumstances, the usual grounds for *refusal* of that request (Labov & Fanshel, 1977: 86ff). It is no accident, for

357

example, that questions about recipient's abilities figure so largely in both indirect speech acts of requesting and pre-requests – they are also the favoured basis for request refusals in conversation:

(109)   *164*
        (*Context : A has asked a third party B for change, C standing by now joins in :*)
        C: How much do you want?
        A: Well a fiver, can you do five?
→   C: Oh sorry, I'd be able to do a couple of quid
(110)   *170*
        A: Hullo I was wondering whether you were intending to go to Popper's talk this afternoon
→   B: Not today I'm afraid I can't really make it to this one
        A: Ah okay
        B: You wanted me to record it didn't you heh!
        A: Yeah heheh
        B: Heheh no I'm sorry about that, ...

Note that in (110) B treats A's first utterance as a transparent pre-request, hence the apologies typical of dispreferreds and the guess at the request that would have been relevant had B been able to attend.

While in conversation inability seems to be the preferred grounds for request refusals (in preference to, say, unwillingness), in service encounters (in shops, offices, bars, etc.) it seems that requests for goods are usually rejected by explaining that the desired goods are not in stock (see Ervin-Tripp, 1976; Sinclair, 1976). Hence the symmetry across the pre-request format and the refusal format below is not accidental:

(111)   *Merritt, 1976 : 325*
→   C: Do you have Marlboros?
→   S: Uh, no. We ran out
        C: Okay. Thanks anyway
        S: Sorry

What is checked in the pre-request is what is most likely to be the grounds for refusal; and if those grounds are present, then the request sequence is aborted.

We now have at least a partial characterization of position 1 turns in pre-requests: they check (and are therefore generally questions) the most likely grounds for rejection. We also have a *motivation* for this particular format – namely avoiding an action (the request) that would obtain a dispreferred second (a rejection), and hence the

checking of the most likely grounds for refusal in position 1
turns.

But there is a further motivation for using pre-requests, namely the
possibility of avoiding requests altogether. As we noted, preference
organization operates not only over alternative seconds but also over
alternative sequences, so that offer sequences seem to be preferred
to request sequences (Schegloff, 1979a: 49).[27] By producing a pre-
request in turn 1, one participant can make it possible for another to
provide an offer in turn (or position) 2, an offer of whatever it was
that the pre-request prefigured, as below:

(112)   *Merritt, 1976: 324*
        C: Do you have pecan Danish today?
→   S: Yes we do. Would you like one of those?
        C: Yes please
        S: Okay ((turns to get))
(113)   (*as in (80)*)
        C: Hullo I was just ringing up to ask if you were going to
           Bertrand's party
        R: Yes I thought you might be
        C: Heh heh
→   R: Yes would you like a lift?
        C: Oh I'd love one
        R: Right okay um I'll pick you up from there ...

There is a further possibility, beyond the preference for offers over
overt requests. For it may be that, after a pre-request, it is preferred
that neither a request nor an offer takes place at all. There are some
parallels for such avoidance of overt actions altogether. In telephone
recognitions, as we noted, there seems to be a preference not only for
the use of minimal resources for mutual recognition, but for the work
of recognition to be actually submerged and hidden altogether in the
exchange of minimal greetings – i.e. a preference for recognition to
appear to be no issue at all. There is another, rather different, parallel:
in repair we noted that there is a preference for self-initiated self-repair
over other-initiated repair either by self or other. But if self fails to
initiate repair, and other is to initiate, then there is a way of doing
this that avoids the use of an NTRI and the consequent three-turn

[27] In addition to the other cases in 6.3.2, we have also seen that, when telling
   bad news, there seems to be a preference for the sequence (a) T_1: pre-
   announcement, T_2: guess, over the sequence (b) T_1: pre-announcement,
   T_2: go-ahead, T_3: announcement.

repair sequence: other can do such repair when his turn naturally comes up, simply by substituting (for example) a 'correct' term for the offending one, as in the following (the relevant terms are in bold face):

(114) *Jefferson, MS.*
(*Hardware store: customer trying to match a pipe-fitting. C = customer, S = salesman*)
C: Mm, the **whales** are wider apart than that.
S: Okay, let me see if I can find one with wider **threads**. ((looks through stock))
S: How's this.
C: Nope, the **threads** are even wider than that.

Here S, the expert, simply substitutes *threads* for *whales*, and C subsequently adopts the suggested usage. So here 'correction' is being effectively achieved without ever becoming the sort of interactional issue that it can become if done through the normal three-position sequence of other-initiated self-repair:

(115) *Jefferson, MS.*
A: ... had to put new gaskets on the oil pan to strop-stop the leak, an' then I put- an then-
R: That was a gas leak.
→ A: It was an oil leak buddy.
→ B: 'T's a *gas* leak.
→ A: It's an oil leak.
((dispute continues for many turns))

Jefferson (MS.) calls correction of the sort in (114) **embedded**,[28] and the sort in (115) **exposed**, and there is reason to think that embedded correction is preferred to exposed, in part perhaps because issues of competence are not overtly raised. So the avoidance of a sequence altogether in favour of a covert solution can sometimes be preferred in repair work also.

Returning to requests, what we may now suggest is that there may also be a preference for the avoidance of requests altogether. So, if you can see that someone wants something, and a pre-request may be an effective clue to that, then it may be most preferred to provide it without more ado, next most preferred to offer, and third in preference to simply solicit the request. If this is correct, then after a pre-request, we have the following preference ranking operating

---

[28] A misleading terminology for linguists – better would be *covert* or *implicit*.

over three kinds of sequences (ignoring those that are aborted when preconditions are not met):

(116)   (i)   most preferred: Position 1: (pre-request)
                         Position 4: (response to non-overt request)
    (ii) next preferred: Position 1: (pre-request)
                         Position 2': (offer)
                         Position 3': (acceptance of offer)
    (iii) least preferred: Position 1: (pre-request)
                         Position 2: (go ahead)
                         Position 3: (request)
                         Position 4: (compliance)

Some examples of sequences of type (i) follow:

(117)   *Sinclair, 1976 : 60*
        S: Have you got Embassy Gold please? ((POSITION 1))
        H: Yes dear ((provides))   ((POSITION 4))

(118)   *Merritt, 1976 : 325*
        C: Do you have Marlboros? ((POSITION 1))
        S: Yeah. Hard or soft?   ((INSERTION
        C: Soft please   SEQUENCE))
        S: Okay   ((POSITION 4))

It may be objected that the initial turns here are just indirect requests – but note that they are in the format of pre-requests, and the difference between, for example, (108) and (117) is simply that position 2 and position 3 turns are missing in the latter. Since (117) might very well have run off similarly to (108), it would be a post-hoc distinction to say of the first turn in (108) that it is a pre-request while to say of the first turn in (117) that it is an indirect request. Sometimes, though, the sequential pattern (i) in (116) is absolutely clear (see also (120) below):

(119)   *178*
        (Context : R and Sheila have delivered a joint lecture course, but failed to provide C, compiler of the relevant examination, with questions for it)
        ((immediately after greetings))
        C: Um (1.5) you and Sheila have been doing some lectures for first year Microbiol//ogy
        R: Right and oh my God it's the third of March or whatever- yes – fourth of March
           (1.0)
        er we'll get them to you (1.0) toda:y ...

We want to say that C's turn here is treated as a pre-request or position 1 turn, which receives in response a position 4 turn, i.e. a response (compliance) as if the request had itself been delivered.

Now the great majority of sequences of this truncated type have pre-requests that are distinctive – namely, they appear to be *built to obtain a position 4 in second turn*. Consider, for example:

(120)   *US : 24*
          M: What're you doing wi' that big bow-puh tank.
          Nothing.
          (0.5)
          V: ((cough)) uh-h-h (1.0) I'm not into selling it or giving it.
          That's it.
          M: Okay

Here a pre-request in the form of a question has tagged on to it a presumption of its answer (*Nothing*). But in supplying the answer to the question that checks the precondition on the request, M invites a position 4 response directly – and gets it (but it is the dispreferred second, a refusal). Note that M's *Okay* in accepting the refusal acquiesces in the request interpretation. Recollect a parallel in the case of pre-announcements, where position 1 turns are often carefully formulated (a) to provide enough information about the upcoming announcement for recipients to judge whether they have already heard it, (b) sometimes so formulated as to extract guesses in position 2 of what would otherwise appear in position 3. Similarly, then, pre-requests can be built *specifically* to invite position 4 responses.

One technique for this formulation is to provide in the pre-request all the information that would be required for recipient to comply with the request. Thus there is a systematic difference in the way the following two sequences run off, given the difference between their first turns:

(121)   *Sinclair, 1976 : 68*
          S: Can I have two pints of Abbot and a grapefruit and whisky?
                                        ((POSITION 1))
          H: Sure ((turns to get))   ((POSITION 4))
          ((later)) There you are ...
(122)   *Sinclair, 1976 : 54*
          S: Do you have any glue?   ((POSITION 1))
          H: Yes. What kind do you want dear? I've got um, I got a jar
          or-

S: Do you have some tubes?   ((another POSITION 1))
H: The tubes? Ah you're lucky, aren't you actually. That's
    twenty five   ((POSITION 2))
S: Oh I'll take that   ((POSITION 3))

In the first example the full specification in position 1 is built to take
a position 4 turn in second turn, whereas in the second the lack of
specification for kind and and quantity of goods does not make such
a second turn possible. Now there are many other properties of
position 1 turns that are designed to get position 4 responses. For
example, there are the range of markers of **interactional pessimism**
(Brown & Levinson, 1979: 320) which occur in position 1 turns like
the following:

(123)   *145B*
             C: You don't have his number I don't suppose
(124)   *151*
             C: I wonder whether I could possibly have a copy of last year's
                tax return

In cataloguing such features of position 1 turns that obtain position
4 responses we would soon find ourselves in the business of noting
all the features of 'indirect requests' – including that same troublesome pre-verbal *please* that causes such difficulties in theories of
indirect speech acts.

We can now say that so-called indirect speech acts are position 1
turns – pre-requests – formulated so as to expect position 4 responses
in second turn. Questions about whether they have 'literal' or
'indirect' (or both) forces or meanings simply do not, on this view,
arise. Such position 1 turns mean whatever they mean; that they can
be formulated so as to project certain conversational trajectories is
something properly explored in the sequential analysis of successive
turns.

Let us just review the ingredients of such an analysis: (i) we make
a distinction between *position* and *turn*, which will allow us to claim
that indirect speech acts are position 1 turns that get position 4
responses in second turn; (ii) we note that preference organization,
in seeking to avoid request refusals, motivates the standard four-
position pre-request sequence; (iii) we show that there's a motivation
provided for the precise content of position 1 turns in such sequences –
namely, in order to avoid request rejections, the material used to
check whether a request is likely to succeed is drawn from the grounds

that would usually be used to reject the request (i.e. position 1 material is drawn from the dispreferred position 4 material), and therefore questions of ability and the existence of goods routinely crop up in pre-requests; (iv) we can find in preference organization a systematic preference for the avoidance of some sequences altogether, and this provides a motivation for the collapse of the four-position sequence into the two-position sequence consisting of a position 1 turn followed by a position 4 turn; (v), given (iv), and the general tendency for pre-s to be so formulated as to prefigure what is to come up next, we can expect position 1 turns to be expressly formulated to get position 4 turns in second turn – and hence for pre-requests of this sort to contain special markers (including *would, could, not, please*, etc.).

Careful comparison of this conversationally based account with the standard accounts of indirect speech acts will show that it renders many of the most problematic aspects of the indirect speech acts issue quite illusory. In actual fact the issue is not of great interest to conversation analysis, and we have covered it in detail only because it illustrates just one of a number of different ways in which CA insights can unravel linguistic problems.

6.5 Conclusions
6.5.1 *Conversation analysis and linguistics*

In this Chapter we have argued that conversation analysis has made important contributions to the understanding of utterance meaning, by showing how a large proportion of the situated significance of utterances can be traced to their surrounding sequential environments. Just as the problems of indirect speech acts can be re-analysed in CA terms, so many of the other central concepts in pragmatic theory may be amenable to CA (or other discourse-analytic) treatments. Grice's maxims are, of course, prime targets in this regard, but so are problems with presupposition (see Sacks, 1968, May 29; Prince, 1978a, 1978b), and even problems with the analysis of deixis (Watson, 1975; Sacks, 1976; Goodwin, 1977).

Less clearly, perhaps, CA has much to contribute too to the study of linguistic form: to prosodics, phonology, syntax and the description of the lexicon. It is worth spelling out here some of the observable relations between conversational and linguistic structure. Let us take some of the conversational organizations we have reviewed and ask how each may be a functional source of, or explanation for, certain linguistic structures and expressions.

The turn-taking system, for example, directly motivates the prosodic and syntactic signalling of turn completion and incompletion. The signalling of incompletion then provides a motivation for syntactic subordination, and predicts a preference for left-branching structures, or traces to the left of right-branching structures that may be forthcoming. Thus the English relative clause in *I am reading the book which I gave you* is more vulnerable to overlap than the equivalent clause in the comparable Dravidian or Japanese sentence, glossable as 'The I to-you given book I am reading'; but the vulnerability is reduced by the location of the WH-word at the head of the clause. On the other hand, the possibility that after completion the speaker may be able to continue, so that a turn may extend over more than one turn-constructional unit, makes it desirable that syntactic structures allow open-ended conjunction or addition to the right. In addition to such very general functional pressures, the turn-taking system provides more specific demands on linguistic structure: for example, the provision in the rules for the selection of next speaker directly motivates tag-formation. There are also many particles in languages that seem to have a function only explicable in relation to the turn-taking system, whether they are floor-holders (like *uh* in English), floor-returners (like *hm* in English), or turn-enders (like tag-particles in many languages).

The repair system also motivates many aspects of linguistic or utterance structure (Schegloff, 1979b). Apart from the markers of self-repair (glottal stops, *I mean*, etc.) and simple understanding or hearing checks (*Pardon?*, etc.), there are special syntactic features of NTRIs or echo-questions (cf. *John went to the what?*). There are also some interesting interactions between segmental phonology and repair (Jefferson, 1974).

Adjacency pair organization likewise motivates aspects of linguistic structure. Indeed a general explanation for the cross-linguistic prevalence of the three basic sentence-types (declarative, interrogative and imperative) may lie in the basic distinction between, respectively, utterances that are not first-pair parts, utterances that are first parts to other utterances, and utterances that are first parts to actions. Adjacency pair organization also motivates other ways of typing first parts of pairs as requiring specific kinds of second part (e.g. *Yes/No* vs. WH-questions; or the conventional sets of summons formats like *Hey!*, *Excuse me*, etc.). While preference organization, working across adjacency pairs, motivates the conventional announcers of dispreferred responses like *Well* and *Actually*.

Sequences of various sorts also have linguistic implications. As we noted for pre-sequences, it is possible to make a distinction between position and turn precisely because positions in a sequence are linguistically marked: thus pre-requests have those syntactic features (pre-verbal *please*, the polite past as in *I was wondering ...*, the *Could you ...* forms, etc.) previously associated with indirect illocutionary force. We have also noted the ways in which given vs. new information is packaged in the structure of pre-announcement sequences.

Topical organization is also an area that has direct linguistic implications, although it should not be thought that there is any direct connection between what has been talked of in linguistics under the rubric of **topic** or **theme** and the notion of discourse topic (see Keenan & Schieffelin, 1976). What is clear, however, is that certain syntactically marked constructions like left-dislocations (as in *John, I like him*) are used in attempts to control the flow of topic in the conversational sense (see e.g. Ochs & Duranti, 1979). Further, phrases like *By the way*, and interjections like *Hey*, mark introductions of new topics, while utterance-initial *Anyway* may mark return to prior topic (cf. Owen, 1982). Much work needs to be done here to clarify linguistic concepts of topic and their relation to discourse or conversational topic; given such clarification, it is possible that many syntactic constructions can be shown to be directly motivated by requirements of topical organization in conversation.

Finally, aspects of overall conversational organization also interact with linguistic structure, most noticeably in the linguistic formulae typical of openings and closings (Irvine, 1974; Ferguson, 1976), but also in the use of particles like *Well* and *Okay* in pre-closings, and the like.

In the present state of our knowledge, remarks of this sort can only be suggestive of the many, largely unexplored, ways in which conversational organization interacts with sentence and utterance structure.

6.5.2   *Some remaining questions*

It is perhaps no accident that the analyses produced by CA so far have a striking (if superficial) resemblance to the structuralist theories of linguistics that predominated before the 1960s. Both kinds of approach are concerned with corpora of recorded materials; both have as a central methodological tool the use of a 'slot and filler' heuristic – i.e. the investigation of how sequential (or *syntagmatic*) considerations restrict the class of items that may expectably follow, and of how items in that class contrast with one another (or stand in *paradigmatic* relations). The parallel is clearest perhaps in CA discussions of **formulation**, where the central issue is why one particular description is chosen from a set of paradigmatic alternatives (see Schegloff, 1972b; also Sacks, 1972 on **membership categorizations**). Just as structuralist analyses of linguistic structure have been shown to be theoretically inadequate as models of human competence, so in the long run CA analyses may perhaps be found deficient as rather simple reconstructions of the no doubt immensely complicated cognitive processes involved in conducting conversations. But meanwhile, at least, no other kind of investigation of conversational organization has yielded such a rich harvest of insights.

A possible puzzle that is raised here is whether, despite the remarks in section 6.1 above, CA is not after all a 'syntactic' model of conversation. For, it is largely concerned with constraints on sequential possibilities. However the differences are in fact substantial. First, some of the rules formulated in CA, e.g. the turn-taking rules described in section 6.2.1.1, are as much **regulative** as **constitutive**, to employ the distinction used by Searle (1969) to distinguish speech act rules (themselves constitutive of each kind of speech act) from, for example, traffic rules (merely regulative of independently existing traffic flow). Secondly, the CA rules describe unmarked expectations rather than the set of possible well-formed sequences or conversations; in this way such rules are much more like Grice's maxims than like linguistic rules. Consider, for example, the rule that given a first part of an adjacency pair, a second part should follow; as the notion of conditional relevance (which we introduced in 6.2.1) makes clear, failure to provide a second is itself a communicational resource that can be used to contribute effectively to conversation. So the adoption of the 'slot and filler' heuristic should not be construed as carrying with it the special sense of rule that is found in linguistics.

Another puzzle that arises is whether the unreflective use of categories like *request, invitation, greeting* and the like, does not embody an implicit theory of speech acts. Might it be that, while speech act theory has been attempting to provide an internal characterization of the function of turns, CA has been concerned with inter-turn relationships, so that some simple synthesis is possible? Workers in CA would reject such suggestions. First, they would point out that the terms *request, invitation, greeting,* and so on, are not the inventions of speech act theory, but rather part of a rich (if largely unexplored) natural language metalanguage (see e.g. Allwood, 1976; Verschueren, 1980). It does not follow from the existence of such terms either that there is a close connection between 'folk' metalanguage and the categories actually utilized in speech production, or that such categories are properly explicated by providing sets of necessary and sufficient conditions for speech act category membership (contrast: Searle, 1969; Levinson, 1979a). In any case, if pressed, CA workers would claim that intuitive use of categories like *request* should in fact be backed up by at least (i) a full sequential explication in terms of the range of expectable responses (like refusals, deferrals, compliances, etc.), (ii) an account of the way that requests are typically formulated in order to obtain the desired responses (see section 6.4.3 above). Secondly, it is incorrect to view CA as primarily concerned with inter-turn relationships: the discussion of examples like (59) or (102) above, as well as the re-analysis of indirect speech acts, should make clear that CA is specifically interested in the relationship between intra-turn structure and inter-turn organization or sequence. It is not clear, therefore, that CA has to yield any quarter at all to speech act theory (see Turner, 1974b).

This raises a final and central issue. To what extent are aspects of conversational organization universal? Or, to what extent are the features of that organization reviewed here restricted to English (or even a sub-variety thereof)? The issue is central for a number of reasons: if basic aspects of conversational organization are universal then: (a) linguists may be able to explain significant linguistic universals by pointing to universal functional pressures exerted by basic patterns of language use; (b) general patterns of child language acquisition may be explained by reference to a single basic learning situation, which is conversational; (c) pedagogical programmes in second language acquisition can take certain basic pragmatic parameters for granted; (d) there are distinct limits to the kind of social variation in the use of language that has been explored in the ethnography of speaking. Further, such universals would throw light on a basic facet of human nature – perhaps humans as a species are as much characterized by conversational activity as they are by differing cultures, complex social systems and tool-making.

At the present we simply do not know to what extent conversational organization is universal – very little comparative work has been done on this level for languages other than the familiar European ones (but see e.g. Moerman, 1977). But it seems safe to say that, of the features reviewed in this Chapter, those that have been described as *local management systems* – e.g. turn-taking, adjacency pair organization, repair systems – have a universal basis, even if the descriptions in this Chapter are culturally skewed in certain ways. Overall structural units – like the notion of a conversation – are much more likely to be culturally variable; indeed this is a significant theme in the ethnography of speaking (see e.g. Bauman & Sherzer, 1974). Intermediate organizations, like preference organization and pre-sequences, probably lie somewhere in between: such things probably exist in all cultures, although the kinds of actions they organize may be quite different (e.g. there is a difference even between American English and British English in the preferred response to a compliment). But these are speculations. Disentangling cultural particulars from universal tendencies can be a difficult job, and given the importance of the issue, this is likely to be a preoccupation of comparative pragmatics and sociolinguistics in the years to come.

Appendix: transcription conventions

The conventions used in this Chapter in all examples from cited sources (except those from Merritt, 1976, Sinclair, 1976 and Labov & Fanshel, 1977) are mostly those employed in Schenkein, 1978: xi–xvi and developed by Jefferson and others. The most important are:

//	point at which the current utterance is overlapped by that transcribed below
*	asterisks indicate the alignment of the points where overlap ceases
(0.0)	pauses or gaps in what is very approximately tenths of seconds

	(closer measurements often being irrelevant because the significance of pauses is linked to some sense of 'the beat' of any particular conversation – see Goodwin, 1981: 114)
(.)	micropause – potentially significant but very short pause, comparable perhaps to an average syllable duration or somewhere below 0.2 seconds' duration
CAPS	relatively high amplitude, or, in double parentheses, analytical labels
italics	syllables stressed by amplitude, pitch and duration
::	lengthened syllables
-	glottal-stop self-editing marker
= =	'latched' utterances, with no gap
?	not a punctuation mark, but a rising intonation contour
.	used to indicate falling intonation contour
,	used to indicate maintained ('continuing') intonation contour
(( ))	used to specify "some phenomenon that the transcriber does not want to wrestle with" or some non-vocal action, etc.
( )	uncertain passages of transcript
→	draws attention to location of phenomenon of direct interest to discussion
hh	indicates an audible out-breath, .hh an in-breath

7
Conclusions

In the history of human inquiry, philosophy has the place of the central sun, seminal and tumultuous: from time to time it throws off some portion of itself to take station as a science, a planet, cool and well regulated, progressing steadily towards a distant final state ... Is it not possible that the next century may see the birth, through the joint labours of philosophers, grammarians, and numerous other students of language, of a true and comprehensive *science of language*? Then we shall have rid ourselves of one more part of philosophy (there will still be plenty left) in the only way we ever get rid of philosophy, by kicking it upstairs. (Austin, 1956: 131–2)

7.0 Introduction

In these conclusions we shall try to tie together some of the loose strands of thought that have run through this book, by considering the relation between pragmatics and other disciplines. One discipline will stand noticeably absent: philosophy, the 'prodigal provider', cannot easily re-absorb the empirical studies that it has spawned (but cf. Atlas, 1979). The general tenor of this book has been the description of how, from original, mostly philosophical concepts, a series of empirical modes of investigation have developed, which jointly form the climate of the Anglo-American tradition in pragmatics. As the quotation indicates, Austin foresaw, and indeed hoped for, just this development of a field that he, perhaps more than any other single individual, did most to promote.

In the sections below, we shall first consider the inter-relations between pragmatics and the other 'core' components of linguistic theory, then between pragmatics and the 'hyphenated' linguistic disciplines (sociolinguistics and psycholinguistics in particular), and finally between pragmatics and less closely related fields.

371

7.1 Pragmatics and 'core' linguistics

A great deal has been said in this book about the relations between pragmatics and semantics; about how pragmatics may simplify semantic analyses (Chapter 3), allow a semantic theory to be built on homogeneous lines, and indeed on a logical base, and remove problems from the semantic field altogether. We have also argued that there must be an interaction between the two components (Chapter 1), and we have speculated on how this interaction may be responsible for many of the inferences we have called pragmatic (Chapters 3 and 4). More specifically, we have reviewed reasons why not all aspects of deixis can properly be thought of as semantic (in the truth-conditional sense), why presupposition in general should not be thought of as an essentially semantic problem, and why the performative analysis, which would have made illocutionary force a semantic notion, ultimately collapses. Further, the theory of implicature has helped immeasurably to tease apart the semantic and the pragmatic content of words and sentences. Finally, we have noted many ways in which pragmatics interacts with the theory and description of the lexicon; for example, we have noted the existence of pragmatic dimensions of meaning in most deictic words, the existence of pragmatic particles (like *well* and *anyway* in English) whose meaning is best explicated in terms of pragmatic concepts, and the predictive power of implicature in the concept of 'possible lexical item'.

However, as was indicated in the Preface, a different textbook might have stressed the relation between pragmatics and linguistic form, i.e. between pragmatics and phonology (including prosodics), morphology and syntax. Here it is worth assembling a set of reminders to indicate just how deep such relations may be. Indeed, the general process of the unburdening of intractable concepts from semantic theory and their absorption or re-analysis in pragmatics has an interesting corollary, namely that many of the putative interactions between semantics and linguistic form that were assembled, especially during the struggle between *generative semantics* and the *standard theory* in the early 1970s, must now be analysed as interactions between pragmatics and linguistic form.

Let us start by bringing together some of the interactions between syntax and pragmatics that we have noted in passing.[1] In discussing

---

[1] For more systematic collections of such interactions, see Green, 1978a; Gazdar, 1980a.

social deixis and conventional implicature, it was noted that honorifics raise significant problems in morphology and the description of predicate agreement. In discussing implicature, we noted that what G. Lakoff (1974) has called **syntactic amalgams** seem to be governed by generalized conversational implicature. There are many possible connections, both synchronic and diachronic, between the exploitative implicatures (the figures of speech) and syntax and semantics (see e.g. Sadock, 1974 on **queclaratives** or rhetorical questions in English). As for presupposition, since many kinds of presupposition-trigger seem to be essentially syntactic (e.g. clefts) or to have syntactic consequences (e.g. factives – see Kiparsky & Kiparsky, 1971), there seem to be intimate relations between syntactic processes and the inferences we call presuppositions. When discussing theories of speech acts we noted that (a) the fundamental syntactic facts about sentence-types (imperative, interrogative, declarative, optative, etc.) which in turn govern all sorts of further syntactic facts, may plausibly be related (though exactly how is a matter of controversy) to concepts of illocutionary force; (b) there are innumerable interactions between indirect illocutionary force and sentence structure. Since the notion of indirect illocutionary force may be re-analysed in conversation analytic terms, as argued in Chapter 6, it follows that there are strong relations between discourse structure and sentence structure in this area too. There are many other kinds of interaction between conversational structure and syntax that were brought up at the end of Chapter 6; for example, there are many general syntactic processes that seem to be motivated by aspects of conversational organization like turn-taking and repair. But perhaps the most interesting lie in the area subsumed by the (rather unclear) notion of topic, for many of the syntactic processes called **movement rules** seem to have the function of indicating how information in the clause relates to what has been talked about before. Here a general speculation, raised in Chapter 1, becomes relevant: perhaps the great bulk of the derivational machinery in the syntax of natural languages can be functionally explained by reference to the specialized conversational jobs that many sentence structures seem to be designed to perform (see papers in Givon, 1979a).

Relations between pragmatics and phonology (including prosodics, and intonation in particular) have received much less attention. But we have remarked in passing how there are connections between social deixis and phonology (e.g. palatalization in Basque; Corum, 1975), and social deixis and prosodics (e.g. Tzeltal polite/formal falsetto; Brown & Levinson, 1978: 272). Grice (1978: 121) has attempted to give an account of the significance of contrastive stress in terms of conversational implicature, while the relation of stress to presupposition has long been noted (Lakoff, 1971; Chomsky, 1972; Wilson & Sperber, 1979). Intonation clearly plays some role in the disambiguation of actual (often indirect) illocutionary force (Liberman & Sag, 1974), and can invoke activities or frames of interpretation, thus acting as **contextualization cues** (Gumperz, 1977). The role of prosodic factors in the governing of conversational interaction has been noted in many places: we have referred to their role in the turn-taking system, in the lengthened syllables of overlapping speech or dispreferred responses, in the marked introduction of new topics, and so on. However, there have been few attempts to provide some systematic account of these phenomena (but see Brazil, Coulthard & Johns, 1980), and this is a field that needs much further attention.

7.2 Pragmatics, sociolinguistics and psycholinguistics

We noted in Chapter 1 that only the most restrictive definitions of pragmatics would draw anything like a clear boundary between sociolinguistics and pragmatics, for sociolinguistics is a field that cross-cuts linguistic levels or components of a grammar. Indeed pragmatics and sociolinguistics share many areas of common interest, and sociolinguists have contributed much to certain areas of pragmatics, especially the study of social deixis and speech acts and their use. However, pragmatics in turn has much to contribute to sociolinguistics; for in trying to understand the social significance of patterns of language usage, it is essential to understand the underlying structural properties and processes that constrain verbal interaction. So, for example, Bernstein (1973: Chapter 6) has attributed sociological causes to patterns of hesitation without understanding the underlying conversational motivations for such patterns (e.g. the role of preference structure). Similarly, sociolinguists have tended to ignore the conversational motivations for the use and location of address forms (contrast Ervin-Tripp, 1972 and Brown & Levinson, 1978: 187ff). Indeed conversation analysis in general has a great deal to offer to sociolinguistics. For example, the view of conversation as

basic or paradigmatic and other forms of talk exchange as speciali-
zations (Sacks, Schegloff & Jefferson, 1978: 45ff; Atkinson & Drew,
1979) may help to put the ethnography of speaking on a sounder
comparative basis (cf. Hymes, 1972). Similarly, the variationist
paradigm associated with Labov (1972a) would benefit greatly from
the systematic application of Labov's own observation that sociolinguistic variables are in part discourse-conditioned (Labov &
Fanshel, 1977: 139). But the fields have so many common concerns
that there is no real danger of the lack of cross-fertilization, especially
amongst sociolinguists with an interest in language understanding
(Ervin-Tripp, 1976; Gumperz, 1977).

Relations between pragmatics and psycholinguistics may be
considered under two heads. First, there are the inter-relations
between pragmatics and cognitive psychology, and especially theories
of language processing and production. Since both disciplines share
a basic interest in the processes of language understanding, they have
a mutual interest in the development of concepts like implicature,
presupposition and illocutionary force. Here, pragmatics is likely to
be the provider, psycholinguistics the tester, refiner or rejector. For,
in the development of pragmatic concepts, there has been little
consideration of issues of psychological plausibility, and pragmatic
theories may have much to gain from rigorous testing by psychologists
(see e.g. Clark & Lucy, 1975, on indirect requests). On the other hand,
advances in discourse analysis may show that certain language
production parameters – e.g. pauses, hesitations and self-editings –
that psycholinguists have taken to be straightforward indicators of
internal cognitive processes are in fact subject to manipulation for
interactional purposes (see e.g. Goodwin, 1981: 6off).

The other branch of psycholinguistics that has much common
ground with pragmatics is developmental psychology concerned with
language acquisition. This is a burgeoning field and, as made clear
in Chapter 1, it has drawn much from pragmatics; it is now beginning
to contribute much in return about the way in which contexts of
language acquisition play a crucial role in how what is learned when.
Developmental pragmatics has not been covered in this book, but
useful sources are Fletcher & Garman, 1979 and Ochs & Schieffelin,
1979.

7.3 **Applied pragmatics: pragmatics and other fields**

Pragmatics has potential application to all fields with a stake in how utterances are understood. Such fields include those, like the study of rhetoric or literature, that are not immediately concerned with practical problems (thus Sperber & Wilson (forthcoming) see a close relation between pragmatics and rhetoric). But they also include fields that are primarily concerned with solving problems in communication, and it is here that the applications of pragmatics are likely to be of direct practical importance. Four areas in particular seem to be especially promising in this regard: so-called applied linguistics (i.e. the theory and practice of second language learning), the study of man–machine interaction, the study of communicational difficulties in face-to-face interaction and the study of communicational difficulties that arise when communicators are not in face-to-face interaction. In these four areas applications of pragmatic insights promise to alleviate communicational problems. Let us take them one by one.

The application of pragmatics to problems in second language learning is based on the assumption that, despite the probable universality of processes like implicature, there are likely to be significant differences not only in the structure of languages but in their use (Hymes, 1972). Even where there are underlying universals of usage, as seems to be the case in the construction of polite expressions (Brown & Levinson, 1978), there is considerable room for cross-cultural misunderstanding: for example, German speakers seem to be significantly more direct, or less polite, in requests and complaints than English speakers (House & Kasper, 1981; see also Walters, 1981). There thus arises the possibility of a systematic contrastive pragmatics, that would isolate potential areas of misunderstanding arising from the learner's assumption that a construction in the language being learnt will have the same implicatures, presuppositions, illocutionary force and conversational uses as some analogous construction in the native language. There is much current research on such issues.

In the field of man–machine interaction (i.e. the study of the difficulties humans experience interacting with computers), pragmatics also has direct applications. The problems here arise from the need for more and more workers with little experience of computers to use them successfully; if computer programmers can make the language shared by machine and human work on principles similar to natural languages and their rules of usage, the computer age will not need to await the massive re-education of the labour force. But such engineering requires a prior analysis of the properties of natural language usage, and it is here that pragmatics promises some help. For example, knowledge that the quantifier *some* can, but need not, implicate 'not all', allows the programmer to avoid making a direct match between the English word and the logical existential quantifier; in translating English input into machine readable programming language, some program component must test for the likely reading in a particular context. Work proceeds apace in the research divisions of the giant computer companies on precisely this sort of problem – on the modelling of presupposition, illocutionary force and conversational routines (see papers in Joshi, Webber & Sag, 1981). In addition, but with applications further in the future, there are projects concerned with speech synthesis and comprehension; as the immediate technical difficulties in these areas are overcome there will be increasing interest here too in the contributions of pragmatics to theories of language understanding.

Finally, there are the contributions that pragmatics can make to problems of communication between humans who speak (more or less) the same language. For example, there can be significant inter-ethnic misunderstandings due to different pragmatic analyses of utterances whose literal content is perfectly well understood; leading questions, probes, hints, etc., may well not be interpreted correctly. Here work by Gumperz (1977; 1982; see also Gumperz, Jupp & Roberts, 1979) has opened up an area of great practical importance. Another area where pragmatic analyses may be of great interest is the design (or more often, re-design) of institutional proceedings; how should, for example, newly introduced small claims courts be organized? Should they be conducted on more conversational lines than ordinary courts of law, or are the traditional procedures actually more conducive to the orderly pursuit of truth (see Atkinson & Drew, 1979)? Similar questions continually arise among those interested in reforming or improving classroom practices. A rather different set of concerns is raised by the possible existence of language pathologies that are essentially pragmatic; for example, there may be difficulties that arise in the rehabilitation of brain-damaged patients that are specifically pragmatic in nature. If this turns out to be the case, again practical help will rely on prior pragmatic analysis of normal language usage (see Lucas, 1981). Finally, there are familiar communicational problems that arise when humans communicate at a remove through space or time, by means of recorded or written messages. In Chapter 2 we explored how natural languages are constructed, so to speak, around the assumption of face-to-face interaction, and we noted how deictic terms can be misinterpreted when this face-to-face condition is not met. Analytical considerations may be quite helpful here to the design of crucial notices (e.g. on roads, or for the maintenance crew of aircraft, etc.), questionnaires, and other down to earth usages of written language. They may also be useful in the design of special programmes of learning for those who have difficulty in literate skills. As another example, quite interesting problems arise when normal conversational turn-taking cannot operate, as in communications by field radio, telex, or the message capabilities of computer terminals; how should substitutes for the normal practices be designed? It is only recently that the possibility has arisen of informed advice on such relatively simple but important issues – advice based on the detailed study of natural language usage.

As always in the application of academic ideas to vital practical issues, there is the very real possibility of the premature acceptance and application of untested concepts and theories (with the sorts of potential dangers made clear by the premature application of sociolinguistic theories to educational practices – see the critique in Dittmar, 1976). Here the pragmaticist has a responsibility to point out the limitations of current approaches, and to demonstrate the empirical basis for the working categories employed. It is for this reason that this book has surveyed a relatively restricted set of issues in a depth that will make those limitations clear, rather than covered a larger area in a relatively superficial way. Austin's vision of a "true and comprehensive *science of language*" still, as he predicted, has some time to wait.

Bibliography

Albert, E. M. (1972). Culture patterning of speech behavior in Burundi. In Gumperz & Hymes (1972: 72–105).

Allwood, J. (1972). Negation and the strength of presuppositions. Logical Grammar Report 2. University of Gothenberg, Department of Linguistics. (Reprinted in Ö. Dahl (ed.) *Logic, Pragmatics and Grammar* (1977). University of Gothenberg, Department of Linguistics, pp. 11–52.

Allwood, J. (1976). *Linguistic Communication in Action and Co-operation: A Study in Pragmatics*. Gothenberg Monographs in Linguistics 2. University of Gothenberg, Department of Linguistics.

Allwood, J. (1977). A critical look at speech act theory. In Ö. Dahl (ed.) *Logic, Pragmatics and Grammar*. University of Gothenberg, Department of Linguistics, pp. 53–69.

Allwood, J., Andersson, L-G., & Dahl, Ö. (1977). *Logic in Linguistics*. Cambridge: Cambridge University Press.

Anderson, S. R. (1971). On the linguistic status of the performative/constative distinction. Mimeograph, Indiana University Linguistics Club.

Anderson, S. R. & Keenan, E. L. (in press). Deixis. In Shopen (ed.) (in press).

Annamalai, E. & Levinson, S. C. (in press). Why presuppositions are not conventional: some cross-linguistic evidence. *Linguistics*.

Aqvist, L. (1972). *Performatives and Verifiability by the Use of Language*. Filosofiska Studier 14. University of Uppsala.

Argyle, M. (1973). *Social Interaction*. London: Tavistock Publications Ltd.

Atkinson, J. M. (1982). Understanding formality: the categorization and production of 'formal' interaction. *British Journal of Sociology*, 33.1, 86–117.

Atkinson, J. M. & Drew, P. (1979). *Order in Court*. London: Macmillan.

Atkinson, J. M. & Heritage, J. (eds.) (in press). *Structures of Social Action*. Cambridge: Cambridge University Press.

Atkinson, M. (1979). Prerequisites for reference. In Ochs & Schieffelin (1979: 229–50).

Atkinson, M. (1982). *Explanations in the Study of Child Language Development*. Cambridge: Cambridge University Press.

Atlas, J. D. (1975a). Frege's polymorphous concept of presupposition and its role in a theory of meaning. *Semantikos*, 1.1, 29–44.

Atlas, J. D. (1975b). Presupposition: a semantico-pragmatic account. *Pragmatics Microfiche*, 1.4, D13–G14.

Atlas, J. D. (1977). Negation, ambiguity, and presupposition. *Linguistics & Philosophy*, 1, 321–36.

Atlas, J. D. (1979). How linguistics matters to philosophy: presupposition, truth and meaning. In Oh & Dinneen (1979: 265–81).

379

Bibliography

Atlas, J. D. (1980). A note on a confusion of pragmatic and semantic aspects of negation. *Linguistics & Philosophy*, 3, 411–14.

Atlas, J. D. & Levinson, S. (1981). *It*-clefts, informativeness and logical form: radical pragmatics (revised standard version). In Cole (1981: 1–61).

Austin, J. L. (1956). Ifs and cans. *Proceedings of the British Academy*, (1956), 109–32. Reprinted in Austin (1970a: 205–32).

Austin, J. L. (1962). *How To Do Things With Words*. Oxford: Clarendon Press.

Austin, J. L. (1970a). *Philosophical Papers*. Oxford: Oxford University Press.

Austin, J. L. (1970b). Performative utterances. In Austin (1970a: 233–52).

Austin, J. L. (1971). Performative–Constative. In Searle (1971: 13–22).

Ayer, A. J. (1936). *Language, Truth and Logic*. London: Victor Gollancz.

Bach, K. & Harnish, R. M. (1979). *Linguistic Communication and Speech Acts*. Cambridge, Mass.: MIT Press.

Ballmer, T. (1978). *Logical Grammar*. Amsterdam: North-Holland.

Barense, D. D. (1980). Tense structure and reference: a first order non-modal approach. Mimeo. Indiana University Linguistics Club.

Bar-Hillel, Y. (1954). Indexical expressions. *Mind*, 63, 359–79. (Reprinted in Bar-Hillel (1970: 69–89).)

Bar-Hillel, Y. (1970). *Aspects of Language*. Amsterdam: North-Holland.

Bar-Hillel, Y. (1971). *Pragmatics of Natural Language*. Dordrecht: Reidel.

Bates, E. (1976). *Language and Context: the Acquisition of Pragmatics*. New York: Academic Press.

Bauman, R. & Sherzer, J. (eds.) (1974). *Explorations in the Ethnography of Speaking*. Cambridge: Cambridge University Press.

Bean, S. (1978). *Symbolic and Pragmatic Semantics*. Chicago: University of Chicago Press.

Beattie, G. (1978a). Floor apportionment and gaze in conversational dyads. *British Journal of Social & Clinical Psychology*, 17, 7–16.

Beattie, G. (1978b). Sequential temporal patterns of speech and gaze in dialogue. *Semiotica*, 23.2, 29–52.

Beaugrande, R. de & Dressler, W. (1981). *Introduction to Text Linguistics*. London: Longman.

Beck, B. (1972). *Peasant Society in Konku*. Vancouver: University of British Columbia Press.

Bernstein, B. (1973). *Class, Codes and Control*, Vol. 1. St Albans, Herts.: Paladin.

Black, M. (1947). Limitations of a behavioristic semiotic. *Philosophical Review*, 56, 258–72.

Black, M. (1962). *Models and Metaphors*. Ithaca, New York: Cornell University Press.

Black, M. (1979). More about metaphor. In Ortony (1979a: 19–43).

Boër, S. G. & Lycan, W. G. (1976). The myth of semantic presupposition. Mimeo. Indiana University Linguistics Club.

Boër, S. G. & Lycan, W. G. (1978). A performadox in truth-conditional semantics. *Pragmatics Microfiche*, 3.3, A3–C12. (Revised version printed in *Linguistics & Philosophy* (1980) 4.1, 71–100.)

Bolinger, D. L. (1967). The imperative in English. In M. Halle, H. G. Lunt, H. McLean & C. H. von Schooneveld (eds.) *To Honour Roman Jakobson: Essays on the Occasion of his Seventieth Birthday*. Janua Linguarum ser. major 31. The Hague: Mouton, pp. 335–62.

Brazil, D., Coulthard, M. & Johns, C. (1980). *Discourse Intonation and Language Teaching*. London: Longman.

Brockway, D. (1979). Semantic constraints on relevance. MS. University College London. Published as Brockway (1981).

Brockway, D. (1981). Semantic constraints on relevance. In Parret, Sbisà & Verschueren (1981: 57–78).

Brown, P. & Levinson, S. (1978). Universals in language usage: politeness phenomena. In E. Goody (ed.) *Questions and Politeness : Strategies in Social Interaction.* Cambridge: Cambridge University Press, pp. 56–311.

Brown, P. & Levinson, S. (1979). Social structure, groups and interaction. In K. Scherer & H. Giles (eds.) *Social Markers in Speech.* Cambridge: Cambridge University Press, pp. 291–347.

Brown, R. & Gilman, A. (1960). The pronouns of power and solidarity. In Sebeok (1960: 253–76). (Reprinted in Giglioli (1972: 252–82).)

Bruner, J. (1975). The ontogenesis of speech acts. *Journal of Child Language,* 2, 1–20.

Bühler, K. (1934). *Sprachtheorie.* Jena: Fisher. (Reprinted Stuttgart: Fisher, 1965.)

Burks, A. W. (1949). Icon, index and symbol. *Philosophy and Phenomenological Research,* 9, 673–89.

Burling, R. (1970). *Man's Many Voices.* New York: Holt, Rinehart & Winston.

Butterworth, B. (1975). Hesitation and semantic planning in speech. *Journal of Psycholinguistic Research,* 1, 75–87.

Butterworth, B., Hine, R. & Brady, R. (1977). Speech and interaction in sound-only communication channels. *Semiotica,* 20.2, 81–99.

Button, G. & Casey, N. (in press). Generating topic. In Atkinson & Heritage (in press).

Carling, C. & Moore, T. (1982). *Understanding Language : Towards a Post-Chomskyan Linguistics.* London: Macmillan.

Carnap, R. (1938). Foundations of logic and mathematics. In O. Neurath, R. Carnap & C. W. Morris (eds.) *International Encyclopedia of Unified Science,* Vol. 1, pp. 139–214.

Carnap, R. (1955). On some concepts of pragmatics. *Philosophical Studies,* 6, 89–91.

Carnap, R. (1956). *Meaning and Necessity.* 2nd ed. Chicago: University of Chicago Press.

Carnap, R. (1959). *Introduction to Semantics.* Cambridge: Harvard University Press.

Charniak, E. (1972). *Towards a Model of Children's Story Comprehension.* MIT Artificial Intelligence Laboratory Monographs, No. 226. Cambridge, Mass.

Cherry, C. (ed.) (1974). *Pragmatic Aspects of Human Communication.* Dordrecht: Reidel.

Chomsky, N. (1957). *Syntactic Structures.* The Hague: Mouton.

Chomsky, N. (1965). *Aspects of the Theory of Syntax.* Cambridge, Mass.: MIT Press.

Chomsky, N. (1972). *Studies on Semantics in Generative Grammar.* The Hague: Mouton.

Clark, H. & Haviland, S. E. (1977). Comprehension and the given-new contract. In R. Freedle (ed.) *Discourse Production and Comprehension.* Hillsdale, NJ: Lawrence Erlbaum, pp. 1–40.

Clark, H. & Lucy, P. (1975). Understanding what is meant from what is said: a study in conversationally conveyed requests. *Journal of Verbal Learning and Verbal Behavior,* 14, 56–72.

Cohen, L. J. (1971). The logical particles of natural language. In Bar-Hillel (1971: 50–68).

Cohen, L. J. (1979). The semantics of metaphor. In Ortony (1979a: 64–77).

Cole, P. (1975). The synchronic and diachronic status of conversational implicatures. In Cole & Morgan (1975: 257–88).

Cole, P. (ed.) (1978). *Syntax and Semantics 9 : Pragmatics.* New York: Academic Press.

Cole, P. (ed.) (1981). *Radical Pragmatics.* New York: Academic Press.

Cole, P. & Morgan, J. L. (eds.) (1975). *Syntax and Semantics 3 : Speech Acts.* New York: Academic Press.

Comrie, B. (1975). Polite plurals and predicate agreement. *Language,* 51, 406–18.

Comrie, B. (1976a). *Aspect : an Introduction to the Study of Verbal Aspect and Related Problems.* Cambridge: Cambridge University Press.

381

Bibliography

Comrie, B. (1976b). Linguistic politeness axes: speaker–addressee, speaker–reference, speaker–bystander. *Pragmatics Microfiche*, 1.7, A3–B1.

Corbett, G. (1976). Syntactic destructors (problems with address especially in Russian). *Pragmatics Microfiche*, 1.7, A3–B1.

Corum, C. (1975). Basques, particles and baby-talk: a case for pragmatics. In *Proceedings of the First Annual Meeeting of the Berkeley Linguistics Society*, pp. 90–9.

Coulmas, F. (ed.) (1981). *Conversational Routine: Explorations in Standardized Communication Situations and Prepatterned Speech*. The Hague: Mouton.

Coulthard, M. (1977). *An Introduction to Discourse Analysis*. London: Longman.

Coulthard, M. & Brazil, D. (1979). *Exchange Structure*. Discourse Analysis Monographs, 5. Birmingham: Birmingham University. (Reprinted in M. Coulthard & M. Montgomery (eds.) *Studies in Discourse Analysis*. London: Routledge & Kegan Paul, pp. 82–106.)

Cresswell, M. (1973). *Logic and Languages*. London: Methuen.

Crystal, D. (1969). *Prosodic Systems and Intonation in English*. Cambridge: Cambridge University Press.

Davidson, D. (1980). What metaphors mean. In Platts, M. (ed.) *Reference, Truth and Reality*. London: Routledge & Kegan Paul, pp. 238–54.

Davidson, D. & Harman, G. (eds.) (1972). *Semantics of Natural Language*. Dordrecht: Reidel.

Davidson, J. (1978). An instance of negotiation in a call closing. *Sociology*, 12.1, 123–33.

Davidson, J. (in press). Subsequent versions of invitations, offers, requests and proposals dealing with potential or actual rejection. In Atkinson & Heritage (in press).

Davison, A. (1973). *Performatives, Felicity Conditions, and Adverbs*. Unpublished PhD dissertation, University of Chicago.

Davison, A. (1975). Indirect speech acts and what to do with them. In Cole & Morgan (1975: 143–86).

Dittmar, N. (1976). *Sociolinguistics: a Critical Survey of Theory and Application*. London: Arnold.

Dixon, R. M. W. (1972). *The Dyirbal Language of North Queensland*. Cambridge: Cambridge University Press.

Dixon, R. M. W. (1980). *The Languages of Australia*. Cambridge: Cambridge University Press.

Donnellan, K. S. (1966). Reference and definite descriptions. *Philosophical Review*, 75, 281–304. Reprinted in Steinberg & Jakobovits (1971: 100–14).

Donnellan, K. S. (1978). Speaker reference, descriptions and anaphora. In Cole (1978: 47–68).

Dore, J. (1975). Holophrases, speech acts, and language universals. *Journal of Child Language*, 2, 21–40.

Dowty, D. R., Peters, S. & Wall, R. (1981). *Introduction to Montague Semantics*. Dordrecht: Reidel.

Dressler, W. (1972). *Einführung in die Textlinguistik*. Tübingen: Niemeyer.

Drew, P. (1981). The organisation and management of corrections in 'instructional' talk: a response to Wells and Montgomery. In P. French & M. MacLure (eds.), *Adult–Child Conversation: Studies in Structure and Process*. London: Croom Helm, pp. 244–67.

Dummett, M. (1973). *Frege: Philosophy of Language*. London: Duckworth.

Duncan, S. (1974). Some signals and rules for taking speaker turns in conversations. In S. Weitz (ed.) *Nonverbal Communication*. New York: Oxford University Press, pp. 298–311.

Duncan, S. & Fiske, D. W. (1977). *Face to Face Interaction: Research, Methods and Theory*. Hillsdale, NJ: Lawrence Erlbaum Associates.

Duranti, A. & Ochs, E. (1979). Left-dislocation in Italian conversation. In Givon (1979a: 377–418).

Edmondson, W. (1978). A note on pragmatic connectives. *Interlanguage Studies Bulletin* (Utrecht), pp. 100–6.

Edmondson, W. (1979). *A Model for the Analysis of Spoken Discourse*. Unpublished PhD dissertation, Ruhr-Universität, Bochum.

Edmondson, W. (1981). *Spoken Discourse : A Model for Analysis*. London: Longman.

Ervin-Tripp, S. (1972). On sociolinguistic rules: alternation and co-occurrence. In Gumperz & Hymes (1972: 213–50).

Ervin-Tripp, S. (1976). Is Sybil there? The structure of American English directives. *Language in Society*, 5, 25–66.

Ervin-Tripp, S. (1979). Children's verbal turn-taking. In Ochs & Schieffelin (1979: 391–414).

Ervin-Tripp, S. (1981). How to make and understand a request. In Parret, Sbisà & Verschueren (1981: 195–210).

Ervin-Tripp, S. & Mitchell-Kernan, C. (eds.) (1977). *Child Discourse*. New York: Academic Press.

Fann, K. T. (ed.) (1969). *Symposium on J. L. Austin*. London: Routledge & Kegan Paul.

Ferguson, C. A. (1964). Diglossia. In Hymes (1964: 429–39). (Reprinted in Giglioli (1972: 252–82).)

Ferguson, C. A. (1976). The structure and use of politeness formulas. *Language in Society*, 5, 137–51. (Reprinted in Coulmas (1981: 21–35).)

Fillmore, C. J. (1966). Deictic categories in the semantics of *come*. *Foundations of Language*, 2, 219–27.

Fillmore, C. J. (1971a). Verbs of judging: an exercise in semantic description. In Fillmore & Langendoen (1971: 273–90).

Fillmore, C. J. (1971b). Towards a theory of deixis. *The PCCLLU Papers* (Department of Linguistics, University of Hawaii), 3.4, 219–41.

Fillmore, C. J. (1973). May we come in? *Semiotica*, 9, 97–116.

Fillmore, C. J. (1975). *Santa Cruz Lectures on Deixis, 1971*. Mimeo, Indiana University Linguistics Club.

Fillmore, C. J. (1981). Pragmatics and the description of discourse. In Cole (1981: 143–66).

Fillmore, C. J. & Langendoen, D. T. (eds.) (1971). *Studies in Linguistic Semantics*. New York: Holt, Rinehart & Winston.

Fischer, J. L. (1972). The stylistic significance of consonantal sandhi in Trukese and Ponapean. In Gumperz & Hymes (1972: 498–511).

Fletcher, P. & Garman, M. (eds.) (1979). *Language Acquisition*. Cambridge: Cambridge University Press.

Fodor, J. A. & Katz, J. J. (eds.) (1964). *The Structure of Language : Readings in the Philosophy of Language*. Englewood Cliffs, NJ: Prentice-Hall.

Fogelin, R. (1967). *Evidence and Meaning*. New York: Humanities Press.

Foley, W. & Van Valin, R. D. (in press). Information packaging in the clause. In Shopen (in press).

Forman, D. (1974). The speaker knows best principle. *Papers from the 10th Regional Meeting of the Chicago Linguistic Society*, pp. 162–77.

Fraser, B. (1974a). An examination of the performative analysis. *Papers in Linguistics*, 7, 1–40.

Fraser, B. (1974b). An analysis of vernacular performative verbs. Mimeo, Indiana University Linguistics Club.

Frege, G. (1952). On sense and reference. In P. T. Geach and M. Black (eds.) *Translations from the Philosophical Writings of Gottlob Frege*. Oxford: Blackwell, pp. 56–78.

Bibliography

(Originally published 1892, as Über Sinn und Bedeutung. In *Zeitschrift für Philosophie und philosophische Kritik*, 100, 25–50.)

Frei, H. (1944). Systèmes de déictiques. *Acta Linguistica*, 4, 111–29.

Furberg, M. (1971). *Saying and Meaning*. Oxford: Blackwell.

Gale, R. M. (1968). Indexical signs, egocentric particulars, and token-reflexive words. In P. Edwards (ed.) *Encyclopedia of Philosophy*, Vol. 4. New York: Collier Macmillan, pp. 151–5.

Garfinkel, H. (1972). Remarks on ethnomethodology. In Gumperz & Hymes (1972: 301–24).

Garner, R. T. (1971). 'Presupposition' in philosophy and linguistics. In Fillmore & Langendoen (1971: 23–44).

Garvin, R. L. & Reisenberg, S. H. (1952). Respect behavior on Ponape: an ethnolinguistic study. *American Anthropologist*, 54, 201–20.

Gazdar, G. (1978). Heavy parentheses wipe-out rules, okay? *Linguistics & Philosophy*, 2, 281–9.

Gazdar, G. (1979a). *Pragmatics: Implicature, Presupposition and Logical Form*. New York: Academic Press.

Gazdar, G. (1979b). A solution to the projection problem. In Oh & Dinneen (1979: 57–89).

Gazdar, G. (1980a). Pragmatic constraints on linguistic production. In B. Butterworth (ed.) *Language Production*, Vol. 1: *Speech and Talk*. New York: Academic Press, pp. 49–68.

Gazdar, G. (1980b). Reply to Kiefer. *Linguisticae Investigationes*, 3, 375–7.

Gazdar, G. (1981). Speech act assignment. In Joshi, Webber & Sag (1981: 64–83).

Gazdar, G. (1982). Phrase structure grammar. In P. Jacobson & G. K. Pullum (eds.) *On the Nature of Syntactic Representation*. Dordrecht: Reidel.

Gazdar, G. & Klein, E. (1977). Context-sensitive transderivational constraints and conventional implicature. *Papers from the Thirteenth Regional Meeting of the Chicago Linguistic Society*, pp. 137–46.

Gazdar, G. & Pullum, G. (1976). Truth-functional connectives in natural language. *Papers from the Twelfth Regional Meeting of the Chicago Linguistic Society*, pp. 220–34.

Gazdar, G. & Rogers, A. (1978). Conventional implicature: a critical problem. MS. Department of Linguistics, University of Texas at Austin.

Gazdar, G., Klein, E. & Pullum, G. (1978). *A Bibliography of Contemporary Linguistic Research*. New York: Garland.

Geach, P. T. (1962). *Reference and Generality*. Ithaca: Cornell University Press.

Geertz, C. (1960). *The Religion of Java*. Glencoe, Ill.: Free Press. (Extract reprinted as Geertz (1972).)

Geertz, C. (1972). Linguistic etiquette. In Pride & Holmes (1972: 167–79).

Geiss, M. & Zwicky, A. (1971). On invited inferences. *Linguistic Inquiry*, 2, 561–5.

Giglioli, P. P. (ed.) (1972). *Language and Social Context*. Harmondsworth: Penguin.

Givon, T. (ed.) (1979a). *Syntax and Semantics 12: Discourse and Syntax*. New York: Academic Press.

Givon, T. (1979b). From discourse to syntax: grammar as a processing strategy. In Givon (1979a: 81–114).

Godard, D. (1977). Same setting, different norms: phone call beginnings in France and the United States. *Language in Society*, 6.2, 209–20.

Goffman, E. (1976). Replies and responses. *Language in Society*, 5, 257–313.

Goldberg, J. (1982). *Discourse Particles: an Analysis of the Role of 'Y'know', 'I mean', 'Well', and 'Actually' in Conversation*. Unpublished PhD dissertation, University of Cambridge.

Goldman-Eisler, F. (1968). *Psycholinguistics: Experiments in Spontaneous Speech*. London: Academic Press.

Goldman-Eisler, F. (1980). Psychological mechanisms of speech production as studied through the analysis of simultaneous translation. In B. Butterworth (ed.) *Language Production*, Volume 1: *Speech and Talk*. New York: Academic Press, pp. 143-54.

Goodwin, C. (1977). *Some Aspects of the Interaction of Speaker and Hearer in the Construction of the Turn at Talk in Natural Conversation*. Unpublished PhD dissertation, University of Pennsylvania. (Revised version published as Goodwin (1981).)

Goodwin, C. (1979a). The interactive construction of a sentence in natural conversation. In Psathas (1979: 97-121).

Goodwin, G. (1979b). Review of Duncan & Fiske (1977). *Language in Society*, 8.3, 439-44.

Goodwin, C. (1981). *Conversational Organization: Interaction between Speakers and Hearers*. New York: Academic Press.

Goody, E. (ed.) (1978). *Questions and Politeness: Strategies in Social Interaction*. Cambridge: Cambridge University Press.

Goody, J. (1977). *Domestication of the Savage Mind*. Cambridge: Cambridge University Press.

Gordon, D. & Lakoff, G. (1971). Conversational postulates. *Papers from the Seventh Regional Meeting of the Chicago Linguistic Society*, pp. 63-84.

Gordon, D. & Lakoff, G. (1975). Conversational postulates. In Cole & Morgan (1975: 83-106). (Reprint of Gordon & Lakoff, 1971.)

Graham, K. (1977). *J. L. Austin: a Critique of Ordinary Language Philosophy*. Hassocks, Sussex: Harvester Press.

Green, G. (1975). How to get people to do things with words: the whimperative question. In Cole & Morgan (1975: 107-42).

Green, G. (1978a). Pragmatic motivation and exploitation of syntactic rules. MS. Dept of Linguistics, University of Illinois, Urbana.

Green, G. (1978b). *Discourse Functions of Inversion Constructions*. Technical Report No. 98, Center for the Study of Reading, University of Illinois, Urbana.

Grice, H. P. (1957). Meaning. *Philosophical Review*, 67. (Reprinted in Steinberg & Jakobovits (1971: 53-9) and in Strawson (1971: 39-48).)

Grice, H. P. (1961). The causal theory of perception. *Proceedings of the Aristotelian Society*, Supplementary Vol. 35, 121-52.

Grice, H. P. (1967). *Logic and Conversation*. Unpublished MS. of the William James Lectures, Harvard University.

Grice, H. P. (1968). Utterer's meaning, sentence-meaning, and word-meaning. *Foundations of Language*, 4, 1-18. (Reprinted in Searle (1971: 54-70).)

Grice, H. P. (1973). Probability, defeasibility and mood operators. Mimeo. Paper delivered at the Texas Conference on Performatives, Presuppositions and Implicatures, 1973.

Grice, H. P. (1975). Logic and conversation. In Cole & Morgan (1975: 41-58). (Part of Grice (1967).)

Grice, H. P. (1978). Further notes on logic and conversation. In Cole (1978: 113-28). (Part of Grice (1967).)

Grice, H. P. (1981). Presupposition and conversational implicature. In Cole (1981: 183-98).

Griffiths, P. (1979). Speech acts and early sentences. In Fletcher & Garman (1979: 105-20).

Grossman, R. E., San, L. J. & Vance, T. J. (eds.) (1975). *Papers from the Parasession on Functionalism*. Chicago: Chicago Linguistic Society.

Grosu, A. (1972). *The Strategic Content of Island Constraints*. Ohio State University Working Papers in Linguistics 13, 1-225.

Gumperz, J. J. (1977). Sociocultural knowledge in conversational inference. In M. Saville-Troike (ed.) *Linguistics and Anthropology*. Washington: Georgetown University Press, pp. 191-211.

Gumperz, J. J. (1982). *Discourse Strategies*. Cambridge: Cambridge University Press.
Gumperz, J. J. & Herasimchuk, E. (1975). The conversational analysis of social meaning: a study of classroom interaction. In B. Blount & M. Sanches (eds.) *Sociocultural Dimensions of Language Use*. New York: Academic Press, pp. 81–116.
Gumperz, J. J. & Hymes, D. H. (eds.) (1972). *Directions in Sociolinguistics*. New York: Holt, Rinehart & Winston.
Gumperz, J. J., Jupp, T. & Roberts, C. (1979). *Crosstalk*. London: Centre for Industrial Language Teaching.
Gundel, J. K. (1977). *Role of Topic and Comment in Linguistic Theory*. Mimeo. Indiana University Linguistics Club.
Haas, M. R. (1964). Men's and women's speech in Koasati. In Hymes (1964: 228–33).
Haimoff, E. (in press). Video analysis of Siamang (Hylobates Syndactylus) call bouts. *Behaviour*.
Halliday, M. A. K. (1973). *Explorations in the Functions of Language*. London: Arnold.
Halliday, M. A. K. (1975). *Learning How to Mean: Explorations in the Development of Language*. London: Arnold.
Halvorsen, P. (1978). *The Syntax and Semantics of Cleft Constructions*. Texas Linguistic Forum 11, Austin: University of Texas, Linguistics Dept.
Hamblin, C. L. (1971). Mathematical models of dialogue. *Theoria*, 37, 130–55.
Hancher, M. (1979). The classification of co-operative illocutionary acts. *Language in Society*, 8.1, 1–14.
Harada, S. I. (1976). Honorifics. In M. Shibatani (ed.) *Syntax and Semantics 5 : Japanese Generative Grammar*. New York: Academic Press, pp. 499–561.
Hare, R. M. (1949). Imperative sentences. *Mind*, 58, 21–39. (Reprinted in Hare (1971: 1–21).)
Hare, R. M. (1952). *The Language of Morals*. Oxford: Clarendon Press.
Hare, R. M. (1970). Meaning and speech acts. *Philosophical Review*, 79, 3–24. (Reprinted in Hare (1971: 74–93).)
Hare, R. M. (1971). *Practical Inferences*. London: Macmillan.
Harnish, R. M. (1976). Logical form and implicature. In T. Bever, J. Katz, & T. Langendoen (eds.) *An Integrated Theory of Linguistic Ability*. New York: Crowell, pp. 464–79.
Harris, R. (1980). *The Language Makers*. London: Duckworth.
Harris, Z. (1951). *Methods in Structural Linguistics*. Chicago: University of Chicago Press.
Haviland, J. B. (1979). Guugu Yimidhirr brother-in-law language. *Language in Society*, 8, 365–93.
Hawkins, J. A. (1978). *Definiteness and Indefiniteness*. London: Croom Helm.
Head, B. (1978). Respect degrees in pronominal reference. In J. H. Greenberg (ed.) *Universals of Human Language*, Vol. 3 : *Word Structure*. Stanford: Stanford University Press, pp. 150–211.
Heath, J., Merlan, F. & Rumsey, A. (eds.) (1982). *The Languages of Kinship in Aboriginal Australia*. Sydney: Oceania Linguistic Monographs. No. 24.
Hedenius, I. (1963). Performatives. *Theoria*, 29, 115–36.
Heinämäki, O. (1972). Before. *Proceedings of the Eighth Regional Meeting of the Chicago Linguistic Society*, pp. 139–51.
Heny, F. & Schnelle, H. (eds.) (1979). *Syntax and Semantics 10 : Selections from the Third Groningen Round Table*. New York: Academic Press.
Heringer, J. T. (1972). *Some Grammatical Correlates of Felicity Conditions and Presuppositions*. Mimeo. Indiana University Linguistics Club.
Heringer, J. T. (1977). Pre-sequences and indirect speech acts. In E. O. Keenan and T.

Bennett (eds.) *Discourse Structure Across Time and Space*, SCOPIL 5. University of Southern California, Linguistics Department, pp. 169–80.

Heritage, J. (in press). A news-receipt token and aspects of its sequential distribution. In Atkinson & Heritage (in press).

Herzberger, H. O. (1971). Some results on presupposition and modality. Mimeo. University of Toronto.

Hilpinen, R. (ed.) (1971). *Deontic Logic : Introductory and Systematic Readings*. Dordrecht: Reidel.

Hintikka, K. J. J. (1962). *Knowledge and Belief*. Ithaca: Cornell University Press.

Hintikka, K. J. J. (1974). Questions about questions. In Munitz & Unger (1974: 103–58).

Horn, L. R. (1972). *On the Semantic Properties of the Logical Operators in English*. Mimeo. Indiana University Linguistics Club.

Horn, L. R. (1973). Greek Grice. *Proceedings of the Ninth Regional Meeting of the Chicago Linguistic Society*, pp. 205–14.

Horn, L. R. (1978). Some aspects of negation. In J. H. Greenberg (ed.) *Universals of Human Language*, Vol. 4: *Syntax*. Stanford: Stanford University Press, pp. 127–210.

Horne, E. C. (1974). *Javanese–English Dictionary*. New Haven: Yale University Press.

House, J. & Kasper, G. (1981). Politeness markers in English and German. In Coulmas (1981: 157–85).

Huddleston, R. (1969). Some observations on tense and deixis in English. *Language*, 45, 777–806.

Hudson, R. A. (1975). The meaning of questions. *Language*, 51, 1–31.

Hudson, R. A. (1980). *Sociolinguistics*. Cambridge: Cambridge University Press.

Hull, R. D. (1975). A semantics for superficial and embedded questions in natural language. In Keenan (1975: 35–45).

Hymes, D. (ed.) (1964). *Language in Culture and Society*. New York: Harper & Row.

Hymes, D. (1971). Competence and performance in linguistic theory. In R. Huxley & E. Ingram (eds.) *Language Acquisition : Models and Methods*. London: Academic Press, pp. 3–28.

Hymes, D. (1972). Models of the interaction of language and social life. In Gumperz & Hymes (1972: 35–71).

Hymes, D. (1974). *Foundations in Sociolinguistics : an Ethnographic Approach*. Philadelphia: University of Pennsylvania Press.

Ingram, D. (1978). Typology and universals of personal pronouns. In J. H. Greenberg (ed.) *Universals of Human Language*, Vol. 3: *Word Structure*. Stanford: Stanford University Press, pp. 213–47.

Irvine, J. T. (1974). Strategies of status manipulation in the Wolof greeting. In Bauman & Sherzer (1974: 167–91).

Irvine, J. T. (1979). Formality and informality in speech events. *American Anthropologist*, 81.4, 773–90.

Jacobs, R. A. & Rosenbaum, P. S. (eds.) (1970). *Readings in English Transformational Grammar*. Waltham: Ginn.

Jaffé, J. & Feldstein, S. (1970). *Rhythms of Dialogue*. New York: Academic Press.

Jakobovitz, L. A. & Gordon, B. (1974). *The Context of Language Teaching*. Rowley, Mass.: Newbury House.

Jakobson, R. (1932). Zur Struktur des russichen Verbums. In *Charisteria G. Mathesio*. Prague: Cercle Linguistique de Prague, pp. 74–84.

Jakobson, R. (1960). Linguistics and poetics. In Sebeok (1960: 350–77).

James, D. (1972). Some aspects of the syntax and semantics of interjections. *Proceedings of the Eighth Regional Meeting of the Chicago Linguistic Society*, pp. 162–72.

Bibliography

James, D. (1973). Another look at, say, some grammatical constraints on, oh, interjections and hesitations. *Proceedings of the Ninth Regional Meeting of the Chicago Linguistic Society*, pp. 242–51.

Jefferson, G. (1972). Side sequences. In Sudnow (1972: 294–338).

Jefferson, G. (1974). Error-correction as an interactional resource. *Language in Society*, 3, 181–200.

Jefferson, G. (1978). Sequential aspects of story-telling in conversation. In Schenkein (1978: 219–48).

Jefferson, G. (MS). On exposed and embedded correction in conversation. MS. University of Manchester, Department of Sociology.

Jefferson, G. (in press). Stepwise transition out of topic. In Atkinson & Heritage (in press).

Jefferson, G. & Schegloff, E. A. (1975). Sketch: some orderly aspects of overlap in natural conversation. Paper delivered at the December 1975 meetings of the American Anthropological Association. Mimeo. Department of Sociology, University of California, Los Angeles.

Joshi, A. K., Webber, B. L. & Sag, I. A. (eds.) (1981). *Elements of Discourse Understanding*. Cambridge: Cambridge University Press.

Kalish, D. (1967). Semantics. In P. Edwards (ed.) *Encyclopedia of Philosophy*, Vol. 7. New York: Collier-Macmillan, pp. 348–58.

Kaplan, D. (1978). Dthat. In Cole (1978: 221–43).

Kaplan, S. J. (1981). Appropriate responses to inappropriate questions. In Joshi, Webber & Sag (1981: 127–44).

Karttunen, L. (n.d.) Presuppositional phenomena. Mimeo. Department of Linguistics, University of Texas, Austin.

Karttunen, L. (1971a). Some observations on factivity. *Papers in Linguistics*, 4, 55–69.

Karttunen, L. (1971b). Implicative verbs. *Language*, 47, 340–58.

Karttunen, L. (1973). Presuppositions of compound sentences. *Linguistic Inquiry*, 4, 169–93.

Karttunen, L. (1974). Presupposition and linguistic context. *Theoretical Linguistics*, 1, 3–44. (Reprinted in Rogers, Wall & Murphy (1977: 149–60).)

Karttunen, L. (1977). Syntax and semantics of questions. *Linguistics & Philosophy*, 1, 3–44.

Karttunen, L. & Peters, S. (1975). Conventional implicature in Montague grammar. *Proceedings of the First Annual Meeting of the Berkeley Linguistic Society*, pp. 266–78.

Karttunen, L. & Peters, S. (1977). Requiem for presupposition. *Proceedings of the Third Annual Meeting of the Berkeley Linguistic Society*, pp. 360–71.

Karttunen, L. & Peters, S. (1979). Conventional implicature. In Oh & Dinneen (1979: 1–56).

Katz, J. J. (1972). *Semantic Theory*. New York: Harper & Row.

Katz, J. J. (1977). *Propositional Structure and Illocutionary Force*. New York: Crowell.

Katz, J. J. & Fodor, J. A. (1963). The structure of a semantic theory. *Language*, 39, 170–210. (Reprinted as Fodor & Katz (1964: 479–518).)

Katz, J. J. & Fodor, J. A. (1964). The structure of a semantic theory. In Fodor & Katz (1964: 479–518).

Katz, J. J. & Langendoen, D. T. (1976). Pragmatics and presupposition. *Language*, 52, 1–17.

Katz, J. J. & Postal, P. M. (1964). *An Integrated Theory of Linguistic Descriptions*. Cambridge, Mass.: MIT Press.

Keenan, E. L. (1971). Two kinds of presupposition in natural language. In C. J. Fillmore & D. T. Langendoen (eds.) *Studies in Linguistic Semantics*. New York: Holt, pp. 45–54.

Keenan, E. L. (1972). On semantically based grammar. *Linguistic Inquiry*, 3, 413–61.

Keenan, E. L. (ed.) (1975). *Formal Semantics of Natural Language*. Cambridge: Cambridge University Press.

Keenan, E. O. (1976a). Unplanned and planned discourse. *Pragmatics Microfiche*, 3.1, A3–D2. (Reprinted as Ochs, E. (1979a).)

Keenan, E. O. (1976b). The universality of conversational implicature. *Language in Society*, 5, 67–80.

Keenan, E. O. & Schieffelin, B. B. (1976). Topic as a discourse notion: a study of topic in the conversation of children and adults. In Li (1976: 335–84).

Kempson, R. M. (1975). *Presupposition and the Delimitation of Semantics*. Cambridge: Cambridge University Press.

Kempson, R. M. (1977). *Semantic Theory*. Cambridge: Cambridge University Press.

Kempson, R. M. (1979). Presupposition, opacity and ambiguity. In Oh & Dinneen (1979: 283–97).

Kendon, A. (1967). Some functions of gaze-direction in social interaction. *Acta Psychologia*, 26, 22–63.

Kiefer, F. (1979). What do conversational maxims explain? *Linguisticae Investigationes*, 3, 57–74.

Kiparsky, P. & Kiparsky, C. (1971). Fact. In Steinberg & Jakobovits (1971: 345–69).

Kroch, A. (1972). Lexical and inferred meanings for some time adverbs. *Quarterly Progress report of the Research Lab. of Electronics, MIT*, 104.

Kuhn, T. S. (1979). Metaphor in science. In Ortony (1979a: 409–19).

Kuno, S. (1973). *The Structure of the Japanese Language*. Cambridge, Mass.: Harvard University Press.

Labov, W. (1972a). *Sociolinguistic Patterns*. Philadelphia: University of Pennsylvania Press.

Labov, W. (1972b). Rules for ritual insults. In Sudnow (1972: 120–69).

Labov, W. & Fanshel, D. (1977). *Therapeutic Discourse: Psychotherapy as Conversation*. New York: Academic Press.

Labov, W. & Waletsky, J. (1966). Narrative analysis: oral versions of personal experience. In J. Helm (ed.) *Essays on the Verbal and Visual Arts*. Seattle: University of Washington Press, pp. 12–44.

Lakoff, G. (1971). Presupposition and relative well-formedness. In Steinberg & Jakobovits (1971: 329–40).

Lakoff, G. (1972). Linguistics and natural logic. In Davidson & Harman (1972: 545–665).

Lakoff, G. (1973). Some thoughts on transderivational constraints. In B. B. Kachru et al. (eds.) *Issues in Linguistics: Papers in Honor of Henry & Renée Kahane*. Urbana: University of Illinois Press, pp. 442–52.

Lakoff, G. (1974). Syntactic amalgams. *Proceedings of the Tenth Regional Meeting of the Chicago Linguistic Society*, pp. 321–44.

Lakoff, G. (1975). Pragmatics in natural logic. In Keenan (1975: 253–86).

Lakoff, G. & Johnson, M. (1980). *Metaphors We Live By*. Chicago: Chicago University Press.

Lakoff, R. (1970). Tense and its relation to participants. *Language*, 46, 838–49.

Lakoff, R. (1973a). Questionable answers and answerable questions. In B. B. Kachru et al. (eds.) *Issues in Linguistics: Papers in Honor of Henry and Renée Kahane*. Urbana: University of Illinois Press, pp. 453–67.

Lakoff, R. (1973b). The logic of politeness: or minding your *p*'s and *q*'s. *Proceedings of the Ninth Regional Meeting of the Chicago Linguistic Society*, pp. 292–305.

Lakoff, R. (1974). Remarks on this and that. *Proceedings of the Tenth Regional Meeting of the Chicago Linguistic Society*, pp. 345–56.

Lakoff, R. (1977). Politeness, pragmatics and performatives. In Rogers, Wall & Murphy (1977: 79–106).

389

Bibliography

Lambert, W. E. & Tucker, G. R. (1976). *Tu, Vous, Usted*. Rowley, Mass.: Newbury House.

Langendoen, D. T. (1971). Presupposition and assertion in the semantic analysis of nouns and verbs in English. In Steinberg & Jakobovits (1971: 341–4).

Langendoen, D. T. & Savin, H. B. (1971). The projection problem for presuppositions. In Fillmore & Langendoen (1971: 55–62).

Leach, E. R. (1964). Anthropological aspects of language: animal categories and verbal abuse. In E. Lenneberg (ed.) *New Directions in the Study of Language*. Cambridge, Mass.: MIT Press, pp. 23–64.

Leech, G. N. (1969). *Towards a Semantic Description of English*. London: Longman.

Leech, G. N. (1974). *Semantics*. Harmondsworth: Penguin Books.

Leech, G. N. (1976). Metalanguage, pragmatics and performatives. In C. Rameh (ed.) *Semantics – Theory and Application*. Georgetown University Round Table on Languages and Linguistics. Washington: Georgetown University Press, pp. 81–98.

Leech, G. N. (1977). *Language and Tact*. L. A. U. T. paper 46. Trier. (Reprinted as Leech (1980).

Leech, G. N. (1980). *Language and Tact*. Pragmatics and Beyond Series. Amsterdam: Benjamins.

Lemmon, E. J. (1962). On sentences verifiable by their use. *Analysis*, 22, 86–9.

Levin, S. (1976). Concerning what kind of a poem a speech act is. In Van Dijk (1976: 141–60).

Levin, S. (1977). *The Semantics of Metaphor*. Baltimore: Johns Hopkins University Press.

Levinson, S. C. (1977). *Social Deixis in a Tamil Village*. Unpublished PhD dissertation, University of California, Berkeley.

Levinson, S. C. (1978). Sociolinguistic universals. Unpublished paper. Department of Linguistics, University of Cambridge.

Levinson, S. C. (1979a). Activity types and language. *Linguistics*, 17.5/6, 356–99.

Levinson, S. C. (1979b). Pragmatics and social deixis. *Proceedings of the Fifth Annual Meeting of the Berkeley Linguistic Society*, pp. 206–23.

Levinson, S. C. (1980). Speech act theory: the state of the art. *Language and Linguistics Teaching: Abstracts*, 13.1, 5–24.

Levinson, S. C. (1981a). The essential inadequacies of speech act models of dialogue. In Parret, Sbisà & Verschueren (1981: 473–92).

Levinson, S. C. (1981b). Some pre-observations on the modelling of dialogue. *Discourse Processes*, 4.2, 93–110.

Levinson, S. C. (in prep.). Explicating concepts of participant-role: on the infelicity of S and H. To appear in P. Brown & J. Haviland (eds.) *Language and Cultural Context*.

Lewis, D. (1969). *Convention*. Cambridge, Mass.: Harvard University Press.

Lewis, D. (1972). General semantics. In Davidson & Harman (1972: 169–218).

Li, C. N. (ed.) (1976). *Subject and Topic*. New York: Academic Press.

Li, C. N. & Thompson, S. A. (1976). Subject and topic: a new typology of language. In Li (1976: 457–89).

Liberman, M. (1973). Alternatives. *Proceedings of the Ninth Regional Meeting of the Chicago Linguistic Society*, pp. 346–55.

Liberman, M. & Sag, I. (1974). Prosodic form and discourse function. *Proceedings of the Tenth Regional Meeting of the Chicago Linguistic Society*, pp. 416–27.

Lieb, H.-H. (1971). On subdividing semiotic. In Bar-Hillel (1971: 94–119).

Lightfoot, D. (1979). *Principles of Diachronic Syntax*. Cambridge: Cambridge University Press.

Longacre, R. E. (1976a). 'Mystery' particles and affixes. *Proceedings of the Twelfth Regional Meeting of the Chicago Linguistic Society*, pp. 468–75.

Longacre, R. E. (1976b). *An Anatomy of Speech Notions*. Lisse: Peter de Ridder Press.

Lucas, E. D. (1981). *Pragmatic and Semantic Language Disorders: Assessment and Remediation*. Germantown, Maryland: Aspen Systems Corporation.

Luce, R. D. & Raiffa, H. (1957). *Games and Decisions*. New York: Wiley & Sons.

Lyons, J. (1968). *An Introduction to Theoretical Linguistics*. Cambridge: Cambridge University Press.

Lyons, J. (1975). Deixis as the source of reference. In Keenan (1975: 61–83).

Lyons, J. (1977a). *Semantics*, Vols. 1 & 2. Cambridge: Cambridge University Press.

Lyons, J. (1977b). Deixis and anaphora. In T. Myers (ed.) *The Development of Conversation and Discourse*. Edinburgh: Edinburgh University Press.

McCawley, J. (1978). Conversational implicature and the lexicon. In Cole (1978: 245–59).

Martin, J. N. (1975). Karttunen on possibility. *Linguistic Inquiry*, 6, 339–41.

Martin, J. N. (1979). *Some misconceptions in the critique of semantic presupposition*. Mimeo. Indiana University Linguistics Club.

Martin, R. M. (1959). *Toward a Systematic Pragmatics*. Amsterdam: North Holland.

Matthews, P. H. (1972). Review of Jacobs & Rosenbaum (1970). *Journal of Linguistics*, 8, 125–36.

Merritt, M. (1976). On questions following questions (in service encounters). *Language in Society*, 5.3, 315–57.

Miller, G. A. (1963). Speaking in general. Review of J. H. Greenberg (ed.) *Universals of Language*. *Contemporary Psychology*, 8, 417–18.

Miller, G. A. (1979). Images and models, similes and metaphors. In Ortony (1979a: 202–50).

Minsky, M. (1977). Frame-system theory. In P. N. Johnson-Laird & P. C. Wason (eds.) *Thinking: Readings in Cognitive Science*. Cambridge: Cambridge University Press.

Mitchell, T. F. (1975). *Principles of Firthian Linguistics*. London: Longman.

Mittwoch, A. (1976). Grammar and illocutionary force. *Lingua*, 40, 21–42.

Mittwoch, A. (1977). How to refer to one's own words: speech act modifying adverbials and the performative analysis. *Journal of Linguistics*, 13, 177–89.

Moerman, M. (1977). The preference for self-correction in a Tai conversational corpus. *Language*, 53.4, 872–82.

Montague, R. (1968). Pragmatics. In R. Klibansky (ed.) *Contemporary Philosophy*. Florence: La Nuova Italia Editrice, pp. 102–21. (Reprinted in Montague (1974: 95–118).)

Montague, R. (1970). Pragmatics and intensional logic. *Synthese*, 22, 68–94. (Reprinted in Montague (1974: 119–147).)

Montague, R. (1974). *Formal Philosophy: Selected Papers*. (Edited by R. H. Thomason.) New Haven: Yale University Press.

Morgan, J. L. (1973). Sentence fragments and the notion 'sentence'. In B. B. Kachru et al. (eds.) *Issues in Linguistics: Papers in Honor of Henry and Renée Kahane*. Urbana: University of Illinois Press, pp. 719–51.

Morgan, J. L. (1977). Conversational postulates revisited. *Language*, 53, 277–84.

Morgan, J. L. (1978). Two types of convention in indirect speech acts. In Cole (1978: 261–80).

Morgan, J. L. (1979). Observations on the pragmatics of metaphor. In Ortony (1979a: 136–47).

Morris, C. W. (1938). *Foundations of the Theory of Signs*. In O. Neurath, R. Carnap & C. Morris (eds.) *International Encyclopedia of Unified Science*. Chicago: University of Chicago Press, pp. 77–138. (Reprinted in Morris (1971).)

Morris, C. W. (1946). *Signs, Language and Behavior*. Englewood Cliffs, NJ: Prentice Hall.

Morris, C. W. (1964). *Signification and Significance*. Cambridge, Mass.: MIT Press.

Morris, C. W. (1971). *Writings on the General Theory of Signs*. The Hague: Mouton.

Bibliography

Munitz, M. K. & Unger, P.K. (eds.) (1974). *Semantics and Philosophy*. New York: New York University Press.

Newmeyer, F. J. (1980). *Linguistic Theory in America*. New York: Academic Press.

Nunberg. G. D. (1978). *The Pragmatics of Reference*. Mimeo. Indiana University Linguistics Club.

Ochs, E. (1979a). Planned and unplanned discourse. In Givon (1979a: 51–80).

Ochs, E. (1979b) Social foundations of language. In R. Freedle (ed.) *New Directions in Discourse Processing*, Vol.3. Norwood, NJ: Ablex, pp. 207–21.

Ochs, E. (1979c). Introduction: What child language can contribute to pragmatics. In Ochs & Schieffelin (1979: 1–17).

Ochs, E. (1979d). Transcription as theory. In Ochs & Schieffelin (1979: 43–72).

Ochs, E. & Duranti, A. (1979). Left-dislocation in Italian conversation. In Givon (1979a: 377–416).

Ochs, E. & Schieffelin, B. B. (eds.) (1979). *Developmental Pragmatics*. New York: Academic Press.

O'Connor, J. D. & Arnold, G. F. (1973). *Intonation of Colloquial English*. 2nd ed. London: Longman.

Oh, C.-K., & Dinneen, D.A. (eds.) (1979). *Syntax and semantics 11 : Presupposition*. New York: Academic Press.

Ohmann, R. (1971). Speech acts and the definition of literature. *Philosophy & Rhetoric*, 4, 1–19.

Ortony, A. (ed.) (1979a). *Metaphor and Thought*. Cambridge: Cambridge University Press.

Ortony, A. (1979b). Similarity in similes and metaphors. In Ortony (1979a: 186–201).

Owen, M. L. (1980). *Remedial Interchanges : a Study of Language Use in Social Interaction*. Unpublished PhD dissertation, University of Cambridge. To appear as Owen (in press).

Owen, M. L. (1981). Conversational units and the use of 'well ...'. In Werth (1981: 99–116).

Owen, M. L. (1982). Conversational topics and activities: final report to the SSRC of the project on Topic Organization in Conversation. Mimeo. University of Cambridge.

Owen, M. L. (in press). *Apologies and Remedial Interchanges*. The Hague: Mouton.

Parret, H., Sbisà, M. & Verschueren, J. (eds.) (1981). *Possibilities and Limitations of Pragmatics : Proceedings of the Conference on Pragmatics at Urbino, July 8–14, 1979*. Amsterdam: Benjamins.

Passmore, J. (1968). *A Hundred Years of Philosophy*. Harmondsworth: Penguin.

Peters, S. (1977). A truth-conditional formulation of Karttunen's account of presupposition. *Texas Linguistic Forum*, 6, 137–49. Revised version published as Peters (1979).

Peters, S. (1979). A truth-conditional formulation of Karttunen's account of presupposition. *Synthese*, 40.2, 301–16.

Pomerantz, A. (1975). *Second Assessments: A Study of Some Features of Agreements/ Disagreements*. Unpublished PhD dissertation, University of California, Irvine.

Pomerantz, A. (1978). Compliment responses: notes on the co-operation of multiple constraints. In Schenkein (1978: 79–112).

Pomerantz, A. (in press). Agreeing and disagreeing with assessments: some features of preferred/dispreferred turn shapes. In Atkinson & Heritage (in press).

Power, R. (1979). The organization of purposeful dialogues. *Linguistics*, 17, 107–52.

Pride, J. B. & Holmes, J. (eds.) (1972). *Sociolinguistics*. Harmondsworth: Penguin.

Prince, E. F. (1978a). A comparison of *wh*-clefts and *it*-clefts in discourse. *Language*, 54.4, 893–906.

Prince, E. F. (1978b). On the function of existential presuppositions in discourse. *Proceedings of the Fourteenth Regional Meeting of the Chicago Linguistic Society*, pp. 362–76.

Prince, E. F. (1981). Towards a taxonomy of given–new information. In Cole (1981: 223–56).

Prior, A. N. (1968). *Time and Tense*. Oxford: Clarendon Press.

Psathas, G. (ed.) (1979). *Everyday Language: Studies in Ethnomethodology*. New York: Irvington.

Putnam, H. (1958). Formalization of the concept 'about'. *Philosophy of Science*, 25, 125–30.

Quine, W. V. O. (1960). *Word and Object*. Cambridge, Mass.: MIT Press.

Quirk, R., Greenbaum, S., Leech, G. & Svartvik, J. (1972). *A Grammar of Contemporary English*. London: Longman.

Rawls, J. (1955). Two concepts of rules. *Philosophical Review*, 64, 3–32.

Reichenbach, H. (1947). *Elements of Symbolic Logic*. London: Macmillan.

Rogers, A. (1978). On generalized conversational implicature and preparatory conditions. *Texas Linguistic Forum*, 10, 72–5.

Rogers, A., Wall, B. & Murphy, J. P. (eds.) (1977). *Proceedings of the Texas Conference on Performatives, Presuppositions and Implicatures*. Washington: Center for Applied Linguistics.

Ross, J. R. (1967). *Constraints on Variables in Syntax*. Unpublished PhD dissertation, MIT. (Extracts reprinted in G. H. Harman (ed.) (1974). *On Noam Chomsky: Critical Essays*. New York: Anchor Books, pp. 165–200.)

Ross, J. R. (1970). On declarative sentences. In Jacobs & Rosenbaum (1970: 222–72).

Ross, J. R. (1975). Where to do things with words. In Cole & Morgan (1975: 233–56).

Rosten, L. (1968). *The Joys of Yiddish*. New York: McGraw-Hill.

Russell, B. (1905). On denoting. *Mind*, 14, 479–93.

Russell, B. (1957). Mr Strawson on Referring. *Mind*, 66, 385–9.

Russell, B. & Whitehead, A. N. (1910). *Principia Mathematica*. Cambridge: Cambridge University Press.

Rutherford, W. E. (1970). Some observations concerning subordinate clauses in English. *Language*, 46, 97–115.

Ryave, A. L. (1978). On the achievement of a series of stories. In Schenkein (1978: 113–32).

Sacks, H. (1967–1972). *Lecture Notes*. Mimeo. Department of Sociology, University of California, Irvine.

Sacks, H. (1972). On the analyzability of stories by children. In Gumperz & Hymes (1972: 325–45).

Sacks, H. (1974). An analysis of the course of a joke's telling in conversation. In Bauman & Sherzer (1974: 337–53).

Sacks, H. (1975). Everyone has to lie. In M. Sanches & B. Blount (eds.) *Sociocultural Dimensions of Language Use*, pp. 57–80. New York: Academic Press.

Sacks, H. (1976). Paradoxes, pre-sequences and pronouns. *Pragmatics Microfiche*, 1.8, E6–G12.

Sacks, H. & Schegloff, E. A. (1979). Two preferences in the organization of reference to persons in conversation and their interaction. In Psathas (1979: 15–21).

Sacks, H., Schegloff, E. A. & Jefferson, G. (1974). A simplest systematics for the organization of turn-taking in conversation. *Language*, 50.4, 696–735. (Variant version published as Sacks, Schegloff & Jefferson (1978).)

Sacks, H., Schegloff, E. A. & Jefferson, G. (1978). A simplest systematics for the organization of turn-taking in conversation. In Schenkein (1978: 7–55).

Sadock, J. M. (1970). Whimperatives. In J. Sadock & A. Vanek (eds.) *Studies Presented to R. B. Lees by His Students*. Edmonton, Canada: Linguistic Research Inc., pp. 223–38.

Sadock, J. M. (1974). *Toward a Linguistic Theory of Speech Acts*. New York: Academic Press.

Sadock, J. M. (1975). The soft interpretive underbelly of generative semantics. In Cole & Morgan (1975: 383–96).

Bibliography

Sadock, J. M. (1978). On testing for conversational implicature. In Cole (1978: 281–98).

Sadock, J. M. (in prep.). A semantic version of the performative hypothesis. (Paper delivered at the University of Cambridge, 1979.)

Sadock, J. M. & Zwicky, A. M. (in press). Sentence types. In Shopen (ed.) (in press).

Samuels, M. L. (1972). *Linguistic Evolution, with Special Reference to English*. Cambridge: Cambridge University Press.

Sayward, C. (1974). The received distinction between pragmatics, semantics and syntax. *Foundations of Language*, 11, 97–104.

Sayward, C. (1975). Pragmatics and indexicality. *Pragmatics Microfiche*, 1.3, D5–D12.

Schegloff, E. A. (1972a). Sequencing in conversational openings. In Gumperz & Hymes (1972: 346–80).

Schegloff, E. A. (1972b). Notes on a conversational practice: formulating place. In Sudnow (1972: 75–119). (Reprinted in Giglioli (1972: 95–135).)

Schegloff, E. A. (1976). On some questions and ambiguities in conversation. *Pragmatics Microfiche*, 2.2, D8–G1. (Reprinted in Atkinson & Heritage (in press).)

Schegloff, E. A. (1979a). Identification and recognition in telephone conversation openings. In Psathas (1979: 23–78).

Schegloff, E. A. (1979b). The relevance of repair to syntax-for-conversation. In Givon (1979: 261–88).

Schegloff, E. A. (in prep. a). Repair after third turn. (Paper delivered to the Conference on Conversational Analysis at the University of Warwick, 1979.)

Schegloff, E. A. (in prep. b). 'Do you know where Mr Williams is'. (Paper delivered to the Conference on Pragmatics, Urbino, July, 1979.)

Schegloff, E. A. & Sacks, H. (1973). Opening up closings. *Semiotica*, 7.4, 289–327. (Reprinted in Turner (1974a: 233–64).)

Schegloff, E. A., Jefferson, G. & Sacks, H. (1977). The preference for self-correction in the organization of repair in conversation. *Language*, 53, 361–82.

Schenkein, J. (ed.) (1978). *Studies in the Organization of Conversational Interaction*. New York: Academic Press.

Schiffer, S. R. (1972). *Meaning*. Oxford: Clarendon Press.

Schmerling, S. F. (1975). Asymmetric conjunction and rules of conversation. In Cole & Morgan (1975: 211–32).

Schmerling, S. F. (1978). Towards a theory of English imperatives. Mimeo. Department of Linguistics, University of Texas, Austin.

Scott, D. (1970). Advice on modal logic. In K. Lambert (ed.) *Philosophical Problems in Logic*. Dordrecht: Reidel, pp. 143–73.

Searle, J. R. (1969). *Speech Acts*. Cambridge: Cambridge University Press.

Searle, J. R. (ed.) (1971). *Philosophy of Language*. Oxford: Oxford University Press.

Searle, J. R. (1974). Chomsky's revolution in linguistics. In G. Harman (ed.) *On Noam Chomsky: Critical Essays*. New York: Anchor Books, pp. 2–33.

Searle, J. R. (1975). Indirect speech acts. In Cole & Morgan (1975: 59–82).

Searle, J. R. (1976). The classification of illocutionary acts. *Language in Society*, 5, 1–24. (Reprinted in Searle (1979b: 1–29).)

Searle, J. R. (1979a). Metaphor. In Ortony (1979a: 92–123). (Reprinted in Searle (1979b: 76–116).)

Searle, J. R. (1979b). *Expression and Meaning*. Cambridge: Cambridge University Press.

Searle, J. R., Kiefer, F. & Bierwisch, M. (eds.) (1980). *Speech Act Theory and Pragmatics*. Synthese Language Library, Vol. 10. Dordrecht: Reidel.

Sebeok, T. (ed.) (1960). *Style in Language*. Cambridge, Mass.: MIT Press.

Sellars, W. (1954). Presupposing. *Philosophical Review*, 63, 197–215.

Shopen, T. (ed.) (in press). *Language Typology and Syntactic Fieldwork*. (Provisional title). Cambridge: Cambridge University Press.

Silverstein, M. (1976). Shifters, linguistic categories, and cultural descriptions. In K. H. Basso & H. A. Selby (eds.) *Meaning in Anthropology*. Albuquerque: University of New Mexico Press, pp. 11–55.

Sinclair, A. (1976). The sociolinguistic significance of the form of requests used in service encounters. Unpublished Diploma dissertation, University of Cambridge.

Sinclair, J. M. & Coulthard, R. M. (1975). *Towards an Analysis of Discourse : the English Used by Teachers and Pupils*. London: Oxford University Press.

Smith, N. V. (ed.) (1982). *Mutual Knowledge*. London: Academic Press.

Smith, N. V. & Wilson, D. (1979). *Modern Linguistics : the Results of Chomsky's Revolution*. Harmondsworth, Penguin.

Snow, C. (1979). Conversations with children. In Fletcher & Garman (1979: 363–76).

Snow, C. & Ferguson, C. (eds.) (1977). *Talking to Children*. Cambridge: Cambridge University Press.

Soames, S. (1979). A projection problem for speaker presuppositions. *Linguistic Inquiry*, 10.4, 623–66.

Sperber, D. & Wilson, D. (1981) Irony and the use/mention distinction. In Cole (1981: 295–318).

Sperber, D. & Wilson, D. (forthcoming). *The Interpretation of Utterances : Semantics, Pragmatics, and Rhetoric*.

Stalnaker, R. C. (1972). Pragmatics. In Davidson & Harman (1972: 380–97).

Stalnaker, R. C. (1974). Pragmatic presuppositions. In Munitz & Unger (1974: 197–214). (Reprinted as Stalnaker (1977).)

Stalnaker, R. C. (1977). Pragmatic presuppositions. In Rogers, Wall & Murphy (1977: 135–47).

Stalnaker, R. C. (1978). Assertion. In Cole (1978: 315–32).

Steinberg, D. & Jakobovits, L. (eds.) (1971). *Semantics : an Interdisciplinary Reader in Philosophy, Linguistics and Psychology*. Cambridge: Cambridge University Press.

Stenius, E. (1967). Mood and language game. *Synthese*, 17, 254–74.

Stevenson, C. L. (1974). Some aspects of meaning. In F. Zabeeh, E. D. Klemke & A. Jacobson (eds.) *Readings in Semantics*. Urbana: University of Illinois Press, pp. 35–88.

Strawson, P. F. (1950). On referring. *Mind*, 59, 320–44.

Strawson, P. F. (1952). *Introduction to Logical Theory*. London: Methuen.

Strawson, P. F. (1964). Intention and convention in speech acts. *Philosophical Review*, 73, 439–60. (Reprinted in Searle (1971: 23–38).)

Strawson, P. F. (ed.) (1971). *Philosophical Logic*. Oxford: Oxford University Press.

Sudnow, D. (ed.) (1972). *Studies in Social Interaction*. New York: Free Press.

Tambiah, S. J. (1968). The magical power of words. *Man*, 3, 175–208.

Tannen, D. (1979). What's in a frame? Surface evidence for underlying expectations. In R. O. Freedle (ed.) *New Directions in Discourse Processing*, Vol. 2. Norwood, NJ: Ablex, pp. 137–82.

Tanz, C. (1980). *Studies in the Acquisition of Deictic Terms*. Cambridge: Cambridge University Press.

Terasaki, A. (1976). *Pre-announcement Sequences in Conversation*. Social Science Working Paper 99. School of Social Science, University of California, Irvine.

Thomason, R. H. (1977). Where pragmatics fits in. In Rogers, Wall & Murphy (1977: 161–6).

Trevarthen, C. (1974). Conversations with a two month old. *New Scientist*, 62, 230–3.

Trevarthen, C. (1979). Instincts for human understanding and for cultural co-operation:

their development in infancy. In M. von Cranach, K. Foppa, W. Lepenies & D. Ploog (eds.) *New Perspectives in Ethology*. Cambridge: Cambridge University Press, pp. 530–71.

Trubetzkoy, N. S. (1939). *Grundzüge der Phonologie*. Travaux du Cercle Linguistique de Prague 7.

Trudgill, P. (ed.) (1978). *Sociolinguistic Patterns in British English*. London: Arnold.

Turner, R. (1972). Some formal properties of therapy talk. In Sudnow (1972: 367–96).

Turner, R. (ed.) (1974a). *Ethnomethodology : Selected Readings*. Harmondsworth: Penguin.

Turner, R. (1974b). Words, utterances and activities. In Turner (1974a: 197–215).

Ullman, S. (1962). *Principles of Semantics*. 2nd ed. Oxford: Blackwell.

Uyeno, T. Y. (1971). *A Study of Japanese Modality : a Performative Analysis of Sentence Particles*. Unpublished PhD dissertation, University of Michigan.

Van Dijk, T. A. (1972). *Some Aspects of Text Grammars*. The Hague: Mouton.

Van Dijk, T. A. (ed.) (1976). *Pragmatics of Language and Literature*. Amsterdam: North Holland.

Van Fraassen, B. C. (1969). Presuppositions, supervaluations and free logic. In K. Lambert (ed.) *The Logical Way of Doing Things*. New Haven: Yale University Press, pp. 67–92.

Van Fraassen, B. C. (1971). *Formal Semantics and Logic*. New York: Macmillan.

Verschueren, J. F. (1978). *Pragmatics : an Annotated Bibliography*. Amsterdam: Benjamins. (Supplements appear annually in the *Journal of Pragmatics*.)

Verschueren, J. F. (1980). *What People Say They Do with Words*. Unpublished PhD dissertation, University of California, Berkeley.

Wales, R. (1979). Deixis. In Fletcher & Garman (1979: 241–60).

Walker, R. (1975). Conversational implicatures. In S. Blackburn (ed.) *Meaning, Reference and Necessity*. Cambridge: Cambridge University Press, pp. 133–81.

Walters, J. (ed.) (1981). *The Sociolinguistics of Deference and Politeness*. Special issue of *International Journal of the Sociology of Language*, 27. The Hague: Mouton.

Watson, R. (1975). The interactional uses of pronouns. *Pragmatics Microfiche*, 1.3, A3–C1.

Watzlawick, P., Beavin, J. H. & Jackson, D. D. (1967). *Pragmatics of Human Communications*. New York: W. W. Norton.

Weinreich, U. (1966). Explorations in semantic theory. In T. Sebeok (ed.) *Current Trends in Linguistics*, Vol. 3. The Hague: Mouton, pp. 395–477.

Werth, P. (ed.) (1981). *Conversation and Discourse*. London: Croom Helm.

Wilks, Y. (1975). Preference semantics. In Keenan (1975: 329–48).

Wilson, D. (1975). *Presuppositions and Non-Truth Conditional Semantics*. New York: Academic Press.

Wilson, D. & Sperber, D. (1978). On Grice's theory of conversation. *Pragmatics Microfiche*, 3.5, F1–G14. (Reprinted as Wilson & Sperber (1981).)

Wilson, D. & Sperber, D. (1979). Ordered entailments: an alternative to presuppositional theories. In Oh & Dinneen (1979: 229–324).

Wilson, D. & Sperber, D. (1981). On Grice's theory of conversation. In Werth (1981: 155–78).

Wittgenstein, L. (1921). *Tractatus Logico-Philosophicus*. (Reprinted and translated as Wittgenstein (1961).)

Wittgenstein, L. (1958). *Philosophical Investigations*. Oxford: Blackwell.

Wittgenstein, L. (1961). *Tractatus Logico-Philosophicus*. Translated by D. F. Pears & B. F. McGuiness. London: Routledge & Kegan Paul.

Wootton, A. (in press). The management of grantings and rejections by parents in request sequences. *Semiotica*.

Wunderlich, D. (ed.) (1972). *Linguistische Pragmatik*. Frankfurt: Athenäum.

Zwicky, A. (1974). Hey, whatsyaname! *Proceedings from the Tenth Regional Meeting of the Chicago Linguistic Society*, pp. 787–801.

SUBJECT INDEX

Page numbers in bold type indicate definitions or main discussions. The first occurrence of abbreviations is indexed; thereafter references will be found after the full form.

ability, pragmatic, 24–5, 53, 367, 377
'aboutness', 89, 220–22
accounts, conversational, 306, 307, 334
acquisition, xii, 43, 47, 60, 61–2, 68, 226, 281–2, 284, 301, 368, 375
  of deixis, 61–2, 68
  of second languages, 368, 376
  of speech acts, 281–2
action:
  theory of, 44–5, 60
  and discourse, 288–94
  and speech acts, 227ff, 240, 246, 259
action-chains, 337–8
actions:
  as conversational responses, 237, 259, 288, 291
  involved in speech, 236; see also under illocutionary acts, speech acts
  mapping of utterances onto, 263–76, 289–94
address, 63, 70–1, 128–9; see also participant-role, summonses, vocatives
  terms or titles of, 53, 70–1, 75, 89, 91, 92, 128–30, 298, 303, 344, 345, 374
addressee, 16, 23, 52, 53, 62, 68–72, 81, 90, 92, 113–14, 248–9, 250, 260; see also participant-role
  honorifics, see under honorifics
adjacency pairs, 289, 293, 303–8, 309–12, 320, 322, 323, 324–5, 327–8, 332–9, 348, 350; see also under pre-sequences, questions, requests, summonses, etc.
  characterization of, 303–4, 306–8
  and conditional relevance, 306, 320
  in closings, 317, 324–5
  first parts, 303, 305ff, 324, 350
  as fundamental unit, 304
  and linguistic structure, 365–6
  in openings, 309–10, 322–3

preference organization in, 307–8, 332–7, 345
  rule for use, 304
  second parts, 303, 304, 306–8, 320, 324, 333ff, 350; dispreferred, see dispreferred turn; range of, 306–7; unforthcoming, 306, 320, 327, 328, 335
adverbs:
  manner, 184n
  performative, 249, 255–8, 262, 263, 266
  place, 54, 62, 79ff
  time, 54, 62, 74ff
advice, 267, 278, 334
agreement:
  of predicates, 70, 91–2, 130, 373
  in conversation, see disagreement
Algonquian languages, 88
all, 38, 123–4, 133–4, 144, 163–4; see also quantifiers
Amahuacan, 78
ambiguity, avoidance of, 102, 272; see also Manner, maxim of
ambiguity:
  claims, 37–8, 98–100, 108–9, 119–20, 132–45, 201, 203, 257–8
  and conversational sequence, 330–2, 353–4
  deictic, 75–6, 82–3
  of literal vs. indirect force, 269–76, 280, 330, 354, 363
  of negation, 171–3, 194, 201, 203, 210, 222
  of scope, 123–4, 171–2, 173, 201, 221–2, 257
Amerindian languages, 42, 75, 77n, 78, 81, 84, 88; see also under individual languages
amplitude, 301, 313, 370
analogy, 155, 159–62
anaphora, 67, 85–7, 188, 247–8, 262
  and discourse deixis, 80n, 85

397

anaphoric usage, of deictic expressions, 67, 80, 85–7
and, 35, 98–9, 108, 119–20, 127, 132, 134, 139, 192; *see also* conjunction
anomaly:
  pragmatic, **6–7**, 25–6, 54–5, 98, 105, 129, 160, 172, 199, 205, 228–30, 232, 235, 248, 265–7, 292–3; *see also* appropriateness
  semantic, 86, 151, 194, 199, 201; *see also* contradiction, falsehoods (categorial)
anyway, 33, 85, 87, 96, 100, 162, 366, 372
answers, 106, 107, 274, **293**, 303, 304, 305–6, 307, 310, 312, 327, 336, 354, 362; *see also* adjacency pairs, questions
'Antithesis', 246ff; *see also under* speech acts
'Applied linguistics', and pragmatics, 368, 376
appreciations, 328–9, 331, 334
appropriateness, 7, **24–7**, 31, 177, 204–5, 229ff, 246
appropriateness-conditions, 25
apologies, 281, 303, 334, 336, 358
article:
  definite, 61n, 83; *see also* definiteness
  indefinite, 126
artificial intelligence, 21, 45, 161–2, 281, 286, 332–3
aspect, 78
assertion:
  concept of, 105, 133, 169ff, 240, 242, 243, 246, 251–5, 256, 261, 265, 266, **277**, 337; *see also* constatives, representatives, speech acts, statements
  and presupposition, 169ff, 180–1, 197; *see also under* presupposition
assessments, 336, **337**, 339
atomic concepts, *see* componential analysis
attributives uses, *see* referential uses
audience, 72, 81, 90; *see also* bystanders
augmenting context, *see under* context (incremental model of)
Australian languages, 43, 71, 72, 82; *see also under individual languages*
authorized speakers/recipients, 91
autonomy:
  of semantics from pragmatics, 20, **34–5**, 59, 94–5; *see also under* components, pragmatics, semantics
  of syntax from pragmatics, xi, 267–8,

372–3; *see also under* pragmatics, syntactic rules

'baby-talk', 8–9, 11, 282
background vs. foreground entailments, 219–20
background knowledge or belief, 4n, 21–2, 23, 51, 53, 113, 125, 143, 146–7, 168, 173, 180–1, 187–8, 190, 197, 199, 204–5, 209, 211, 215, 219, 221, 276, 281, 285, 332, 352, 354–5; *see also* common ground, mutual knowledge
backgrounding, of information in clause, 41, 219–20, 221–2, 225, 373; *see also* given/new, presupposition
Basque, 93
because-clauses, 214–15, 256, 262
before-clauses, 179, 182, 187, 215
belief, 3, 101, 105, 136, 277; *see also* background knowledge, Moore's paradox
believe, 136, 137
biconditional, 146
bivalence, 174n, 175, **176**, 201; *see also* truth values
brevity, 102, 107–8, 112, 135, 136
but, 120, 127, 129, 211, 338
bystanders, 68, 90
  honorifics for, 90–1

C, 307n; *see* caller
CA, 286; *see* conversation analysis
calculability, of implicatures, 117, 119, 120, 128, 129; *see also under* conversational implicature
calendrical measurement, of time, 73, 75–6
caller, in telephone calls, 307n, 309ff, 327–8, 343–5
cancellability:
  of inferences, 114–16; *see also* defeasibility, suspension
  of conversational implicatures, 114–16, 119, 120, 134, 143–4, 224–5
  and conventional implicatures, 128, 129
  of presuppositions, 173, 187–90, 191–8, 207–9, 212–16, 224
canonical situation, of utterance, *see* situation of utterance
channel, of communication, 23, 63, 310, 320
Chinantec, 84
Chinese, 78
child language, *see* acquisition

Chinook, 73
classroom interaction, 39, 279, 284, 318, 377
clausal implicatures, *see under* Quantity
cleft sentences, 125, 217–22
  implicatures of, 125, 217–22
  implicit, 183
  presuppositions of, 182–3, 189, 206, 217–22, 373
  truth conditions of, 125, 206, 217
closings, conversational, 46, 49, 71, 79, **316–18**, 320, 324–5, 346; *see also under* overall organization
  elements of, 317
  pre-closings, 317–18, 322, 325
  re-opened, 322
coding time, 62, 73ff, 85
coherence, in conversation, 51, 107, 286, 288, 313–15; *see also under* conversation
come, 51–2, 64, 83–4; *see also* verbs of motion
comment, *see* topic/comment
commissives, 240
commitment, of speaker, 24n, 134, 135–6, 143, 212n, 240, 276–8
common ground or knowledge, 190, 205, 209; *see also* mutual knowledge
communication, **15–18**, 24, 25, 26–7, 29, 38–40, 49, 97–8, 101, 112–13, 241, 282, 376; *see also* meaning-nn
communicative competence, 25; *see also* ability (pragmatic)
communicative content, of utterances, 14, 15, 98, 131–2, 143; *see also* sentence-meaning, utterance-meaning, meaning-nn, word-meaning
communicative intention, *see* intention
communicative power, of a language, 112–13; *see also* expressibility
comparison, across languages, xi, 10, 42–3, 45–6, 47, 69–72, 75–8, 81–4, 88–94, 121n, 201, 216, 233, 242, 270, 276, 296, 301, 313n, 343n, 368–9, 376; *see also* universals
comparison:
  and implicature, 35
  and presupposition, 183
  vs. simile, 154; *see also* similes
competence/performance, 7–9, 24, 33–5, 36
complex sentences, 191n
  and projection, *see* projection problem
compliments, 339, 369
componential analysis, of meaning, 12, 69, 148ff, 199, 203–4

components of linguistic theory, 8, 9, 13–15, 22, 29, 33–5, 36, 59, 129–30, 145, 156, 267–8, 372–4
compositionality, 191, 207ff, 268, 270
compound sentences, 191n, 192ff; *see also* logical connectives
conative function, of speech, 41
conditional relevance, 293, **306**, 310, 320, 367
conditionals, 115, 137, **141–2**, 145–6, 188, 192–3, 195, 196–8, 200, 202, 208, 213–4, 224, 266–7
  counterfactual, 184
conjunction, 35, 98–9, 108, 119–20, 127, 129, 132, 134, 137, 139, 146, 197, 209, 211; *see also and, but,* logical connectives
  asymmetric, 35, 98–9, 108n, 119, 146, 165
connectives, *see* logical connectives
  and discourse, 288
connotation, 49, 150; *see also* incidental vs. defining characteristics
consistency, of inferences, *see* context (incremental model of), inference (inconsistency of)
constancy under negation, *see under* negation
constatives, 229ff, 234–5; *see also* assertion, statements
constitutive vs. regulative rules, 238, 367
context, x, 5, 7, 8–10, 13–14, 19–21, **22–3**, 24, 27, 30–1, 47ff, 54–9 passim, **63**, 79ff, 89ff, 95, 99, 115–16, 121–2, 143, 151, 161, 177, 186–90 passim, 205, 210–11, 212–15, 220, 237, 245, 271, 275, 276–83 passim, 291, 295
  definitions of, 22–4, 63, 212
  discourse-, 102, 115–16, 186–90, 199, 211, 291, Ch. 6 passim; *see also* sequence
  encoded in sentences, 9–11, 31, 47ff, Ch. 2 passim, 180ff
  incremental model of, 23n, 31, 143–4, 212–15, 276–8
  and indirect speech acts, 271ff, 278–83, 291
  and inference cancellation, *see* cancellability, defeasibility
  and inference generation, *see* conversational implicature, frames, inference
  'institutional' vs. conversational, 39, 279–81, 284, 301
  intra-sentential, or linguistic, 115, 144, 186, 190–8; *see also* projection problem

context (*cont.*)
  null, 8–9
  as sets: of indices, 58–9, 95; of
    propositions, 23n, 143–4, 212–15,
    276–8
context-change theory:
  of pragmatics, 31
  of speech acts, **276–8**
context-dependent (or -sensitive)
    meaning, 13–14, 20–1, 26, 37, 54–61,
    94–5, 115–16, 137, 143, 145, 161,
    186–90, 197, 200, 204, 233, 269ff,
    278–80, 291, 326–32; *see also*
    defeasibility
context-description, 23
contextualization-cues, 23, 29, 374
contradiction, 99, 109, 138, 140, 194, 201
contraction, 267
convention, 14n, 17, 216
conventional aspects of meaning, 12n, 14,
    15, 17–18, 19, 55, 112–13, 127–31,
    206–7, 212, 216ff, 229–30, 237, 241,
    243, 264, 282, 367; *see also*
    conventional content,
    grammaticalization,
    sentence-meaning
  non-truth-conditional, 13–14, 19, 96,
    127–9, 206ff; *see also* conventional
    implicature, non-truth-conditional
    aspects of meaning, presupposition
conventional content, 12n, **14**, 15, 17, 19,
    49, 97, 113, 128, 159; *see also*
    sentence-meaning
conventional implicature, 19, 88, 96, 117,
    127–131, 207
  Karttunen & Peters' theory of, 131,
    207–12
  and presupposition, 131, 216, 217
  properties of, 128, 129, 216
  reduction of, 128ff
  and syntax, 130, 373
conventionalization, of implicatures, 166
conversation, 43, 46–7, 278–9, Ch. 6
  analysis of, *see* conversation analysis
  centrality of, 284–5, 321, 374–5
  closings of, *see* closings
  vs. conversational activity, 318
  coherence in, *see* coherence
  cultural variations in, 296, 301, 313n,
    343n; *see also* universals of
  definition of, 284, **318**
  and inference, 39, 49, Ch. 3, 279, 287,
    326–33, 364
  vs. 'institutional' discourse, 284, 301,
    318, 321
  intuitions about, 287, 292–3

local systems in, *see* local management
    systems
  openings of, *see under* overall
    organization
  overall organization of, *see* overall
    organization
  and pragmatics, 284–5, 364–6, 373
  sequencing rules in, 288, 289–94, 367
  sequential organization of, *see under*
    pre-sequences, sequence
  speech act models of, 288–94, 303, 304,
    368
  structure of, 49–50, Ch. 6.
  'syntactic' models of, 286–7, 289–94,
    304, 367
  and syntax, 365–6, 373
  turns in, *see* turns, turn-taking
  units of, 288–91, 297; *see also* turns
  universals of, 296, 301, 368–9
conversation analysis, ix, 47, 278–9, 282,
    286–7, 294ff
  and context, 295
  data of, 287, 295–6, 326
  vs. discourse analysis, 284–94
  functionalism in, 319, 322–5, 365–6
  and linguistics, 364–6, 373
  methods of, 286–7, 318–326
  'rules' in, 367; *see also* turn-taking
  and sentence or turn structure, 287,
    297, 302–3, 368; *see also under* turns
conversational activity vs. conversation,
    318
conversational implicature, 10, 14, 45,
    Ch. 3; *see also* implicature
  actual vs. potential, 134
  calculability of, *see* calculability
  calculation of, 113–14, 122–5, 126,
    134–6, 218
  cancellability of, *see under* cancellability
  clausal, *see under* Quantity
  and communication, 97–8, 101
  definition of, 113
  and felicity conditions, 105, 241, 258–9
  and figures of speech, *see* figures of
    speech
  'filters' of, 224
  by flouting, *see under* exploitation,
    floutings
  generalized, 14, **104**, 122, 123, **126–7**,
    132–47, 143n, 163, 166, 188n
  indeterminacy of, 118, 128, 160
  and indirect speech acts, 270, 273–4
  kinds of, 126–7, 131
  and language structure, 97, 162–6, 373
  and logical connectives, *see under*
    conversational implicatures

conversational implicature (*cont.*)
    and logical form, 122–5, 218, 220–3
    and meaning-nn, 101
    and metaphor, 147–62
    particularized, 14, **126–7**, 166
    and presupposition, 125, 196, 213–14,
        217–25
    projection of, 224–5; *see also under*
        projection problem
    properties of, **114–22**, 223–5; *see also*
        caculability, cancellability,
        defeasibility, non-conventionality,
        non-detachability
    scalar, *see under* Quantity
    and simplification of semantics, 98–100,
        132–47, 372
    standard, **104**, 106, 107, 118, 126
    and syntax, 164–5, 373
    tests for, 118–22; *see also* properties of
    and truth conditions, 122–5
    universality of, 103, 120–7
conversational implicatures:
    of clefts, 125, 218, 222
    of conditionals, 115, 137, **141–2**, 145–6,
        188n, 213–14, 224
    of conjunctions, 35, 98–9, 108, 119–20,
        132, 134, 137, 139, 146–7
    of disjunctions, 134, 136–7, **138–40**,
        141, 142, 188n, 211, 213, 214, 224
    of negative sentences, 217–22
    of non-entailed clauses, *see under*
        Quantity (clausal implicatures)
    of quantifiers, 37–8, 100, 121, 133–4,
        138, 143–4
    of scales, *see under* Quantity (scalar
        implicatures)
    see also under individual lexical items and
        'triggers'
conversational postulates, 271–2, 282, 291
conveyed meaning, 15n, 98; *see also*
    implicature, indirection, utterance-
    meaning
co-operation, 45, 50, 51, 101ff, 109, 121
    and Ch. 3 passim, 167, 209, 241, 273,
        354
    and court proceedings, 121–2
co-operative principle, **101**, 109, 113, 117
co-ordination, in interaction, 45, Ch. 6
    passim
co-reference, 67, 85–7, 248
corrections, 330, 341, 360; *see also* repair
    'embedded' vs. 'exposed', 360
CT, 62; *see* coding time
courtroom interaction, 121–2, 284, 318, 377
cross-linguistic generalizations, *see*
    universals

Cubeo, 88
cultural variation, *see* comparison (across
    languages), universals, variation
    (socialinguistic)

DA, 286; *see* discourse analysis
days of the week, words for, *see* diurnal
    spans
declarations, 240
declaratives, 40, 228, 242, 243, 244, 250,
    251–5, 263–78 passim, 350, 365; *see*
    also sentence-types
deductive inference, 114–15
deep or underlying structure, 247–51,
    260–2, 268; *see also* logical form,
    semantic representation
defeasibility, 13–14, 25, 114–16, 121–2,
    137, 138, 142, 143–4, 145, 186–91,
    199, 204, 210ff, 223, 293; *see also*
    cancellability, *and under*
    conversational implicature,
    presupposition
    and discourse context, 115–16, 186–90,
        211, 220
    and linguistic context, 115–16, 186,
        190, 191ff, 220
definite article, *see under* article
definite descriptions, 60, 170–4, 181, 214
definite expressions, 86; *see also* article,
    demonstratives
definiteness, 83
deictic centre, 64, 73
deictic expressions, 64
deictic projection, 64, 68, 73–4
deictic simultaneity, 73
deictic usage, kinds of, 64–8, 95; *see also*
    anaphoric, gestural, symbolic usage
deixis, 3–4, 9, 27, 45, 51–3, Ch. 2,
    249–50, 284, 364, 372
    acquisition of, 61–2; *see also* acquisition
    descriptive frameworks for, 61ff
    discourse, **85–9**; *see also* discourse
        deixis
    and indices, *see under* pragmatic indices
    and logic, 3–4, 58–9
    person, **68–73**; *see also* participant-role,
        pronouns
    philosophical approaches to, *see under*
        philosophy
    place, **79–85**; *see also* place deixis
    reducibility of, 57–8
    relativized to text, 67n
    social, **89–94**; *see also* social deixis
    and semantics/pragmatics border, 55,
        59, 94–6, 249–50
    time, 73–79; *see also* time deixis

deixis (*cont.*)
  and truth-conditions, 20, 53, 58–61,
    87–8, 94–6
delay, in conversation, 307, 334, 336–7,
  339, 341; *see also* pauses
demonstratives, 54, 60, 61n, 62, 65, 72,
  79–83, 85
deniable inferences, 105, 115, 129, 143,
  186, 194–5
deontic modality, 192, 202, 277
descriptions, theory of, 170–4
detachability, 116, 128, 206, **223–4**; *see
  also* non-detachability
determiners, 82–3; *see also*
  demonstratives, *and under* article
diachrony, and deixis, 64
  and implicature, 165–6
dialect, 29
diglossia, 91, **93**
directives, 240, 241; *see also* orders,
  requests
disagreement, in conversation, 308, 334,
  336, 338–9
disambiguation, contextual, 7–9, 27–8, 76,
  119, 136, 233, 269ff, 278–80, 330ff;
  see also ambiguity
discourse, 27, 33, 35, 64, 162, 189–90; *see
  also* conversation
  non-conversational, 64, 284, 288, 301,
    318, 321
  well- vs. ill-formed, 286, 291–3, 306,
    321n
discourse analysis, 286–94
  data of, 286–7, 352
  categories of, 286, 288–9
  critique of, 289–94, 352–3
  interactional vs. text-grammatical, 288
  intuitions in, 286, 287, 292–3
  methods of, 286, 287, 319
  sentences in, 287, 288
  sequencing rules in, 286–7, 289–294,
    306, 367
  speech acts in, 288–94, 352
discourse context, and presupposition
  cancellation, 189–90, 199–200, 211;
  see also conversation, discourse deixis
discourse deixis, 62, 77n, 79, **85–9**,
  128–9
  and conventional implicature, 128–9
  impure, 87
  and truth-conditions, 96, 128–9
disjunction, 134, 136–7, **138–40**, 141, 142,
  188n, 193, 196–8, 200, 202–3, 211,
  213, 214
  exclusive vs. inclusive, 138–40
dispreferred turns, 50, 307–8, 320–1,

332–9, 357–8; *see also under*
  preference organization
  avoidance of, 333, 346, 356, 357ff
  characteristics of, 333–6
  typical contents of, 336
dispreferreds, 308; *see* dispreferred turns
distal demonstratives, *see* proximal vs.
  distal demonstratives
distributional constraints, *see under*
  syntactic rules
diurnal spans, words for, 52–3, 74–6
domain of discourse, 80n, 87
Dravidian, 365
Dyirbal, 72, 82, 90–1, 93

echo-questions, 341, 351, 365; *see also*
  next turn repair initiators
egocentric particulars, 57
ellipsis, 165n
emotive function, of speech, 41
empathetic deixis, 81
encoding, **10–11**, 21, 31; *see also*
  grammaticalization
encyclopaedic knowledge, 21–2, 80,
  146–7, 150–1, 204; *see also*
  background knowledge, mutual
  knowledge
entailment, 14, 52, 96, 103, 115, 116, 128,
  133–8 passim, 143, 173, **174**, 175–6,
  178, 185, 191ff, 199–203, 213–15,
  217, 219–20, 223, 258–9; *see also*
  logical consequence
  background vs. foreground, 219–20
  definition of, 174
  and felicity conditions, 258–9
  focal scale of, 219
  and implicature, 103, 115, 116, 123,
    133, 134, 135, 136, 137, 138, 143,
    213–14, 217, 223
  and presupposition, 173, 174–6, 178,
    185, 191ff, 199–203, 213–15
epistemic logic, 135–6, 137, 141, 144, 213,
  278n; *see also* knowledge
epistolary tenses, 74
equi-NP deletion, 249
essential condition, *see under* felicity
  conditions
eternal sentences, *see* tenseless sentences
ethnography of speaking, 279, 369,
  375
ethnomethodology, 46–7, **295**
even, 127
euphemism, 165
exclamatives, 42, 242n
exclusive vs. inclusive disjunction, *see
  under* disjunction

existential quantifier, 38; *see also*
quantifiers, *some*
existential statements, 215; *see also*
definite descriptions
explanation, 40ff; *see also* functionalism
exploitation:
of a communicative convention, 26,
112–13, 367
of the maxims of conversation, 109–13,
118n, 126, 143n, 147–62, 292; *see also*
flouting, maxims
expressibility, principle of, 233, 241–2
expressives, 240
extension expression, 207ff

face-to-face interaction, 43–7, 54, 63,
71–2, 237, 282, 284–5, 287, 294, 295,
309 and Ch. 6 passim, 378
vs. relayed communication, 52, 68–9,
72, 73–4, 297, 309
factives, *see under* presuppositions of,
verbs
falsehoods, categorial, 110, 151, 157
feature theories of meaning, 12, 148–51,
203–4; *see also* componential analysis,
semantic features
feedback, in interaction, 337
felicity, 24, 204–5; *see also*
appropriateness, felicity conditions
felicity conditions, 14, 25, 105, 113n,
168n, 217, **229–31, 238–40**, 244–5,
251, 258–9, 266–7, 271–2, 273, 280–1
ability, 259, 271, 358ff
classification of, 229, 239, 244
constitutive of forces, 238–40, 244–5
as entailments, 258–9
essential, 238, 239, 241, 244
as implicatures, 105, 241, 258–9
and indirect speech acts, 271–2, 273
inflexibility of, 238n, 273n, 280–1,
368
as pragmatic presuppositions, 259
preparatory, 239, 244, 259, 271
of promises, 238–9
propositional content, 239, 244, 272
of requests, 239–40
sincerity, 239, 244, 271
speaker- vs. hearer-based, 271
and truth conditions, 247, 258–9
of warnings, 239–40
figures of speech, or tropes, 38, 109–12,
126, 147ff, 161, 373; *see also under*
exploitation, irony, metaphor,
rhetorical questions, etc.
classification of, 148
interpretation of, 157–8, 160

filtering conditions, for presuppositions,
196–8, 208, 209–10, 224
'filters', of presuppositions, *see under*
presupposition
filters, syntactic, *see under* syntactic rules
first parts, *see under* adjacency pairs
flouting, of the maxims of conversation,
104–5, 109–13, 126, 147–62, 292; *see
also* exploitation
force, *see* illocutionary force
foreground vs. background, 219–20; *see
also* background knowledge
foregrounding, of information in clause,
41, 219–20; *see also* backgrounding,
topic/comment
formality, 23, 46, 90–1, 93
formulae, polite, 46, 71, 366
formulation, 285, 347, 367
frames, for interpretation, 281, 282, 332,
374
frankly, 255, 262
French, 28, 65, 177, 343n
functions of language, 36, 41ff, 239–42,
278–83, 311, 326ff; *see also* speech
acts
functional pressures on language, 40–7,
166, 368; *see also* functionalism
functionalism, 7, **40–7**, 97, 319, 322–5,
368, 373

game theory, 44
games, language, *see under* language-
games
gamma-operator, 221–2
gap, vs. silence, 299–300
gaze, 302; *see also* visual contact
generalized implicatures, *see under*
conversational implicature
generative semantics, 4, 36, 176, 272
German, 72
gesture, 52n, 54, 60, 65, 66, 281, 291; *see
also* gestural usage
gestural usage, of deictic expressions,
65–8, 71, 80, 95
given/new, 88, 220, 221, 225, 285, 354–5,
366; *see also* foregrounding,
presupposition, topic
go, 52, 83–4; *see also under* verbs (of
motion)
goals:
of actors, 44–5, 294; *see also* intention
of a pragmatic theory, 7, 29–32, 59, 76
of a semantic theory, 30, 204
grammar, overall theory of, 8, 9, 12, 29,
33, 129–30, 162; *see also* components,
and under pragmatics

Subject index

grammaticalization, 8–11, 21, 32, 43, 54,
55, 62, 63, 68–9, 89, 91–3, 162–6,
181–4, 206ff, 244
greetings, 26, 46, 71, 72, 79, 281n, 289,
293, 303, 308n, **309–12**, 327–8, 343–5
Gricean argument, *see under*
conversational implicature (calculation
of)
Gricean principles of inference, *see*
implicature
Grice's maxims, *see* maxims of
conversation
Grice's theory of meaning, *see* meaning-nn
group-operator, 221–2
Guugu Yimidhirr, 90–1, 93

hearer, vs. addressee, 72
hearing/understanding checks, 298, 303,
340ff, 348, 365; *see also* next turn
repair initiators, repair
hereby, 57, 232, 234, 255
heritage expression, 208–9
hesitation, 308, 313, 326, 334, 352, 353n,
374, 375; *see also* pauses
hey, 313, 314, 366
Hindi, 75
history, of pragmatics, 1–5, 35ff
'holes', *see under* presupposition
holophrases, 281
home-base, 84
honorific concord, 70, 90, 93, 130, 249;
see also agreement
honorifics, 25, 28, 63, **90–4**, 129, 130, 166,
216, 249
addressee, 90, 92–3
bystander, 90–1
referent, 90ff; *see also* T/V pronouns
hybrid theory of meaning, 15, 132, 145,
225

idealization, 33
identification, of speaker, *see under*
speakers
idioms, 268–70
if, 137, 141–2, 145–6, 192–3, 266–7; *see
also* conditionals
IFID, 238; *see* illocutionary force
(indicating devices)
illocutionary acts, 231, **236–7**; *see also*
speech acts
vs. locutionary acts, 236
vs. perlocutionary acts, 236–7; *see also*
perlocutionary acts
illocutionary force, 236ff, 277, 285; *see
also* performatives, speech acts
acquisition of, *see under* speech acts

constituted by felicity conditions,
238–40, 244–5
conventional nature of, *see under* speech
acts
indicating devices, 238, 239, 244, 245,
246, 264
indirect, *see* indirect speech acts
and intention, 241, 282
kinds of, 239–42; *see also under* speech
acts (classification of)
literal vs. indirect, 263–76, 291; *see also*
indirect speech acts
multiple, 261, 290–1
vs. perlocution, 236–7, 241–2; *see also*
perlocutionary acts
vs. propositional content, 236, 242, 243,
245
reduction to truth conditions, 246–7,
250, 251–60
and syntax, 247–51, 260–3, 265–8, 269,
272–3
imperative, 40, 107, 234, 242, 243, 244,
249, 250, 263–76 passim, 350, 365
implication, logical or material, 103, 116;
see also conditionals, entailment
pragmatic, 13ff, 21–2, 48–53; *see also*
inference
implicational scale, *see* scale
implicature, 10, 27, 33, 37–8, Ch. 3, 285,
292, 372; *see also* conversational
implicature, conventional
implicature, maxims or conversation
kinds of, **126–32**
and language structure, 162–6, 373
and meaning-nn, 101
problems for theory of, 118–22, 136,
145–7
universality of, 103, 120–1, 128
implicature expression, 207–9
implicitness in communication, 17–18,
38–9; *see also* indirection
imprecatives, 42
inappropriate utterances, *see* anomaly,
appropriateness, felicity, infelicity
incidental vs. defining characteristics, 110,
150–1; *see also* connotation
indeterminacy, of implicatures, 118, 160
index, *see* pragmatic indices
indexicals, 55ff, 57; *see also* deixis
indices, *see* pragmatic indices
indirect speech acts, 50, 51, 165, 262,
263–76, 291, 254, **356–64**
comprehension problem, 269ff, 281
definition of, 263–4
and felicity conditions, 271–3
idiom theory of, 268–70, 275

indirect speech acts (*cont.*)
  inference theory of, 268, 270–6, 278–82, 291
  and intonation, 269, 374
  politeness of, 273–4
  and pre-requests, 361–4
  rules for, 271–3, 289, 291
  and syntax, 265–8, 269, 270, 272–3, 363–4 366, 373
  universality of, 270, 276
indirect requests, *see under* requests
indirection, 17–18, 263–76, 335; *see also* indirect speech acts
Indo-European languages, 88; *see also under individual languages*
inductive inference, 114–15
infelicity, 26, 229, 234–5; *see also* anomaly, appropriateness, felicity
inference, pragmatic, 13–14, 21–2, 48ff, 76, Ch. 3 passim, Ch. 4 passim, 269–76, 278–82, 287, 326–33, 364; *see also* defeasibility, implicature, presupposition, indirect speech act
  context-sensitive, 13–14, 37, 55ff, 99, 115–16, 167, 121–2, 126–7, 137, 145, 177, 186ff, 197, 279–81; *see also* defeasibility
  in conversation, 39, 49, 279, 287, 290, 312, 321n, **326–33**, 364
  as corollary of usage constraints, 132, 279–80
  defeasible, *see* defeasibility
  frames for, 281, 282, 332, 374
  of illocutionary force, 269–76, 278–82, 356–64
  inconsistency of, 143–4, 145–7, 189, 190, 213–5, 224–5; *see also under* context (incremental model of), contradiction
  inductive vs. deductive, 114–15
  kinds of, 13–14, 38–40, 126–132
  linguistic structure and, 167, 265–8, 363–4
  and meaning-nn, 101
  rules of, 270–2, 279, 291
  vs. semantic inference, 8–9, 13–14, 37–8, 55, 94–6, 98–9, 132–47, 167, 177, 199–225, 246–63
  and sequential location, *see* inference (in conversation)
  and speech events, 279–80
informativeness, 101, 106, 111, 133, 135, 146–7, 218, 222
  principle of, 131, **146**, 218, 222
input to a pragmatic theory, *see under* autonomy, goals

insertion sequences, 304, 305–6, 348
intention, communicative, 11, 15–17, 29, 60, 101, 241, 273, 277, 282, 319
interaction, *see* face-to-face interaction, conversation
'interactional pessimism', 274, 363
interrogatives, 40, 184, 242, 243, 244, 250, 263–76 passim, 350–1, 365
  meaning of, 274–5
interruption, 299, 320, 330
intonation, x, 36, 233, 269, 296, 302, 313, 344, 374
invitations, 328, 333–4, 336, 346
invited inferences, 145–6
irony, 8, 17, 26, 28, 93, **109**, 116, 126, 161, 165, 273
ISA, 263; *see* indirect speech acts
island constraints, 40

Japanese, 69, 75, 77, 83, 88, 90, 91, 92, 93, 94, 129, 365
Javanese, 42, 90, 92, 93, 94, 216

kinship terms, 70–1; *see also* vocatives, *and under* address (terms of)
know, 136, 186
knowledge, *see* background knowledge, epistemic logic, mutual knowledge
Korean, 77n, 90, 93, 94, 129
Kwakwala, 77n

L-tense, 77–8
lambda-extraction, 221–2
language change, *see* diachrony
language-games, 227, 280–1; *see also* speech events
language structure vs. language use, 7–11, 43, 89, 93, 161, 162–6, 364–6, 372–4
language user, 1ff, 23
language understanding, 21–2, 24, 48ff, 76, 97–8, 146–7, 269ff, 279–81, 332, 364, 375, 377; *see also* artificial intelligence, communication, inference
lapse, *see under* pause
Latin, 74, 81
laughter, 291, 324, 331
left-dislocation, 89, 366; *see also* movement rules
lengthening, of syllables, 301, 337, 341, 374
levels, of grammar, *see* components of linguistic theory
lexical decomposition, 256
lexical items, *see* lexicon, word-meaning

Subject index

lexicalization, 163–4
lexicon:
  pragmatic constraints on, 37, 100,
    163–4, 372
  pragmatic information in, 8–9, 33–4,
    100, 127–30, 162–3, 179, 181–4,
    206–7, 212, 216, 268–70, 372
  reduction of complexity in, 37–8,
    98–100, 137–42, 145, 163–4, 216,
    225, 268–9
LFH, 263; *see* literal force hypothesis
literacy, 46, 378
literal meaning, 14n, 17n, 49, 97, 98, 102,
    117, 156; *see also* sentence-meaning,
    conventional content, conveyed
    meaning, literal force hypothesis
  vs. figurative use, 150, 151, 155, 156,
    160, 161, 165–6
literal force hypothesis, **263–5**, 268, 270,
    274–6, 282–3, 278, 282–3
literal vs. indirect force, 263–76 passim,
    357, 363; *see also* indirect speech acts,
    literal force hypothesis
literary criticism, *see* stylistics
local management systems, in
    conversation, 297, 300, 318, 329, 369
local vs. overall organization, *see* local
    management systems, overall
    organization
localism, 85
locutionary acts, **236**
logic, 6, 38, 57–9, 77, 100, 114–16, 138ff,
    140–1, 145, 169ff, 174, 176–7, 199ff,
    201, 202, 251ff, 277
  classical, 57, 58, 175–6; *see also*
    bivalence
  and defeasibility, 114–16
  deontic, 277
  epistemic, *see* epistemic logic
  and natural language, 6, 58–9, 100,
    138ff, 145, 169ff, 174, 175n, 176–7,
    199–203, 251ff
  modal, 140–1, 202
  predicate, 38; *see also* quantifiers
  three-valued, 176, 201
  second-order, 152n
  tense, 77
logical connectives, 100, 138–40, 141–2,
    145–6, 164, 191n, 192–3, 208,
    211–12; *see also* conditionals,
    conjunction, disjunction
logical consequence, 58, 95, 103, 140–1,
    174, 199; *see also* entailment, valid
    inference
logical form, 111, 218, 220–5; *see also*
    semantic representation

of cleft sentences, 125, 218
of definite descriptions, 170–2
and implicature, 122–5, 218, 220–5
and presupposition, 170–7, 218, 220–5
and speech acts, 251ff
logical models, of language, *see*
    truth-conditional semantics, *and*
    under logic (and natural language)
logical positivism, xii, 227–8
logical priority, of components of
    grammar, *see* autonomy (of
    semantics), components of linguistic
    theory

M-tense, 77–8
Madurese, 93
Malagasy, 81
man–machine interaction, 376–7
manage, 178–9
Manner, maxim of, **102**, 103, 107–8, 112,
    116, 117, 120, 122, 125, 135, 146,
    165, 218
marked vs. unmarked turns, 307–8, 313,
    322, 333, 342, 366
markedness, 307–8, **333**
maxims of conversation, **101ff**, Ch. 3
    passim, 218, 241, 293, 364, 367; *see*
    also Manner, Relevance, Quality,
    Quantity
  hedges on, 162
  non-linguistic analogues of, 103
  flouting vs. observing of, *see* flouting,
    observing, *and under* exploitation
meaning:
  hybrid theory of, 15, 132, 145, 225
  kinds of, 13–14; *see also* inference
  pragmatics as branch of the theory of, 11ff
  see also inference, literal meaning,
    meaning-nn, pragmatics, semantics,
    sentence-meaning, utterance-
    meaning, word-meaning
meaning postulates, 271
meaning-nn, **16**, 49, 101, 113, 131, 238, 241
meaningfulness, 170–1, 227
measures:
  of time, 73ff
  of space, 79ff
medium, of communication, 23, 63, 93
mention, *see* use vs. mention
metalinguistic uses of language, 7n, 41,
    228n, 247n, 368; *see also*
    token-reflexivity, use vs. mention
metaphor, 85, 100, 110, 118, 127, **147–62**,
    165, 273
  and analogy, 155, 159–62
  and category violation, 151, 153, 157

metaphor (*cont.*)
classification of, 152–3
comparison theory, **148**, 151–6
construal rules for, 149, 151, 158
correspondence theory, 159–60
feature transfer model of, 148–51
focus of, 148, 150
frame of, 148
and identity relation, 152n, 160n
indeterminacy of, 118, 160
interaction theory, **148–51**
and language change, 165–6
and models, 147, 159–60
nominal, 152
paraphrases of, 150, 156, 159–60
pragmatic theories of, 156–62
predicative, 152–3
and psychology, 147, 152, 158ff
recognition of, 157, 158, 159, 161
and semantic anomaly, *see* and category
    violation
and semantic representation, 154–5
semantic theories of, 148–56
sentential, 153
and simile, 151–6
and syntax, 154, 156, 166
'triggers' for, 151
metonym, 148
misleading utterances, 106, 117; *see also*
    anomaly
misplacement markers, 313, 322
misunderstandings, 279, 331, 353–4, 376,
    377; *see also* ambiguity, repair
'mitigators', 274, 334, 335, 341
modal contexts, and presuppositions, 192,
    193, 209, 211, 220
modal logic, *see under* logic
modality, 78, 135
modals, 99–100, 135, 138, **140–1**, 192, 202
modus tollens, 176
monitoring, audio-visual, 44, 65, 95
Montague grammar, 95, 131, **207**, 208
mood, 233, **243**; *see also* sentence-types
Moore's paradox, 100, 105, 235
morphemes, distribution of, *see under*
    syntactic rules
morphology, 63, 70, 77–8, 92, 130, 249
moves, interactional, 288, 303, 310, 311
movement rules, 373
mutual knowledge, **16**, 44–5, 113–14, 187,
    190, 205, 285; *see also* background
    knowledge, common ground

narrative, *see* stories
natural vs. artificial languages, 6, 138,
    145, 174, 176, 376–7; *see also*

artificial intelligence, defeasibility,
    logic (and natural language)
necessity vs. possibility, 134, 135, 137,
    140–1; *see also* modality, *and under*
    logic (modal)
negation, 139n, 163–4, 169–76, 218
ambiguity of, 171–3, 194, 201, 203,
    210, 222
constancy under, 168ff, 177–9, 184–5,
    193, 199
definitions of, 175, 178
external vs. internal, 201, 221–2
lexicalization of, 163–4
scope of, 171–2, 201, 218, 221–2
and presupposition, *see under*
    presupposition
test, for presuppositions, *see* constancy
    under
negative polarity items, 165
negatives, *see* negation
neustic, 242
New Guinea, languages of, 82
news, in conversation, 311n, 350ff; *see*
    also given/new, *oh*
next-speaker selection, 298, 300, 303, 320,
    365
next turn repair initiators, 334, 339, 341,
    342, 351, 359, 365
null context, 8–9
non-conventional aspects of meaning,
    12n, 15, 101, 112–3, 117, 119, 131–2;
    see also conversational implicature,
    and under speech acts (and
    intentions), presupposition (reduction
    of)
non-conventionality, of implicatures, 117,
    119
    of presuppositions, 206ff, 216ff
non-co-operation, 121-2; *see also*
    co-operation
non-deictic usage, of deictic expressions,
    65–8; *see also* anaphoric usage of
    deictic expressions
non-detachability, **116–17**, 119–20, **144**,
    206, 233–4
and conventional implicatures, 128, 129
and presupposition, 116, 223–4
non-synonymy, and implicature, 125, 144
non-truth-conditional aspects of meaning,
    13–14, 19, 59, 87–8, 94–6, 127–30,
    Ch. 3 passim, 188n, 199–225, Ch. 5
    passim
non-verbal cues, 337; *see also* gaze,
    pauses, prosody
NTRI, 339; *see* next turn repair
    initiators

observing, of the maxims of conversation, 104, 105–9, 113, 126–7; *see also* exploitation

offers, 240, 259, 272, 289, 290, 293, 303, 310, 334, 336, 343, 344, 359
    preferred to requests, 343, 355, 359

oh, 2, 3, 33, 129, 162, 311, 353

okay, 317–18, 322, 325, 346, 366

openings, of conversations, *see under* overall organization

optatives, 42

or, 134, 136, 137, 138–40, 141, 188n, 211; *see also* disjunction

order, of reported events, 35, 102, 108, 146; *see also* Manner, stories

orders, 242, 243, 246, 263–4, 272, 276, **277**, 278

orientation:
    to conversational principles, 103, 319ff
    spatial, *see* deixis
    mutual, in interaction, 44–5

ostension, *see* gestural usage

ostensive definition, of pragmatics, 27, 31–2

overall organization, of conversation, 49–50, **308–18**, 322, 328, 329, 366, 369
    closing sections in, 316–18, 322, 366; *see also* closings
    opening sections in, 309–12, 322, 323, 327–8, 343–5, 366; *see also* greetings
    and topic, 309, 312–16, 325

overhearers, 72; *see also* bystanders

overlap, 296–7, 299, 302, 303, 334, 365
    vs. interruption, 299, 319–20
    resolution system for, 300–1, 319

overstatement, 165–6

Pacific languages, 91; *see also under individual languages*

paralanguage, 63; *see also* gaze, prosody

parataxis, 120

parenthetical clauses, 179, 183–4, 266

participants, 1–5, 23, **68**, **72**, 83, 89ff, 102, 205, 212, 229, 295, 297, 300, 337, 354–5; *see also* addressees, bystanders, mutual knowledge, participant-role, speakers

participant-role, 23, 62, 63, **68ff**, 72, 73, 84, 89, 91; *see also* person, turn-taking

particles, 42, 87–8, 92, 93, 129, 162–3, 225, 233, 365, 372; *see also anyway*, *oh*, *well*, etc.

particularized implicatures, *see under* conversational implicature

partings, *see* closings, conversational

passive, 41

pauses, 255, **299–300**, 307, 320, **326–9**, 334, 337, 338–9, 341–2, 344, 370, 375
    'filled', 51
    vs. gaps, 299
    vs. lapses, 299, 300, 302, 320, 322
    psychological theories of, 326
    vs. silence, 299–300, 320–1, 324, 326–9, 337, 339, 341–2

'performadox', 257–8; *see also under* adverbs (performative)

performance, *see* competence/performance

performative adverbs, *see under* adverbs

performative analysis, *see* performative hypothesis

performative clause, 247–63 passim
    deletion of, 248–9, 250, 260–2

performative hypothesis, 247–63, 271, 272–3
    collapse of, 251–63
    semantic basis for, 246–7, 251–60
    strong version of, 250–1
    syntactic basis for, 247–50, 260–3

performative prefix, 244, 246, 247, 249, 253–5

performative verbs, 42, 232, 233–4, 244, 248–9, 250, 256, 258–9, 263
    classification of, 234, 239–41, 245
    performative vs. descriptive uses of, 232–3, 245–6, 252–5, 259

performatives, **228–37** passim, 244–63 passim, 282; *see also under* speech acts
    vs. constatives, 229–31, 234–5
    explicit, 231–3, 237, 244, 251–5; truth conditions of, 245–6, 246–7, 251–9, 263–4, 275
    implicit, 231, 233, 234, 244, 247–8, 251–5, 274–5
    normal form of, 231–3, 235, 244, 247ff
    tense/aspect of, 231–2, 247n
    truth vs. felicity of, 228–31, 234–5, 246–7, 251–60

perlocutionary acts/effects, **236–7**, 241–2, 290, 292
    properties of, 237, 292
    responses to, 290, 292

permissions, 276, 277, 280

person deixis, 20, 56, 62, **68–73**; *see also* person, social deixis

person:
    first, 54, 62, 69, 186, 231, 248; inclusive vs. exclusive, 69, 280n
    second, 54, 62, 65, 69, 92, 248, 249

person (*cont.*)
  third, 62, 65, 69, 70, 72
  fourth, 88
perspicuity, 102, 104; *see also* Manner
PH, 247; *see* performative hypothesis
phatic function of language, 41
phonology, 34, 93
philosophy, of language, 1–5, 36, 285, 371
  and deixis or indexicals, 55ff, 68, 80,
    87, 94–6
  and presupposition, 167, 169–76, 225
  and speech acts, 227–46
phrastic, 242
place deixis, 51–2, 62, **79–85**; *see also*
    space
  and discourse deixis, 85
  and time deixis, 84–5
please, 50, 265–6, 268, 269, 270, 272, 363,
    364
'plugs', *see under* presupposition
pluperfect, 77; *see also* tense
poetic function of language, 41
poetry, 147, 156
'point', of an utterance, 98, 180–1, 219,
    221
point of view, 64, 72, 83; *see also* deictic
    projection
polite pronouns, *see* T/V pronouns
politeness, 43, 83, 131–2, 165, 249, 273–4,
    300, 376
Ponapean, 91
position:
  sequential, 348ff
  characterizations of, 346–7, 349–52
  vs. turn, 348–9
possibility, 99, 134, 135, 137, **140–1**, 192,
    202, 209; *see also* modals, necessity
'pragmantax', 267
pragmatic constraints, on syntax, *see*
    under syntactic rules
pragmatic indices, or co-ordinates, 57,
    58–9, 94–5 249–50
pragmatic inference or implication, *see*
    implication, inference
pragmatic presupposition, *see under*
    presupposition
pragmatics:
  applications of, 376–7
  borders or bounds of, 1–5, 12–21, **27–9**,
    55, 59, 93–6, 374
  as competence vs. performance, 7–9,
    24–5, 33–5, 36
  as component of linguistic theory,
    33–5; *see also* components
  and 'core' linguistics, 7–8, 33–5, 372–4
  definitions of, 1–34

empirical vs. theoretical, 33, 279, 285
generative linguistics and, xii, 35–8, 40,
    130, 167, 176, 247–51, 260–3, 372–4
goals of, 7, **29–32**, 59, 76
motivations for, 35ff;
  and philosophy, *see* philosophy
  and phonology, 372, 373–4; *see also*
    prosody
  and psycholinguistics, 27, 375; *see also*
    psychology
  pure vs. descriptive, 1–2, 3
  reduction of, to semantics, 94–6, 176–7,
    199–204, 246–63
  and semantics, 1ff, 12–21, 33–5, 55,
    59, 94–6, 176, 199–204, 219–22, 225,
    372
  and syntax, xi, 1ff, 41, 89, 92, 125, 130,
    164–5, 181–4, 247–51, 260–3, 265–8,
    269, 272–3, 297, 364–6, 372–3
  universal vs. language-specific, 10,
    42–3, 45–6; *see also* comparison
    (across languages), universals
pragmatism, 1, 57
pre-announcements, *see under* pre-
    sequences
pre-closings, *see under* pre-sequences
pre-emptive use, of deictic words, 75–6
preference organization, **307–8**, 327,
    332–45, 355–6, 357–64 passim, 368,
    369;
  of turns, 332–9; *see also* dispreferred
    turns, preferred turns
  of sequences, 339–45; *see also* preferred
    sequences
preferreds, 308; *see* preferred turns,
    dispreferred turns
preferred sequences, 339–45, 355ff
  guesses vs. tellings, 350n, 356, 359n
  offers vs. requests, 343, 344, 355–6,
    359, 360–1
  in openings, 343–5
  recognitions vs. self-identifications,
    343–5
  in repair, 339–42
preferred turns, 307–8, 332–4; *see also*
    dispreferred turns
preparatory condition, *see under* felicity
    conditions
pre-requests, *see under* pre-sequences
presentatives, 65
pre-s, 345; *see under* pre-sequences (first
    turns of)
pre-sequences, 308, **345–64**, 369
  aborted, 347, 352, 358
  characterization of, 346–9
  composed of adjacency pairs, 349–50

pre-sequences (*cont.*)
  first turns of, 345, 346, 350, 352, 353,
    357–9, 362–3, 364
  motivations for, 347, 354–6, 357–9, 363
  in openings, 345–6
  positions vs. turns in, 348–9, 350
  pre-announcements, 323, **349–56**, 362
  pre-arrangements, 347–8
  pre-closings, 317–18, 322, 325, 346
  and preference organization, 355–6,
    357–64 passim
  pre-invitations, 346–7
  pre-offers, 349
  pre-requests, 321, 327, 343, 344, 347,
    348, **356–64**; and indirect requests,
    361ff
  pre-self-identifications, 344, 346
  truncation of, 361–4
presupposition, 9, 14, 25–6, 27, 45, 52,
  113n, 115n, 116, 117, 120n, 128, 131,
  Ch. 4, 235, 242, 251, 259, 284–5,
  364, 372, 373
  actual vs. potential, 212
  and assertion, 169–70, 173, 180, 197,
    242
  and background belief, *see* background
    knowledge, common ground, mutual
    knowledge, presupposition (and
    mutual knowledge)
  cancellation of, 189–90, 191–8, 207–9,
    211, **212–15**
  and conditionals, 184, 185, 188, 193,
    195, **196–8**, 200, 202, 208, 209–10,
    213–14, 224; *see also* 'filters' of
  and conjunction, 197, 209, 211
  and conventional implicature, 131,
    207–12, 216, 217
  conventionality of, 206–7, 212, 216ff
  and conversational implicature, 116–17,
    136–7, 186, 194n, 196, 213–14,
    217–25
  defeasibility of, 186–91, 199, 204, 210ff,
    220
  definitions of, 172, **175**, 176, 184–5
  denial of, 171–3, 190, **194–5**, 201, 210,
    214–15
  detachability of, 206, **223–4**
  and disjunctions, 188, 193, **196–8**, 200,
    202–3, 211, 213, 224
  and entailment, 174–7, 178–9, 191–8,
    199–203, 213–15, 217–25
  entailment/implicature analysis of,
    217–25
  and felicity conditions, 168, 259
  'filters' of, 196–8, 200, 208, 209–10,
    211, 216, 224

heterogeneity of, 180, 217
'holes' for, 193, 195, 198, 208, 211,
  216
and modal contexts, 192, 193, 202
and mutual knowledge, 25–6, 113n,
  205, 210–11, 212, 215
and negation, 168, 169–76, 178–9,
  184–5, 193, **201**, 203, 210, 215,
  217–8, 219, 221–2
and philosophy, *see under* philosophy
in positive sentences, 193, 194–5, 197
'plugs' for, 195–6, 198, 208, 211, 215,
  216
pragmatic, 96, 177, **204–25**, 259
projection of, 190, 191–8, 199, 200–3,
  207–10, 212–16, 223–5
properties of, 185–98
re-allocation of, 216–25
reduction of, 194n, **217–25**
semantic, 174–7, 178n, **199–204**
and sentence structure, 167, 206
sentences vs. utterances, as bearers of,
  170–3, 175, 178, 207–9, 212
speaker-, 170, 173, 177, 178n
Strawson's concept of, 172, **175**, 178, 179
survival, in modal contexts, 192, 202,
  224; in compound sentences, 184,
  193; through 'holes', 193, 195, 196,
  198
suspension of, 115n, 195
and syntax, 206, 373
triggers of, 179, **181–5**, 205–6, 207, 212,
  216, 218
and truth conditions, 199–203, 212
and truth values, 169–77, 178
universality of, 216
presuppositions:
  of adverbs, 184n
  of change-of-state verbs, 174, 181–2,
    188
  of clefts, 125, 182–3, 189, 206, 217–22
  of comparisons, 183
  of counter-factuals, 184
  of definite descriptions, 172, 174, 181
  of factive verbs, 25–6, 179–80, 181, 188,
    189–90, 193, 373
  of implicative verbs, 178–9, 181
  of iteratives, 52, 182, 193
  of proper names, 169, 174, 179
  of quantifiers, 174
  of questions, 184
  of relative clauses, 179, 183–4
  of singular terms, 174
  of stress, 183, 219, 374
  of temporal clauses, 174, 179, 182
  of verbs of judging, 182

principles, of language use, 9–11, 32, 35, 38, 272; *see also* expressibility (principle of), implicature, informativeness (principle of)
projectability, of turn completion, 297
projection problem, 13
  for implicatures, 133–4, 136–7, **142–4**, 145–7, **224–5**
  for presuppositions, 190, **191–8**, 199–203, 207–10, 212–16, 223–5
  for topics, x
promises, 106, 230, **238–9**, 240, 259, **277**; *see also* commissives
pronominalization, 86
pronouns, 3–4, 69ff, 85–7
  and anaphora, 85–7
  componential analysis of, 69
  and discourse deixis, 85–7
  of laziness, 86–7
  and social deixis, 90ff
propositions, 30–1, **58–9**, 80, 95, 117, 242, 245
propositional attitudes, 195, 241
propositional content, 228n, 239, 240, 242, **245**
propositional content condition, *see under* felicity conditions
prosody, x, 36, 71, 93, 183, 225, 255, 269, 296, 302, 311, 313, 344, 364, 374; *see also* intonation, lengthening, stress
proverbs, 151
proximal vs. distal demonstratives, 62, 80ff, 87
psychology, and pragmatics, 2, 4, 5, 27, 159–61, 281, 295, 302, 326, 332, 375

Quality, maxim of, **101**, 103, 105–6, 109–10, 157; *see also* irony, metaphor
quantifiers, 37–8, 100, 121, 133–4, 138, 143–4; *see also* all, existential quantifier, *some*, universal quantifier, *and under* conversational implicatures, presuppositions
Quantity, maxim of, **101**, 102, 103, 106–7, 110–11, 123, 131, 132–47, 163–4, 213–14, 354, 355
  clausal implicatures of, 132, 136–45, 188n, 213–14, 225
  conflicting inferences, 145–7
  scalar implicatures of, 132–6, 138–46, 163–4, 213–14, 224
queclaratives, 373
questions, 105–6, 107, **184**, 239, 242, 263–5, 266–7, 270, 274–5, 276, 278, 281n, 289, 290, 293, 298, 327, 330,

336, 352, 353–4; *see also* interrogatives
  and answers, 289, 293, 303, 305, 307, 320, 330; *see also* adjacency pairs, answers
  kinds of, 184, 273n, 274–5, 327, 366; *see also* echo-questions
  as requests to tell, 256, 275
  rhetorical, 110, 157, 165, 274, 373
Quileute, 43

R, 307n; *see* receiver
radical pragmatics, 37n, 221n
rationality, 44, 101, 103, 121, 168, 241, 259, 276
receiver:
  of signals, 16, 63; *see also* recipient
  of telephone calls, 307n, 309ff, 327–8, 343–5
receiving time, 62, 73ff
recipient, of message, 16, 68ff, 91, 241; *see also* addressees, participant-role, receiver
reckoning, of time, 73, 76
recognition, of speakers by hearers, *see under* speakers (identification of)
recorded messages, and deixis, 73–4, 378
redundancy, 120, 163, 164, 194; *see also* tautology
reference:
  and deixis, 58–61, 79
  and presupposition, 169 74
  and topic, 313–15
reference points, deictic, 58, 95, 249–50
  reference time, 77–8, 84
referent honorifics, 90ff
referential function of language, 41, 46; *see also* functions of language
referential vs. attributive uses of referring expressions, 60
reflexives, 248, 273
refusals, 334ff, 357–9, 364; *see also* dispreferred turns, *and under* requests
regret, 25–6, 179–80, 181, 188, 223; *see also* factives
regulative rules, *see* constitutive vs. regulative rules
reinforceability, 120
relative clauses:
  non-restrictive, 165, 183–4, 261
  restrictive, 183
Relevance, maxim of, **102**, 103, 106n, 107, 109n, 111–12, 127, 135, 157, 164, 219, 292

repair, conversational, 303, 308, 319, 330, 334, **339–42**, 348, **359–60**
  opportunities for, 340, 341
  other-initiated vs. self-initiated, 340–2, 359, 365
  other-repair vs. self-repair, 340–2
  preference in, 341–2
  and syntax, 365
representatives, 240, 241
requests, 50–1, 98, 107, 239–40, 242, 243, 258, 259, 261, 263–76 passim, 280, 281, 282, 298, 305, 336, 347, 348, 356–64; *see also* pre-requests
  indirect, 264–5, 266, 268, 270, 272, 356–64
  refusals vs. acceptances of, 308, 333–7, 357–9
  replaced by offers, 343, 344, 355–6, 359, 360–1
respect, *see* honorifics, politeness
rhetoric, 38, 147, 158, 376
rhetorical questions, *see under* questions
ritual-constraints, 44, 45–6
'ritual' formulae, *see* formulae, politeness
role, of participants in speech event, *see* participant-role

S. E. Asian languages, 77n, 90, 129; *see also under individual languages*
'said' vs. implicated, 97–8, 112ff, 127, 131, 132
Samal, 72, 81
scalar, implicatures, *see under* Quantity
scale, linguistic, **133**, 138, 163–4, 213
scope, ambiguities of, *see under* ambiguity
seconds, or second parts, *see under* adjacency pairs
selectional restrictions, 110
self-editing, 313, 334, 341, 365, 375; *see also* repair
self-identification, *see under* speaker
self-referring expressions, *see* token-reflexivity
'semantax', 267
semantic entailment, 174, 199ff; *see also* entailment
semantic features, *see* componential analysis
semantic presupposition, *see under* presupposition
semantic relations, 174, 199
semantic representation:
  and implicature, 122–5, 220–5
  and presupposition, 207, 219–25
  and speech acts, 246–63, 268
semantic shift, 165–6

semantics:
  border with pragmatics, *see under* pragmatics
  interaction with pragmatics, 13–15, 20, 30–5, 55, 59, 94–5, 98–100, 122–47, 156ff, 162–6, 174–7, 199ff, 217–25, 236, 245, 246–7, 251–60, 268–9, 274–6, 372
  kinds of theories of, 12–13, 148ff, 199ff, 203ff, 245; *see also* truth-conditional semantics
  scope of, 1–5, 12ff, 28, 38, 55, 59, 94–6, 98–100, 132, 148–56, 199–204, 275
  simplification of, 37–8, 98–100, 108–9, 132–47
  see also truth-conditional semantics
semiosis, *see* semiotics
semiotics, branches of, 1–5, 6, 33
semi-sentences, 165n
sender of signals, 16, 63
sense vs. reference, 170
senses, proliferation of, 99, 108–9, 132–47; *see also under* ambiguity
sentence, 17, **18–19**, 25, 30–1, 35, 55–6, 59, 68–9, 94, 104n, 133–4, 172, 175, 178, 207–9, 211, 212, 231n, 242–3, 247ff, 251, 263ff, 275–6, 288, 291, 365–6, 372–4; *see also* sentence-fragment, sentence-meaning, sentence-types, utterance
  as unit of conversation, 288, 291, 294, 297
  vs. utterance, *see under* utterance
sentence-fragment, 16, 18, 164, 165n, 291
sentence-meaning, 17, 18–20, 59, 273; *see also* conventional content, literal meaning
sentence-tokens, 19
sentence-types, 40, 42, 233n, 242, **243**, 244, 250, 263–5, 274–5, 276, 350, 357, 365, 373
  meaning of, 233, 244, 250, 274–5, 276
  minor, 242n
  vs. sentence-tokens, 19
  syntax of, 250, 373
  and truth conditions, 247ff, 251ff, 274–5
  universals, 40, 242, 276
sequence, conversational, 49, 279, 286, 308, 310, 326ff, 339–69 passim; *see also* adjacency pairs, pre-sequences, repair, *and under* conversation
  of positions vs. turns, 348–9, 350
  location in, 312, 326–32, 345ff; *see also* slots

sequencing rules, in conversation, *see under* conversation
setting, *see* context, formality
'setting selection', theory of, 7–9; *see also* disambiguation
shared knowledge, *see* background knowledge, common ground, mutual knowledge
signs:
  indexical, 57
  systems of, *see* semiotics
silence, *see under* pauses
similes, 151–6
sincerity, 51, 103, 105; *see also* felicity conditions, Quality
situation of utterance, canonical 63, 73; *see also* context, deixis, speech event
slots, conversational, 312ff, 325, 331, 337, 340, 346, 367
social constraints on language use, x, 45–6, 89, 279; *see also* ritual-constraints
social deixis, 46, 62–3, 64, 70, 77n, **89–94**, 128–9, 166, 177, 374; *see also* honorifics, T/V pronouns
  absolute vs. relational, 90–1
  and conventional implicature, 128–30, 177
  and pragmatic presupposition, 177
  and truth-conditions, 96, 128–9, 177
social rank, *see* social status
social relationship, 69–71, 89–94, 129, 280, 295; *see also* honorifics, social deixis, social status
social status, 10, 23, 25, 63, 69–70, 129; *see also* honorifics, social deixis
sociolinguistics, and pragmatics, 2, 25, **27–9**, 33, 93–4, 295, 369, 374–5; *see also* variation
some, 37–8, 119–20, 121–2, 133–4, 142–4, 163–4, 377; *see also* quantifiers
source, of message, 68, 72–3
space:
  deictic categories of, *see* place deixis
  conceptualization of, 68, 79, 82–3
Spanish, 83
speakers, 1–5, 8, 9, 16, 17–18, 20, 23, 24n, 51–2, 53, 56, 58, 62, 64, **68–73**, 81, 90–2, 101–2, 104n, 113, 134–6, 143, 157–8, 170, 173, 177, 205, 212n, 213–14, 218, 238–9, 240, 248–9, 250, 260, 271, 272, 276, 277, 296ff, 311–12, 337, 343–5
  identification of, 56, 309, 311–12, 328, 343–5, 346, 354
  selection of, *see* next-speaker selection

transition between, *see* turn-taking
speaker-meaning, 17; *see also* intention, meaning-nn, utterance-meaning
speaker-reference, vs. semantic reference, 60
speech acts, 9, 27, 42, 45, 71, 89, 105, Ch. 5, 285, 288ff, 332, 352, 354, 357ff, 368, 373; *see also* illocutionary force, performatives
  abuse vs. misfire of, 230
  acquisition of, 281–2
  ambiguity of term, 236, 243
  'Antithesis' theory of, 246–63
  characterization of, 233–4, 238–42, 244–5, 276–8; *see also* felicity conditions
  classification of, 234–5, 239–42, 245
  consequences of, 237, 259
  context-change theory of, 276–8
  conventional nature of, 229–30, 237, 241, 243, 264, 282
  and conversation, 278ff, 285, 288–94, 332, 368
  definition of, 236
  'family relations' of, 238n, 274–5, 278
  felicity conditions on, *see under* felicity conditions
  mapped onto utterances, 263–76, 278–83, 288–92
  indirect, *see* indirect speech acts
  institutional preconditions for, 229, 240, 241, 247n, 260
  and intentions, 229, 238, 241, 282
  interactional aspects of, 237, 259–60
  irreducibility of, 246, 251–60; *see also* 'Thesis'
  multiple, per sentence, 261, 290–1
  vs. perlocutions, **237**, 241, 243–4, 290
  reduction of, 246, 251, 255, 258; *see also* 'Antithesis'
  and reference, 60
  and sincerity, 230, 235
  and syntax, 247–50, 260–3, 265–8, 373
  'Thesis' theory of, 243–6, 254, 257, 263
  and truth-conditional semantics, 246–63
  uptake of, 230, 237, 260
  universals of, 270, 276
speech event, 83, 84, 95, **279–81**, 282
speech levels, 90; *see also* honorifics
standard implicatures, 104, 106, 107, 118, 120
statements, 58–9, 172ff, 234–5, 242, 263–4, 276, 277, 281n; *see also* assertion, constatives, representatives
  vs. sentences, *see under* utterance (vs. sentence)

stories:
  'main line' of, 88
  in conversation, 323–4, 328–9, 331–2,
    349, 352, 353; *see also* order, Manner
strength, semantic, 133, 137, 146; *see also*
  informativeness, scale
stress, x, 36, 139n, 183, 219, 341, 370,
  374; *see also* prosody
structuralism, 36, 367
style, 91; *see also* diglossia, formality,
  politeness
stylistic options, non-synonymy of, 125
stylistics, 147, 226
subject:
  of imperatives, 249
  logical vs. syntactic, 170–1, 220–2
  and topic, 88, 220
suggestions, 50–1, 261, 267, 278, 334, 337
summonses, 71, 92, 281n, 310, 365
  reasons for, 310–11, 312, 315, 345–6
summons–answer sequences, **309ff**, 320,
  321, 345–6
suppletion, and honorifics, 92
surface structure:
  and implicature, 122–5
  interpreted, 125n
  and presupposition, 179, 186; *see also*
    under triggers
  and speech acts, 247–50, 260–1, 265–7
  and turns in conversation, 297, 302–3
suspension:
  vs. cancellation, of implicatures, 115,
    142
  of presuppositions, 115n, 194–5
switch, of deictic centre, 64, 68; *see also*
  turn-taking
symbolic usage, of deictic expressions,
  65–8, 71
synecdoche, 148
synonymy, 116, 119–20, 125, 144
syntactic amalgams, 164–5, 261, 373
syntactic models, of discourse, *see under*
  conversation
syntactic rules:
  pragmatic constraints on, xi, 36, 41,
    88–9, 92, 130, 164–5, 206, 263,
    265–8, 269, 272–3, 274, 363–4, 372–3
  pragmatic filtering of, xi, 36, 92, 130,
    268, 272–3
syntax, 1, 5, 36; *see also* syntactic rules
  and pragmatics, *see under* pragmatics
system-constraints, 44
system-sentence, 19

taboo 'languages', 72, 90; *see also*
  bystanders, social deixis

Tagalog, 88
tag-questions, 47, 261, 298, 365
Tamil, 70, 72, 91, 92, 93
target, of message, 68, 72–3, 260
tautology, 100, 110–11, 124–5, 127
telephone, conversation on, 52, 72, 296,
  297, 302, 307n, 309–18, 327–8,
  343–5
tense, 20, 56, 74, **76–8**, 250
tense logic, 77
tenseless languages, 77–8
tenseless sentences, 77, 250–1
text deixis, *see* discourse deixis, deixis
text grammar, 286, 288
text-sentence, 19
Thai, 91
'Thesis', 243ff; *see also under* speech
  acts
third person, 61n, 62; *see also* person deixis
three-valued logic, 176; *see also*
  truth-value gaps, truth values
time:
  adverbs of, *see* adverbs
  reckoning of, 73
  semantics of, 73
  units of, 73ff
time deixis, 62, **73–9**
  and discourse deixis, 85
  and place deixis, 84–5
Tlingit, 81
token-reflexivity, 57, 62n, 86, 95, 254n
topic, in conversation, 51, 111, 293,
  312–16, 324, 325, 366
  change of, 313, 314
  collaborative construction of, 315
  vs. sentence-topic, 77n, 88–9, 366; *see*
    also 'aboutness'
  first, 312–13, 315, 318, 323, 325
  and linguistic structure, 366
  in monotopical calls, 316
  and reference, 313–15
topic/comment, x, 88–9, 225; *see also*
  'aboutness', backgrounding,
  given/new, mutual knowledge,
  presupposition
topicalization, 41
transcription:
  broad vs. narrow, 295
  notation, 369–70
  limitations of, 295, 348n
  of prosody, x, 296
transderivational constraints, 272–3
transition relevance place, **297**, 298, 299,
  300, 303, 323, 324, 354
transition space, 340
'triangular' kin terms, 71

trichotomy, syntax/semantics/pragmatics, 1ff, 33; *see also* components of linguistic theory
'triggers', of inferences, 49ff
of implicatures, 108
of indirect force interpretations, 270–1, 273
of metaphors, 151, 157
of presuppositions, 179, 181–5
tropes, *see* exploitation, figures of speech, irony, metaphor, understatement, *and under* questions (rhetorical)
tropic, 242
TRP, 297; *see* transition relevance place
truth, and falsity, 3–4, 20, 55ff, 77, 86, 101, 105, 109–10, 114–15, 117, 124, 136, 153, 155, 170–7, 217, 227, 228n, 229, 234–5, 240, 242, 246–7, 252–3; *see also* verifiability
pragmatic vs. semantic, 252–3
truth-conditional semantics, 12–15, 28, 34, 35, 55, 94–6, 128, 138ff, 164, 174ff, 199–203, 227, 246–7, 251–60, 372
limitations of, 12ff, 34–5, 48ff, 59, 94–6, 97–8, 114–16, 124–5, 128–9, 199–203, 219–20, 227ff, 246, 251–60
truth-conditions, 12–15, 20, 28, 34, 35, 55–9, 77–8, 94–6, 97, 119, 122ff, 127–9, 164, 170ff, 220, 227, 246–7, 251–60
of declaratives, 251–5, 257–8
and felicity conditions, 258
and implicatures, 122–32
and indexicals, 20, 55–61, 94–6
of non-declaratives, 246–50, 251, 258
of performatives, 246–7, 251–60
and presuppositions, 169–77, 178–9, 199–203, 212
and speech acts, 227ff, 234–5, 246–63
and tautologies, 111, 124–5
of tenses, 77–8
of utterances vs. sentences, *see under* utterance
truth-functional connectives, *see* logical connectives
truth tables, 99
truth-value gaps, 174n, **176**, 201
truth values, 170, 175–6, 228ff
preconditions for having, 169–76
two vs. three, 175–6; *see also* bivalence
utterances lacking, 228ff; *see also under* presupposition, speech acts
see also truth, truth-conditions
Tunica, 42, 91

Turkish, 81
turns, **296–303**, 307, 317, 321, 331–2, 332–9, 345–64 passim, 365, 368
constructional units of, 297–8, 300, 302, 365
delayed, 334ff
design of, 337, 351, 362–3, 364, 365
extended, 323–4, 354
gaps between, 299–300, 302
interactive construction of, 336–7, 339, 368
overlap of, *see* overlap
vs. positions, 348–9, 350
prefaces to, 334
size of, 300
surface-structural nature of, 297, 302–3
turn-taking, 47, 68, **296–303**, 318, 319–21, 322–5, 326–7, 330, 331–2, 354, 378
auditory motivation for, 301n
ethological basis of, 301
and gaze, 302
initiation of, 322–3, 324
locally-managed vs. pre-allocated, 297, 300, 301, 318
and pauses, 299–300, 302, 326–7
precision of, 297, 298
properties of, 296–7
and prosody, 297, 302, 374
rules for, 297, **298**, 299–303 passim, 326
'signalling' model of, 301–2
suspension of, 323–4, 328, 331, 348
and syntax, 365
termination of, 324–5
universals of, 301
T/V pronouns; 28, 70, 89, 90, 92, 128–30, 166
and truth conditions, 96, 128–9, 177
Tzeltal, 93

understanding, *see* language understanding, uptake
display of, 321, 331–2, 339–40
understatement, 157, 161
universal quantifier, 38, 123–4, 133–4, 144, 163–4; *see also* quantifiers
universals, of pragmatics, xi, 10, 40, 45–7, 69, 78, 90, 103, 120–1, 201, 216, 221, 242, 270, 272, 276, 296, 301, 368–9, 376; *see also* comparison (across languages)
uptake, 230, 237, 260, 285; *see also under* speech acts
usage conditions, 245, 247
usage theory of meaning, 227ff, 245–6

use vs. mention, 7n, 86, 109n, 139n, 247n
users of language, 1–5, 23; *see also* addressees, participants, speakers
uses of language, *see* functions of language
utterance, 3, 16, **18–19**, 24–6, 30–2, 34–5, 55–9, 95, 101, 104n, 132, 143, 146, 170–3, 175, 178, 205, 211, 212–13, 219–20, 231n, 242–3, 244, 259, 274–5, 278–83, 288ff, 289n, 326ff, 332, 364
  definitions of, 18–19, 19n, 289n
  non-linguistic, 16–17, 291, 321
  vs. sentence, as bearer of truth-conditions, 17–20, 34–5, 55–7, 58–9, 95, 104n, 133–4, 172, 175, 199ff, 228ff, 247, 251ff, 274–5; as bearer of force, 231n, 242–3, 274–5; as bearer of implicatures, 104n, 122–32, 133–4; as bearer of presuppositions, 170–3, 175, 178, 207–9, 211, 212, 219–20, 225
  as unit of conversation, 288, 291, 294
utterance-act vs. utterance-product, 19
utterance-meaning, 18–21, 59, 364
utterance-type vs. utterance-token, 19
utterance-unit, 289ff, 290–1

vagueness, 99, 138, 352–3
valid inference, 114–15, 140, 174
variables, sociolinguistic, *see* variation
variation, sociolinguistic, 25, 29, 375

verbs:
  change-of-state, 174, 181–2, 188
  factive, 25–6, 179–80, 181, 188, 189–90, 193
  of judging, 182
  of motion, 83–4
  performative, *see* performative verbs
  of propositional attitude, 195
  of saying, 195, 215, 256; *see also* performative verbs
verifiability, 227
  by use, 247, 251
visible/invisible, deictic category of, 63n, 77n, 82
visual contact, in communication, 72, 95, 297, 302
vocabulary, general, 138, 145; *see also* lexicon
vocatives, 53, 63, **70–1**, 89n, 91, 92; *see also* address, pronouns
voice-quality, 311, 327, 344

warnings, 234, 238, 239–40, 247
well, 33, 88, 98n, 162, 307, 334, 338, 366, 372
word-meaning, 33, 137, 148–9, 162–3, 204, 228n, 247, 258–9; *see also* lexicon
word-order, 88–9, 225
writing, 23, 93; *see also* diglossia, literacy, recorded messages

Yoruba, 78

INDEX OF NAMES

Albert, E. M., 301
Allwood, J., 25, 30n, 58, 77, 135, 152n, 176n, 201, 221, 241, 259, 271, 314, 368
Anderson, S. R., xi, 43, 62, 63n, 67n, 77n, 81, 82, 88, 260
Andersson, L.-G., 25, 30n, 58, 77, 135, 152n, 176n, 221, 271, 314
Annamalai, E., 216
Aqvist, L., 254n
Argyle, M., 302
Aristotle, 100, 140, 147, 175n, 227n
Arnold, G. F., 296n
Atkinson, J. M., 39n, 46, 91, 287, 294n, 300, 309, 333-4, 336n, 345-6, 375, 377
Atkinson, M., 41, 47, 60
Atlas, J. D., xiv, 60, 125, 131, 136, 147, 170, 182, 201, 206, 210, 217, 220, 221n, 242, 371
Austin, J. L., 25, 36, 227-31, 233-40, 243, 245-7, 259-60, 264, 279, 371, 378
Ayer, A. J., 227

Bach, K., 241
Ballmer, T., 277
Bar-Hillel, Y., 4, 18, 19, 23, 58, 59, 60
Bates, E., xii, 226, 281
Bateson, G., 2
Bauman, R., 279, 369
Bean, S., 1n, 57
Beattie, G., 302
Beaugrande, R. de, 286, 314
Beavin, J. H., 2
Beck, B., 70
Bernstein, B., 326, 374
Bierwisch, M., 6
Black, M., 2, 159
Boër, S. G., 204, 217, 257, 258n, 262
Bolinger, D. L., 275
Brady, R., 302

Brazil, D., xi, 287, 288, 296n, 374
Brockway, D., 88, 162
Brown, P., xiv, 10, 40, 46, 70, 89, 93, 121n, 132, 162-3, 165-6, 267, 269n, 270, 271n, 272-4, 363, 374, 376
Brown, R., 28, 90, 92, 166
Bruner, J., 226, 281
Bühler, K., 41, 46, 61
Burks, A. W., 57
Burling, R., 69
Butterworth, B., 302-3, 326
Button, G., 315n

Carling, C., 150
Carnap, R., 2-5, 10, 20, 271
Charniak, E., 22, 281, 332
Casey, N., 315n
Cherry, C., 2
Chomsky, N., xii, 4, 7, 24, 33, 34, 36, 40, 183, 219, 250, 374
Clark, H., 225, 285, 375
Cohen, L. J., 147, 149, 151
Cole, P., xiii, 37n, 166, 221n
Comrie, B., 42, 70, 78, 90, 92, 130, 333
Corbett, G., 92
Corum, C., 93, 374
Coulthard, M., xi, 279, 286-8, 293, 294n, 296n, 304, 315n, 356n, 374
Cresswell, M., 95, 257
Crystal, D., 296n

Dahl, O., 25, 30n, 58, 77, 135, 152n, 176n, 221, 271, 314
Davidson, J., 328, 337
Davison, A., 256, 266
Dinneen, D. A., xiii, 168
Dittmar, N., 378
Dixon, R. M. W., 43, 72, 82, 93
Donnellan, K. S., 34, 60, 61
Dore, J., 281
Dowty, D. R., 207n
Dressler, W., 286, 314

Index of names

Drew, P., xiv, 39n, 282, 294n, 300, 309, 327, 333–4, 336n, 345–6, 356n, 375, 377
Dummet, M., 242
Duncan, S., 302
Duranti, A., 89, 366

Edmondson, W., 288, 292
Ervin-Tripp, S., 47, 93, 264, 275, 280, 297, 302, 358, 374–5

Fann, K. T., 228n
Fanshel, D., 274, 286–9, 294, 352, 357, 369, 375
Feldstein, S., 302
Ferguson, C. A., 46, 47, 93, 366
Fillmore, C. J., xi, xiv, 47n, 53, 54, 61–2, 64–7, 69, 70, 73–6, 78–81, 83–6, 89, 91, 94, 182, 226
Firth, J. R., xii
Fiske, D. W., 302
Fletcher, P., 375
Fodor, J. A., 7, 22, 27, 148, 204, 288
Fogelin, R., 100n
Foley, W., 225
Forman, D., 271
Fraser, B., 260
Frege, G., 169–70, 173–4, 177, 179, 181–2, 225, 242
Frei, H., 61, 81
Freud, S., 4
Furberg, M., 227n, 228n

Gale, R. M., 57
Garfinkel, H., 295
Garman, M., 375
Garner, R. T., 175n
Garvin, R. L., 91
Gazdar, G., xi, xiii, xiv, 4, 9, 12, 17n, 24n, 26, 31, 34, 36n, 37, 69n, 105n, 115n, 120, 122–3, 125n, 126, 130, 132, 134, 136, 139–41, 143, 145, 164–5, 186, 195, 201, 203–5, 209, 211–12, 214–16, 224, 242, 245, 250–1, 252n, 255, 260, 262–3, 267, 272, 273n, 274, 276–7, 372n
Geach, P. T., 86
Geertz, C., 42, 90, 92
Geiss, M., 145
Gilman, A., 28, 90, 92, 166
Givon, T., 40, 373
Godard, D., 343
Goffman, E., 44, 72, 304, 356n
Goldman-Eisler, F., 301n, 326
Goodwin, C., 72, 289n, 296n, 297, 301n, 302, 337, 353n, 364, 375
Goody, E., 280
Goody, J., 46

Gordon, B., 226
Gordon, D., 37, 266–7, 271–3, 275
Graham, K., 228n
Green, G., xi, 36n, 261, 269, 372n
Greenbaum, S., 242n
Grice, H. P., 16–18, 24, 26, 27, 36, 49, 88, 96, 100–4, 105n, 108n, 109, 111–19, 120n, 126–9, 132, 134, 139n, 147, 156–8, 161, 188n, 207, 218, 222–3, 238, 241, 270, 273, 282, 292, 354, 364, 367, 374
Griffiths, P., 281–2
Grosu, A., 40
Grossman, R. E., 40
Gumperz, J. J., xiv, 23, 29, 39n, 279, 281, 374–5, 377
Gundel, J. K., x, 88, 89n, 225

Haas, M. R., 42, 91
Haimoff, E., 301
Halliday, M. A. K., 42, 282
Halvorsen, P., 125n, 178n, 182
Hamblin, C. L., 24n, 277
Hancher, M., 241
Harada, S. I., 70, 90, 92, 130
Hare, R. M., 242, 275
Harnish, R. M., 108n, 146, 147, 241
Harris, Z., 19n
Haviland, J. B., xiv, 90, 93
Haviland, S. E., 225, 285
Hawkins, J. A., 61n, 83
Head, B., 92
Heath, J., 43, 71
Hedenius, I., 86, 247
Heinämäki, O., 182, 187
Heny, F., 86
Herasimchuk, E., 39n
Heringer, J. T., 266, 272, 356n
Heritage, J., xiv, 129, 287, 294n, 311n, 353, 356n
Herzberger, H. O., 202n
Hilpinen, R., 277
Hine, R., 302
Hintikka, K. J. J., 135, 275
Horn, L. R., 37, 38, 115n, 132, 134, 139n, 140–1, 163, 164n, 195, 201
Horne, E. C., 92
House, J. 376
Huddleston, R., 78
Hudson, R. A., 261
Hull, R. D., 274
Hymes, D., 25, 72, 73, 279, 375–6

Ingram, D., 69
Irvine, J. T., 46, 91, 366

Jackson, D. D., 2

418

Jaffé, J., 302
Jakobovitz, L. A., 226
Jakobson, R., 41, 46, 333n
James, D., 163
Jefferson, G., 284n, 295n, 298–9, 301,
    303, 315n, 318, 321, 324, 339–42,
    355, 360, 365, 369, 375
Johns, C., xi, 296n, 374
Johnson, M., 159
Joshi, A. K., 377
Jupp, T., 279, 377
Jung, C., 4

Kalish, D., 4
Kaplan, D., 34, 61
Karttunen, L., 86, 116, 127, 131, 181, 185,
    187–8, 193, 195–8, 202, 207–10, 212,
    214–17, 274
Kasper, G., 376
Katz, J. J., 7, 8, 20, 22, 27, 30, 33, 148,
    184, 203, 204, 241, 250, 288
Keenan, E. L., xi, 43, 62, 63n, 67n, 77n,
    81, 82, 88, 96, 176–7, 189, 217
Keenan, E. O. (see also Ochs, E.), x,
    121n, 282, 313, 366
Kempson, R. M., 8, 33, 127, 128, 201,
    204, 217, 245, 247n
Kendon, A., 302
Kiefer, F., 6, 122
Kiparsky, C., 181, 373
Kiparsky, P., 181, 373
Klein, E., xi, xiii, 37, 130, 272
Kroch, A., 122, 147
Kuhn, T. S., 159
Kuno, S., 90

Labov, W., 29, 274, 286–9, 294, 324, 352,
    357, 369, 375
Lakoff, G., xiv, 37, 116, 159, 164–5, 176,
    183, 250–3, 261, 266–7, 271–3, 275,
    373, 374
Lakoff, R., xiv, 74, 78, 81, 98, 162, 255, 274
Laing, R. D., 2
Lambert, W. E., 28, 92
Langendoen, D. T., 180, 191, 203, 212
Leach, E. R., 159n
Leech, G. N., 46, 73, 79, 203, 242n, 260,
    271n, 274
Lemmon, E. J., 247
Levin, S., 148–9, 226
Levinson, S. C., x, 10, 21, 25, 40, 46,
    69–70, 73, 88–9, 92–3, 121n, 122,
    125, 131–2, 136, 147, 162–6, 182,
    206, 216–17, 220, 267, 269n, 270–5,
    279–81, 290, 363, 368, 374, 376
Lewis, D., 14n, 16n, 58, 113n, 251–2,
    255, 275

Li, C. N., 88
Liberman, M., 211, 269, 374
Lieb, H.-H., 3
Lightfoot, D., xi, 37
Locke, J., 1
Longacre, R. E., 42, 88, 163, 286, 288
Lucas, E. D., 378
Luce, R. D., 44
Lucy, P., 375
Lycan, W. G., 204, 217, 257, 258n, 262
Lyons, J., xiii, xiv, 1n, 6, 12, 19, 20, 23,
    25, 33, 41, 54, 58, 60–4, 69, 73, 77–9,
    80n, 81, 83, 85–7, 94, 148, 184, 191n,
    241–3, 254n, 255, 258n, 272, 275,
    289n, 333n

McCawley, J., 37, 145
Martin, J. N., 202n, 204
Martin, R. M., 3
Matthews, P. H., xiv
Merritt, M., 39n, 304, 347, 356n, 357–9,
    361, 369
Miller, G. A., 151, 153–5, 157, 160, 301n
Minsky, M., 281
Mitchell, T. F., 280n
Mitchell-Kernan, C., 47
Mittwoch, A., 256, 258n, 262, 267
Moerman, M., 369
Montague, R., 4, 5, 58, 59, 94, 95, 207,
    208
Moore, G. E., 100, 105, 235
Moore, T., 150
Morgan, J. L., xiii, 14n, 160, 165n, 166
Morris, C. W., 1–5, 10
Murphy, J. P., xiii

Newmeyer, F. J., 4, 36n
Nunberg, G. D., 74

O'Connor, J. D., 296n
Ochs, E., xii, 23, 47, 89, 295, 366, 375
Oh, C.-K., xiii, 168
Ohmann, R., 226
Ortony, A., 147, 155
Owen, M. L., xiv, 88, 129, 162, 281,
    284n, 314n, 315n, 334, 366

Passmore, J., 227n
Peirce, C. S., 1, 57
Peters, S., 116, 127, 131, 196, 200,
    207–10, 212, 214, 216–17
Petöfi, J. S., 286
Pomerantz, A., 286, 334, 337–9
Postal, P., 250
Power, R., 45, 286
Prince, E. F., 182, 205, 364
Prior, A. N., 77

Index of names

Psathas, G., 287, 294n
Pullum, G., xiii, 164
Putnam, H., 220, 313

Quine, W. V. O., 60
Quirk, R., 242n

Raiffa, H., 44
Rawls, J., 238
Reichenbach, H., 77
Reisenberg, S. H., 91
Roberts, C., 279, 377
Rogers, A., xiii, 259
Ross, J. R., xi, 34, 37, 40, 89, 165, 247–8, 267
Rosten, L., 68
Rumsey, A., xiv
Russell, B., 170–3, 174, 175n, 194n, 242
Rutherford, W. E., 257
Ryave, A. L., 324

Sacks, H., 70, 286, 292, 294n, 297, 298–9, 302–3, 309, 313–16, 318, 321–5, 329, 339–41, 354–5, 364, 367, 375
Sadock, J. M., xi, xiv, 40, 42, 119–20, 122, 144, 165, 205, 226, 242–3, 247, 249–50, 252–3, 255–6, 259, 261, 263, 266–7, 269, 273, 275, 373
Sag, I. A., 269, 374, 377
Samuels, M. L., 166
San, L., 40
Saussure, F. de, 14n
Savin, H. B., 191, 212
Sayward, C., 3
Schegloff, E. A., 26, 39n, 71, 72, 285–6, 294n, 297–9, 301, 303–4, 306, 309–13, 318, 320–2, 327–9, 339, 340–5, 348, 353n, 354, 356n, 359, 365, 367, 375
Schenkein, J., xiii, 287, 294n
Schieffelin, B. B., xii, 47, 314, 366, 375
Schiffer, S. R., 16n, 17, 113n, 241, 243, 282
Schmerling, S. F., 108n, 274
Schnelle, H., 86
Scott, D., 58
Searle, J. R., 6, 8n, 14n, 17n, 25, 36, 40, 42, 60, 155–6, 158, 160, 226, 233, 237–45, 264, 273, 367–8
Sellars, W., 174, 181
Sherzer, J., 279, 369
Silverstein, M., 1n
Sinclair, A., 358, 361–2, 369
Sinclair, J. M., 279, 286, 288
Smith, N. V., 8, 16n, 88, 98, 113n, 126
Snow, C., 47, 282

Soames, S., 215
Sperber, D., 106n, 109n, 112, 116, 118n, 126n, 157–8, 160, 183, 217, 219–20, 374, 376
Stalnaker, R. C., 20, 27, 34, 59, 204, 205, 277
Stenius, E., 246
Strawson, P. F., 20, 24, 36, 60, 172–5, 177–8, 181, 241–3, 282
Svartvik, J., 242n

Tambiah, S. J., 226
Tannen, D., 281
Tanz, C., 60, 62, 64
Terasaki, A., 309, 324, 349–51, 353, 355, 356
Thomason, R. H., 21
Thompson, S. A., 88
Trevarthen, C., 301
Trim, J., xiv
Trubetzkoy, N. S., 333n
Trudgill, P., 29, 65n
Tucker, G. R., 28, 92
Turner, R., 280, 295, 368

Ullman, S., 166
Uyeno, T. Y., 70

Vance, T. J., 40
Van Dijk, T. A., 23, 24n, 25, 149, 286, 292
Van Fraassen, B. C., 176
Van Valin, R. D., 225
Verschueren, J. F., xiii, 368

Wales, R., 62
Waletsky, J., 324
Walker, R., 101
Wall, R., xiii, 207n
Walters, J., 376
Watson, R., 70, 364
Watzlawick, P., 2
Webber, B. L., 377
Weinreich, U., 149
Whitehead, A. N., 242
Wilks, Y., 150
Wilson, D., xiv, 8, 34, 88, 96, 98, 106n, 109n, 112, 116, 118n, 126–7, 157–8, 160, 182–3, 189, 194–5, 201, 203–4, 210, 217, 219, 220, 374, 376
Wittgenstein, L., 227, 228n, 280
Wootton, A., 282, 307, 334–5
Wunderlich, D., 2

Zwicky, A., xi, 40, 42, 71, 92, 145, 242–3